ARCHITECTS OF CONSPIRACY

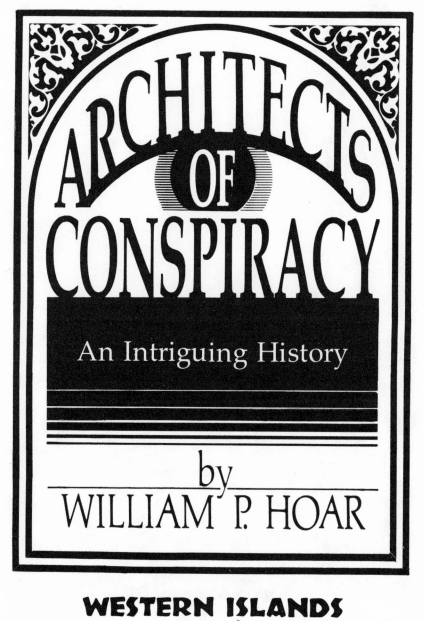

ARCHITECTS OF CONSPIRACY

An Intriguing History

by
WILLIAM P. HOAR

WESTERN ISLANDS

PUBLISHERS

BOSTON   LOS ANGELES

Published by
WESTERN ISLANDS
395 Concord Avenue
Belmont, Massachusetts 02178

Manufactured in the United States of America
ISBN: 0-88279-237-7 (hardbound)
ISBN: 0-88279-132-X (paperbound)

To my mother and father

Table of Contents

Author's Preface

HISTORY doesn't just happen. Men have deliberate goals for which they strive individually and collectively, the results of which — regardless of the success of their missions — become history. Private ambitions and public posturings are seldom the same, so it is healthy to be wary of the ostentatiously altruistic. It was not without reason that Henry David Thoreau prepared to flee whenever he heard that someone was on the way to do him good.

That man is flawed, fallible, and roguish is no surprise to any outside the nursery, and it should not be shocking that the collective record seems worse than the sum of the parts. The historian Edward Gibbon had a professional understanding of the game, complaining that history is often "little more than the register of the crimes, follies and misfortunes of mankind."

Such a registration by name, date, and place has frequently been all that the "accidentalists" want to discuss, ignoring the questions of why the world is run the way that it is, how, and by whom. Culpability is assigned by the winners, for the men who run things know what they are doing and do it anyway. Feathering one's own nest is applied in the making of history, economics, politics, sociology, psychology, and morality. It is also applied in writing about them. As Adam Smith observed two centuries ago in *The Wealth Of Nations*: "It is not from the benevolence of the butcher, the brewer, or the baker that we expect our dinner, but from their regard to their self-interest." So it is with history and the historians.

The currents beneath the surface are usually the strongest and determine direction, while the casual observer sees but the reflections on top. With this in mind, we set out in the writing of these chapters to see and make clear to our readers what had been made murky by years of fashionable obfuscation.

Have men conspired throughout the ages? Have they cheated and pillaged, inflated and warred, and then labored to have the best light shone upon their motives? Such questions answer themselves, but apparently must be repeatedly asked. For, as Edmund Burke expressed it: "People will not look forward to posterity who never look backward to their ancestors." Or inward to themselves.

Some will say that the evidence here or there in this survey is only circumstantial, or that some case is not sufficiently made because the perpetrators didn't plead guilty. To suggest that conspiracy might have been involved would be too, well, too *revisionist*. But the long arm of coincidence can only stretch so far. Propaganda is expected to fool most of the people some of the time, so one can only ask the honest reader to be at least equally skeptical of Establishment interpretation. Circumstantial? Take all the proof presented here, collate it with experience, and remember with Thoreau that "some circumstantial evidence is very strong, as when you find a trout in the milk."

Of course, this book does have a point of view; there is a *leitmotiv*. Human nature being what it is, few will enjoy being reminded of the vast evil at large in the world. During the French Revolution, for instance, the conspirator Mirabeau seriously declared that liberty "should have for her bed mattresses of corpses." Accordingly, at one time, the French revolutionists had plans to kill half the population — just as was done by their Twentieth Century successors in Cambodia! The framers of the American Constitution, on the other hand, saw the terrible potential for collective evil and labored to avoid what George Washington called the "leveling principles." The runaway "turbulence and follies of democracy," in Edmund Randolph's phrase, must be resisted.

That is why Randolph urged the Constitutional Convention to "check . . . and to restrain, if possible, the fury of Democracy." Gouverneur Morris, our Minister to France during its bloody gyrations in the name of equality, actually called the unrestrained masses of people a "reptile." Jefferson realized: "In questions of power . . . let no more be heard of confidence in man, but bind him down from mischief by the chains of the Constitution." As the historians Charles and Mary Beard put it in 1939, "when the Constitution was framed no respectable person called himself a democrat." Which is why they created the Republic for which we stand.

It is that Republic which conspirators have been laboring to wreck and submerge into a New World Order, or an all-powerful United Nations, or some way station of regional government. It would be, we are told when we dare to demand an answer, for our own benefit. Despots just *love* to do good, the means to that end notwithstanding. Take John Dewey, the demigod of the "Liberal" Education Establishment. In 1916, in *Ethics*, Dewey maintained that whether the use of force "is justifiable or not . . . is, in substance, a question of efficiency (including economy) of means in the accomplishing of ends . . . . The criterion of value lies in the relative efficiency and economy of the expenditure of force as a means to an end." Bowing to bare efficiency is still obsequity.

Consider the founder of the American Civil Liberties Union, Roger Baldwin, who in 1935 admitted: "Communism is the goal." By age 96, in 1981, he had evolved this notion to a contention that "world order, a one-world order, is necessary to human survival." One is also reminded of John Adams's writings to Thomas Jefferson: Rousseau and other revolutionary philosophers, said Adams, "preached to the French nation *liberty*, until they made them the most mechanical slaves; *equality* till they destroyed all equity; *humanity* till they became weasels and African panthers; and *fraternity* till they cut one another's throats like Roman gladiators."

How much better were the results of following the truly revolutionary precepts of Adam Smith. He did not appeal to the *benevolence* of bakers and butchers, you will recall. "We address ourselves," Smith said, "not to their humanity, but to their self-love, and never talk to them of our necessities, but of their advantages." The consequence was the freed marketplace and the Industrial Revolution that lifted millions in the West from squalor.

Time and again, however, statists and worshippers of big government reemerge, much like the Lernaean Hydra with multiple heads replacing each that is beaten back. José Ortega y Gasset rightly saw the greatest danger threatening civilization as "State intervention" which is "the absorption of all spontaneous social action by the State," and which can lead only to the people being "converted into fuel to feed the mere machine which is the State." As he predicted in 1930 in *The Revolt Of The Masses*: "The result of this tendency will be fatal. Spontaneous social action will be broken up over and over again by State intervention; no new seed will be able to fructify. Society will have to live *for* the State, man *for* the governmental machine."

Government is at root simple force and/or the threat of using it. Too much government has sapped us, just as Alexis de Tocqueville anticipated: "The will of man is not shattered, but softened, bent, and guided; men are seldom forced by it to act, but they are constantly restrained from acting. Such a power does not destroy, but it prevents existence; it does not tyrannize, but it compresses, enervates, extinguishes, and stupefies a people, till each nation is reduced to nothing better than a flock of timid and industrious animals, of which the government is the shepherd.''

There are those who are enervated by the fear of stigma, of not being seen as an orthodox interpreter of history, of being accused of seeing incipient totalitarians plotting under the beds. In the name of modernism, however, it is they who surrender skepticism. They will look at our long list of national and international ''errors'' and deny even the possibility that the fix is in. From the top, Establishment historians will contend that *none* of this happened because men connived to make it happen. The less such popinjays of the hour know about what they scoff at as the ''conspiracy theory'' — as if there were one set by dogma — the more they disavow its validity.

If everyone on your side of the street says, for instance, that the Emperor has such a fine set of clothes, and how nice it is that he has recorded its details with the People's Academy of Haphazard History, you may think it odd to note in the face of official history to the contrary that the Emperor is naked as a jaybird. There really is none so blind as the man who will not see. Moreover, as Machiavelli pointed out: ''One who deceives will always find those who allow themselves to be deceived.''

* * *

A word on style: Most material in this book appeared over a decade, from 1975 to 1984, in a different format in *American Opinion* magazine. The emphasis has been on making the information flow in a popular and readable fashion rather than to litter the landscape with legions of *op. cits.* and other paraphernalia of merely academic tomes. By incorporating cited works into the body of this history we have sought to minimize the page-turning to minute type. A bibliography of volumes referred to in the text is included at the back.

Finally, let me add my gratitude to my parents, John P. Hoar and Helen R. Hoar; my friend and Editor, Scott Stanley Jr.; and, my wife, Louisa Miller Hoar.

W.P.H.

Arlington, Massachusetts
August 1984

Introduction

THOSE CONSPIRATORS who would by degrees reduce the sovereignty of the United States of America to raise in its stead a New World Order are the subjects of this intriguing yet scholarly work by William P. Hoar. Writing of such machinations, of the movers and shakers conspiring behind the scenes, the author indicates that, because of exposure by Conservatives, members of the Trilateral Commission (as one example) now comprise "anything but a conspiracy of silence; it is in fact a relatively open collusion of the powerful, and brazen enough to own up to at least some of its aims. These admissions against interest need examining."

Indeed. Consider how these people manipulate government. One name that springs to mind is that of international banker James P. Warburg. His father had been the chief architect of the Federal Reserve System. He was himself an early New Dealer; at age thirty-five, he was president of the International Acceptance Bank, with its interlocks to the Morgans, Rockefellers, and the funding of the Bolshevik Revolution; and, by 1932, he was director of the Bank of Manhattan. Warburg was in charge of American propaganda during World War II; supported universal disarmament after the war as well as the United World Federalists; and, was not only a member of the Council on Foreign Relations but also was a trustee of the Institute for Policy Studies, an important and influential Marxist think-tank in Washington, D.C. In short, here was a man who *knew* how policy was made. He admitted in his 1966 book *The United States In The Postwar World* that:

There is a group of " . . . bankers, industrialists, businessmen, lawyers and educators who are now and then consulted informally by the White House. Some two hundred of these prominent citizens, in various parts of the country, most of whom are on first-name terms with each other and communicate with each other by telephone, might appropriately be called

'The Establishment.' They are closely connected to the nation's major corporate interests and, perhaps more important, to its major universities; they are on the boards of the major foundations.''

Another witness to the sort of conspiracy with which Mr. Hoar's book is concerned was the late Georgetown professor Carroll Quigley, who acknowledged in his voluminous 1966 history *Tragedy And Hope*: ''There does exist, and has existed for a generation, an international Anglophile network which operates, to some extent, in the way the radical Right believes the Communists act. In fact, this network, which we may identify as the Round Table Groups, has no aversion to cooperating with the Communists, or any other groups and frequently does so. I know of the operations of this network because I have studied it for twenty years and was permitted for two years, in the early 1960's, to examine its papers and secret records. I have no aversion to it or to most of its aims and have, for much of my life, been close to it and to many of its instruments. I have objected, both in the past and recently, to a few of its policies . . . . but in general my chief difference of opinion is that it wishes to remain unknown . . . . ***

''. . . the American branch of this organization (sometimes called the 'Eastern Establishment') has played a very significant role in the history of the United States in the last generation.''

Professor Quigley noted that before World War I there were ''organized semisecret groups, known as Round Table Groups, in the chief British dependencies and the United States. These still function in eight countries.'' After 1914, fronts were organized in target nations. One, ''called the Royal Institute of International Affairs, has as its nucleus in each area the existing submerged Round Table Group. In New York it was known as the Council on Foreign Relations, and was a front for J.P. Morgan and Company in association with the very small American Round Table Group . . . .''

These are not paranoid imaginings rising like vapors from the fever swamps, but admissions of participant members of the reigning foreign-policy elite, who are proud of what they have been doing.

In *Architects Of Conspiracy: An Intriguing History*, William Hoar is not letting fanciful bugbears run amok either. His message is too important to need exaggeration, and this compilation speaks for itself.

Chapters I and II go to the roots of things by comparing and contrasting the French, American, and Industrial Revolutions. Whereas Thomas Paine claimed ''the cause of the French people is that of . . . the whole world,'' George Washington denounced Jacobins in America for trying to ''destroy the government.'' Our first President warned against ''self-created societies'' which ''sow seeds of jealousy and distrust.'' If they were not exposed, said Washington, "adieu to all government in this country, except mob and club government." Economic freedom was the message carried by Adam Smith, who called the regulations of mercantilism the "impertinent badges of slavery." Little else, contended Smith, "is required to carry a state to the highest degrees of affluence . . . but peace, easy taxes, and a tolerable administration of justice." The Industrial Revolution was itself made possible by repeal of the income tax.

Counterpoints are the growth of a free America and the destruction sought and wrought by those who would, through anarchy, bring down all. Under James Polk, for example, American territory increased by 1.2 million square miles; Andrew Jackson, a believer in Manifest Destiny (Chapter III), thwarted the central bank and paid off the National Debt. On the other hand, anarchists here and abroad (Chapter VI) were already being used by conspirators to try to create a vacuum in which carefully organized revolutionary forces might seize political control.

Hatred and plunder at government behest are central to Chapters IV and V. During the so-called Reconstruction of the American South, the radical Republicans looted the defeated states and organized a black voting bloc, while denying white former Confederates the right to vote or hold office and taxing them further into poverty. The celebrated Robber Barons wanted subsidies; sought restrictive government-backed monopolies; and, bought legislators, the judiciary, and regulators — using government to expand their power.

The manipulations of Andrew Carnegie, a prototypical insider, whose legacy of conspiracy remains with us today, are outlined in Chapter VII. Carnegie funds, for example, were used to propagandize for the United Nations (his political heirs having failed to get us into the League of Nations), with the U.N.'s founding Secretary General, Soviet agent Alger Hiss, subsequently becoming a president of the Carnegie Endowment.

The watershed year of 1913 is examined in Chapter VIII, when the federal income tax was authorized and implemented; when the American states were weakened and "democracy" enhanced by the direct election of Senators; and, when insiders of international finance pushed through the Federal Reserve Act that allowed inflation and depression at the will of its masters.

World War I, the Versailles Treaty, and the League of Nations are subjects of Chapters IX and X. We learn how Colonel E.M. House, Woodrow Wilson's "alter ego," began work on what he called "A World Constitution" in 1915; but how, despite the best efforts of conspirators, the U.S. Senate refused ratification of American participation in the League of Nations with which House and his co-conspirators hoped to initiate their scheme.

Men who made a difference for freedom are featured in Chapters XI and XII. There we see Henry Ford cutting the ground from under Marxist propaganda by paying the highest industrial wage in America, inaugurating the eight-hour day, and sharing profits with the workers — leading to greater efficiency and more profits. "This is neither charity nor wages," said Ford, "but . . . efficiency engineering." We also learn how the Lindberghs, father and son, fought the power brokers. The senior Lindbergh, for example, opposed those who would control our money through the Federal Reserve Act; aviator hero Charles Jr., like his father, strove fiercely against efforts to drag us into world war.

In Chapters XIII and XIV, Mr. Hoar shreds many of the myths spread about facism, national socialism, and populism. He quotes a top Italian fascist as claiming that the "maximum of liberty coincides with the maximum of state force"; he quotes Hitler as saying in 1941 that "basically National Socialism and Marxism are the same." As for the Populists, Hoar explains: "While they were swinging battering rams at the front door, their programs were slipped in the back door by the major parties. By asking for more federal government they simply played into the hands of the would-be monopolists."

We discover in Chapters XV and XVI that it was Herbert Hoover who first tried to spend us out of penury and the Great Depression. For example, government spending rose forty-two percent in 1931 alone. While there had been a vast credit expansion through the Twenties, the brakes had been suddenly applied by the Fed which depressed the money stock by more than one-third between 1929 and 1933. As a result, under Hoover, the Gross National Product fell by almost a half.

A world in economic depression was about to become a world aflame. Hitler so admired Stalin that he made him a partner in "a new distribution of the world." This included their mutual smashing of Poland after the pact of the dictators, as described in Chapters XVII and XVIII, and the starting of World War II. The Kremlin congratulated Hitler on his Blitzkrieg even as Soviet agents preached "pacifism" in the West. As for Poland, F.D.R. covered up the Red massacre of captured Polish officers, and (as the Communists gained control) Churchill declared he would not "wreck the peace of Europe because of a quarrel between Poles."

Franklin Roosevelt, who said in 1932 that he regarded "reduction in Federal spending as one of the most important issues of this campaign," is the centerpiece of Chapters XIX and XX. When they failed to ignite an "incident" to bring the U.S. into the European war, Roosevelt and Churchill agreed on provoking Japan. The question was how to maneuver Tokyo "into firing the first shot." Churchill (Chapter XXI) was an old hand at intrigue who had initiated the terror bombing of cities four months before the first air strike on London. Like F.D.R. at Pearl Harbor, he subsequently had advance knowledge of a retaliatory raid on Coventry but, hoping to rally his people by the outrage, refused to warn the population.

Truman became a belated member of the "Big Three," and it was he who arranged the postwar "peace" with Stalin. Ignoring intelligence reports, the President paid a huge price for "Uncle Joe's" one-week war against Japan — one of many points touched in Chapter XXII. Though the Japanese were suing for peace, Truman ordered that atom bombs be dropped on them. During the Korean War (Chapter XXIII), he fired General MacArthur — after the brilliant Inchon landing and destruction of the North Korean Army. Granting sanctuary to the Communist Chinese and recalling MacArthur prevented victory.

As shown in a survey of much more serious Presidential offenses in Chapter XXIV, we learn that Watergate was far from the crime of the century. And the destruction of Indochina, with the concomitant attempts to suppress the results of our betrayal (as seen from the vantage point of the Seventies in Chapter XXV) is a brutal example of what has happened over and over again. Ask the Afghans. This is typical Communism in practice, as bestial as the Reign of Terror in the days of the French Revolution. Nevertheless, there are still those who press for America to "negotiate" with the Communist gangsters in the Kremlin, despite the shameful record of past summits, which Mr. Hoar summarizes in Chapter XXVI.

Who exerts the push for dealing with the Communists? None other than the same self-perpetuating Establishment that has been in charge of our disastrous foreign policy for decades. It was riding high before and during the Carter Administration (Chapter XXVII) when a spokesman for a World Order "project," funded by the Carnegie Endowment and the Rockefeller Foundation, claimed there "is no longer a question of whether or not there will be world government by the year 2000." Of necessity, according to a prominent member of the influential Trilateral Commission and the Council on Foreign Relations, the " 'house of world order' will have to be built from the bottom up rather than the top down. . . . an end run around national sovereignty, eroding it piece by piece, will accomplish much more than the old-fashioned frontal assault."

That Trilateral Commission, once criticized by Ronald Reagan, now apparently has his support. These are supposedly the "best brains in the world," yet (as described in Chapter XXVIII) they want the U.S. to disarm and avoid missile defenses; to increase funding to the backward nations; and, to become partners with the Communist regimes we continue to strengthen. The head of the Commission is David Rockefeller, the longtime chairman of Chase Manhattan Bank which has a branch in Moscow. Rockefeller says, however, that he is not the ''cabalist-in-chief'' of a conspiracy in ''cahoots with the Kremlin.'' Of course, remarks an apologist for the Rockefellers, the C.F.R., and the Trilateralists, ''what some critics see as a vast international conspiracy,'' Rockefeller considers ''just another day's work.''

To buy that nonsense would be to accept the notion that men do not will the obvious consequences of their actions and to embrace a mockery and a delusion.

What we are seeing today is the most obvious push that the advocates of the New World Order dare to muster. But we believe we can take heart in the Roman historian's maxim: ''Treachery, though at first very cautious, in the end betrays itself.'' And, as William Pitt put it: ''You may ravage, you cannot conquer. It is impossible. You cannot conquer the Americans.''

The reason, of course, is that once aware of the nature and treachery of their would-be conquerors, Americans fight fiercely for their liberties. This up-to-date compendium of the sinister deeds of those who conspire to rule the world promises to make a huge contribution to that needed awareness. Which is why, as Chairman of The John Birch Society, I am very happy to introduce this important work by William P. Hoar.

A. CLIFFORD BARKER

Newport News, Virginia

Chapter I

American Republic And French Revolution

It WAS the best of times, it was the worst of times. It was the epoch of constitutional government in the United States, it was the epoch of revolution in France. And the French Revolution not only split America's Founding Fathers, but left its mark on revolutionary strategies for centuries. As Russian anarchist Prince Kropotkin wrote in 1908: "What we learn today from the study of the Great Revolution is that it was the source and origin of all the present communist, anarchist, and socialist conceptions."

To many, what was happening in France at first seemed benign if not beneficent. "A great revolution had commenced in that country," wrote John Marshall, later Chief Justice of the U.S. Supreme Court, "the first stage of which was completed by limiting the powers of the monarch, and by the establishment of a popular assembly. In no other part of the globe was this revolution hailed with more joy than in America. The influence it would have on the affairs of the world was not then distinctly foreseen; and the philanthropist, without becoming a political partisan, rejoiced in the event. On this subject, therefore, but one sentiment existed." (*The Life Of John Marshall*, Volume II, Albert J. Beveridge, Boston, Houghton Mifflin, 1916)

But the fact is that a number of Americans were skeptical of the French Revolution from its beginning. Among these was the always perceptive John Adams. Biographer Page Smith reports that Adams "from the first moment viewed it with misgivings . . . . At the same time he could not forbear to point out 'that the form of government they have adopted' could be 'nothing more than a transient experiment. An obstinate adherence to it' would involve France 'in great and lasting calamities.' A single assembly would be dominated by demagogues and the result would be repeated upheavals and disorder — a succession of bloody contentions." (*John Adams*, Volume II, Garden City, Doubleday, 1962)

Adams proved no mean prophet. While the French Revolution is presented in the government schools as a peasants' revolt against bloody tyranny, this was so only in the fiction of such brilliant polemicists as Charles Dickens, for it resulted from nothing short of a conspiracy against the very best of French civilization. After all, as Professor Douglas Johnson has noted, the Eighteenth Century "had not been a bad one for France as a whole. The population had risen from about twenty to twenty-six millions; no great plagues or other catastrophes had occurred; no wars had been fought on French soil; industry had thrived; the general rise of prices from about 1730 to the eve of the Revolution was a sign of the prosperity of the producing classes; overseas trade multiplied. The Bourbon monarchy was the first monarch of Europe, and no signs of disloyalty to it could be detected in France." (*The French Revolution*, New York, G.P. Putnam's Sons, 1970)

Even Thomas Jefferson, who had been led to believe otherwise by radical Frenchmen, told Lafayette in 1787: "I have been pleased to find among the people a less degree of physical misery than I had expected. They are generally well clothed, and have plenty of food, not animal indeed, but vegetable, which is as wholesome."

Unfortunately, the good times were not to continue. By 1789, the year in which the Revolution is normally said to have begun, shortages of food were being consciously created by one of the prime conspirators, the Duc d'Orléans. There can be no doubt, confirmed historian Nesta Webster in *The French Revolution*, "that the famine of 1789 was deliberately engineered by the agents of the duke, and that by this means the people were driven to the pitch of desperation necessary to produce the Revolution." And the Orléanistes were joined in such intrigues by agents of the Barvarian-bred Illuminati who operated out of the Club Breton and were later known as the Jacobins. Ruffians and street toughs were hired and moved about Paris like pawns on a board; the Bastille, with but *seven* prisoners, was beseiged to make a show; and, the gory Revolution was begun. Soon one of the Jacobins devised a scheme which produced "the Great Fear" when a phony story was spread simultaneously throughout France that a foreign invasion was imminent. The panic that resulted provided the conspirators with the disruption and chaos they desired to persuade King Louis XVI to accept one radical political concession after another.

On the scene as our Minister in Paris was Gouverneur Morris, the conservative statesman who had been the architect of much of the U.S. Constitution. Morris wrote from France in July of 1789 that "this country is at present as near to anarchy as society can approach without dissolution. . . . The authority of the King and the nobility is completely subdued, but yet I tremble for the constitution.'' (*The Diary And Letters Of Gouverneur Morris*, Volume I, New York, Charles Scribner's Sons, 1888)

The French merchants controlling the market had soon turned the contrived food shortages into large profits by raising the prices, observed historians Will and Ariel Durant, and "barges carrying food to the towns were attacked and pillaged en route; disorder and insecurity disrupted transportation. Paris was running riot with criminals. The countryside was so subject to marauding robbers that in several provinces the peasants armed themselves in their 'Great Fear' of these lawless hordes; in six months 400,000 guns were acquired by the alarmed citizens. When the Great Fear subsided, the peasants decided to use their weapons against tax collectors, monopolists and feudal lords.'' (*The Age Of Napoleon*, New York, Simon and Schuster, 1975)

It was less than three months after the inauguration of George Washington that the Bastille was stormed. But even at this early date, and with worldwide favorable propaganda for the Revolution, it is instructive to see the diplomatic reaction of our first President when he was sent by Lafayette the "main key" of the "fortress of despotism." It was "a tribute which I owe as a son to my adoptive father, as an aide-de-camp to my general, and as a missionary of liberty to its patriarch," declared Lafayette. President Washington did hang the key to the Bastille "in the Presidential Mansion, but added, so as not to prejudice the foreign policy of the United States, an engraved portrait of Louis XVI.'' (*Washington: The Indispensable Man*, James T. Flexner, Boston, Little, Brown, 1969)

Indeed, there were a number of Americans, wrote the senior Henry Cabot Lodge, who were never deceived by the French Revolution, "even by their hopes. Hamilton, who 'divined Europe,' as Talleyrand said, and Gouverneur Morris, studying the situation on the spot with keen and practical observation, soon apprehended the truth, while others more or less quickly followed in their wake. But Washington, whom no one ever credited with divination, and who never crossed the Atlantic, saw the realities of the thing sooner, and looked more deeply into the future than anybody else.'' (*George Washington*, Volume II, Boston, Houghton Mifflin, 1898) Nevertheless, President Washington, Alexander Hamilton, and James Madison were named citizens of the new French Republic, being among only eighteen foreigners so honored. Also in this group was Prussian baron Anacharsis Clootz, an Illuminist conspirator who was later guillotined when the Revolution began to devour its own. (*James Madison: Father Of The Constitution, 1787-1800*, Irving Brant, Indianapolis, Bobbs-Merrill, 1950)

Another favorite of the French, revolutionist or otherwise, was Benjamin Franklin — probably the most famous and popular American in

Europe, who was ever ready to engage in intrigue. Leading conspirators of the Revolution consulted with the Doctor: men such as Mirabeau (dubbed a scoundrel by Gouverneur Morris), the fanatical Marat and the bloody-handed Robespierre, who supposedly "wanted information on the lightning rod." (*The Private Franklin*, Claude-Anne Lopez and Eugenia W. Herbert, New York, Norton, 1975)

Franklin had in fact hailed the 1787 Assembly of the Notables, and contended that having served an apprenticeship to Liberty in the United States the French were now prepared to take the message to all Europe. But, reports Franklin's biographer James Parton, by 1789 the good Doctor "began to tremble for his old friends, and for France. The chief actors in the fearful scene, Lafayette, Mirabeau, Necker, Brissot, the King, the Queen, de Vergennes, and others, he had been in the habit of meeting for nine years, entertaining and entertained; and for many of them he cherished the warmest regard. The news of the dissensions in the States-general, of the famine, of the fall of the Bastille, the march on Versailles, the lamppost executions, the confinement of the King and Queen in their palace, filled him with anxiety . . . . Franklin feared for his friends more than he hoped for France." (*Life And Times Of Benjamin Franklin*, Volume II, Boston, Ticknor and Fields, 1867) Whatever the case, Ben Franklin died in 1790 before the worst of the terror had begun.

Still, there was already terror enough. Gouverneur Morris, our first Minister to France under the Constitution, wrote to his business associate Robert Morris (no relation) concerning the owner of a French quarry who brought legal action because so many corpses had been dumped there that the bodies "choked it up so that he could not get men to work at it." These victims were, said Morris, "the best people," slaughtered "without form of trial and the bodies thrown like dead dogs into the first hole that offered." Morris wrote in his diary: "At dinner I sit next to M. de Lafayette who tells me I injure the cause, for that my sentiments are continually quoted against the good party. I seize this opportunity to tell him that I am opposed to the democracy from regard to liberty."

This was of course no Revolution of liberation, but one of oppression. Thus a Nazi idealogue like Goebbels could later declare with pleasure that he "paid homage to the French Revolution for all the possibilities of life and development which it had brought to the people. In this sense, if you like, I am a democrat." In fact Hitler called the Nazi revolt "the exact counterpart of the French Revolution." (*Leftism*, Erik von Kuehnelt-Leddihn, New Rochelle, Arlington House, 1974)

Despite its horrors, the French Revolution enjoyed considerable support from influential Americans. Thomas Jefferson, James Madison, James Monroe, and the Anglo-American Thomas Paine, to cite a few, were all enthusiastic about it. In this matter, as in so many others, Secretary of State Jefferson found himself at odds with Treasury Secretary Alexander Hamilton. Whereas Jefferson hoped in 1791 that ''so beautiful a revolution'' would sweep the world, Hamilton assuredly did not. (See *To Covet Honor*, Holmes Alexander, Boston, Western Islands, 1977.) In France, said Hamilton of our former Minister to Paris, Jefferson had seen ''government only on the side of its abuses. He drank freely of the French philosophy, in religion, in science, in politics. He came from France in the moment of fermentation, which he had a share in exciting, and in the passions and feelings of which he shared both from temperament and situation.''

Jefferson became a near fanatic in his revolutionary zeal. He claimed to believe that ''most Frenchmen were Jacobins. Their excesses, if one called them such, reflected that national will.'' (*George Washington & The French Revolution*, Louis Martin Sears, Detroit, Wayne State University Press, 1960) Which certainly would have astonished the French revolutionaries. Even Danton said in September of 1792 that ''the Republicans are an infinitesimal minority . . . the rest of France is attached to the monarchy.'' Actually it was the liberality of King Louis in his regard for the French people that led to his downfall; each reform to which he acceded, each change, was followed by new demands — and when violence broke out the King hesitated to send troops against his own people.

Jefferson, meanwhile, was willing to overlook the drumhead execution of the innocent best of France because ''time and truth will rescue & embalm their memories, while their posterity will be enjoying that very liberty for which they would never have hesitated to offer up their lives. The liberty of the whole earth was depending on the issue of the contest. . . . '' Rather than see the French Revolution fail, wrote State Secretary Jefferson in 1793, ''I would have seen half the earth desolated. Were there but an Adam & Eve left in every country, & left free, it would be better than it now is.'' To the Virginian, ''the form our own government was to take depended . . . on the events of France.'' (*John Adams*)

It is hard to imagine a more outrageous declaration. Even *before* the Massacres of September and the Reign of Terror, here is how the supposed liberty of France was acquired, and the monarchy deposed. Nesta Webster draws this compilation from historians of the time:

'' ' . . . a wretched undercook, who had not time to escape, was seized by these tigers, thrust into a copper, and in this state exposed to the heat of the furnace. Then falling on the provisions every one seizes what he can lay hands upon. One carries off chickens on a spit; another a turbot; that one a carp from the Rhine as large as himself . . . monsters with human faces collected in hundreds under the porch of the Escalier du Midi, and danced amidst torrents of blood and wine. A murderer played the violin beside the corpses, and thieves, with their pockets full of gold, hanged other thieves on the banisters.' Still worse horrors took place that cannot be written, nameless indecencies, hideous debaucheries, ghastly mutilations of the dead, and again, as after the siege of the Bastille, cannibal orgies. Before great fires, hastily kindled in the apartment, 'cutlets of Swiss [*Guards*]' were grilled and eaten; the actor Grammont — one of the earliest hirelings of the Duc d'Orléans, and the last man to insult the Queen on her way to the scaffold — in a fit of revolutionary frenzy drank down a glass of blood.''

The instigators of this mob, trained in the Jacobin Clubs, were nowhere to be seen. The revolutionary leaders, you see, were in hiding until the danger had passed. They were indeed the same Jacobins who professed belief in the natural goodness of man, and declared their desire to install a puritanical regime without vices. (See *The Jacobins*, Clarence Crane Brinton, New York, Russell & Russell, 1961.)

Certainly Thomas Jefferson knew what was being done in the name of liberty. He had personally seen the first brands of the fire of revolution, and had written as follows to John Jay in 1789: ''The city [*Paris*] is as yet not entirely quieted. Every now and then summary execution is done on individuals by individuals, and nobody is in condition to ask for what, and by whom . . . . The details from the country are as distressing as I had apprehended they would be . . . . Abundance of châteaux are certainly burnt and burning, and not a few lives sacrificed. The worst is probably over in this city, but I do not know whether it is so in the country.'' (*Jefferson: The Scene Of Europe, 1784-1789*, Marie Kimball, New York, Coward-McCann, 1950)

Jefferson proved a poor oracle, for the terror in the cities was just beginning. Perhaps if he had lived through the experience of being a military commander like Hamilton or Washington he would have had less to say about being willing to see ''half the earth desolated'' by burnings and massacres to feed the Revolution.

In England a great friend of the American Revolution named Edmund Burke had meanwhile published his scathing *Reflections On The Revolution In France*, which ran through ten editions in its first year. An attempt to refute Burke was made by the revolutionary Thomas Paine in *Rights Of Man*, an appeal to revolution in England that received the endorsement of Jefferson; got Paine indicted for treason in England; and, helped make him an honorary citizen of Revolutionary France. In Paris and named a member of the French Convention in 1792, Paine voted *against* the death of Louis XVI. Always intriguing, he was imprisoned for a year (1793-1794) by the Revolutionary Government and released only at the request of U.S. Minister to France James Madison.

It was widely believed that Paine's incendiary writings made possible the murder of Louis. A baronet informed George Washington of Paine that true, "he voted against it, but his principles were too deeply rooted in the minds of the People; that Idea of Equality stimulated the Dregs of the People to all the Massacres; I hope in God, he will never revisit America, for he might distract your now happy Government." (*George Washington & The French Revolution*) In 1802, Jefferson did invite Paine to return to the United States. But by then reports of the massacres of the French Revolution had resulted in his being discredited and Paine died seven years later an ostracized and obscure man.

Tom Paine's involvement in conspiracies had made him many enemies, among whom was Gouverneur Morris. Paine had written to Jefferson to oppose Morris's appointment to France. Indeed he was not alone among radicals opposing Morris, whose nomination passed the Senate by a vote of sixteen to eleven. Though both were influential in America's War for Independence, Tom Paine and Gouverneur Morris were poles apart. " 'Cocksure,' was the way Morris described him," reports Yvon Bizardel. "Paine was eaten up with vanity and undoubtedly suffering the effects of too much whiskey. In his journal Morris wrote of their conversation: 'I tell him that the disordered state of things in France works against all schemes of Reformation, both here and elsewhere. He declares that the riots and outrages in France are nothing at all. It is not worthwhile to contest such declarations, I tell him therefore that as I am sure he does not believe what he says, I shall not dispute it.' " (*The First Expatriates*, translated by June Wilson and Cornelia Higginson, New York, Holt, Rinehart and Winston, 1975)

Likewise, Gouverneur Morris did not gladly suffer Thomas Jefferson, saying he was once with the fiery Virginian for an hour, "which was at least fifty minutes too much." Morris called him a theorist who "is desirous of annihilating distinctions of order. How far such views may be right respecting mankind in general is, I think, extremely problematical, but with respect to this nation [*France*], I am sure it is wrong and cannot eventuate well." (*Gouverneur Morris: Witness Of Two Revolutions*, Daniel Walther, New York, Funk & Wagnalls, 1934) As Morris saw developments in 1792: "France is on the high road to despotism. They have made the common mistake that to enjoy liberty it is necessary only to abolish authority." In fact, Morris predicted in a letter to Washington in 1793 that the result would be a consulship of probably three men, from which would come a single dictator. Which is exactly how Napoleon came to power.

In the meantime, France was suffering military difficulties and had declared war on Britain. Now the Revolutionary Government in Paris seemed even more important in America and the debate about what was happening raged among our Founding Fathers. France's example, worried the thoughtful John Adams, could "produce anarchy among us." Men like Danton, Robespierre, and Marat are furies, he wrote his wife. "Dragons' teeth have been sown in France and come up as monsters." The U.S., the Vice President contended, has its own "Robespierres and Marats whose wills are good to do mischief but the flesh is weak. They cannot yet persuade the people to follow them."

A point of contention was a 1778 treaty with France which committed us to be a fighting ally and to defend the French West Indies. But this was a European war, and so young a country as our own could hardly be helped by being drawn into further war with Great Britain. Alexander Hamilton argued that we should stand aside and leave the matter to a test of arms among the principals. "This effort is not prudent, is not commendable," he said. All patriots "will scorn to stand on any but purely *American* ground." (*To Covet Honor*) While Jefferson claimed to dislike the idea of war he nonetheless called our neutrality "pusillanimous."

The country was in a frenzy of seriously mistaken enthusiasm over what had happened in France. "The papers were full of news of a celebration at Boston in honor of the masters of the Terror. A tax of three dollars a head was imposed to pay for a great 'Civic Feast' in honor of the French comrades, and the Boston Federalists were afraid not to pay it for fear of being denounced as aristocrats. The democratical distemper was worse than the smallpox, and Adams was pleased at the news that John Quincy had dared to decry this infatuation within the sacred walls of Faneuil Hall." (*John Adams*)

From Charleston to Boston, cannons were fired to salute French victories. "One observer noted that in America more gunpowder was fired in celebrating French triumphs than the French ever spent in achieving them." In a Philadelphia waxworks, the most popular exhibit was the execution of Louis XVI. Families "saw the knife fall and the King's lips turn from red to blue. Children were admitted at half price." John Adams called all of this "sound and fury," but to Thomas Jefferson "it was music." (*John Jay*, Frank Monaghan, New York, Bobbs-Merrill, 1935)

Radical propaganda aligned the French cause in the popular mind with that of American liberty. "Americans decried titles and all that smacked of monarchy. Men and women addressed each other as 'Citizen' and by such contrived female variants as 'Citess.' They raised liberty poles and wore the tricolored cockade everywhere; they sang French songs; and they drank toasts to French principles.'' (*Entangling Alliance*, Alexander DeConde, Durham, Duke University Press, 1958)

It was at this time that George Washington issued the Proclamation of Neutrality — though at Jefferson's suggestion the word *neutrality* was left out in the hopes that Great Britain might make some diplomatic concessions to be absolutely assured of American neutrality.'' (*A Diplomatic History Of The United States*, Samuel Flagg Bemis, New York, Holt, Rinehart and Winston, 1965) Britain made no further concession, but the proclamation was soon taken on both sides of the ocean as declaring us neutral.

As for the 1778 alliance, Washington here accepted Jefferson's advice and chose to postpone consideration of all treaties made with the pre-revolutionary Government. (Hamilton had wanted them declared inapplicable, and they were eventually dissolved under President John Adams.) For the French a neutral United States might prove more helpful than if we had confirmed the military treaties since our country did not have the naval strength to keep open our ports in the face of war with Britain.

The new French Minister, Citizen Edmond Genêt, had plans to use this country as a base from which to organize raids on the commerce and colonies of Britain and Spain, to fit out ships for attacks against the British fleet, and also to enlist Americans aboard French ships. Secret instructions from Revolutionary France directed Genêt to propagandize among the Americans, says Professor Alexander DeConde, ''to influence them so they would favor France in her struggle. Assured of the favorable disposition of Jefferson and Madison, he had orders to tamper with American domestic politics for whatever advantage might accrue to France.'' (*Entangling Alliance*)

Fortunately the U.S. Government moved quickly to prohibit the fitting out of French privateers or recruitment of American crews. President Washington ignored Secretary of State Jefferson, who was of course favorable to Revolutionary France, and gave the job of enforcing the neutrality to Treasury Secretary Hamilton's customs officers. Jefferson offered to resign.

Genêt, who had been received with wild approval in several large U.S. cities, was busy inland as well as at sea. ''Hatching or abetting various plots, he had planned to launch hostile military expeditions from American soil with American troops against Spanish and English possessions in North America.'' (*Entangling Alliance*) And the French Revolution became even more entangled in our affairs with the rise here of French-hatched communes — or Democratic Clubs, as Citizen Genêt called them. Despite America's neutrality policy, these revolutionary anti-Federalist societies were pro-French and anti-British, and their incendiary propaganda was soon pandemic. They appeared, in Genêt's words, "as if by magic from one end of the continent to the other."

These revolutionary cells were organized to make serious trouble, and their influence was subversive to say the least. At a gathering in Philadelphia, for example, guests toasted Citizen Genêt but refused to extend the same courtesy to President Washington. Here was an association, said Noah Webster, "which must be crushed in its infancy or it would certainly crush the government." In the words of John Quincy Adams, these so-called Democratic Clubs "are so perfectly affiliated to the Parisian Jacobins that their origin from a common parent cannot possibly be mistaken." (*Entangling Alliance*)

Soon even the patient George Washington became convinced that these "self-created societies" were meant to "sow seeds of jealousy and distrust among the people." (*To Covet Honor*) And this was certainly happening. Mobs in city streets threatened the Federalists who stood with Hamilton. Washington later recalled: "I early gave it as my opinion to the confidential characters around me that if these societies were not counteracted (not by prosecutions, the ready way to make them grow stronger), or did not fall into disesteem" about their real purposes instituted "by their father Genêt, . . . they would shake the government to its foundations." (*Washington: The Indispensable Man*) Later Washington would speak more directly about the spread of the "doctrine of the Illuminati, and the principles of Jacobinism," as a result of the Democratic Societies established in our country by Revolutionary France.

President Washington believed the revolutionary Democratic Clubs were responsible for the so-called Whiskey Rebellion. Whatever the case, it was certainly the spirit of the French Revolution that sustained it. Albert Beveridge comments that "when the troops sent out to put down the insurrection reached Harrisburg, they found the French flag flying over the courthouse." President Washington said: "I consider this insurrection as the first *formidable* fruit of the Democratic Societies . . . instituted by *artful and designing* members [*of Congress*] . . . . I see, under a display of popular and fascinating guises, the most diabolical attempts to destroy . . . the government." He further declared: "That they have been the fomenters of the western disturbance admits of no doubt." If "the daring and factious spirit" is not crushed, "adieu to all government in this country, except mob and club government." (*The Life Of John Marshall*)

The Presidential denunciations devastated the neo-Jacobin clubs. By 1795-1796 "most of them had apparently disappeared. Weakened from within and assailed from without, they did not survive Washington's second term." (*Entangling Alliance*) At least they had gone underground.

As for Citizen Genêt, he became reckless and alienated former friends in Jefferson's Republican party. His progress in this country had been "marked by founding Jacobin clubs corresponding roughly to the Communist cells of our own time." (*The Oxford History Of The American People*, Samuel Eliot Morison, New York, Oxford University Press, 1965) Genêt "appealed to the people over the head of their government to support him. This was next to encouraging revolution. It had been done with success by French republican diplomatists in the smaller states of Europe, but it did not succeed in the United States." (*A Diplomatic History Of The United States*) Even Thomas Jefferson now called him a madman.

Washington requested Genêt's recall, and it was eventually accepted in return for the recall from Paris of the conservative Gouverneur Morris. But the President charitably allowed the French conspirator, who correctly feared the guillotine, to live out his life in our country — a nation whose orderly traditions he had labored to subvert.

The subversion spun off by the conspirators behind the French Revolution did not disappear at once, nor was it forgotten overnight. New England clergymen continued to insist from their pulpits "that the French Revolution was a vast conspiracy directed by the Illuminati of Bavaria against all government, religion and morality." And John Jay and others agreed that "the Jacobins are still more numerous, more desperate, and more active in this country than is generally supposed." (*John Jay*) Indeed, the Jacobin clubs in our country proved "so divisive that popular feeling forced the passage of the Alien and Sedition Acts. The acts were, of course, eventually repealed; but by that time they had succeeded in dispersing the subversive influence of the American Jacobins." (*Seventeen Eighty Nine*, American Opinion Preview Series, 1968)

Popular resentment of Revolutionary France was further aroused with the attempted bribe of the U.S. Government by Talleyrand's agents — the so-called XYZ Affair, made public in 1798. And "an undeclared naval war between the countries did take place, 1799-1800." (*The Rebirth Of Liberty*, Clarence B. Carson, New Rochelle, Arlington House, 1973) France's conduct, said Patrick Henry in 1799, "has made it the interest of the great family of mankind to wish the downfall of her present government." For she destroys. said Henry, "the great pillars of all government and of social life, — I mean virtue, morality, and religion. This is the armor, my friend, and this alone, that renders us invincible."

Shortly thereafter, of course, there was a *coup* in France with Bonaparte becoming First Consul. The 1778 treaties with France were completely abandoned as Europe continued its bloody marches in the

Napoleonic wars. The young and independent Republic of the United States had survived subversion by a European conspiracy and now had breathing space in which to recuperate. The disease, however, had not been conquered and would appear again.

Chapter II

Industrial Revolution:
Freeing The Market

MERCANTILISM was the economic system that dominated Western Europe from around 1500 to the time of the Industrial Revolution. It was a system of state control and national economic rivalry, which sought to accumulate precious bullion for the state through a politically planned economy involving taxation of imports, promotion of favored exports, and exploitation of colonies. Regulation was the byword of the day.

Like contemporary Marxism, mercantilism held "that there is an irreconcilable conflict of interests among men and groups of men. The gain of one is invariably the damage of others; no man profits but by the loss of others . . . . It was the essence of the teachings of Mercantilism. . . ." (*Theory And History*, Ludwig von Mises, New Rochelle, Arlington House, 1969)

Colonies such as those Great Britain had in America were viewed as economic markets whose purpose was to serve Mother England. Such colonies, observed Edward P. Cheyney, "were controlled by the English government largely for their commercial and other forms of economic value. The production of goods needed in England but not produced there, such as sugar, tobacco, tar, and lumber, was encouraged. But the manufacture of such goods as could be exported from England was prohibited. The purchase of slaves in Africa and their exportation to the West Indies was encouraged, partly because they were paid for in Africa by English manufactured goods, partly because their use in the colonies made the supply of sugar and some other products plentiful and cheap." (*An Introduction To The Industrial And Social History Of England*, New York, Macmillan, 1929)

Under the Navigation Acts, for example, certain English merchants were assured of a monopoly of trade with the colonies in America, the East Indies, and Africa. Movement of cargoes to and from the colonies could only be legally done on English ships built in the motherland and crewed by British seamen. Indeed, our own War for Independence was in large part a reaction to the government controls imposed by British mercantilism. London's economic prohibitions and regulations, said America's friend Edmund Burke in the House of Commons, resulted in "the system of a monopoly. No trade was let loose from that constraint, but merely to enable the colonists to dispose of what in the course of your trade you could not take; or to enable them to dispose of such articles as we forced upon them, and for which, without some degree of liberty, they could not pay."

Doubtless the most famous critic of the mercantilist system was Adam Smith, professor of moral philosophy at Glasgow University and author of *The Theory Of Moral Sentiments* (1759) and *An Inquiry Into The Nature And Causes Of The Wealth Of Nations* (1776). Smith urged a Free Market approach to political economy, observing in 1755, for instance: "Little else is required to carry a state to the highest degree of affluence from the lowest barbarism but peace, easy taxes, and a tolerable administration of justice; all the rest being brought about by the natural course of things. All governments which thwart the natural course are unnatural, and, to support themselves, are obliged to be oppressive and tyrannical." (*The Roots Of Capitalism*, John Chamberlain, Indianapolis, Liberty Press, 1976)

The regulations of mercantilism, said Professor Smith, were "impertinent badges of slavery" imposed "by the groundless jealousy of the merchants and manufacturers of the mother country." You see, it was not that Smith loved businessmen but that he knew the destructive consequences of legally assured monoply. As he remarked in an oft-quoted passage: "People of the same trade seldom meet together, even for merriment and diversion, but the conversation ends in a conspiracy against the public, or in some contrivance to raise prices." But Smith's point was and is, reflects Benjamin Rogge, that "in the absence of government backing, such conspiracies do not survive." (*Can Capitalism Survive?*, Indianapolis, Liberty Press, 1979)

The argument made by Adam Smith applies today even as it did two hundred years ago: In the absence of government interference the freedom of all to follow self-interest will enrich the individual as it rewards the public. In the words of the great Scots economist: "The uniform, constant, and uninterrupted effort of every man to better his condition, the principle from which public and national, as well as private opulence is originally derived, is frequently powerful enough to maintain the natural progress of things toward improvement, in spite of the extravagance of government, and of the greatest errors of administration." (*The Wealth Of Nations*, edited by Edwin Cannan, New York, Modern Library, 1937)

It will doubtless surprise many to learn that the meddlesome bureaucrats of today are mirror images of those under which Adam Smith suffered. Regulation under mercantilism was overwhelming. And the penalties, as Smith described them, were enough to set a bureaucrat at the Federal Trade Commission longing for the good old days. For instance, wrote Smith, ''the exporter of sheep, lambs or rams, was for the first offense to forfeit all his goods forever, to suffer a year's imprisonment, and then have his left hand cut off in a market town upon a market day, to be there nailed up; and for the second offense to be adjudged a felon, and to suffer death accordingly. To prevent the breed of sheep from being propagated in foreign countries, seems to have been the object of this law.'' Poor Ralph Nader; like Miniver Cheevy, born too late. How he would have loved mercantilism!

Consider the typical regulation of the trading of English wool, as described in *The Wealth Of Nations*:

''In order to prevent exportation, the whole inland commerce of wool is laid under very burdensome and oppressive restrictions. It cannot be packed in any box, barrel, cask, case, chest, or other package, but only in packs of leather or pack-cloth, on which must be marked on the outside the words *wool* or *yarn,* in large letters not less than three inches long, on pain of forfeiting the same and the package, and three shillings for every pound weight, to be paid by the owner or packer. It cannot be loaden on any horse or cart, or carried by land within five miles of the coast, but between sun-rising and sunsetting, on pain of forfeiting the same, the horses and carriages. The hundred next adjoining to the sea coast, out of or through which the wool is carried or exported, forfeits twenty pounds, if the wool is under the value of ten pounds; and if of greater value, then treble that value, together with treble costs, to be sued for within the year. . . . These regulations take place through the whole kingdom.

''But in the particular counties of Kent and Sussex the restrictions are still more troublesome. Every owner of wool within ten miles of the seacoast must give an account in writing, three days after shearing, to the next officer of the customs, of the number of his fleeces, and of the places where they are lodged. And before he removes any part of them he must give the like notice of the number and weight of the fleeces, and of the person to whom they are sold, and of the place to which is intended they should be carried.''

All of this, so similar to what our modern bureaucrats demand, was of course fearfully inefficient. In its place Smith proposed what became known as the *laissez-faire* theory. The idea was to restrict government to protecting the nation from foreign invasion: administering justice in connection with personal injury, contract disputes, and violence; and, "certain public works and certain public institutions." Many of Smith's more temperate successors, notes Edward Cheyney, "would have cut off the last duty altogether."(*An Introduction To The Industrial And Social History Of England*) But it was Adam Smith's popular volume, a contemporary correctly predicted, that "would persuade the present generation and govern the next." (*Rousseau And Revolution*, Will and Ariel Durant, New York, Simon and Schuster, 1967)

As even so "Liberal" an economist as Robert L. Heilbroner admits, "Smith was the first to understand the full philosophy of action which such conception demanded, the first to formulate the entire scheme in a wide and systematic fashion. He was the man who made England, and then the whole Western World, understand just how the market kept society together and the first to build an edifice of social order on the understanding he achieved." (*The Worldly Philosophers*, New York, Simon and Schuster, 1953)

Not that Adam Smith lived to see England transformed from economic dictatorship into a practitioner of economic liberty. When he died, in 1790, the consequences of his ideas were only beginning to flower. What is important to note here is that the basis for restraining the state in favor of the Free Market had first to be laid in a great educational campaign fostered by Adam Smith's important book. As Smith had noted in *The Wealth Of Nations,* mercantilism considered production to be the key to industry and commerce, virtually ignoring the role of the free play of the market in determining what ought to be produced and how. The producers had therefore contrived to control the system with the power of government. It would take widespread public understanding of the inefficiencies of this before politicians would appear on the scene — such as the precocious William Pitt II, Chancellor of the Exchequer at age twenty-three and Prime Minister the next year — who would attempt to implement the theory of limited government.

As John Chamberlain explains, Pitt the Younger took Smith's philosophy "as his guiding light of policy. If the shadows of the French Revolution and the long Napoleonic struggles had not intervened, the full Smith doctrine might have become English government policy long before 1835 or 1848."

The times were surely suited for change as Great Britain suffered horribly under the heel of economic regulation. Ludwig von Mises described the situation in his monumental *Human Action* (Third Edition, Chicago, Regnery, 1963):

"The truth is that economic conditions were highly unsatisfactory on the eve of the Industrial Revolution. The traditional social system was not elastic enough to provide for the needs of a rapidly increasing population.

Neither farming nor the guilds had any use for the additional hands. Business was imbued with the inherited spirit of privilege and exclusive monopoly; its institutional foundations were licenses and the grant of a patent of monopoly; its philosophy was restriction and the prohibition of competition both domestic and foreign. The number of people for whom there was no room left in the rigid system of paternalism and government tutelage of business grew rapidly. They were virtually outcasts. The apathetic majority of these wretched people lived from the crumbs that fell from the tables of the established castes. In the harvest season they earned a trifle by occasional help on farms; for the rest they depended on private charity and communal poor relief. Thousands of the most vigorous youths of these strata were pressed into the service of the Royal Army and Navy; many of them were killed or maimed in action; many more perished ingloriously from the hardships of the barbarous discipline, from tropical diseases, or from syphilis. Other thousands, the boldest and most ruthless of their class, infested the country as vagabonds, beggars, tramps, robbers, and prostitutes. The authorities did not know of any means to cope with these individuals other than the poorhouse and the workhouse. The support the government gave to the popular resentment against the introduction of new inventions and labor-saving devices made things seem quite hopeless.''

Yet with the first efforts to deregulate came fear and violence. Among the opponents of labor-saving devices were the so-called Luddites, who demanded the continued ''protection'' of the government from industrial advances that they viewed as threatening their jobs. Parliament had ended the regulation of the wool industry and thus made possible the first ventures that would lead to the Industrial Revolution. Throughout 1811 and 1812 mobs rioted in Lancashire, Yorkshire, and Nottingham, breaking up machinery such as wool frames. ''They issued letters signed by 'King Lud,' or 'Ned Lud,' and so gave the movement of machine-breaking its name. In nearly a year, from March 1811 to February 1812, they broke over a thousand frames . . . . Sympathy with them was general.'' (*Modern Britain*, Pauline Gregg, New York, Pegasus, 1965)

Eventually, remembering the French Revolution, the government broke the Luddite movement and continued to deregulate. In 1813, report J.L. and Barbara Hammond in *The Rise Of Modern Industry* (New York, Harcourt, Brace, 1926), Parliament repealed ''the Acts authorizing magistrates to fix wages; in 1814 the apprenticeship sections of the Statute of Artificers; in 1815 the Act establishing the Assize of Bread in London. The repeal, in each case, registered a decision taken and applied much earlier . . . . industry, like agriculture, escaped sooner in England than on the Continent from the restraints that the institutions and the temper of the Middle Ages had placed upon it.''

The factories developed in an atmosphere of dramatic political change accompanied by prejudice, vestigial regulations, and fear over the loss of vested interests. Mises recounts in *Human Action*:

''That the factories could thrive in spite of all these hindrances was due to two reasons. First there were the teachings of the new social philosophy expounded by the economists. They demolished the prestige of Mercantilism, paternalism, and restrictionism. They exploded the superstitious belief that labor-saving devices and processes cause unemployment and reduce all people to poverty and decay. The laissez-faire economists were the pioneers of the unprecedented technological achievements of the last two hundred years.

''Then there was another factor that weakened the opposition to innovations. The factories freed the authorities and the ruling landed aristocracy from an embarrassing problem that had grown too large for them. They provided sustenance for the masses of paupers. They emptied the poorhouses, workhouses, and the prisons. They converted starving beggars into self-supporting breadwinners.

''The factory owners did not have the power to compel anybody to take a factory job. They could only hire people who were ready to work for the wages offered to them. Low as these wage rates were, they were nonetheless much more than these paupers could earn in any other field open to them.''

The resultant growth and prosperity were extraordinary. The consumption of raw cotton, for example, increased from eight thousand tons in 1760 to one hundred thousand tons in 1830; coal production over roughly the same period nearly quadrupled; and, the iron output was four times as great in 1835 as in 1800.

The key to all of this growth was the political philosophy of Prime Minister William Pitt II, a disciple of Adam Smith. (See *The Younger Pitt*, John Ehrman, New York, Dutton, 1969.) As Winston S. Churchill put it, Pitt ''was the first English statesman to believe in Free Trade, and for a while his Tory followers accepted it. The antiquated and involved system of customs barriers was now for the first time systematically revised. There were sixty-eight different kinds of customs duties, and some articles were subject to many separate and cumulative imposts. A pound of nutmegs paid, or ought to have paid, nine different duties. In 1784 and 1785 Pitt was able to bring a degree of order into this chaos, and the first visible effect of his wide-ranging revision of tariffs was a considerable drop in smuggling.'' (*History Of The English-Speaking People*, New York, Dodd, Mead, 1957)

But Pitt was soon faced with a general war, and to finance it he imposed a variety of new taxes. "He first put a tax on racehorses, carriage-horses, hackney carriages, personal servants, shopkeepers, windows, hair-powder, dogs, watches and clocks, and various other articles," records S.E. Ayling. "Later, under the demands of war, he both trebled his original taxes on many of these items, and also underlined the element in them of taxing luxuries; a man with ten servants would pay more than ten times the tax of a man having one only, and so forth. Some of these taxes were failures, others open to criticism; the window tax has been blamed for encouraging the bricking-up of windows and exclusion of light . . . . the national lottery begun in 1784 (it lasted forty years) was attacked by some on moral grounds. But, in any case, the great expenses of war with France eventually forced altogether more radical thoughts on taxation; and Pitt in 1799 . . . imposed a tax on income itself, again using the principle of a higher rate of tax on the rich . . . ." (*The Georgian Century*, London, Harrap, 1966)

All of this had not only slowed the move toward an unregulated economy, it had in consequence frustrated the Industrial Revolution. But, after twenty-two years of war the income tax, supposedly a war measure only, was scheduled for abolition. The trouble is, as we know, that government has a tendency to expand, not contract, and it is always reluctant to surrender its revenues. That is, unless the public demands otherwise. This time, because of the growing influence of the advocates of the Free Market, it did so. And the great tax rebel of the time was a champion of the middle class named Henry Brougham, a lawyer and journalist with the *Edinburgh Review*, who helped to found London University. According to former *Wall Street Journal* editor Jude Wanniski:

"What made the Industrial Revolution and the Pax Britannica possible was the audacity of the British Parliament in 1815. Spurred by middle-class agitators such as Henry Brougham, the legislature rejected the stern warnings of the fiscal experts and in one swoop eliminated Pitt's income tax, which had been producing £14.6 million or a fifth of all revenues and tariffs and domestic taxes that had been producing £4 million more. Had the British left their tax rates high in an attempt to quickly pay down their debts, the sixty-year bull market that followed would not have been possible . . . . As the economy surged in the following decades, expanding revenues were used both to pay down the debt and reduce other tax rates." (*The Way The World Works*, New York, Simon and Schuster, 1978)

England went to work with determination. Furthermore, in 1816, she returned to the gold standard; three years later, bullion and coins were allowed to pass in and out of the country with impunity. Mercantilism was on its way to the graveyard. As Will and Ariel Durant observe:

"Inspired by Adam Smith . . . English industry was geared to private enterprise, spurred by the profit motive, and largely free from government regulation. It obtained capital from its own unspent earnings, from prosperous merchants, from landlords gathering agricultural revenues and urban rents, and from bankers who knew how to make money by hugging it, and who lent money at lower rates of interest than their French compeers. So individuals and associations provided funds for entrepreneurs who proposed to unite the products of farm and field with the service of machines and the labor of men, women, and children on a larger scale and to greater gains than England had ever known. The providers of capital kept watch on its use, and gave its name to the economic system that was about to transform the Western world." (*The Age Of Napoleon*, New York, Simon and Schuster, 1975)

Capitalism in a free market responded by providing products not mainly to the rich, as under mercantilism, but for the great masses. Workers became more affluent consumers and, because of business expansions and economies of scale, could afford the results of their mechanically enhanced production. Ludwig von Mises elaborates:

"The laissez-faire ideology and its offshoot, the 'Industrial Revolution,' blasted the ideological and institutional barriers to progress and welfare. They demolished the social order in which a constantly increasing number of people were doomed to abject need and destitution. The processing trades of earlier ages had almost exclusively catered to the wants of the well-to-do. Their expansion was limited by the amount of luxuries the wealthier strata of the population could afford. Those not engaged in the production of primary commodities could earn a living only as far as the upper classes were disposed to utilize their skill and services. But now a different principle came into operation. The factory system inaugurated a new mode of marketing as well as of production. Its characteristic feature was that the manufactures were not designed for the consumption of a few well-to-do only, but for the consumption of those who had hitherto played but a negligible role as consumers. Cheap things for the many, was the objective of the factory system." (*Human Action*)

Not that government regulation of the economy which had been the norm for centuries was easily set aside. In 1820, for example, the *Edinburgh Review* was still complaining of: "Taxes upon every article which enters into the mouth, or covers the back, or is placed under the foot . . . . taxes upon warmth, light, and locomotion . . . . taxes on the raw material — taxes on every fresh value that is added to it by the industry of man . . . . The schoolboy whips his taxed top — the beardless youth manages his taxed horse, with a taxed bridle on a taxed road: and the dying Englishman pouring his medicine, which has paid seven per cent., into a spoon that has paid fifteen per cent. — flings himself back upon his chintz bed which has paid twenty-two per cent. — makes his will on an eight pound stamp, and expires in the arms of an apothecary who has paid a license of £100 for the privilege of putting him to death. His whole property is then immediately taxed from two to ten percent. Besides the probate, large fees are demanded for burying him in the chancel; his virtues are handed down to posterity on taxed marble; and he is then gathered to his fathers, — to be taxed no more.''

But one by one such taxes were repealed or reduced as the middle class began to exert its growing power. For example, the ''wine excise was abolished in 1825, the tea excise in 1833, the beer tax in 1830, the tobacco excise in 1840. The transit duties on coal were reduced, the law prohibiting the emigration of artisans was repealed in 1824; the export of machinery was permitted under licence.'' (*Modern Britain*) A potato blight in 1845 and 1846 led to the abolition of the Corn Laws (grain in general), which had heavily taxed foodstuffs imported from a foreign country. Because of the failure of the potato crop, reports Jude Wanniski, ''the starving Irish could not be fed from the inadequate British granaries. The Corn Laws simply had to be ended to permit entry of grains from the United States. Even so, a half million Irish died of starvation in 1846-47.''

Prime Minister Robert Peel, a Tory, not only dealt with the Corn Laws but also ''abolished the excise duties on livestock, meat, and potatoes; he reduced those on sugar, cheese, and butter. Gladstone's budgets of 1853 and 1860 completed the work and Britain was virtually a Free Trade country.'' (*Modern Britain*) Gone, too, were the relics of the guilds, legal monopolies, emigration bans, and the whole slate of mercantilist regulations.

And what were the consequences of this introduction of *laissez faire*, of leaving each individual free to act in the market? It made Britain the economic colossus of the world, gave her supremacy on the seas for some one hundred fifty years, and provided a rich Empire upon which the sun never set. As Professor George Woodcock has written:

''. . . from imperial defeat in 1783, Britain rose to become the most dominant naval power the world has known, and to assemble an Empire that in size and population dwarfed any of its predecessors or contemporaries. With its fleet and its Empire, Britain — whose army was negligible by the standards of continental Europe — became a major power and, for most of the nineteenth century, the world's exemplar and leader, whose achievements other nations emulated and whose aura of strength and self-confidence was so intimidating that its real power was rarely even tested.'' (*Who Killed The British Empire?*, New York, Quadrangle, 1974)

Great Britain thrived under economic freedom not only in Empire and prestige, but in other spheres as well. As K.B. Smellie observes in *Great Britain Since 1688* (Ann Arbor, University of Michigan Press, 1962):

''Between 1816 and 1875 Britain was to become the world's workshop, the world's banker, and the world's trader . . . . By 1860 she was supplying half the world's output of coal and manufactured goods. In 1830 world production of coal was about 30 million tons, of which Britain produced four-fifths; in 1870 it was about 220 million tons, of which Britain produced half . . . . In 1870 the external trade of the United Kingdom was greater than that of France, Germany, and Italy combined and three times that of the United States. The output of pig iron had risen from 700,000 tons a year in 1830 to about 3,800,000 in 1869-71, and to over 6,500,000 in 1871-73. While many industries were dependent on the coal fields, the main growth had been in cotton. Cotton was the one industry into which mechanization had cut deep by 1820. Textile operatives were more than 10 percent of the working population in 1841 . . . .

''Between 1815 and 1851 occurred the most rapid development of domestic resources in the whole of British economic history.''

There seemed no stopping Great Britain, which was soon the leading creditor in the world. Historian K.B. Smellie recounts: ''It was this vigorous, competitive, hideous and yet dazzling community which was the great exporter of the capital which made it possible to open up the vast but hitherto untapped resources lying in the hinterlands of new continents. All the underdeveloped parts of the world were calling for investments. Nearly a quarter of the £2.4 billion which was added to the capital of the United Kingdom between 1865 and 1875 was placed abroad, while a sixth went into houses and a tenth into railways at home . . . . It has been argued that the effort and the expense which went into the development of the colonial empire were at the cost of improvements which might have been made at home. This is to ignore the indirect gains which came from bringing new areas with new products into a worldwide system of multilateral trade. The small volume of direct trade with many new colonies often contained an element which played a vital part in some more complex interchange.''

All of this was great and splendid. But it did not suit the purposes of collectivist conspirators who saw government as the ultimate monopoly. They made their counterattack at about the time of the release of the *Communist Manifesto*, in the mid-Nineteenth Century, by arranging for Great Britain to readopt the income tax. As the country entered the

Twentieth Century, that tax was gradually made more progressive, even as conspirator Karl Marx had urged. And, as the influence of the Fabian Socialists waxed before and after World War I, economic freedoms waned. There developed a movement for a return to "protectionist" tariffs and a "planned" economy. And as these found political favor in the aftermath of war, Britain moved away from *laissez faire* and . . . ceased to be Great.

There is of course a lesson in all of this for the United States. It is that we can free the market and return to greatness as Britain once did under the influence of Adam Smith and his successors, or we can continue with the neo-mercantilism of regulation, paternalism, taxation, and decay. Only fools fail to learn from history.

Chapter III
Manifest Destiny

It WAS IN 1845 that a New York editor spoke for the nation by coining the phrase *Manifest Destiny*. According to editor John L. O'Sullivan, it was "our manifest destiny to overspread the continent allotted by Providence for the free development of our yearly multiplying millions." Expansion of the United States was looked at, variously, as reaching our natural frontiers at the Pacific and Rio Grande, conveying the benefits of republican government to those anxious to embrace them, and just plain pioneering.

"Many felt that it was the right, the duty, and the opportunity of Americans," reported historian Glyndon G. Van Deusen, "to expand the area of freedom and to enrich it, whether by the development of domestic resources, by continental conquest, or by the extension of American influence and American ideals to more distant quarters of the globe. Expansionism in this period pushed the American nation to the Pacific and to the Rio Grande, and sent clipper ships into the seven seas. It fostered dreams of great trade development in the Orient. 'Our population,' wrote William Henry Seward in 1846, 'is destined to roll its resistless waves to the icy barriers of the north, and to encounter Oriental civilization on the shores of the Pacific.' " (*The Jacksonion Era, 1828-1848*, New York, Harper & Row, 1959)

Yes, young America was feeling her oats and sowing them as well. In the forty years following our Second War for Independence in 1812, the size of the country doubled — adding Florida at the expense of Spain, Texas through its fight for independence, the Oregon Country from Britain, and the Mexican Cession and Gadsden Purchase as a result of the Mexican War. "It took American people one hundred and seventy-five years to build up and achieve independence for thirteen colonies with about three million inhabitants," observe Charles and Mary Beard. "In less than one-third that span of years seven new states were established in the region immediately westward and occupied by a population larger than that of the whole United States when the census of 1790 was taken. In less than half that number of years five additional states were formed in the Louisiana Territory, still further west, Texas was brought into the Union, a vast area to the southwest wrested from Mexico, and California admitted to statehood.'' *(The Beards' New Basic History Of The United States*, Garden City, Doubleday, 1960)

There was something special about the character of the early American, armed with liberty and a will to succeed, that even a foreigner could sense. Alexis de Tocqueville, a French aristocrat, visited us and wrote of our countrymen during the Jacksonian era in *Democracy In America*:

''In the United States, the greatest undertakings and speculations are executed without difficulty, because the poorest as well as the most opulent members of the commonwealth are ready to combine their efforts for these purposes. The consequence is, that a stranger is constantly amazed by the immense public works executed by a nation which contains, so to speak, no rich men. The Americans arrived but as yesterday on the territory which they inhabit, and they have already changed the whole order of nature for their own advantage. They have joined the Hudson to the Mississippi, and made the Atlantic Ocean communicate with the Gulf of Mexico, across a continent of more than five hundred leagues in extent which separates the two seas.''

Even earlier than de Tocqueville's visit to this country, President James Monroe and Secretary of State John Quincy Adams spelled out the now famous doctrine that proclaimed there would be no future European colonies in the Americas; nor transfer to other European powers of possessions already held; and, that the United States would in turn stay out of European wars just as the U.S. expected Europeans to stay out of conflicts in this Hemisphere. President Monroe and Secretary Adams proposed this policy, but it would have to be left to others — especially James Polk — to enforce it.

In Monroe's second Inaugural, says Pulitzer Prize historian George Dangerfield, the President ''recalled the passing of the War of 1812, the building of coast fortifications from the St. Croix to the Sabine in a spirit of 'peace and goodwill,' the ratification of the Florida Treaty, the 'peculiar felicity' of the United States in being altogether unconnected with the causes of war which seemed to menace Europe. He noted that he had been able to repeal the internal taxes, and he expressed his belief that 'the present depression in prices' would be temporary; while, as a proof of the 'extraordinary prosperity' of the nation, he offered the payment of nearly $67,000,000 of the public debt. He declared that no serious conflict had arisen between national and state governments, and announced that 'there is every reason to believe that our system will soon attain the highest degree of perfection of which human institutions are capable.' '' (*The Era Of Good Feelings*, New York, Harcourt, Brace, 1952)

So, at times, it seemed. The Erie Canal, for example, was built without federal help. But the success of this project only motivated those who would have a central government finance similar internal improvements. "The American republic had come into existence," noted George Dangerfield, "by overthrowing a tyrant who ruled from afar: was it now to put itself into the hands of another tyrant, ruling only a little less remotely on the borders of Virginia and Maryland? Was it not always true that political power in remote hands was almost certain to be abused? Before the dismayed eyes of those who remembered and cherished the warnings of Thomas Jefferson, and before the eyes of Jefferson himself at Monticello, there spread a vision of a mass of internal-improvement legislation, entangled in local schemes, confused by jealousies, and saturated with greed and with corruption." There is nothing new under the sun.

Secretary of State John Quincy Adams was in fact an expansionist not only for the United States but also for American government. It is of course well known that during the Monroe Administration he pressed the Adams-Onis Treaty of 1819 through which Spain "ceded East Florida to the United States, gave recognition to an American seizure of West Florida, and transferred Spanish claims to the Pacific Northwest north of the line of 42° to the United States." (*Manifest Destiny And Mission In American History*, Frederick Merk, New York, Knopf, 1963) Less well known is the fact that later, as President, John Quincy Adams asked Congress in his first annual message for what were then considered vast national powers — including scientific expeditions, an astronomical observatory, a national university, various internal improvements, and creation of a Department of the Interior. These measures, complained Thomas Jefferson, "will be to them [*the Federalists*] a next blessing to the monarchy of their first aim, and perhaps the surest stepping stone to it." Adams had affronted representative government by demanding that the Establishment of the day not be "palsied by the will of our constituents . . . ."

Such sentiments, aired in public, led many to believe that the Adams family was a nest of monarchists. And all of this prepared the climate for the 1828 election of war hero Andrew Jackson. Old Hickory's policy was simply summarized by him: "The Federal Constitution must be obeyed, state rights preserved, our national debt must be paid, direct taxes and loans avoided, and the Federal Union preserved. These are the objects I have in view, and regardless of all consequences, will carry into effect."

Growth and change in the nation before Jackson became President were profound, and they continued dramatically during his term in office.

"While General Jackson was President," reports Bray Hammond, "the federal union came to include twice as many states as it had begun with and held territory that recently had belonged to Spain and France. It was shortly to add regions in the South and West taken from Mexico and regions in the Northwest that Great Britain claimed. Its expansion seemed irresistible." (*Banks And Politics In America*, London, Oxford University Press, 1957)

Indeed, migration, growth, and expansion were watchwords of the era. John Quincy Adams had spoken of "our natural dominion in North America." But all did not swoon over the frontier. We learn in *The Growth Of The American Republic*: "Major [*Stephen*] Long's expedition of 1819 reported the Great Plains 'almost wholly unfit for cultivation,' and laid down on the map of that region, which now supports a thriving population of several millions, the legend 'Great American Desert.' " (Samuel Eliot Morison and Henry Steele Commager, New York, Oxford University Press, 1937) Daniel Webster opposed even a postal route from Missouri to the Oregon territory, saying: "What do we want with this vast, worthless area? This region of savages and wild beasts, of deserts, or those endless mountain ranges, impenetrable, and covered to the very base with eternal snow? What can we ever hope to do with the western coast, a coast of three thousand miles, rock-bound, cheerless, uninviting, and not a harbor on it?"

But the people thought otherwise. Europeans were moving to America even as Americans were focusing their attention on the West. The invaluable de Tocqueville reported of his visit here:

"It is the Americans themselves who daily quit the spots which gave them birth, to acquire extensive domains in a remote region. Thus the European leaves his cottage for the transatlantic shores, and the American, who is born on that very coast, plunges in his turn into the wilds of central America. This double emigration is incessant; it begins in the middle of Europe, it crosses the Atlantic Ocean, and it advances over the solitudes of the New World. Millions of men are marching at once towards the same horizon; their language, their religion, their manners differ; their object is the same. Fortune has been promised them somewhere in the West, and to the West they go to find it.

"No event can be compared with this continuous removal of the human race, except perhaps those eruptions which caused the fall of the Roman Empire. Then, as well as now, crowds of men were impelled in the same direction, to meet and struggle on the same spot; but the designs of Providence were not the same. Then every newcomer brought with him destruction and death; now everyone brings the elements of prosperity and life.''

There was life indeed. In 1790 the population of the United States was estimated at four million; by 1848, we Americans numbered an impressive twenty-two million. Virtually in the middle of that expansion Andrew Jackson commented:

''[F]rom the earliest ages of history to the present day there never have been thirteen millions of people associated in one political body who enjoyed so much freedom and happiness as the people of these United States. You have no longer any cause to fear danger from abroad . . . . It is from within, among yourselves — from cupidity, from corruption, from disappointed ambition and inordinate thirst for power — that factions will be formed and liberty endangered . . . .'' (*The Meaning Of Jacksonian Democracy*, edited by Edwin C. Rozwenc, Boston, Heath, 1963)

The conduct of the nation's financial affairs concerned President Jackson as much as America's frontiers. In fact, though Andy Jackson would himself die in debt, in 1835 he saw to it that our National Debt was paid. And his famous fight with the Bank of the United States was an epoch battle against conspiracy and monopoly. As George Roche has observed of the Age of Jackson: ''The assault on economic privilege carried over from the banking struggle and came to include tariffs and subsidies. The Jacksonians were squarely in the American tradition of insisting upon free competition and a minimum of interference, whether public or private, with the independence and opportunity of the individual. Jackson himself was a westerner whose primary appeal to a rising middle class was equality before the law and resistance to unwarranted centralization, whether in economics or politics.'' (*The Bewildered Society*, New Rochelle, Arlington House, 1972)

Contemporary critics of Jackson portrayed him as a monarch, but his sympathies and policies were motivated by the welfare of the Middle American. Indeed, even among the influential business community, reported Claude G. Bowers, ''the feeling was germinating that Jackson was not far wrong in the conclusion that a moneyed institution possessing the power to precipitate panics to influence government action, was dangerous to the peace, prosperity, and the liberty of the people.'' (*The Party Battles Of the Jackson Period*, Boston, Houghton Mifflin, 1922)

Rechartering the Bank of the United States became a campaign issue in 1832, and when Congress voted to maintain the *status quo* with the central financial institution, President Jackson vetoed the legislation and removed government funds from the Bank. Nicholas Biddle, president of the Bank, fought to maintain his power, contracting credit to punish the

Government for its action — to the point where discount rates rose as high as thirty-six percent. By flexing the Bank's muscles, however, Biddle proved Jackson's point about its potential as a nefarious force. By 1841 it was forced to liquidate.

Here is part of the famous veto message that President Andrew Jackson sent Congress, calling the central bank unconstitutional: "It is to be regretted that the rich and powerful too often bend the acts of government to their selfish purposes . . . . In the full enjoyment of the gifts of Heaven and the fruits of superior industry, economy, and virtue, every man is equally entitled to protection by law; but when the laws undertake to add to these natural and just advantages, artificial distinctions, to grant titles, gratuities, and exclusive privileges, to make the rich richer and the potent more powerful, the humble members of society — the farmers, mechanics, and laborers — who have neither the time nor the means of securing like favors to themselves, have a right to complain of the injustice of their Government . . . . In the act before me there seems to be a wide and unnecessary departure from . . . just principles." (*Jackson Versus Biddle: The Struggle Over The Second Bank Of The United States*, edited by George Rogers Taylor, Boston, Heath, 1949)

President Jackson was easily re-elected. There were more Middle Americans, it seems, than big bankers. "The Jacksonian revolution," reports *Banks And Politics In America*, "was a consequence of the Industrial Revolution and of a farm-born people's realization that now anyone in America could get rich and through his own efforts, if he had a fair chance . . . . The humbly born and rugged individualists who were gaining fortunes by their own toil and sweat, or wits, were still simple Americans, Jeffersonian, anti-monopolistic, anti-governmental, but fraught with the sense of what soon would be called manifest destiny. . . . [*Such Americans*] made the age of Jackson a festival of *laisser faire* preclusive to the age of Grant and the robber barons."

After the bitter winters of the late 1830s, Americans again turned to the West in ever greater numbers, aided by the rapid development of canals, roads, and railroads. "As soon as it became evident that little help could be expected from the Federal Government for internal improvements," note Samuel Morison and Henry Commager, "other states followed New York [*with its Erie Canal*] in constructing canals, or lending their credit to canal corporations. Ohio linked the Great Lakes with the Mississippi valley by canal in 1833-34. Cleveland rose from a petty frontier village to a great lake port by 1850; Cincinnati, at the other end of the state canal system, sent pickled pork down the Ohio and Mississippi by flatboat and steamboat, shipped flour by canal boat to New York, and in 1850 had a population of 115,000 — more than that of New York in 1815." (*The Growth Of The American Republic*)

Jackson's Secretary of State, Martin Van Buren, failed in his attempt to purchase Texas from Mexico. But, later as President, Van Buren stayed aloof from the Texas question, and in so doing lost much of his popularity for refusing to annex Texas as the Lone Star Republic wanted. Van Buren's temporizing on the Texas issue, as well as economic panic in the country during his Administration, cost him the 1840 election to William Henry "Tippecanoe" Harrison. President Harrison's running-mate was John Tyler, who succeeded him in very short order and annexed Texas just before he left the White House to make room for James Polk. President Polk was elected on an expansionist platform over Henry Clay, the straddling Whig.

The Polk election came in the midst of more Westward expansion. According to *The Growth Of The American Republic*: "The Oregon Trail and the Lone Star Republic appealed to a people recovering confidence after the hard times of 1837 to 1840. The 'manifest destiny' of the United States to expand westward and southward . . . became the theme of countless newspaper articles, Fourth of July orations, and political speeches. Much talk there was, too, of Anglo-Saxon genius in colonization and self-government . . . . The slogans of 1844, 'Reoccupation of Oregon and reannexation of Texas,' 'Fifty-four forty or fight,' rallied the same sort of people who shouted 'Tippecanoe and Tyler too' in 1840 . . . ."

The Oregon Country was made up of not only the present state bearing that name, but also Washington, Idaho, a part of Montana, and British Columbia up to the aforementioned 54° 40´. All of this, said Polk, was American territory "clear and unquestionable." As it turned out, of course, Polk compromised with the British, with whom we had been jointly occupying Oregon, and agreed to a settlement — opposed for a time by Secretary of State James Buchanan — at the forty-ninth parallel. Polk followed his own advice to a Congressman whom he considered timid towards London — namely, that "the only way to treat John Bull was to look him straight in the eye, that he considered a bold and firm course on our part the pacific one."

As a matter of fact the U.S. had long been willing to accept the forty-ninth parallel, but had been rebuffed by the British. Furthermore, Polk did not want war simultaneously with Mexico (which seemed imminent) and Britain. The compromise gave both Canada and the United States a Pacific outlet. And, observed Samuel Morison, except "for a minor controversy over the islands of Puget Sound, this western end of the lengthy frontier between Canada and the United States gave no further trouble.'' (*The Oxford History Of The American People*)

The signing of the Oregon treaty meant the American Republic now reached from Atlantic to Pacific. President Polk surely felt, wrote historian Glyndon Van Deusen, ''that ports on the Pacific were more important than territory; that the area north of the 49th parallel was not worth a war, so long as the United States had access through the Vancouver Straits to the ocean; and that compromise with the British in Oregon was necessary, if they were to be kept from getting a slice of a greater prize, California.'' (*The Jacksonian Era*)

Young Hickory, as James Knox Polk was called, was carrying on as Old Hickory wished. (Polk was the youngest President elected to date.) Andy Jackson, says Frederick Merk, still ''lent glamour to Manifest Destiny.'' The former President ''sent repeated letters in the years preceeding his death [*in 1845*] to friends urging the annexation of Texas and the occupation of Oregon, and these were usually promptly transmitted to the press. Jackson urged annexation to insure the national safety and interest and to checkmate the machinations of the British.'' (*Manifest Destiny And Mission In American History*)

Above all was that matter of Texas, over which Henry Clay had lost the Presidency in 1844, alienating both North and South, abolitionist and slaveowner. Clay viewed the annexation as a judgment about states' rights and slavery. On the one hand, Mr. Clay ''declared that he personally had no objection to the annexation of Texas, but that he was unwilling to see it made an issue which 'jeoparded' [*sic*] the Union. He protested against the positions of the extremists of South Carolina who wished to make the recent rejection of the Texas treaty an occasion to dissolve the Union.'' (*Henry Clay And The Art Of American Politics*, Clement Eaton, Boston, Little, Brown, 1957)

But, as we have said, the Polk people wanted annexation — or ''reannexation,'' since it was considered to be part of the Louisiana Purchase given up by J.Q. Adams. And that was not all that Young Hickory had in mind. Indeed, President Polk told his Navy Secretary: ''There are four great measures which are to be the measures of my administration: one, a reduction of the tariff; another, the independent treasury; a third, the settlement of the Oregon boundary territory; and lastly, the acquisition of California.'' (*The Mexican War, A Compact History: 1846-1848*, Charles L. Dufour, New York, Hawthorn, 1968) The first three were *faits accomplis* by 1846, but the latter required war with Mexico.

Polk saw in California a ground for possible European intrigue proscribed by the Monroe Doctrine. The same was true of the Oregon

Country and Mexico, "where the United States had interests of its own," notes Harvard Professor Emeritus Frederick Merk. "There, especially, he wished Europe held at bay. Again, in Monroe's case, the emphasis had been upon military adventures by Europe, upon interferences, by force or other means, to oppress or control New World governments. Polk was concerned about other kinds of interferences and seemed to include aid to, and even advice to, independent American governments among the forbidden activities. The Polk version of the Monroe message attained major importance in American history. It swayed decisions until well into the twentieth century." (*The Monroe Doctrine And American Expansionism*, New York, Knopf, 1966)

As it happened, in an era when the United States was seriously thinking of abolishing the Military Academy at West Point, the war with Mexico broke out . . . and the anti-militarists were put to flight. We were soon defeating Mexico with but 7,200 troops in our regular Army compared to some 27,000 well-trained Mexican forces whose leaders contended their "Eagle and Serpent [*would be*] flying over the White House." (*Home Of The Brave*, John Alexander Carroll and Odie B. Faulk, New Rochelle, Arlington House, 1976) American troops were quickly in the Halls of Montezuma.

"Acquisition of territory by conquest was a question the Cabinet had considered the day the war was formally declared," noted Frederick Merk in *Manifest Destiny And Mission In American History*. "It had been broached by Buchanan. He proposed issuing a declaration to foreign governments that the war was not for conquest or for any dismemberment of Mexico, that its purpose was simply self-defense. This proposal was a characteristic exhibit of his weakness. It was squashed immediately and completely by the President. Such a declaration, Polk said, would be improper and unnecessary. The war would not be fought for conquest, 'yet it was clear that in making peace we would if practicable obtain California and such other portion of the Mexican territory as would be sufficient to indemnify our claimants on Mexico and to defray the expenses of the war.' "

Eventually four American Presidents would be elected as a result of fame resulting from their roles in the war with Mexico — they were General Zachary Taylor, Franklin Pierce, James Buchanan, and Confederate President Jefferson Davis. When the war with Mexico was over, having cost us thirteen thousand dead, we "emerged from it with 529,000 square miles of additional territory, a magnificent outlet to the trade of the Pacific, and hundreds of millions in California gold, a bonanza the news of which was just beginning to spread as the treaty reached the final stages of ratification." (*The Jacksonian Era*)

The Mexican War sent a message that we meant to determine our own destiny and that Texas was indeed a part of the Union. Foreigners were made to understand, concluded Burt Hirschfield, that "the war underscored certain truths — it meant the continent was rounded under American rule, putting an end to any European hopes of re-establishing a foothold in North America, foreshadowing at the same time the growing might of the United States." (*After The Alamo: The Story Of The Mexican War*, New York, Messner, 1966)

In fact, from the period before Texas was brought into the Union to 1848, the United States added 1.2 million square miles to its dominion, and in 1853 filled out part of Arizona with a $10 million deal known as the Gadsden Purchase. (*The United States To 1865*, Michael Kraus, Ann Arbor, University of Michigan Press, 1959) The Mexican War had concluded with President Polk paying for title to the conquered land — a sum that was no more than he had offered before the conflict began.

Despite the controversies, such as the slavery issue in the new territory, "the United States had gained an immense new domain, and the dream of some of her greatest leaders — a two-ocean nation — had been fulfilled. With the later Gadsden Purchase, all the present states of Texas, New Mexico, Arizona, California, Utah, and Nevada, together with portions of Kansas, Colorado, and southern Wyoming were acquired. It was a territory for the most part completely wild and in many parts even unexplored, but it was destined to exert enormous influence on the later course of American history." (*The House Divides*, Paul I. Wellman, Garden City, Doubleday, 1966) In short, James K. Polk oversaw the greatest territorial expansion in the history of the Republic.

The wilderness had been opened and American government spread coast to coast. Manifest Destiny had in fact caused the American Eagle to spread her wings over the entire land. As editor John O'Sullivan had said: "Yes, more, more, more! . . . till our national destiny is fulfilled and . . . the whole boundless continent is ours." From sea to shining sea.

Chapter IV

Reconstruction: Carpetbaggers And Scalawags

"I<small>T IS OUR</small> duty to live," said the surrounded Robert E. Lee. "What will become of the women and children of the South if we are not here to protect them?" Issuing General Order Number Nine in April of 1865 before surrendering at Appomattox Court House, General Lee told his troops he was "compelled to yield to overwhelming numbers and resources." (*Robert E. Lee*, Peter Earle, New York, Saturday Review Press, 1973) The terms of capitulation were magnanimous, and within a month the War Between the States was effectively over. But the so-called Reconstruction that followed was a mockery of that name and amounted to destruction and tyranny for half the nation.

President Abraham Lincoln had in 1863 proposed leniency toward the South, planning widespread pardons and a "ten percent plan" whereby a rebelling state would be recognized as having regained all rights in the Union when ten percent of the 1860 voters took a loyalty oath and agreed to end slavery. This was done in Louisiana, Arkansas, and Tennessee even before the hostilities on the battlefield had ceased.

Opposing Lincoln's plans were the Radical Republicans, a gang of conspirators out for vengeance and power. For example, in 1864 the Radical-dominated Congress passed a bill sponsored by Senator Benjamin Wade[*] of Ohio and Congressman Henry Davis of Maryland which set as the price of readmission an oath of *past* loyalty to the Union of a majority of a state's 1860 voters — a practical impossibility. President Lincoln pocket vetoed it. Clearly the President and the conspirators had very different plans for post-war America.

A subsequent Wade-Davis Manifesto sneered at the President's "dictation of his political ambition," berated the veto as a "stupid outrage on

---

[*]Wade would have succeeded President Andrew Johnson had the latter been successfully impeached and convicted, and Ben Wade was so sure of the outcome he had his own Cabinet chosen before the vote in the Senate was taken.

the legislative authority of the people,'' warned that Mr. Lincoln had
''presumed on the forebearance which the supporters of his Administration had so long practiced,'' and bluntly told the President of the United States to ''confine himself to his executive duties.''

It was in such a climate that Lincoln was assassinated less than a week after Appomattox by a conspiracy that also struck at key members of his Cabinet. Senator Benjamin H. Hill of Georgia, a pro-Union man who like Robert E. Lee had rallied to the Stars and Bars, immediately declared of the murder: ''God help us if that is true. It is the worst blow that has yet been struck the South.'' (*The Angry Scar*, Hodding Carter, Garden City, Doubleday, 1959)

Certainly that was true in the matter of what was to be done with the freed Negroes. Radical Republicans were well aware that Abraham Lincoln had asserted: ''I am not, nor ever have been in favor of bringing about in any way the social and political equality of the white and black races. I am not nor ever have been in favor of making voters or jurors of Negroes, nor of qualifying them to hold office, nor to intermarry with white people. And I will say in addition to this that there is a physical difference between the white and black races which I believe will forever forbid the two races living together on terms of social and political equality.'' (*South Of Appomattox*, Nash K. Burger and John K. Bettersworth, New York, Harcourt, Brace, 1959)

Succeeding the murdered Lincoln was Andrew Johnson, his Vice President on a coalition Union ticket, a former Democrat Senator and military governor of Tennessee. At the onset, the Radicals thought they had their own man in the White House. Had not Johnson talked of hanging ''traitors'' and stated ''treason must be made infamous, and traitors must be impoverished''? But the new President attempted to carry out Lincoln's plan to bind up the wounds of the nation and restore liberty to the South, causing him to meet quick and venomous opposition from the Congress. The Radicals had misread Johnson. Like Lincoln, comments historian Claude G. Bowers, Johnson ''did not like slavery; like Lincoln, he recognized the constitutional rights of slavery; like Lincoln, he did not care for abolitionists; like Lincoln, he was more interested in the preservation of the Union, with or without slavery; and like Lincoln, he thought the war was waged for the preservation of the Union and for no other purpose.'' (*The Tragic Era*, New York, Blue Ribbon Books, 1929) In fact, contrary to the legalistic posturing of the Radicals, both held that the Southern states had *not* seceded — a constitutional impossibility — but had merely tried unsuccessfully to secede.

President Johnson's Amnesty Proclamation of May 29, 1865, effectively renewed Lincoln's pledge of December of 1863. The new

President's terms for restoration to the Union were repudiation of Confederate debt; repeal of the secession ordinances; and, abolition of slavery. Indeed, by December of 1865 every Confederate state (except Texas, which followed four months later) had accepted the terms to be returned to good standing in the Union. "In the subsequent elections, Alexander E. Stephens, former Vice-President of the Confederacy, 4 Confederate generals, 5 Confederate colonels, 6 Confederate Cabinet officers, and 58 Confederate Congressmen were elected to the 39th Congress from the South. The prevalence of recent rebels in state and local governments was no less emphatic." (*The Reconstruction*, James P. Shenton, New York, G.P. Putnam's Sons, 1963)

To be sure, these men *were* the leaders in the South. But the election of the former rebels was fanned by propaganda into outrage in the North. After all, it was noted, only white males had the vote. And this for a paltry pledge of allegiance to the Union against which they had so recently made war.

Meanwhile, emancipation of the slaves was formalized as the now occupied Southern states ratified the Thirteenth Amendment. The former slaves, mostly illiterate, were led to believe they would each receive "forty acres and a mule" and the right to confiscate the property of their former masters. To compound the hostility and further humiliate the South, Negro troops were sent to oversee the white population. One out of four white Southern males between the ages of seventeen and forty-five had died in the war and a like number was wounded. Bitterness and chaos thrived in occupied Dixie. Claude Bowers writes:

"This, then, was the combination against the peace of a fallen people — the soldiers inciting the blacks against their former masters, the [*Freedmen's*] Bureau agents preaching political and social equality, the white scum of the North fraternizing with the blacks in their shacks, and the thieves of the Treasury stealing cotton under the protection of Federal bayonets. And in the North, demagogic politicians and fanatics were demanding immediate negro suffrage and clamoring for the blood of Southern leaders. Why was not Jeff Davis hanged; and why was not Lee shot?" (*The Tragic Era*)[*]

Vagrancy, drunkenness, and violent crime mounted, with no little help from Northern carpetbaggers and Southern scalawags. In an attempt to bring order, a number of states legally adopted so-called Black Codes prohibiting the often ignorant and naïve Negroes from sitting on juries, carrying weapons, committing adultery, being vagrants, and violating

---

[*]Yet, even in 1867, Negroes could vote in only six Northern states. (*Reconstruction* [*1865-1877*], edited by Richard N. Current, Englewood Cliffs, Prentice-Hall, 1965)

curfew and segregation laws. The Black Codes did, report John Alexander Carroll and Odie B. Faulk, "recognize the right of freedmen to own and inherit property, to make contracts, and to sue in court — and they made it very plain that blacks were expected to return to work, for they said that blacks had to have a steady occupation and they carried heavy penalties for violations of labor contracts." (*Home Of The Brave*)

But the Northern Radicals would have none of this, and the Congress that convened in December of 1865 refused to seat the duly elected Representatives from the former Confederacy. Never mind that these controversial codes which the Radicals so self-righteously castigated "did not differ materially from similar statutes in the Northern States. Even some of the harshest laws, those which were received with wide-spread indignation throughout the North, could almost be duplicated by laws at that time in force in such states as Rhode Island and Connecticut. Even the phraseology, the using of the words master, mistress and servant, which was deemed objectionable and suggestive by Northern Republicans, could be found in Northern statutes." (*The Struggle Between President Johnson And Congress Over Reconstruction*, Charles E. Chadsey, New York, AMS Press, 1967)

Northern Radicals — led by Senator Charles Sumner of Massachusetts and Representative Thaddeus Stevens of Pennsylvania — meant to treat the states of the South like conquered provinces. "I have never," claimed the vengeful Stevens, "desired blood punishment to any great extent. But there are punishments quite as appalling and longer remembered than that. They are more advisable, because they would reach greater numbers. Strip proud nobility of their bloated estates; reduce them to a level with plain republicans; send them forth to labor and teach their children to enter the workshops or handle a plow, and you will thus humble the proud traitors." (*The Angry Scar*) The land belonging to Confederates, he urged, should be taken from them and sold to their slaves at ten dollars an acre.

Stevens, by the way, was a bachelor who lived with a mulatress — though historians disagree on the extent of her role in his household.

In February of 1866, President Johnson vetoed an extension of the notorious Freedmen's Bureau which was causing so much trouble in the South. Moreover, he reiterated that the states should determine the matter of suffrage as directed by the Constitution. Each move the President made deepened his political grave in the North. But the President believed that the Radical conspirators wanted nothing less than destruction of the Republic. In a public speech he decried the attempt to centralize power in the hands of a few at the federal level, and referred to the Joint Committee on Reconstruction as an "irresponsible central directory" which had assumed "nearly all the powers of Congress" without "even consulting the legislative and executive departments of the Government. *** Suppose I should name to you those whom I look upon as being opposed to the fundamental principles of this Government, and as laboring to destroy them. I say Thaddeus Stevens, of Pennsylvania; I say Charles Sumner, of Massachusetts; I say Wendell Phillips [*president of the Anti-Slavery Society*], of Massachusetts." (*The Struggle Between President Johnson And Congress Over Reconstruction*)

The battle was joined. And the Radical-led Congress overrode Johnson's veto of not only the Freedmen's Bureau but also of the Civil Rights Bill. When the President pointed out the unconstitutionality of granting full citizenship to four million former slaves while eleven states were not recognized in the Congress, the Radicals incorporated language from their Civil Rights Act into the Fourteenth Amendment and submitted it to the states. With the exception of Tennessee, ten of the eleven Southern states rejected it — as did California, Delaware, Kentucky, and Maryland.

During this period, Robert E. Lee was avoiding politics as much as possible. But in an interview he had to observe: "The [*Congressmen of the*] Radical party are likely to do a great deal of harm, for we wish now for good feeling to grow up between North and South, and the President, Mr. Johnson, has been doing much to strengthen the feeling in favor of the Union among us. The relations between the Negroes and the whites were formerly friendly, and would remain so if legislation be not passed in favor of the blacks, in a way that will only do them harm. [*The Radicals*] are working as though they wished to keep alive by their proposals in Congress the bad blood in the South against the North. If left alone the hostility which must be felt after such a war would rapidly decrease, but it may be continued by incessant provocation." (*South Of Appomattox*) And the Radicals knew how to be provocative.

Since the Southern states refused to ratify the Fourteenth Amendment, Congress arbitrarily and unconstitutionally put them out of the Union. "The newly elected 40th Congress convened in March rather than in December of 1867, and on March 2 passed an act dividing the old Confederacy, with the exception of Tennessee, into five military districts." (*The Reconstruction*) Negroes in these districts were enfranchised, though they were still without the vote in much of the North, while white former Confederates were disenfranchised. Under this series of Reconstruction Acts, only when the new "reconstructed" non-Union governments passed the Fourteenth Amendment could they be admitted to the Union, a clear violation of the Constitution which stipulates that only the legislatures of sovereign states may vote on Amendments.

As the constitutional scholar Dan Smoot has pointed out: "Congress denied the southern states judicial relief, by intimidating the Supreme Court into silence — threatening to abolish the Court's appellate jurisdiction, or to abolish the Court itself, by constitutional amendment. Army bayonets escorted illiterate negroes and white carpetbaggers to the polls, keeping most southern whites away. In Louisiana, an Army general even presided over the state legislature which 'ratified' the Fourteenth Amendment.''

Even so, counting the votes of six "reconstructed" governments plus two more Northern states, ratification left the total of those states approving at one short of the required three-fourths because New Jersey and Ohio became outraged at the power grab and withdrew their ratifications. The obliging Secretary of State nonetheless determined, and the Radical Congress agreed, that the unratified Fourteenth Amendment was now part of the Constitution. We live with that decision and its many destructive consequences to this day.

Also over President Johnson's veto, the Congress passed the Tenure of Office Act, prohibiting the President from removing Cabinet officers without approval of Congress; and the Command of the Army Act, violating his constitutional authority as Commander-in-Chief. The Radicals were strengthened in the elections, having encouraged mobs around the country to attack the President when he sought to take his case to the people. "Never in history had a President gone forth on a greater mission — to appeal for constitutional government and restoration of union through conciliation and common sense; and never had one been so scurvily treated. City officials in Baltimore, Philadelphia, Cincinnati, Indianapolis, and Pittsburgh had refused an official welcome; the Governors of Ohio, Indiana, Illinois, Michigan, Missouri, and Pennsylvania had not appeared; and in the more than forty congressional districts traversed, but one Radical Congressman had paid a call of courtesy.'' (*The Tragic Era*) All Democrats were murderers, went the cry, and the air was filled with charges of "copperhead," "rebel hounds," impeachment of the President, and even the implication that Johnson was involved in the assassination of Lincoln.

The Freedmen's Bureau in the South joined in preaching this liturgy of hate. Carpetbaggers and scalawags organized the Negroes into voting blocs in Union or Loyal Leagues. Historian Bowers reports: "Night meetings, impressive, flamboyant ceremonies, solemn oaths, passwords, every possible appeal to the emotions and senses, with negroes on guard down the road to challenge prowlers, much marching and drilling — all mystery. And then incendiary speeches from Northern politicians promising the confiscation of the white man's land. Discipline, too — iron discipline. Intimidation, likewise — the death penalty for voting the Democratic ticket. Strangers arriving mysteriously in the night with warnings that the native whites were deadly enemies. Promises of arms, too — soon to be fulfilled. And the negroes moved as a race into the clubs. And woe to the negro who held back, or asked advice of an old master. This, they were taught, was treason to race, to party. Persuasion failing, recourse was had to the lash, and many a negro had welts on his back.'' The white reaction to this was the original Ku Klux Klan, headed at its founding by the legendary Confederate General Nathan Bedford Forrest.

In Washington, even though his power over the Executive departments and the military had been usurped by the conspirators, the Radicals now decided to impeach President Johnson and replace him with one of their own, Senate president *pro tempore* Benjamin Wade. The President had decided to test the constitutionality of the Tenure of Office Act by discharging Secretary of War Edwin Stanton, a conspirator and Radical informant who had, in fact, been appointed not by him but by Lincoln. The Joint Committee on Reconstruction, that ''irresponsible central directory,'' responded by bringing eleven charges against the President. Eight of these referred to the Stanton firing; one to the Army Act; one, drawn up by the Radical haranguer Benjamin Butler, charged the President with having in ''a loud voice'' made ''certain intemperate, inflammatory and scandalous harangues'' against Congress, bringing ''the high office of president of the United States into contempt, ridicule, and disgrace, to the great scandal of all citizens''; and, finally, a catchall charge was added by Thaddeus Stevens on the ground that it would be easiest to pass.

Johnson was indeed impeached by the House and tried in the Senate with Chief Justice Salmon Chase presiding. After a trial of more than two months and every conceivable sort of pressure and bribery, the Senate failed in May of 1868 to convict on what was thought the most promising charge. The margin was one vote — a vote generally credited to Senator Edmund Ross of Kansas, though a total of seven Radicals had refused to follow the party line. Not one of the seven ever again held elective office.

The hamstrung Andrew Johnson finished out his term, and was denied nomination in 1868 as a Democrat. The Republicans gained control of both the Executive and Legislative branches in the fall of 1868 with the election of Ulysses S. Grant. His platform endorsed Radical Reconstruction and called for giving the Negroes the vote in the South but leaving it up to the states elsewhere. With the South under occupation and effectively disenfranchised, the people of the North were inflamed by politicians ''waving the bloody shirt.'' As one Radical politician put it:

"The cure for all the evils we endure — all of them spawned by rebellion — is not to be found in conciliation . . . but in sustaining the party that restored the Union to the Fathers, clad now in the white robes of freedom, unsullied and irreproachable." Indeed, in short order, the voters of the State of Mississippi — such as they were — sent a Negro to fill the seat in the U.S. Senate formerly held by Jefferson Davis.

In 1869 the Radicals passed the Fifteenth Amendment, providing for male Negro suffrage — even in the North — and approval of the Amendment was made a condition of "readmission" to the Union for Virginia, Texas, Mississippi, and Georgia. A Force Act became law in 1870 and a Ku Klux Klan Act the following year, authorizing the suspension of a writ of *habeas corpus*. Martial law was in force. Claude Bowers writes of South Carolina:

"Came then the terror, with wholesale arrests, with business all but suspended, with every citizen at the mercy of a dishonest enemy with a private grudge. The trials were mockeries of justice, the United States Circuit Court at Columbia a shambles . . . . The juries were defiantly packed with partisans, and an astonishing number of Radical politicians became jurors. Thus a dastardly conspiracy was manipulated by officials of the Federal Government! In Charleston, the scenes were similar. As if by magic the Democrats and Conservatives seemed to disappear. The courts could find no one for jury service but negroes, carpetbaggers, and scalawags. Some of the accused were deservedly convicted; others were youths of little education who had joined the Klan for a lark . . . ."

Louisiana was especially hard hit by its "reconstruction" government, which incurred a debt of forty-eight million dollars in four and a half years, prompting an outraged citizen to remark: "We are all ruined here and to hold property is to be taxed to death by our African communists." In South Carolina printing costs in fifteen months under the Republicans exceeded the total cost for seventy-eight years before the war. Three-quarters of the South Carolina legislators in 1873 were blacks who were uneducated in matters of government but knew a good time when they saw it. "In refurnishing the state house, five-dollar clocks were replaced by new ones costing $600; $4 looking glasses by $600 mirrors; and $1 chairs by new ones at $60 each. Taxes paid for a free restaurant for members where ham, oysters, and champagne were served." (*Quest Of A Hemisphere*, Donzella Cross Boyle, Boston, Western Islands, 1970) A carpetbagger named "Honest" John Patterson was quoted as saying "there are five years more of good stealing in South Carolina."

Indeed, enough liquor was consumed in the office next to the clerk of the South Carolina Senate to have amounted to one gallon per legislator per day. Not to mention the fine foods and furnishing for the homes of the legislators' mistresses. *The Tragic Era* paints the scene:

" . . . amid the cracking of peanuts, the shouting, laughing, stamping, members are seen leaving and returning in a strange state of exaltation — they come and go in streams. Let us follow the trail to the room adjoining the office of the clerk of the Senate. We learn that it is open from eight in the morning till two or four the next morning, and now, as we push in, it is crowded. A barroom! Solons are discussing politics over sparkling glasses of champagne, supplied by taxpayers. Here gallons of wine and whiskey are consumed daily. Members enter blear-eyed in the early morning for an eye-opener or a nightcap — some are too drunk to leave at 4 A.M. Champagne? Wine? Whiskey? Gin? Porter? Ale? — and the member orders to his taste. Does a special brand of liquor or fine cigars appeal especially? Boxes are ordered to the member's hotel or boarding-house. 'One box of champagne, one box of sherry wine, three boxes cigars' — this is the order for one negro member. When the chairman of the Claims Committee found one box of wine delivered to his lodging, he indignantly wrote: 'This is a mistake; the order calls for two boxes of wine. Please send the other.' ✱✱✱

"A clubby crowd, too, these 'loyal' men of South Carolina; for when Speaker Moses and Whipper, a negro member who owned fast horses, arranged a race on a thousand-dollar bet, and Moses lost, did not the Legislature within three days vote a gratuity to the Speaker to cover his loss, 'for the dignity and ability with which he has presided.' "

But the disenfranchisement of whites was gradually lifted in the South, and in 1874 the Democrats won a majority in the U.S. House of Representatives for the first time since the War. Grant had easily been re-elected in 1872 and was now more conciliatory, being also confronted with scandal after scandal in his own Administration. In fact, by the end of 1875 only the Southern states of Louisiana, South Carolina, and Florida were ruled by the Radicals. At long last the Reconstruction period was drawing to a close.

"Much was lost in the destruction of the Old South that men have not ceased to regret," observed Richard M. Weaver in his classic *The Southern Tradition At Bay*. "Most of the poetic virtues — honor, dignity, fealty, valor — were made to look outmoded and futile, and have since had to sneak in by the back door and apologize for themselves." (New Rochelle, Arlington House, 1968) Indeed the period ended with a stolen election.

The Presidential returns of 1876 saw Democrat Samuel Tilden win the popular vote over Republican Rutherford B. Hayes, and in an honest count he probably won the electoral vote as well. However, the Radical

Republicans still controlled the voting boards in three contested Southern states — South Carolina, Louisiana, and Florida — and there would be no honest tally there. Congress decided the dispute by one vote in an Electoral Commission. The commission was to have been made up of five Republicans and five Democrats from Congress, two Democratic Justices from the Supreme Court and two Republican Justices, and one independent. But the Illinois Legislature then elected the one independent Justice to the U.S. Senate, leaving but four remaining Justices from which to choose, all of them being Republicans. Each vote by the resulting Commission was eight to seven along straight partisan lines, accounting for a one-vote electoral margin in favor of Hayes.

The Democrats threatened to filibuster in the House, which they controlled, but were appeased by the Compromise of 1877, which promised a withdrawal of federal troops from the three remaining "reconstructed" states; various federal aid; and, appointment of an ex-Confederate to the patronage-laden post of Postmaster General.

With these conditions fulfilled to seat Hayes as President, and in the absence of federal bayonets, the three remaining carpetbag-scalawag governments soon fell. The conservative Democrats were back in control of the then Solid South, and could begin what reconstruction they could as each state saw fit — starting with repeal of local Radical legislation. The South might forgive, but it would not forget.

Chapter V

Robber Barons: Moguls And Manipulation

"LAW! What do I care about law?" demanded Cornelius Vanderbilt. "Hain't I got the power?" Indeed, by manipulating and corrupting government, Vanderbilt had proved his contempt of the legal canons many times over. Not that Mr. Vanderbilt was the worst of those who obtained vast wealth by conspiring to have government serve their purposes. In fact, he was sometimes outmaneuvered in this by those even more unscrupulous. It was the era between the end of the Civil War and the conclusion of the Nineteenth Century — the era of the Robber Barons.

So arrogant was Cornelius Vanderbilt, however, that he actually proposed a monument be built in New York's Central Park to honor the country's two greatest heroes — George Washington and himself . . . not necessarily in that order. Vanderbilt was not above manipulating an entire state government so that he could drive down the price of, say, the New York Central Railroad to buy in at bargain rates. In fact, he did so. Accordingly, even John Chamberlain (in his informative if propitiatory book *The Enterprising Americans*) reported: "Legislators, to him, were holdup men who had to be bribed to keep them from selling out to his opponents, who in most cases happened to be [*Jim*] Fisk, [*Daniel*] Drew and [*Jay*] Gould, the pirates of the Erie Railroad 'ring.' " (New York, Harper & Row, 1963)

The unprecedented growth in the power and corruption of government during the War Between the States raised many ugly problems besides Reconstruction. Among those out to take advantage of this power and corruption, recounts Columbia University historian John A. Garraty, "there developed in these years the 'Robber Baron,' an unscrupulous, greedy industrial and financial type who competed ruthlessly with his fellows, exploited his labor force callously, bilked investors and other public officials without conscience, all the while masquerading behind a facade of unctuous respectability. Ever since 1871, when Charles Francis

Adams, Jr. described the unsavory practices of Jay Gould and Cornelius Vanderbilt in their battle to control the New York Central Railroad, historians have been uncovering fresh evidence of the antisocial actions and attitudes of these piratical characters.'' (*The New Commonwealth: 1877-1890*, New York, Harper & Row, 1968)

Of course in later years Commodore Vanderbilt enjoyed a reputation better than that of a pirate, or even of the notorious Jay Gould. Which only proves that writers can be as venal as legislators. Even before the outbreak of the Civil War, however, Members of Congress were asking questions of the Pacific Mail Company, for example, about certain dubious Vanderbilt dealings. According to Meade Minnigerode, they wanted to know if ''the company, which received a government subsidy, had been paying the Commodore $480,000 a year 'in order to prevent all competition to their line'? And the Pacific Mail later testified that it was true; that for more than four years the greater part of their earnings 'was wrongfully appropriated to Vanderbilt for blackmail,' because 'the terror of his name and capital would be effectual upon others who might be disposed to establish steamship lines.' A state of affairs which induced Senator Toombs to exclaim that 'you give $900,000 a year to carry the mails to California, and Vanderbilt compels the contractors to give him $56,000 a month to keep quiet.' The Pacific Mail was plundering the Government, but 'old Vanderbilt' was 'the kingfish that is robbing the small plunderers.' '' (*Certain Rich Men*, New York, G.P. Putnam's Sons, 1927)

What Vanderbilt did was a crime, punishable by years in jail, but of course he was by now a power behind the scenes in government and was not prosecuted. After all, the Commodore was merely practicing on a larger scale the means by which he began to make his fortune in steamships — namely bribing the New York Common Council to give him dock privileges and deny them to competitors. His policy, records historian Gustavus Myers, was simply to use fraud and the power of government to ''bankrupt competitors, and then having obtained a monopoly, to charge exorbitant rates. The public, which welcomed him as a benefactor in declaring cheaper rates and which flocked to patronize his line, had to pay dearly for their premature and short-sighted joy.'' (*History Of The Great American Fortunes*, New York, Modern Library, 1909, revised 1936)

Carrying the mail for the government, as we noted above, was most lucrative because of the accompanying subsidies and the receipts for postage. One got these contracts by paying off government officials in positions to award contracts. As Mr. Myers has reported: ''By means of this systematic corruption the steamship owners received many millions of dollars of Government funds. This was all virtually plunder; the returns from the 'postages' far more than paid them for the transportation of mails. And what became of these millions in loot? Part went in profits to owners, and another part was used as private capital by them to build more and newer ships constantly. Practically none of Vanderbilt's ships cost him a cent; the Government funds paid for their building.''

During the Civil War, with privateers threatening his commercial ships, the Commodore turned his attentions to railroads, acquiring through shady means the New York and Harlem, New York and Hudson River, and New York Central railroads. Then Vanderbilt plucked the Erie Railroad from Daniel Drew, though he reinstated the freebooter Drew as a director of the line and Drew in turn brought in as fellow directors Jay Gould and Jim Fisk. The latter in time wrested away the Erie line, which had been built largely with public funds, by a classic case of stock watering.

Ostensibly the infamous Erie bond issue was to be used for repairs (which were badly needed), but what it was in reality was a means for Vanderbilt's own directors to use the printing press in a *coup* against him. "Gould and Fisk set their presses whirring in the Erie basement," reports Richard O'Connor, "and ran off the ten million in bonds, which were promptly converted to 100,000 shares of stock and thrown on the market. They were undeterred by a new Vanderbilt injunction ordering that no more capital stock be issued. Flooded with this watered stock, Erie quotations kept falling and falling, and Vanderbilt kept buying and buying, driving the price up only to see it fall an hour or two later. In this struggle even the Vanderbilt fortune, not to mention his platoon of lawyers and any number of compliant judges, were not equal to the power of that printing press. 'Give us enough rag paper,' gloated Jim Fisk, 'and we'll hammer the everlasting tar out of the mariner from Staten Island.' '' (*Gould's Millions,* Garden City, Doubleday, 1962)

Thus was eight million dollars transferred from the Vanderbilt pockets into money satchels belonging to Gould and his co-conspirators, who skipped town to New Jersey just ahead of the law which the Commodore had sicced on them. From a Jersey City hotel the Gould conspirators operated in exile, obtaining passage of a bill from the New Jersey legislature enabling Erie's directors to issue stock at will. Delighted with their use of the power of government, they also set out to obtain a similar law from the dissolute New York legislators. Albany now became the setting for a bribery contest.

"Ineffectually did Vanderbilt bribe the legislators to defeat [*the bill legalizing the fraudulent stock issue*]; as fast as they took and kept his money, Gould debauched them with greater sums. One Senator in particular . . . accepted $75,000 from Vanderbilt, and $100,000 from

Gould, and pocketed both amounts.'' (*History Of The Great American Fortunes*) In the end, Gould's side prevailed, although Vanderbilt (who sold his interest) was later to force Erie to repay him for his part of the bribery. In 1873 an investigation of the events that had occurred five years before showed that the Gould conspirators had spent more than a million dollars in ''extra and legal services'' — the euphemism for bribing government officials in Albany.

In fact, in the 1873 investigation Jay Gould spoke candidly of his bought political power in several states: ''In a Republican district I was a Republican; in a Democratic district, a Democrat; in a doubtful district I was doubtful; but I was always for Erie.''

There being no honor among thieves, Drew was overthrown by Fisk and Gould and he died a bankrupt, saying of Jay Gould: ''His touch is death.'' But Cornelius Vanderbilt called the corrupt Gould ''the smartest man in America,'' no doubt since he had more than met his match with him. Indeed, his last scrap with Gould proved a psychological crusher when the Commodore decided to start a price war with the Erie Railroad, slashing the cattle carload rates of his New York Central line. The public benefitted from such competition as Gould went even lower, then Vanderbilt went lower still — until the rate was but one dollar a carload. Then, ''Erie suddenly restored its $125 rate and the Commodore gloated, believing Gould had been licked. A few weeks later he learned that he had been celebrating a false victory. Gould had bought every head of cattle his agents could find west of Buffalo and was shipping them via the New York Central at $1 a carload, taking a sizable profit at Vanderbilt's expense. Vanderbilt 'nearly lost his reason' at learning how he had been tricked.'' (*Gould's Millions*)

The corrupt Tammany Hall Ring headed by William ''Boss'' Tweed also switched allegiance from Vanderbilt to Gould, helping to control politicians and legislators while milking Erie of some twelve million dollars — most of which Gould pocketed. Indeed, by the time Jay Gould resigned from Erie its funded debt had jumped by sixty-four million dollars and it was so debilitated that its common stock was unable to pay one cent in dividends for sixty-nine years. (*The Age Of The Moguls*, Stewart H. Holbrook, Garden City, Doubleday, 1953)

''Gould's Erie Railroad operations, were, however, only one of his looting transactions during those busy years,'' records Gustavus Myers. ''At the same time, he was using these stolen millions to corner the gold supply. In this 'Black Friday' conspiracy (for so it was styled) he fraudulently reaped another eleven million dollars to the accompaniment of a financial panic, with a long train of failures, suicides and much disturbance and distress.''

The Black Friday scandal reached to the very doors of the White House, as Fisk and Gould corrupted the brother-in-law of President Ulysses S. Grant in order to get inside information on what the President intended to do with the government's gold. As summarized in *Home Of The Brave*: "Railroad speculators Jay Gould and Jim Fisk convinced the president that the sale of government gold would hurt farm prices. With Grant's assurance that no government gold would be released, Gould and Fisk began buying up gold and soon cornered much of the market. Prices soared to astronomical heights as businesses sought to exchange gold to meet their foreign commitments. On September 24 [*1869*] the stock exchange was in such a panic that a collapse of the economic system seemed imminent. Grant at last realized on September 24, known as 'Black Friday,' what was afoot and ordered the Treasury Department to release $4 million in gold — and the conspiracy collapsed."

There were rumors that Gould had lost thirty million dollars when the price broke, but in fact during the days before Black Friday — when Gould was urging others to buy — he was selling quietly at high prices (having obtained from his government sources inside knowledge of what was coming) while making a show of more purchases. While Jay Gould did have some outstanding contracts for purchases which would have bankrupted him, he found enough collusion in the judiciary to enjoin Gould's creditors from settling on these contracts. As the *New York Tribune* reported at the time, speculators such as Gould "use lawyers' injunctions to prevent the payment of honest debt; obey the rules of the Gold Exchange when they make by it and repudiate when they lose; betray each other's counsels, sell out their confederates and consent to the ruin of their partners . . . ."

But then that was in the days before such things were managed with the open collusion of government — as in the effort in the early 1980s by silver speculators to swindle the Hunt family of Texas.

Another celebrated scandal of the Robber Baron era involved the Union Pacific Railroad which, as it turned out, would also fall into Gould's grasp. At the end of the Civil War the Union Pacific was reported not to be raising sufficient private funding. Since it was in fact being built at government expense for private profit this was only part of the con game. A scheme was cooked up to create a corporation, the Crédit Mobilier Company, which would supposedly build the railroad and reap vast profits. Fair enough, but it was a scam and a front. Massachusetts Congressman Oakes Ames, head of the Union Pacific, protected this confidence game by seeing to it that he had a little help from his friends in setting up Crédit Mobilier. In the winter of 1867-1868 Mr. Ames "distributed his first discreet gifts of free shares of Crédit Mobilier 'where they would do the most good,' that is, among prominent Senators and Representatives. With the transcontinental line completed in 1869, amid nation-wide celebrations, both Ames and [*Collis Huntington, promoter of the western half of U.P., the Central Pacific*] organized 'junkets' for politicians, who traveled over their lines at a cost of $10,000 per private train." (*The Politicos,* Matthew Josephson, New York, Harcourt, Brace, 1963)

Crédit Mobilier was in fact owned by the board members of the Union Pacific Railroad. Eventually it was discovered that Members of Congress were involved with the stock "as a precaution against an investigation. It was the plan that these statesmen should buy at par, but since a large dividend had been assigned the stock, and another dividend was soon due, it meant, in reality, a 'purchase' at a price far below par, and an assured profit. It was, in truth, intended as a bribe. It *was* a bribe." (*The Tragic Era,* Claude G. Bowers)

Difficulty arose when it became apparent that Crédit Mobilier was not only well stocked with legislators but totally crooked. All of which proved an embarrassment to the politicians in on the scam, including former Vice President Schuyler Colfax, Vice President Henry Wilson, Republican leader James G. Blaine, and future President James A. Garfield, among others. A whitewash was arranged by a friendly Congressional Committee which found "that as far as their participation was concerned 'nothing was proved,' but, protest their innocence as they vehemently did, the tar stuck, nevertheless.

"As to the loot of Crédit Mobilier Company, the committee freely stated its conclusion. Ames and his band, the evidence showed, had pocketed nearly $44,000,000 outright, more than half of which was in cash . . . . [*T*]he committee found . . . that the total cost of building the Union Pacific Railroad was about $50,000,000. And what had the Crédit Mobilier Company charged? Nearly $94,000,000 . . . . The committee admitted that the 'road had been built chiefly with the resources of the Government.' A decided mistake; it had been entirely built so." (*History Of The Great American Fortunes*)

Less than a hundred thousand dollars, which was the bribe to the politicians, had brought the conspirators manipulating government some forty million dollars and a railroad worth fifty million more. It was publicly embarrassing if not financially so. Prominent financier Jay Cooke, who was later to lose his shirt in backing the Northern Pacific Railroad, "using all his mighty influence in Washington, had been unable to stop the exposures, which he declared were 'nonsense' and would damage our credit abroad . . . ." (*The Robber Barons,* Matthew Josephson, New York, Harcourt, Brace 1934)

Congressman Ames did not perjure himself as did his colleagues and was impeached by the House, in Claude Bowers' witty view, "as a warning to corrupt Congressmen against turning State's evidence." A similar fate befell Congressman James Brooks, who in fact had either abstained from votes in Union Pacific matters or voted against the lobbying efforts of the railroad. But Brooks, you see, was the lone Democrat caught. All the tarnished Republicans, except for the now fabulously wealthy and belatedly honest Ames, were exonerated. As Oakes Ames put it: "It's like the man in Massachusetts who committed adultery, and the jury brought in a verdict that he was guilty as the devil, but that the woman was as innocent as an angel. These fellows are like that woman." (*The Tragic Era*)

If the conspirators had stolen only from one another it would have been one matter, but the big money was in looting the taxpayers. The privately held railroads over which they contended, especially before the early 1870s, were in the main built with public money and with the connivance of corrupted politicians. As summarized in the *History Of The Great American Fortunes*: "The money lavishly poured out for the building of railroads was almost wholly public money drawn from the compulsory taxation of the whole people. At this identical time practically every railroad corporation in the country stood indebted for immense sums of public money, little of which was ever paid back. In New York State more than $40,000,000 of public funds had gone into the railroads; in Vermont $8,000,000 and large sums in every other State and Territory. The whole Legislature and State Government of Wisconsin had been bribed with a total of $800,000, in 1856, to give a large land grant to one company alone . . . . The State of Missouri had already disbursed $25,000,000 of public funds; not content with these loans and donations two of its railroads demanded, in 1859, that the State pay interest on their bonds."

It cannot be over-emphasized that the Robber Barons were not capitalists trying to make a profit in a free market, but seekers of subsidies, restricted competition, grants, and other aid that only government could provide. Without crooked government they could never have operated. The Central Pacific half of the Union Pacific Railroad, for example, became widely known as "the Octopus" because of its stranglehold on California. But its grip was due to a monopoly granted by the state to a group of conspirators called The Associates who controlled the legislature. They were Collis Huntington, Leland Stanford, Charles Crocker, and Mark Hopkins. With competition kept out by government, Central Pacific was able to raise rates so high that it was estimated it would be cheaper to ship a keg of nails from New York around Cape Horn to

California rather than move it overland where the Central Pacific could add its excessive fees.

The three dry-goods merchants and the former peddler who comprised The Associates had naturally managed to build their line with government money. There were even instances, says Matthew Josephson, "where in their strenuous progress they encountered existing lines, such as the Sacramento Valley Railroad built for a short distance in 1859, through a rich region. Faced with the option of buying, instead they built their own line around it over a somewhat lengthier distance in a queer and crazy course through the same valley, 'because it was cheaper to build at the government expense than to buy a railroad already existing . . . .' The fruits of the great project went to the construction [*the so-called separate construction outfit, similar to U.P.'s Crédit Mobilier*] company, one authority holds. 'The Federal government seems . . . to have assumed the major portion of the risk and the Associates seem to have derived the profits.' " (*The Robber Barons*)

Profiteering at the expense of the taxpayers was not the only negative aspect of government intervention in the railroad industry. As economic historian Clarence B. Carson puts it: "Premature railroad building induced by government grants left a trail of disaster in its wake . . . . Government aid fostered a boom in railroad building that extended beyond those railroads receiving it. There was overbuilding in some areas; many roads were left in shaky financial conditions; there were bankruptcies. Hapless settlers were lured by government and railroads to buy farms in the semi-arid West; many would return eastward after years of failure. Unscrupulous financiers moved into railroading, sometimes made their quick profits, then left the railroads in disarray. *** There is every reason to believe that America would have had such a railroad system as was needed and could have been afforded without the government aid and without the manifold infelicities that accompanied premature building." (*Throttling The Railroads*, Indianapolis, Liberty Press, 1971)

So that fateful meeting at Promontory Point, Utah, between the locomotives from the Central Pacific and Union Pacific railroads was something far less than a crowning glory wrought by Free Enterprise. Indeed, reflecting on the looting of the taxpayers, Massachusetts Senator George Hoar put it this way: "When the greatest railroad in the world, binding together the continent and uniting two great seas which wash our shores, was finished, I have seen our national triumph and exaltation turned to bitterness and shame by the unanimous reports of three committees of Congress that every step of that mighty enterprise had been taken in fraud." (*Iron Wheels And Broken Men*, Richard O'Connor, New York, G.P. Putnam's Sons, 1973)

Such looting was by now no secret. The failure of Jay Cooke & Company struck hard on the heels of the scandals of the Erie Railroad, the Tweed Ring, and the Crédit Mobilier. "The leading bankers and brokers who had been close to railroad jobbers followed Cooke in their collapse; runs spread to commercial and savings banks believed to be burdened with unsalable railroad securities; money went into hoarding; and during the remaining three months of 1873 more than five thousand business houses closed their doors." (*The Politicos*) Union Pacific stock also plunged, and the ubiquitous Jay Gould used his swag from the Erie Railroad virtually to take over U.P., as well as other smaller railroads which were then "sold" at highwayman rates to the Gould-controlled Union Pacific to allow further looting by Gould. "It was a plan which, although theoretically regarded in law as fraudulent, was nevertheless audaciously carried on with complete immunity" from the law. (*History Of The Great American Fortunes*)

Then William Vanderbilt's Western Union was taken to the cleaners by Gould, painfully reminding him of his father's warning to steer clear of Jay. Gould began buying Western Union stock, but was rebuffed in his demand to join its board. So the prideful Gould set up the rival Atlantic & Pacific telegraph company and raided Vanderbilt's firm for officers. Gould now bought the *New York World* for propaganda purposes, and the newspaper had an immediate change in editorial policy. As related by Stewart Holbrook:

"First, he turned the *World's* guns on Western Union, the largest of the many telegraph companies. Readers of the *World* were soon learning that Western Union was an expensive and un-American near monopoly that was sucking the lifeblood of business. In the same paper, readers also saw that a new concern, the Atlantic & Pacific Company, was laying telegraph lines along the railroads which just happened to be in the control of Jay Gould. Within twelve months, the business of Western Union declined by approximately two million dollars, and the company made up its mind it would be best to pay Gould's blackmail: Western Union purchased Atlantic & Pacific for a sum variously reported as 'exceeding ten million dollars.'

"Within weeks, the New York *World* was describing in most favorable light another new telegraph outfit, the American Union, sponsored by Jay Gould. Western Union bought it, paying considerably more than its worth. Whereupon, Gould prepared to take Western Union itself into camp . . . . Gould set the *World* on a campaign to wreck Western Union's credit, while his hatchet men used all the tricks of manipulation they knew so well to depress the stock still lower. It was a savage war and brief. In

1881, when he was forty-five, Gould had control of Western Union."
(*The Age Of Moguls*)

Jay Gould was perhaps the prototypical Robber Baron, but others who emerged with rosier reputations were little better. For example, Andrew Carnegie (see Chapter VII) knowingly sold the U.S. Navy defective armored plating, secretly treated to defraud the government, and was even fined for it by President Grover Cleveland. J. Pierpont Morgan managed to stay out of the Civil War, but profitted from it by selling back to the government its own defective rifles bought at $3.50 each and then resold at $22 apiece. These weapons were so bad they would tear off the thumbs of Union soldiers firing them. The master conspirator Morgan, of course, went into the railroad business as well as international banking.

Like the others, J.P. Morgan opposed competition in favor of controlled stability. Government, after all, was far easier to manipulate than the market. "The dominant fact of American political life at the beginning of this century," contends Gabriel Kolko, "was that big business led the struggle for federal regulation of the economy. *** The first federal regulatory effort, the Interstate Commerce Commission, had been cooperative and fruitful; indeed the railroads themselves had been the leading advocates of extending federal regulation after 1887." (*The Triumph Of Conservativism*, New York, Free Press of Glencoe, 1963) Indeed, the I.C.C. quickly came to be seen, said one railway owner, as something merely to satisfy "the public clamor for a government supervision of railroads," becoming "a sort of barrier between the railroad corporations and a sort of protection against hasty and crude legislation hostile to railroad interests." (*The Politicos*) Or as another railroad executive admitted, by 1890 "there is not a road in the country that can be accused of living up to the rules of the Interstate Commerce Law." (*The New Commonwealth*)

Another archetype of the Robber Barons was John D. Rockefeller, about whom there have been hundreds of thousands of pages written. Rockefeller believed competition to be literally a sin, and exclaimed with relief in his own writings that "the day of individual competition in large affairs is past and gone." (*Random Reminiscences Of Men And Events*, New York, Doubleday, Doran, 1909) This, of course, was his position after having attained a near monopoly in the refining business through espionage, bribery, secret kickbacks, and other fraudulent and illegal means. As Matthew Josephson puts it in *The Robber Barons*: "Rockefeller's instinct for conspiracy [*was*] marked."

The secret kickbacks or "rebates" were one of the ramps to Rockefeller ascendancy, and as his strength grew so did his demands for more kickbacks on oil shipped by rail. Indeed it reached the point where Rockefeller's interests were being given rebates on oil shipped by other refiners! Right from the start the man who would by 1878 control ninety-five percent of all U.S. pipelines and refineries had been thinking of monopoly. "To accomplish the [*local*] monopoly he first went to the Lake Shore Railroad, which brought the crude oil from the producing fields to Cleveland, to demand a secret rebate of fifteen times that openly allowed the other and smaller refiners . . . . He got it. Within a short time Cleveland's refineries were reduced to ten. The others had done one of two things: they either joined Rockefeller and associates, or went out of business." (*The Age Of The Moguls*)

Then there was the infamous matter of the South Improvement Company, a front which was intended "to guarantee large profits for the railroads by turning the oil business of the country over to a cartel of a few large refiners, who could at their will extinguish all competition. The profits of the refiners would come, in the end, from the raising of prices of oil products to consumers . . . ." (*John D. Rockefeller's Secret Weapon*, Albert Z. Carr, New York, McGraw-Hill, 1962)

One learns in *The History Of The Standard Oil Company* that Mr. Rockefeller's early competitors were all "feeling more or less the discouraging effects of the three or four years of railroad discriminations in favor of Standard Oil Company. To the owners of these refineries Mr. Rockefeller now went one by one, and explained the South Improvement Center. 'You see,' he told them, 'this scheme is bound to work. It means an absolute control by us of the oil business.' " (Ida M. Tarbell, New York, Macmillan, 1904) When this conspiracy against the Free Market was exposed it was soundly denounced as piracy. In Titusville, Pennsylvania, a symbolic John D. Rockefeller was ". . . hanged, then burned in effigy. A hurriedly organized Congressional investigation termed Rockefeller's attempt to bring what he liked to call order into the oil business 'one of the most gigantic and dangerous conspiracies ever conceived.' " (*The Age Of The Moguls*)

John D. wanted the public to think the South Improvement plan was killed. In fact, reports biographer Jules Abels, "over the years the arrangements Rockefeller made with the rails were suspiciously akin to the main features of South Improvement." (*The Rockefeller Billions*, New York, Macmillan, 1965) As John D. Rockefeller had boasted, the oil business became substantially his. Or, as he said: "We have sufficient money laid aside to wipe out any concern that starts in this business."

But of course money, alone, was not sufficient. Since what was being done was clearly illegal, it was necessary to corrupt and harness the power of government. Like J.P. Morgan, Rockefeller manipulated the powers of government to create monopoly as best he could. In this he was brother to Morgan, of whom it was said, "every corporation he formed or influenced did away with real competition." (*The Robber Barons*) The best way to do that was by government regulation, which in turn was controlled by those it supposedly regulated.

Thus, the Communist newspaper *The Worker* was right when it smirked in 1901 that the socialists "are not making the Revolution. It would be near the truth to say that Morgan and Rockefeller are making it." Certainly they were soon financing the leading Leftwing press. The bigger the government the better their chance of manipulating it for greater power over the nation and its economy.

Only governments can perpetuate monopolies, whether through connivance, corruption, or conspiracy. In fact, during the 1880s a popular slogan was "Scratch a monopoly and you will find the Government underneath." (*The Politicos*) Which is precisely why it was less government that was needed during the days of the Robber Barons, and why the same holds true today. The proper role of government in business is one and one only — the provision of justice under the common law, which guarantees contracts and prohibits fraud, theft, deception, duress, and conspiracy. That is the only way to have a truly free market and by natural means prevent monopoly, impoverishing maladjustments, and the looting of the consumer.

Chapter VI

Anarchists Reviewed

T HE WORD *anarchy* comes from the Greek *anarchos*, meaning rulerless. As a political theory it is based upon the notion that government should be abolished and replaced by a voluntary association of persons and groups maintaining no private property. The forebears of ideological anarchism include Zeno the Stoic of Citium (c. 300 B.C.), the Anabaptists (1525-), and William Godwin (1756-1836). Will and Ariel Durant call Godwin "the most influential English philosopher of his generation." (*The Age Of Napoleon*)

More interesting is the role of Jean Jacques Rousseau (1712-1778), a frequent advocate of extreme libertarianism. Anarchists would later find, says Professor James Joll, that "it was perhaps Rousseau's ideals of Nature and of education which were to have the most influence. To the belief in the perfectibility of man and of human institutions, Rousseau added in particular the notion of the Noble Savage, a figure dear to all anarchists' hearts. 'Man was born free and is everywhere in chains' [*the first line of* Du Contrat Social] becomes, in fact, a first principle of anarchist thought. The idea of a happy primitive world, a state of nature in which, so far from being engaged in a struggle of all against all, men live in a state of mutual cooperation, was to have a powerful appeal to anarchists of all kinds."(*The Anarchists*, Boston, Little, Brown, 1964)

The fact that the hypothesis is fatuous seems only to make it more alluring to utopians. As the astute Joseph Schumpeter observed, "anarchism was utopianism with a vengeance." (*Capitalism, Socialism And Democracy*, New York, Harper & Row, Third Edition, 1950)

Communists and other totalitarians who claim to do what they do to bring on some future utopia also owe much to Rousseau. Especially, says Eugene H. Methvin, to his "absolute, nihilistic belief that existing society is all evil, corrupt, unjust and hateful, and that to achieve the golden age, since man is naturally good, the established order must be destroyed first." (*The Rise of Radicalism*, New Rochelle, Arlington House, 1973) The Red Flag of the Communist and the Black Flag of the Anarchist may thus be used to cloak the revolutionary purposes of any conspirator against the established order.

Like Rousseau, William Godwin contended in his influential *Enquiry Concerning Political Justice And Its Influence On General Virtue And Happiness* that man could be perfected to faultlessness. Though Godwin sought abolition of government, he opposed violent revolution, declaring that "a revolution of opinion is the only means of attaining a better distribution of wealth." (*The Age Of Napoleon*) His *opinions* embraced free love, anarchy, and atheism. As it happened, ironically, Godwin was horrified when his daughter ran off with the poet Shelley and produced a macabre tale of what may occur should man usurp the role of the Creator. Godwin's daughter, child of the radical Mary Wollstonecraft, was author of *Frankenstein*.

Revolutionary anarchism grew out of experiences of the French Revolution, which the fanatic Gracchus Babeuf gloated "is only the forerunner of a much bigger, much more solemn revolution, which will be the final one." Babeuf was not an anarchist, but did believe in the abolition of private property and thus became a role model for some later followers of the Black Flag by virtue of his Conspiracy of Equals in 1796.

Though executed, Babeuf is viewed as the prototype revolutionist for his promotion of secrecy, conspiracy, and crowd control. Of the latter, he wrote: "From the start, force the people to commit acts which will prevent them from deserting the revolution and retreating. All reflection on the part of the people is to be prevented." And what anarchist could fail to agree with Gracchus Babeuf's contention that: "Private property is the principal source of all the ills which burden society . . . . The sun shines on everyone and the earth belongs to no one. Go on then, my friends, batter, upset, overturn this society which does not suit you. Take what suits you everywhere. What is superfluous belongs by right to him who has nothing." (*The Anarchists*)

So it was no surprise when the man who first applied the term *anarchism* to the theory, Frenchman Pierre Joseph Proudhon (1806-1865), achieved prominence with a pamphlet offering the premise: "What is property? Property is theft." As Proudhon's revolutionary Russian disciple Mikhail Bakunin (1814-1876) later claimed: "He was the master of us all." Certainly this "Father of Anarchism" was an enemy of religion. Proudhon declared that God "is stupidity and cowardice; God is hypocrisy and falsehood; God is tyranny and poverty; God is evil . . . ." (*By Bullet, Bomb And Dagger*, Richard Suskind, New York, Macmillan, 1971)

Proudhon's choicest bile, however, was reserved for government, which he claimed should not even be changed by political means, declaring: "Universal suffrage is counterrevolution." Any and all government was seen by Proudhon "as a fund-squandering parasite," reports James D. Forman, "necessitating expensive armies, colonial conquests, taxes and custom houses. Instead, he advocated small free communities where each man could voluntarily assent to decisions affecting his life . . . . Proudhon accepted Rousseau's conviction that mankind was perfectible, and he assumed that, without the exploitative owner-worker relationship, an equality of fortunes would result. Man would not be deprived of property; rather, he would have the right of occupation subject to his using it directly. To rent it out, thereby reaping the profit from another's labor, was the 'theft' Proudhon intended to avoid." (*Anarchism*, New York, Franklin Watts, 1975)

The strength of the anarchists is in their negative appeal, for it is a matter of ideology with them that they will not replace what they destroy. Thus Proudhon emphasized: "To be governed is to be watched over, inspected, spied on, directed, legislated at, regulated, docketed, indoctrinated, preached at, controlled, assessed, weighed, censored, ordered about, by men who have neither the right nor the knowledge nor the virtue. To be governed means to be, at each operation, at each transaction, at each movement, noted, registered, controlled, taxed, stamped, measured, valued, assessed, patented, licensed, authorized, endorsed, admonished, hampered, reformed, rebuked, arrested. It is to be, on the pretext of the general interest, taxed, drilled, held to ransom, exploited, monopolized, extorted, hoaxed, robbed; then at the least resistance, at the first word of complaint, to be repressed, fined, abused, annoyed, followed, bullied, beaten, disarmed, garotted, imprisoned, machine-gunned, judged, condemned, deported, flayed, sold, betrayed and finally mocked, ridiculed, insulted, dishonoured. That's government, that's its justice, that's its morality!"

And that, we are supposed to believe, is the inevitable collective action of Nature's otherwise unblemished children!

One of these unblemished children was Mikhail Bakunin, foremost of the Russian anarchists, who turned from the life of an aristocrat to that of an active participant in five revolutions — acting on the theory of Proudhon. Devoted to creating a political vacuum, he labored to destroy every institution. "In a word, we reject all legislation," explained Bakunin, "all authority, and all privileged, licensed, official, and legal influence, even though arising from universal suffrage, convinced that it can turn only to the advantage of a dominant minority of exploiters against the interests of the immense majority in subjection to them . . . . This is the sense in which we are really Anarchists.'' (*The Essential Works Of Anarchism*, edited by Marshall Shatz, New York, Bantam Books, 1971)

There was another, more bloody sense. As Bakunin and co-author Sergei Nechayev (1847-1882) wrote in a pamphlet entitled ''Principles Of Revolution'': ''We recognize no other activity but the work of extermination, but we admit that the forms in which this activity will show itself will be extremely varied — poison, the knife, the rope, *etc.* In this struggle revolution sanctifies everything alike.''

As we have noted, Bakunin took part in five revolutions, including that in Paris in 1848 and the Dresden insurrection the next year. Thanks to the labors of an international conspiracy, revolt was then sweeping the European continent, and revolutionary anarchists served the purpose of every conspirator. As Bakunin recalled: ''It seemed as if the entire world was turned upside down. The improbable became commonplace, the impossible possible . . . . In a word, people found themselves in such a state of mind that if someone had said, 'God has been driven from heaven and a republic has been proclaimed there,' everyone would have believed it and no one would have been surprised.'' (*Bombs Beards And Barricades*, Anthony Esler, New York, Stein and Day, 1971)

So impetuous an advocate of destruction was Bakunin that he was calling for rebellion in Paris even after there was nothing left against which to rebel, prompting the revolutionary Prefect of Police to proclaim: ''What a man! On the first day of a revolution he is a perfect treasure. On the second, he ought to be shot!'' (*By Bullet, Bomb And Dagger*) As it happened, the revolts of 1848 and 1849 were put down, and Bakunin was sentenced to death for his participation in the Dresden uprising. The sentence was later commuted, he was deported to Russia, and then sent to Siberia from where he escaped to Japan, the United States, and thence to England where he worked with Marx and Engels. The followers of Marx and Bakunin had different goals: the former, conquest; the latter, destruction. And the latter could be made to serve the former only in times of uprising. Accordingly, Bakunin was expelled from the First International in 1872 because it was said his anarchism was undisciplined. He had in the meantime, however, produced a series of manifestos, including *The Catechism Of The Revolutionary*, which were later used by Lenin. The anarchist creed declared, in part:

''The revolutionist is a doomed man . . . . The revolutionist despises every sort of dogma and has renounced the peaceful scientific pursuits. . . . He despises and hates the existing social order and code of morals with all its manifestations. For him morality is everything which contributes to the triumph of the revolution. *** All soft and tender affections arising from kinship, friendship, love, gratitude, and even honor itself must be obliterated. *** We must join hands with the bold gangs of bandits — the only genuine revolutionists in Russia. To weld these people into a single force which is wholly destructive and wholly invincible — such is the sole object of our organization; this is our conspiracy and our task.'' (*The Rise Of Radicalism*)

The anarchists were in fact stalking horses for Reds waiting to pick up the pieces. As Austrian scholar Erik von Kuehnelt-Leddihn has remarked: ''In Russia the Anarchists (S.R., 'Social Revolutionaries') were the ones who committed practically all the acts of violence. The Communists were too shrewd, too clever to engage in mere terrorism. Conspiracy, organization and mass rising were their means.''(*Leftism*)

As Lenin stated in 1918: ''The majority of anarchists think and write about the future without understanding the present. That is what divides us communists from them.'' But such anarchist groups as the Nihilists and Narodniki — the Party of the People's Will — made possible the rise of the Bolsheviki. Ivan Turgenev describes them in his fictional *Fathers And Sons*: ''A nihilist is a person who does not bow to any authorities; who doesn't accept any principle on faith, no matter how hallowed and venerated . . . .'' They were the radical sons of ''Liberal'' fathers. One was an associate of Nechayev named Peter Tkachev, who remonstrated: ''We should kill everyone over 25 and make a new start.'' Comrade Tkachev, after all, was still twenty-four.

As part of the prescribed ''propaganda of the deed,'' anarchists assassinated six Heads of State in the two decades before World War I. These were President Carnot of France; Premier Canovas of Spain; Empress Elizabeth of Austria; King Umberto of Italy; President McKinley of the United States; and, Premier Canalejas of Spain. This series of terrorist acts and others in Russia, ''even if their aim was not the anarchist one of abolishing the state, derived their techniques from the movements with which Bakunin and Nechayev had been associated. All over Europe and elsewhere, terrorism was to become an accepted political weapon; and in some cases, as in that of the conspiracy which led to the murder of Archduke Francis Ferdinand in 1914, it was directly inspired by the anarchist example.'' (*The Anarchists*)

Despite this unquestionably tawdry heritage, there are those even in recent years who argue that ''Anarchism is the purity of rebellion.'' (*Social Anarchism*, Giovanni Baldelli, Chicago, Aldine Atherton, 1971) Ah, purity. Never mind that the program of the Narodniki declared: ''Terrorist activity, consisting in destroying the most harmful person in government, aims to undermine the prestige of the government and arouse in this manner the revolutionary spirit of the people and their confidence in the success of the cause.''

What was the result in Russia? "In 1881 the Narodniki struck a blow that startled the world: they assassinated the Czar, Alexander II. It was a triumphant coup, equal, they imagined, to the battering down of the Bastille [*which got more sympathetic media coverage*]. It would shout aloud their protest, summon the oppressed and terrorize the oppressors. Instead it ushered in reaction." (*The Proud Tower*, Barbara W. Tuchman, New York, Macmillan, 1966) Czar Alexander, as it happened, had committed the crime of liberating the serfs.

In addition to Bakunin and his heirs, the other major Russian anarchist figure was Prince Petr Kropotkin, a direct descendant of the original rulers of Russia. He too preached "propaganda of the deed" — to be distributed by "speech and written word, by dagger, gun and dynamite." (*By Bullet, Bomb And Dagger*) His newspaper *Le Révolté* in Switzerland called for: "Permanent revolt by word of mouth, in writing, by the dagger, the rifle, dynamite . . . . Everything is good for us which falls outside legality." (*The Anarchists*) Yet Kropotkin is now described in all too many histories as a harmless scholar. In point of fact he demanded terrorism and expropriation of property. And among his early converts was a young man named Benito Mussolini.

There were times when Kropotkin professed ambivalence toward terrorist tactics . . . always, of course, when he was himself likely to be held responsible. And he wrote of one of the murderers of Czar Alexander: "By the attitude of the crowd she understood that she had dealt a mortal blow to the autocracy. And she read in the sad looks which were directed sympathetically towards her, that by her death she was dealing an even more terrible blow from which the autocracy will never recover."

The aristocratic anarchist declared: "Outside of anarchy, there is no such thing as revolution." And he was a clever conspirator. Kropotkin "favored two organizations [*of anarchists*], one open and large in size, the other secret and smaller, much as Bakunin had arranged in the early 1870s. The larger, open group should be 'an organization of resistance, of strikes' while the secret one should be composed of a smaller number of trusted people who will involve themselves in a 'workers' conspiracy.' Kropotkin envisioned the secret group as the [*coordinating*] international body . . . ." (*Kropotkin*, Martin A. Miller, Chicago, University of Chicago Press, 1976) Far from being a kindly theorist, the man was an active conspirator.

Prince Kropotkin supported the Russian Revolution. He had been predisposed to feeling guilty about things over which he had no control, a character flaw that is highly developed today. The young prince said he asked himself, "what right had I to those highest joys when all around me was nothing but misery and struggle for a mouldy bit of bread; when whatsoever I should spend to enable me to live in that very world of higher emotions must needs be taken from the very mouths of those who grew the wheat and had not bread enough for their children?'' (*Memoirs Of A Revolutionist*, Boston, Houghton Mifflin, 1899)

Less sentimentally, Kropotkin wrote: ''A single deed is better propaganda than a thousand pamphlets.'' Acts, he said, are needed ''to excite hate for the exploiters, to ridicule the Rulers, to show up their weaknesses and always to awaken the spirit of revolt.'' As historian Barbara Tuchman observed: ''The acts he loftily called for on paper were performed, but not by him.'' (*The Proud Tower*) Virtually under house arrest after the Bolshevik Revolution took over from Kerensky, the Reds let him live — perhaps to avoid enraging his revolutionary followers, and perhaps because he was a conscious conspirator in their rise to power.

Kropotkin's lesser-known colleagues were not so lucky. As Aleksandr Solzhenitsyn has wryly commented: ''. . . the Mensheviks, the Anarchists, the Popular Socialists — had for decades only pretended to be revolutionaries; . . . and for that they went to hard labor, still pretending. Only during the violent course of the Revolution was the bourgeois essence of these socialist traitors discovered. What could be more natural than to begin arresting them!'' (*The Gulag Archipelago, I-II*, New York, Harper & Row, 1973) It was all historical inevitability, don't you see.

Prominent observers in the West who were sympathetic to the Reds remained silent. One of these was George Bernard Shaw. When ''the bolsheviks shot down their old comrades and (in his own words) 'fellow sufferers' of the Tsarist era, the anarchists and syndicalists, he refused to reproach them.'' (*The Fellow-Travellers*, David Caute, New York, Macmillan, 1973) What would one expect of a Fabian Socialist founder?

There were of course others who long refused to speak ill of the Bolsheviki. Lenin personally reassured American anarchist Emma Goldman: ''Anarchists of ideas are not in our prisons.'' Red Emma eventually awakened to the con, but not before spending years of her life serving a conspiracy which found her incendiary radicalism useful.

Emma Goldman had been drawn into the anarchist movement after the Haymarket Square riots at Chicago in 1886. The McCormick Harvester works was the scene that year of a May Day demonstration, and when radicals returned two days later shots were fired. A German anarchist editor named August Spies quickly ran off a propaganda screed headed: ''Revenge! Working man! To Arms!'' and announced a May fourth protest at which ''Good Speakers will be present to denounce the latest atrocious act of the police, the shooting of our fellow-workmen yesterday afternoon.'' Editor Spies declared: ''A pound of dynamite is worth a bushel of bullets.'' At the resultant gathering in the Haymarket, a crowd of mostly foreign-born radicals was quickly inflamed by revolutionary speakers. Among them was one Samuel Fielden, head of an international anarchist organization. Fielden railed:

"The law is only framed for those that are your enslavers . . . . You have nothing more to do with the law except to lay hands on it and throttle it until it makes its last kick. It turns your brothers out on the wayside and has degraded them until they have lost the last vestiges of humanity and are mere things and animals. Keep your eye on it, throttle it, kill it, stab it, do everything you can to wound it.***

"The skirmish lines have met. People have been shot. Men, women and children have not been spared by the capitalists . . . . What matters it whether you kill yourselves with work to get a little relief, or die on the battlefield resisting the enemy? What is the difference? Any animal, however loathsome, will resist when stepped upon. Are men less than snails and worms? . . . " (*By Bullet, Bomb And Dagger*)

Hearing this incitement to riot, Chicago police ordered the assembly peaceably to disperse. A bomb was then thrown at the ranks of police. Seven officers were killed and their colleagues fired into the mob. One of the anarchists who was arrested admitted delivering fifty of his bombs to a known radical hangout on the morning of May fourth. Eventually three anarchists were given prison sentences; the bomb maker blew off his head on the night before execution; and, four were hanged in November of 1887 and immediately became anarchist martyrs. As Red Emma saw it, the trial had "proved the worst frame-up in the history of the United States." (*Living My Life*, New York, Knopf, 1931)

Radicalized by all of this, Emma joined the anarchists' cause and became, among other things, the mistress of anarchist leader Johann Most — who had called the murder of Alexander II an "heroic act," declaring that the Czar had been "croaked like a dog." Before bringing his hate message to the United States, Johann Most had been imprisoned in Great Britain for "inciting the murder of crowned heads."

Emma, a practitioner of what was then called "free love," soon took another lover named Alexander "Sasha" Berkman and the two anarchists worked on a bombing plot to "revenge" themselves on the strike-breaking activity at Carnegie Steel in 1892. When their bomb proved a dud, Sasha decided to shoot Carnegie chairman Henry Clay Frick. To help raise funds to finance the proposed murder it was decided that Emma would work as a street-walker. She felt guilty about her hesitation. "Weakling, coward," said her inner reproaching voice, "Sasha is giving his life, and you shrink from giving your body, miserable coward." (*Living My Life*) This effort also proved a dud when the lady anarchist's only customer gave her ten dollars, refused to touch her, and sent her home with the advice: "You haven't got it, that's all there is to it."

Sasha managed to shoot Frick anyway, though not fatally, and Miss Goldman naturally bewailed the sentence he received as entirely too harsh for this "propaganda of the deed." So angry was Emma that she publicly horsewhipped her former lover Johann Most for disavowing the efficacy of Frick's attempted murder.

Emma the Anarchist continued to have her problems — almost one thousand pages' worth of them in her fascinating autobiography. For instance, there was the occasion at a Detroit church which allowed her to speak. After her lecture, as the female anarchist told it, an elderly woman arose. " 'Mr. Chairman,' she demanded, 'does Miss Goldman believe in God or does she not?' She was followed by another. 'Does the speaker favor killing off all rulers?' Then a small, emaciated man jumped to his feet and in a thin voice cried: 'Miss Goldman! You're a believer in free love aren't you? Now, wouldn't your system result in houses of prostitution at every lamp-post?'

" 'I shall have to answer these people straight from the shoulder,' I remarked to the minister. 'So be it,' he replied.

" 'Ladies and gentleman,' I began. 'I came here to avoid as much as possible treading on your corns. I had intended to deal only with the basic issue of economics that dictates our lives from cradle to grave, regardless of our religion or moral beliefs. I see now that it was a mistake. If one enters a battle, he cannot be squeamish about a few corns. Here then are my answers: I do not believe in God, because I believe in man. Whatever his mistakes, man has for thousands of years past been working to undo the botched job your God has made.' The house went frantic. 'Blasphemy! Heretic! Sinner!' the women screamed. 'Stop her! Throw her out!' "

"When order was restored, I continued: 'As to killing rulers, it depends entirely on the position of the ruler. If it is the Russian Tsar, I most certainly believe in dispatching him to where he belongs. If the ruler is as ineffectual as an American president, it is hardly worth the effort. There are, however, some potentates I would kill by any and all means at my disposal. They are Ignorance, Superstition, and Bigotry — the most sinister and tyrannical rulers on earth. As for the gentleman who asked if free love would not build more houses of prostitution, my answer is: they will be empty if the men of the future look like him.'

"There was instant pandemonium."(*Living My Life*) Emma, you see, was delighted with her performance.

She was less cocky in 1901 when it was revealed that Leon Czolgosz, an anarchist who had attended Emma's lectures, took her fiery polemics so seriously that he shot and killed the President of the United States. The anarchist boasted: "I killed President McKinley because I done my duty and because he was an enemy of the good working people . . . . I don't believe we should have rulers. It is right to kill them . . . . I don't believe in voting. It is against my principles. I am an Anarchist. I don't believe in marriage. I believe in free love."

Czolgosz killed President William McKinley in September, was electrocuted in October, and his body and clothing were promptly destroyed. Moreover, the Immigration Act was thereafter amended to prevent entry of foreign anarchists. Though arrested, Emma Goldman was found innocent of complicity in the shooting.

Emma and the anarchists she led were certainly not, however, innocent of complicity in promoting the Russian Revolution and supporting its Red masters. As she admitted in her autobiography: "In the columns of *Mother Earth Bulletin*, from the platform, and by every other means we defended the Bosheviki against calumny and slander."

When she was deported to Russia for anti-draft activity she had led during World War I, Emma saw first-hand what she and the Bolsheviks had wrought. Finally the bitter truth became all too plain. The Reds had eliminated "from responsible positions . . . everyone who dared think aloud, and the spiritual death of the most militant elements whose intelligence, faith, and courage had really enabled the Bosheviki to achieve their power. The anarchists and Left Socialist Revolutionists had been used as pawns by Lenin in the October days and were now doomed to extinction by his creed and policies. It was the system of taking hostages for political refugees, not exempting even old parents and children of tender age. The nightly *oblavas* (street and house raids) by the Cheka, the population frightened out of sleep, their few belongings turned upside down and ripped open for secret documents, the dragnet of soldiers left behind to haul in the crop of unsuspecting callers at the besieged house.

"The penalties for flimsy charges often amounted to long prison terms, exile to desolate parts of the country and even execution. Shattering in its cumulative effect, the essence of the story was the same as told me by my Petrograd comrades. I had been too dazzled then by the public glare and glitter of Bolshevism to credit the veracity of the accusations. I had refused to trust their judgment and their viewpoint. But now Bolshevism was shorn of its pretence, its naked soul exposed to my gaze. Still I would not believe, I would not see with my inner eye the truth so evident to my outer sight. I was stunned, baffled, the ground pulled from under me. Yet I hung on, hung on by a thread as a drowning man. In my anguish, I cried: 'Bolshevism is the *mene, tekel* over every throne, the menace of craven hearts, the hated enemy of organized wealth and power. Its path has been thorny, its obstacles many, its climb steep. How could it help falling behind at times, how could it help making mistakes? But to belie itself, to play Judas to the fervent hope of the disinherited and oppressed, to betray its own ultimate aims? No, never could it be guilty of such an eclipse of the world's most luminous star!''

It seems she had discovered that some of the Noble Savages were simply savages.

It took two years in Soviet Russia to disillusion America's best-known anarchist . . . but it did not sway her from her faith in the anarchist cause. When Emma Goldman died in 1940 she was buried beside the Haymarket Square radicals.

The last gasp for the anarchists in the United States had meanwhile come and gone in the propaganda that arose around the conviction of Sacco and Vanzetti in 1921 and their execution in 1927 for murder and robbery in Massachusetts. Leftists to this day ignore the undeniable evidence of their guilt. But, as Erik von Kuehnelt-Leddihn has observed: ''. . . to the outside world the *least* important of all [*aspects*] was the question of the two men's guilt or innocence. Whatever the answer might be, they themselves never admitted any guilt except their belief in political anarchism.'' (*Leftism*)

It was a propaganda ploy all the while. As Katherine Anne Porter discovered while she was agitating on behalf of the anarchists amidst ''Liberals'' led by Reds, the Communists had co-opted the anarchist cause and ''organized to promote disorder . . . . I remarked to our Communist leader [*in her protest group*] that even then, at that late time, I still hoped the lives of Sacco and Vanzetti might be saved and that they would be granted another trial. 'Saved,' she said, ringing a change on her favorite answer to political illiteracy. 'Who wants them saved? What earthly good would they do us alive?' '' (*The Never-Ending Wrong*, Boston, Atlantic-Little, Brown, 1977) Indeed, the Communists raised millions of dollars purportedly for defense of anarchists Sacco and Vanzetti, but their Defense Committee received a scant six thousand dollars from the Comrades. (*By Bullet, Bomb And Dagger*)

The anarchists were, as usual, only cannon-fodder for the Communists. During the Spanish Civil War the same scenario was played as the two revolutionary groups fought both the Nationalists and each other. The Red and Black battled openly for Barcelona. And certainly the Reds had no monopoly on terrorism and horrible atrocities. Consider that in Spain, just like the Communists, the *Federación Anarquista Ibérica* ''killed several thousand priests, monks and nuns, shooting some, crucifying others, hurling still others off high walls or into deep wells — so carried away by the blood-madness that they even dug up the mummified bodies of nuns, danced with them in the streets, and threw the corpses onto bonfires.'' (*By Bullet, Bomb And Dagger*)

It wasn't out of squeamishness but out of rivalry that the Reds turned on the anarchists, just as George Orwell explained in *Homage To Catalonia*. They would be cleaned out, as *Pravda* said, just as had the Trotskyists in the Soviet Union. The Comintern, reported John P. Diggins, simply "ordered Spanish communists to put down a popular uprising [*sic*] in Barcelona and to liquidate . . . anarchist leaders. In the United States only a handful of isolated anti-Stalinists publicized the repression." (*The American Left In The Twentieth Century*, New York, Harcourt Brace Jovanovich, 1973)

In Spain as in Russia the anarchists murdered in the name of liberty, created a vacuum and invited reaction, while the Communists waited their time to institute the so-called dictatorship of the proletariat. Regardless of the alleged idealism of the anarchists, who claimed they sought a simple life, they only paved the way for organized tyranny. Utopia with a vengeance, indeed!

Chapter VII

Andrew Carnegie: A Prototype And A Legacy

ANDREW CARNEGIE, the son of a radical father and a Chartist mother, left Scotland with his parents in the 1848 panic over Illuminist revolution. Settling near Pittsburgh, he took a job at age thirteen as a bobbin-boy, then as a telegrapher, and soon became secretary to Thomas Scott, of the Pennsylvania Railroad — writing to friends in Scotland that the radical Chartist ideas of their 1848 adventure were being effectively promoted in America. His family motto, he claimed, was "death to privilege." When Scott became Assistant Secretary of War after the firing on Fort Sumter, young Carnegie went along to organize the military telegraph system. The Civil War, says Joseph Frazier Wall (*Andrew Carnegie*, New York, Oxford University Press, 1970), was a conflict "that Carnegie had so often predicted and so eagerly awaited." As he was twenty-eight and unmarried he was drafted, but bought a substitute (an Irish immigrant named John Lindew) for $850 and settled into the role of profiteer.

By the end of the war Carnegie was invested in the first railroad sleeping car, the first major U.S. oil field, and was a partner in a Pittsburgh iron business. In fact, says historian Louis M. Hacker, "Just as the war was ending, Carnegie was the chief money man and the active manager of four such concerns, of which the one closest to his heart was the Keystone Bridge Co. The others were Union Iron Mills (which rolled beams for railroad bridges), the Superior Rail Mill, and the Pittsburgh Locomotive Works." (*The World Of Andrew Carnegie: 1865-1901*, Philadelphia, J.P. Lippincott, 1968)

Carnegie was a master at manipulating government for profit. In the 1880s he made much noise about all the reasons why America should not modernize her aging naval fleet. While doing so he was angling to obtain the contract to supply armor plating — getting the job as a result of inside information from his friends in the office of the Secretary of War.

Carnegie apparently charged three hundred percent over his cost of production, writing a friend: "Best speciality going sure. Millions in it."

Like his contemporary, John D. Rockefeller, Andrew Carnegie quickly learned that a reputation for humanitarian philanthropy is a most effective means of overcoming public resistance to the use of vast personal power for looting the Treasury. He donated thousands of church organs and buildings for public libraries, he funded the fabulous research facilities of the Carnegie Institution, he established the Carnegie Hero Fund Commission, and on and on and on.

In 1901 Carnegie sold his steel holdings alone for about $250 million. There is far more to the story of Andrew Carnegie, however, than the Horatio Alger tale of his rise from being a $1.20 per week bobbin-boy to become, as J.P. Morgan put it, "the richest man in the world."

The carefully created myth is that there was nothing for which the radical war profiteer Andrew Carnegie was more eager to sacrifice his millions than world peace. For example, there was the construction of his three "Temples of Peace," as Carnegie called them: the Central American Court of Justice; the Pan American Union (for "the union of all the republics of this hemisphere"); and, the Palace of Peace at The Hague to headquarter a Permanent Arbitration Court for the world. He called his "Temple of Peace" at The Hague, which he paid $1.5 million to construct in 1903, "the most holy building in the world." By 1904, as Joseph Frazier Wall has observed: "Carnegie was increasingly drawn to the idea, not of disarmament, but of a coalition of great powers which would police the world."

Thus Andrew Carnegie was among the first to call for "a League of Nations," declaring that nationalism was the cause of war.* The richest man in the world favored an internationalist "peace army" — a concept that, as chance would have it, nicely paralleled the scheme of a wealthy Machiavellian from Maryland named Theodore Marburg. The Marburg Plan foresaw international financiers, the Fabian Socialists, and the wealth of Andrew Carnegie being harnessed "in a movement to compel the formation of a league to enforce peace." (*Woodrow Wilson: Disciple Of Revolution*, Jennings C. Wise, New York, Paisley Press, 1938)

In the opinion of Marburg, writes Jennings Wise, "It was imperative, therefore, that its financial aspects be screened, that the money interests behind it be held under cover, that the whole movement be cloaked with the guise of pure humanism." The aim of this conspiracy was World

---

*Carnegie exercised the rights of an American citizen, but biographer Wall points out that he never became a U.S. citizen, though "no government official or court was prepared to gainsay" Carnegie's usurpation.

Government, says Professor Wise, with the ultimate power remaining in the hands of international financiers "to control its councils and enforce peace." From these seeds, writes Professor Antony Sutton in *Wall Street And The Bolshevik Revolution* (New Rochelle, Arlington House, 1975), grew the modern internationalist movement, which included not only the famous Andrew Carnegie, John D. Rockefeller, Paul Warburg, Otto Kahn, Bernard Baruch, and Herbert Hoover, but also the Carnegie foundations and their progeny.

The Carnegie Endowment for International Peace, created in 1910, was active in intriguing for America's entry into the war to establish a League of Nations and thereby "end all wars" through World Government. In 1915, at a time we were supposedly neutral, Andrew Carnegie, J.P. Morgan, Otto H. Kahn, and others helped float a half-million-dollar Anglo-French loan in anticipation of pushing America into the conflict. (*America's 60 Families*, Ferdinand Lundberg, New York, Vanguard Press, 1937) Step by step the way was being laid to send Americans "over there." The connivance of conspirators in the United States and Britain in arranging the sinking of the *Lusitania*, for example, has been amply documented. (See *The Lusitania*, Colin Simpson, Boston, Little, Brown, 1972.)

Meanwhile Woodrow Wilson, who was a frequent visitor at Carnegie's Skibo Castle in Scotland and was a virtual captive of the insiders angling to push us into the European bloodbath, campaigned for re-election in 1916 on the theme "he kept us out of war." Wilson had already made secret commitments to the internationalist conspirators at the time he said in his acceptance speech that the U.S. must remain neutral "because it was the fixed and traditional policy of the United States to stand aloof from the politics of Europe . . . ." Wilson did what he was told. Which may be why "Colonel" Edward M. House, Wilson's alter ego and Presidential liaison with Carnegie and other international financiers, wrote the president of the College of the City of New York that Woodrow Wilson "is a great man, with great ideas, and ought to be made 'dictator' of the United States."

On February 14, 1917, Carnegie wrote to Wilson urging that he go ahead with world war for world peace. The Carnegie Endowment for International Peace openly supported the senseless American participation. When war was declared by the United States, less than two months later, Carnegie cabled Wilson that he had "triumphed at last." The doughboys were soon in the trenches, fighting to make the world safe for the insiders of international finance. By war's end, Russia would be in the hands of Communists who were at this point biding time in Switzerland and New York. Wilson would himself arrange a passport for Trotsky.

At the conclusion of war Colonel House, Dr. James Brown Scott of the Carnegie Endowment, and other Carnegie-financed conspirators in England and the United States laid the groundwork for the peace conference that produced the Versailles Treaty — a vindictive pact that looted the Central Powers, stripped them of their political traditions, nearly brought the Communists to power in Hungary and Germany, and made World War II inevitable. The Carnegie-planned League of Nations, designed to pick up the pieces, became a dead letter only because Middle-American outrage at the machinations of the international bankers, profiteers, and conspirators who had suckered us into the war emboldened the U.S. Senate and it refused to be a party to another internationalist trap.

The conspirators responded by establishing the Foreign Policy Association in 1918 and the Council on Foreign Relations in 1919 — both of which have continued to receive Carnegie support to this day. They would persist in working for the Carnegie dream of World Government. Both would play major roles in helping to involve the United States in World War II, secure the Communist base in Eastern Europe, and create the United Nations.

In recent years, the Carnegie Endowment has worked with the United Nations to "establish universal peace" through a stepped-up attack on strategic anti-Communist nations. For instance, there was the Endowment "Project on Rhodesia," headed by Anthony Lake, which fought for sanctions against the little African country that declared its independence from Britain in much the same way as had the United States. What was the Carnegie interest here? According to Mr. Lake: ". . . the Rhodesian issue is really a very special one. It represents the only effort by the United Nations actually to impose comprehensive mandatory sanctions against any territory." That was of course before Rhodesia became Marxist Zimbabwe, thus fulfilling the plans of the international Left.

Another such Carnegie project was its 1965 study, published as *Apartheid And United Nations Collective Measures*, which went through at least three printings. It included a blueprint for U.N. invasion of South Africa, specifying the necessary troop strength, cost, and casualties it would take to conquer that anti-Communist country.

One begins to understand what kind of "peace" the Carnegie Endowment is laboring to inflict.

From the internationalist standpoint, traditional American values still stand in the way of their New World Order. Defeat of the League of Nations taught them this, as has growing popular rejection of the United Nations. Like Winston Smith in *Nineteen Eighty-Four*, the total breakdown will not be complete until we can be made to *love* Big Brother. Accordingly, every effort is being made to indoctrinate American youth with courses in "peace" and "world order," as well as clever propaganda designed to teach youngsters that they are "world citizens" rather than Americans. The younger the children can be removed from the influence of their parochial parents the better.

As early as 1934 the Carnegie Corporation (established in 1911 by Andrew Carnegie) spent $340,000 on the Commission on Social Sciences of the American Historical Association, which laid out a program for indoctrinating students through social studies courses in the public schools. This was necessary, said the Carnegie-financed report, because: "Cumulative evidence supports the conclusion, that, in the United States as in other countries, the age of individualism and laissez faire in economy and government is closing and that a new age of collectivism is emerging." Indeed, according to Fabian Socialist Harold Laski, this Carnegie project "at bottom, and stripped of its carefully neutral phrases," was "an educational program for a socialist America."

Textbooks financed by the Carnegie Corporation's "Project Read" have been even more flagrant in pushing radicalism at our children. Intended for "culturally deprived areas" and produced through Behavioral Research Laboratory of Palo Alto, the Carnegie series was reviewed by columnist Edith Kermit Roosevelt in 1968 as follows: "These foundation-funded books reveal a fire pattern that amounts to an incitement to the sort of arson and guerrilla warfare that took place in Watts, Washington, D.C., and elsewhere. ***

". . . Pictures in the Carnegie-funded, supposedly educational texts include a comparison of a flag with a rag, the ransoming of an American soldier in a Chinese prison, a picture that shows people kneeling in a church to say their prayers beside a picture of a horse being taught to kneel in the same way, a reference to a candidate elected to public office as a "ruler," a picture of a boy stealing a girl's purse, and another boy throwing pointed darts at a companion whom he uses as target practice."

The idea is to radicalize American youth. The 1971 Carnegie Commission on Higher Education, for instance, urged that universities establish a "bill of rights" for the campuses to protect "dissenters," and conducted "the largest poll" of undergraduates ever, announcing (in what was no doubt viewed as a self-fulfilling report) that fifty-nine percent of the students and thirty-two percent of the faculty wanted to abolish grades. Its successor commission, the Carnegie Council on Policy Studies, was chaired by Clark Kerr, the former cream-puff president of the University of California at Berkeley. The council warned in March of 1975 that it was "imperative" that the federal government "preserve" private colleges by instituting a multibillion-dollar program of tuition subsidies. The merest tyro would know that once federal dollars were handed out, federal control of the private schools would follow.

The point is that tax-exempt Carnegie interests are actively involved in trying to indoctrinate, control, and manipulate America's youth for the purpose of expanding conspiratorial control from the top.

The philanthropies of Andrew Carnegie were, as we have noted, a mixture of cosmetic humanitarianism and insidious subversion. One cheers, for example, his generous support of Booker T. Washington and his Tuskegee Institute. More in character was Carnegie backing of the National Urban League, whose executive director, Whitney M. Young, became a leading racial extortionist in the Sixties, declaring: "We are asking the Establishment to fund a social revolution to offset a violent armed revolution."

In fact, it was a Carnegie-funded study, *An American Dilemma*, authored by Swedish Marxist Gunnar Myrdal in 1944, which provided the intellectual padding used to justify the Supreme Court's 1954 desegregation edict. Myrdal, allegedly chosen not because he was a Communist but because Sweden had no race problem, was supposed to be unbiased. Yet he certainly had no respect for the U.S. Constitution, which he described as "impractical and unsuited to modern conditions." Americans, he said, had a "relatively low degree of respect for law and order." Our legal culture was "anarchistic." Adoption of the U.S. Constitution "was nearly a plot against the common people."

It should come as no surprise that Comrade Myrdal prepared his $250,000 Carnegie study with the help of sixteen collaborators — all with Communist Front affiliations and at least four of them members of the Communist Party. Which may be why we read in *An American Dilemma* that liberty must be forsaken in order to acquire "social equality." Nonetheless, in 1973, the Carnegie Corporation granted fifteen thousand dollars for another Myrdal study on race to be prepared at the radical Center for the Study of Democratic Institutions.

Promoting racial animosity has for years been a favorite Carnegie technique. The busing hustle is typical of Carnegie innovation. Troubled Boston was long a special target. As Waldemar A. Nielsen has pointed out: "In 1966 and again in 1968, the foundation [*Carnegie Corporation*] funded a program in Boston to bus school children from the inner city to suburban schools." (*The Big Foundations*, New York, Columbia University Press, 1972) Massive "white flight" and heightened racial tensions were two results when neighborhood schools were in effect outlawed and the federal judiciary took over.

There is little doubt that Andrew Carnegie would have approved what is now being done with his money to expand collectivism in America.

Professor Gabriel Kolko quotes Carnegie in 1908, after he had sold Carnegie Steel to J.P. Morgan, as declaring that "it always comes back to me that Government control, and that alone, will properly solve the problem" of pricing. (*The Triumph Of Conservatism*) "And so, quite easily and quickly," records Joseph Frazier Wall, "Carnegie tossed aside any laissez-faire or Social Darwinian scruples he might have professed and became an outspoken proponent of legislation that would permit the state government to intervene directly in the conduct of a private business enterprise" — at one point even threatening (as would Whitney Young years later) that mob violence would otherwise result. Andrew Carnegie wrote to President Theodore Roosevelt: "Interstate problems require extension of Federal power. We must be a Nation, one central power. Not a Confederacy of States."

Carnegie also worked hard for a federal central banking system as proposed in the *Communist Manifesto*. According to biographer Wall, he "anticipated [*sic*] much of Woodrow Wilson's Federal Reserve Banking System," which has since been used by Establishment insiders as the engine for their controlled, and for them highly profitable, booms and busts. Another feature of the *Communist Manifesto* for which he fought was the graduated income tax — from which he protected his own fortune in trusts and foundations. Writing to a "Liberal" English friend he commented in his idiosyncratic spelling: "So we have a tax at last — 1% on everyone's revenue over 5000$. So we go. Untaxt wealth and Rank to become things of the past. Common sense."

According to Carnegie biographer Joseph Frazier Wall: "A decade before his death he had written that the day of the free enterprise, competitive system of American capitalism had ended, and that these new 'virtual monopolies' must be controlled by the national government." Which may explain why the Carnegie foundations so lavishly supported Ralph Nader and his war on American business. In fact, the first major project of Nader's radical Center for the Study of Responsive Law was financed by a grant from the Carnegie Corporation.

Not that you are likely to miss the point, but the Conspiracy's international view on this theme was nicely summarized in the Carnegie Endowment's 1934 *Yearbook*, which declared that "economic nationalism, which is still running riot . . . is the greatest obstacle to the reestablishment of prosperity and genuine peace." That is, as it happens, just how the Communists see it.

According to Louis Budenz, the former editor of the *Daily Worker* who turned American, the Communists have long realized the importance of the great tax-free foundations. Particular favorites, he reported, "were the Carnegie, Rockefeller, and Guggenheim Foundations . . . ."

So we can assume it was no accident when John Foster Dulles, who had been warned that Alger Hiss was a Communist, invited that Soviet agent to become president of the Carnegie Endowment. Nor was it an accident, after Hiss was publicly exposed, that his successor was Joseph E. Johnson, a Hiss protégé who quit the State Department after a leak of Top Secret information was traced to his department. Mr. Johnson became President Emeritus of the Endowment, as well as Honorary Secretary General for the American continent of the conspiratorial Bilderberg operation — a secret international Establishment whose U.S. operations have been run from the Carnegie offices. In fact the Carnegie Endowment has picked up the tab for those lovely Bilderberg meetings.

Carnegie funds flow to conspiracy as certainly as water runs downhill. Consider the following, from *American Legion Magazine* for August of 1952: "Alger Hiss . . . became a vested interest in the world of the foundations. Besides enjoying a $20,000-a-year job as president of the Carnegie Endowment for International Peace, an 11-million-dollar trust, from 1946 to 1949 when trials laid bare his perfidy, Hiss had a hand in several other foundations. He was a trustee of both the Woodrow Wilson Foundation and the World Peace Foundation. He was also a director of the American Institute of Pacific Relations, the American Peace Society, and the American Association for the United Nations.

"Hiss had a friend named Laurence H. Duggan, likewise a former State Department official. Duggan succeeded his father as head of the Institute of International Education. This organization has had the financial support not only of the Carnegie Endowment for International Peace and the Carnegie Corporation but of more than a dozen other foundations, as well as handsome contracts from the State Department. In December of 1948 Laurence H. Duggan jumped or was hurled to his death from his New York office window. He had been questioned a few days earlier by agents of the Federal Bureau of Investigation about his association with Alger Hiss and other suspected red agents. ✳✳✳

"One of the greediest feeders at the foundation trough was the late Louis Adamic. Adamic, who either shot himself or was murdered in his New Jersey home, was a member of some fifty communist-front organizations. He devoted most of his literary life to glorifying the Soviets and became the chief apologist in the United States for Tito, communist dictator of Yugoslavia. The Carnegie Corporation gave him grants-in-aid while he was writing his book. He also received money from the Rockefeller Foundation over the years.

"Adamic was editor of a magazine called *Common Ground*, a publication largely financed with Carnegie money. On his editorial board was [*Communist*] Langston Hughes, the Negro poet who has sustained himself during much of his adult life on foundation grants. Hughes' best known poem, 'Goodbye Christ,' urges Jesus to 'beat it on away from here now' to 'make way for Marx, Communist Lenin, Peasant Stalin, Worker Me.' ''

One of the most important of the subversive Carnegie operations was its backing of the Institute of Pacific Relations, officially cited as "an instrument of Communist policy, propaganda and military intelligence." The Carnegie and Rockefeller foundations contributed millions to the I.P.R., which labored tirelessly to support U.S. betrayal of China to the Communists.

A key I.P.R. figure was Owen Lattimore, beneficiary of the Social Science Research Council, supported by six million dollars that came mostly from the Carnegie and Rockefeller foundations. It was Lattimore, of course, who in the unanimous opinion of an investigating Senate Subcommittee, was "a conscious and articulate instrument of the Communist conspiracy." Other "Old China Hands" actively selling Mao through the Carnegie-funded I.P.R. included nearly fifty persons identified in sworn testimony as members of the Communist Party.

As we have noted, another Carnegie-supported outfit is the Foreign Policy Association, which for thirty years employed Vera Micheles Dean as research director and editor. A veteran Communist Fronter, Mrs. Dean served on the subversive Congress of American Women with two of the world's top Red agents, including Tsola N. Dragoichev of Red Bulgaria. She told American and foreign delegates attending a meeting of this group that they must "whittle away their conception of national sovereignty" and pull themselves out of the "ancient grooves of nationalism."

John Goormaghtigh, head of the Carnegie Endowment's European Center in Geneva, a decade ago enthused about having established a "kind of working relationship with the Socialist [*Iron Curtain*] countries which I think is unique among American foundations." The Endowment, along with the Twentieth Century Fund, has even urged a merger of the U.S. and U.S.S.R. satellite systems.

Myriad indeed are the ways of the subversion. How many Africans, for instance, have died at the hands of Communist terrorists funded by the World Council of Churches? One can bet that very few know that it was an initial contribution of two million dollars to the Church Peace Union by an unreligious man named Andrew Carnegie, and other Carnegie grants directly to the Federal Council of Churches, which resulted in the founding of the World Council.

Alger Hiss, Laurence Duggan, Louis Adamic, Vera Dean, Owen Lattimore, the masters of the Communist slave states in East Europe — these are all benefactors of the Carnegie foundations. How could it be?

Such subversion is, in fact, in the Carnegie tradition. The steel man himself (Carnegie, not Stalin) was charged near the end of the Nineteenth Century by the Conservative *St. James's Gazette* with being engaged in a conspiracy to destroy the British Empire. Carnegie responded that he was "no conspirator," but his radicalism alarmed even his friends in Britain's Liberal Party. As he put it: ". . . I should not have been honest had I not admitted that I would destroy, if I had the power, every vestige of privilege in England . . . ." In his *Autobiography* (Boston, Houghton Mifflin, 1920), Andrew Carnegie boasted of buying eighteen British newspapers in order to begin "a campaign of political progress upon radical lines." Not only did he favor the dissolution of the British Empire, he urged abolition of the House of Lords and the monarchy, favored "land reform," and urged the disestablishment of the Church of England.

Like his friend Cecil Rhodes, who is known to have engaged in assorted conspiracies to encourage a merger of the United States and Britain, Andrew Carnegie saw the establishment of regional governments as a first step toward the New World Order. In Carnegie's words: "Let men say what they will, I say that as surely as the sun in the heavens once shone upon Britain and America united, so surely it is one morning to rise, shine upon, and greet again the Reunited States — the British-American Union."* Crackpot stuff? Perhaps . . . but remember that the speaker was the richest man in the world, a man whose "perpetual" philanthropies still support his grand design to restructure the world. For instance, according to the 1941 *Yearbook* of the Carnegie Endowment: "It is this kind of planning for a *new world order* on a cooperative basis which furnishes the constructive program of the peace movement . . . ." (Emphasis ours.)

One of the mergers supported by Carnegie as a step toward World Government was the Continental Union movement, founded in the 1880s by a Britisher named Goldwin Smith, to combine the United States and Canada. And he went so far as to tout a "Race Alliance" of the English-speaking people, which he said would become a *"Kriegsverein* [*literally, a war union*] with power so overwhelming that its exercise would never be necessary."

Andrew Carnegie's idea was that by ever escalating regional governments one could establish a World Government with strong central power and tight regulation to replace Free Enterprise, all enforced by what he called a "peace army." The successor to Carnegie's "League of Nations," the U.N., is still very much with us. And the Carnegie Endow-

---

*The Carnegie Endowment joined the Rockefellers in supporting *Union Now*, a book published by Clarence Streit of Atlantic Union, part of an effort to force the surrender of our national sovereignty to a regional avatar of a contemplated World Government.

ment for International Peace is a chief supporter and propagandist for the United Nations. As we have seen, the conspiratorial Council on Foreign Relations and the Foreign Policy Association have been financed by Carnegie funds as supportive mechanisms through which the Establishment insiders continue to press for the New World Order.

All of this sounds arcane. There is, however, no secret at all about it among the cognoscenti. Historian Arthur M. Schlesinger, a member of the C.F.R., wrote in *A Thousand Days* (Boston, Houghton Mifflin, 1965) of "the New York financial and legal community — that arsenal of talent which had so long furnished a steady supply . . . to Democratic as well as Republican administrations. This community was the heart of the American Establishment . . . its front organizations [are] the Rockefeller, Ford and Carnegie foundations and the Council on Foreign Relations; its organs, the *New York Times* and *Foreign Affairs*."

Back in 1947, when Soviet agent Alger Hiss was running the Carnegie Endowment and was a member of the Council on Foreign Relations, he wrote in the Endowment *Yearbook* urging "close collaboration with other organizations principally engaged in the study of foreign affairs, such as *The Council on Foreign Relations, The Foreign Policy Association, The Institute of Pacific Relations*," and other Establishment groups including the World Affairs Council.*

Carnegie funds have over the years supported Henry Kissinger, and not only the conspiratorial Bilderberg meetings but their secret hemispheric equivalent called *Encuentros Siglo XX*. The goal of all of these is repeatedly stated as being a New World Order.

The Trilateral Commission, founded by C.F.R. Chairman David Rockefeller, is another of the conspiratorial organizations working with the Carnegie Endowment. This commission, not surprisingly, also sees itself as becoming "a major factor in building a new world order." C. William Maynes Jr., a member of the C.F.R. who headed the Endowment's International Organization Program, boasted in the Seventies of having "two new organizations . . . the African American Institute . . . and the Trilateral Commission which will deal with the whole cluster of political and economic issues confronting the U.S., Western Europe, and Japan. They join such old and close friends of the Endowment as the Foreign Policy Association, the United Nations Association USA, and others."

One does detect a pattern. And what these men are doing is all too clear. In fact they don't even bother to deny it. The Carnegie Endowment's

---

*The World Affairs Council even prepared a preamble for a 1976 Declaration of Interdependence, written by Professor Henry Steele Commager, which stated: "Two centuries ago our forefathers brought forth a new nation; now we must join with others to bring forth a new world order." (See Chapter XXVII.)

William Maynes Jr. has admitted that "the Endowment participated in the World Order Models Project, an attempt by scholarly teams from several continents to posit a desirable 1990 world order and *concrete steps to achieve it.*" (Emphasis ours.)

As Andrew Carnegie's friend Woodrow Wilson put it: "There is a power somewhere so organized, so subtle, so watchful, so interlocked, so complete, so pervasive that they better not speak above their breath when they speak in condemnation of it." The Carnegie interests continue to be an important part of that power, about which the captive Establishment media dare not whisper so much as a discouraging word.

Chapter VIII
The Watershed Year: 1913

THE AMERICAN system was so badly battered in 1913, wrote the astute Taylor Caldwell, that the Republic never recovered. Three things happened that make her assertion hard to refute. On February 3, 1913, the Wyoming legislature approved the Sixteenth Amendment, becoming the last of the thirty-six states needed to authorize the progressive income tax. Henceforth the federal government would have virtually unlimited financial power. Then, on May 31, 1913, our republican form of government was changed dramatically by adoption of the Seventeenth Amendment, requiring the popular election of U.S. Senators and further reducing the power of the states. Finally, on December 23, 1913, the Federal Reserve bill became law, giving central bankers and the conspiratorial combines that control them the power to create booms and busts through expansions and contractions of the supply of our money.

"Years he number'd scarce thirteen," wrote Ben Jonson in another context, "When Fates turn'd cruel." The Fates had indeed dealt our country three crushing blows.

In Article I of the Constitution the Founding Fathers stipulated that "direct taxes shall be apportioned among the several States" according to population. And that "No capitation or other direct tax shall be laid, unless in proportion to the census." In other words, a direct tax graduated by income was clearly unconstitutional. Accordingly, the "years from 1789 to the Civil War were a period of almost complete reliance upon customs receipts from imports, but a few miscellaneous excises were imposed from time to time." In 1791, for example, "taxes were levied on distilled spirits and carriages. A little later there were added levies on sugar, salt, snuff, proceeds of auction sales, legal instruments, and bonds." (*The Federal Income Tax: Its Sources And Applications*, Clarence F. Miller *et al.*, Englewood Cliffs, Prentice-Hall, 1968)

"And so," wrote the late Frank Chodorov, "the government of the United States got along with what it could get out of tariffs and a few excise taxes until the Civil War; it is interesting to note that the excise levies were dropped in 1817, and not restored until the Civil War. As a consequence, it was a weak government, in the sense that it could not become bothersome; and the freedom of the people made them strong, so that wealth multiplied and the country flourished. *** [*T*]he Founding Fathers, agreeing with John Locke, with whose writings they were familiar, thought of government principally as *an instrument for safeguarding private property* . . . . " (*The Income Tax: Root Of All Evil*, Old Greenwich, Devin-Adair, 1954)

Under the emergency dictatorship wrought by the War Between the States, however, the federal government ignored the Constitution in order to finance the conflict. As Professor C. Northcote Parkinson has reported: "It began with the Act of Congress of August 5, 1861, which imposed a 3 per cent federal income tax. This was superseded almost at once by an Act of March, 1862, signed in July, which, while maintaining a 3 per cent tax on income below $10,000, increased the rate to 5 per cent above that level. This tax was levied in 1863, increased in 1864 and not abolished until 1872. *** [*T*]he importance of the Act of 1862 lies in its differentiated incidence. In this Act we see the beginning of disproportional or progressive taxation . . . . Until that date the Congressman who voted for a tax did so in the knowledge that it would fall as heavily on himself as upon others — a safeguard some might think important . . . ." (*The Law And The Profits*, Boston, Houghton Mifflin, 1960)

By today's standards of course the tax rates of the Civil War do not seem excessive. After all, these were the highest levels: From six hundred dollars in income to five thousand, one paid five percent taxation; from five to ten thousand dollars, seven and one-half percent; and, above ten thousand dollars, ten percent. It was the principle and the precedent that were wrong. As Victorian economist J.R. McCulloch explained:

"Even if taxes on income were otherwise the most unexceptional, the adoption of the principle of graduation would make them among the very worst that could be devised. The moment you abandon, in the framing of such taxes, the cardinal principle of exacting from all individuals the same proportion of their income or their property, you are at sea without rudder or compass, and there is no amount of injustice and folly you may not commit." (*The Law And The Profits*)

Though the war taxes ended with the military emergency, an expanding hunger for revenue led to the adoption of a second income tax in 1894, which was sold to the people on the ground that it would only soak the rich. But a Mr. Charles Pollock of Massachusetts brought suit over the tax, correctly claiming this direct levy which exempted incomes under four thousand dollars and was not apportioned according to the population was unconstitutional. And as Gerald Carson has observed: "In 1894-1895 the circumstances were very different from the exigencies of wartime, and a court of different complexion was sitting. It was deeply conservative, in temper a Marshall court . . . ." (*The Golden Egg*, Boston, Houghton Mifflin, 1977)

During the Civil War "the Justices had unanimously sustained the collection of a similar tax," but in 1895 the Court ruled that direct taxation of incomes was unconstitutional. (*The Constitution And What It Means Today*, Edward S. Corwin, New York, Atheneum, 1969) A concurring opinion, written by Justice Stephen Field, denounced the tax as follows: "The present assault on capital is but the beginning. It will be but a stepping stone to others, larger and more sweeping, till our political contests will become a war of the poor against the rich; a war constantly growing in intensity and bitterness. If the Court sanctions the power of discriminating taxation, and nullifies the uniformity mandate of the Constitution, it will mark the hour when the sure decadence of our government will commence." (*The Development Of The American Constitution*, Loren P. Beth, New York, Harper & Row, 1971)

In Britain, freeing up the marketplace had led to vast economic expansion. (See Chapter II.) Indeed, spurred by the repeal of their income tax, the British enjoyed for sixty years — between 1830 and 1890 — the greatest increase of living standards in their history while government expenditures dropped as a percent of the Gross National Product from fifteen to eight percent. On this side of the Atlantic, the G.N.P. of the United States grew four times as fast as government spending until application of the income tax in 1914. After that, it was growth of government which had the upper hand.

Professor C. Northcote Parkinson marks 1909 as the "key date" in taxation for the English-speaking world. In Britain, Prime Minister Lloyd George introduced a huge Budget with vastly increased taxes to meet what he called a "war budget." It was, he said, "for waging implacable warfare against poverty and squalidness." This scheme became law in 1910. "Until then," notes Parkinson, "the tide of western expansion was flowing. The British, for example, made their last deliberate colonial acquisitions in 1909."

That same year, 1909, saw President William Howard Taft recommend a "compromise" to those seeking a personal income tax. Taft proposed a corporate income tax as a sop to the Populists and called for a Constitutional Amendment which would permit a personal income tax if approved by three-quarters of the states. (*Our Times*, Volume Four, Mark Sullivan, New York, Charles Scribner's Sons, 1932) The "compromise" was quickly approved by Congress and the Sixteenth Amendment was submitted to the states — with Republicans contending there would never be enough support to ratify it.

While Taft was doubtless deluded, others knew exactly what they were doing. Among these was Senator Nelson Aldrich of Rhode Island, the chief political agent of the senior John D. Rockefeller and, as it happens, the maternal grandfather of Nelson Aldrich Rockefeller. The tax "compromise" became part of the Payne-Aldrich tariff bill, and the Amendment proposal read briefly: "The Congress shall have power to lay and collect taxes on incomes, from whatever source derived, without apportionment among the several states and without regard to any census or enumeration."

The Democrats and Progressives both campaigned in 1912 for approval of the Sixteenth Amendment, and state after state began ratifying this open-ended invitation for looting. With Teddy Roosevelt drawing off votes for his Progressive "Bull Moose" Party, the Republicans lost the White House and the final state approved the Sixteenth Amendment while President Taft's baggage was being packed. (*The Golden Egg*) The tax Amendment became law on February 25, 1913, and Woodrow Wilson took his oath of office on March fourth. Because of the "compromise," the Constitution had been altered for the first time in forty-three years.

It took Congress little time to use its new taxing power. Enabling legislation was written by Representative Cordell Hull of Tennessee, later F.D.R.'s Secretary of State. Hull was a radical "and 'a quiet fanatic' on the particular issue of the income tax as an equalizer . . . . " (*The Golden Egg*) The loose wording of the Sixteenth Amendment made possible a graduated tax as proposed by Karl Marx, and though Cordell Hull was said to favor a flat rate, "Representative John Nance Garner of Texas succeeded in gaining acceptance for the principle of graduation. Lenin prophesied that the United States would spend itself to destruction. Toward that end this graduated tax was the first and essential step." (*The Law And The Profits*) Under the Hull measure the corporate income tax of 1909, used to carry the day with the Progressives, was ended as under the law corporations became "people" to be taxed according to the tables of the new personal income tax. All of which was "part of the 'New Freedom' program of President Woodrow Wilson . . . . " (*A Biography Of The Constitution Of The United States*, Broadus and Louise Pearson Mitchell, New York, Oxford University Press, 1964) The New Freedom, you see, was taxation for ever bigger government; the Old Freedom was the lack of it.

Still, the income-tax portion of the new tariff law covered but fourteen pages in the statute books, as compared to more than two thousand in the late Seventies. It was a light burden at first: "A tax of 1 per cent was levied on the net taxable income of every citizen or resident, with a personal exemption of $3000. The system of graduation was represented by a surtax payable on incomes of $20,000 and over. Beginning at a mere 1 per cent, this was to reach 6 per cent on income of $500,000 and upward; not a very onerous tax in itself but a foretaste of all that was to follow." (*The Law And The Profits*) Indeed, taxation today is more than a third of our Gross National Product. From its meager beginnings, Americans were working in 1929 until February ninth to pay their taxes; until April fifteenth by 1959; and, last year, every dollar earned until May first was taken for taxes.

A quiet but terrible revolution had occurred. As Frank Chodorov has explained: "The great debate in the Constitutional Convention of 1789 was over the question as to whether this country should have a republican or democratic form of government; the question was finally resolved in 1913, when the door was opened for the introduction of the socialistic form." Those who controlled the tax laws, and attendant exemptions, would control the nation's wealth. And there would now be money with which to buy and bribe the masses into acquiesence. Bread and circuses were only a matter of time.

The sovereign states had by passage of the income tax been set up to become vassals of a federal government upon which they would gradually become dependent for funds. The republican checks and balances were destroyed not only by the Sixteenth Amendment but also through a move to make the Senate more "democratic." The wisdom of the Founding Fathers was ignored. Edmund Randolph, for example, had conceived the Senate as a small, dependable, body to check "the turbulence and follies of democracy." And George Mason had proposed election of U.S. Senators by the legislatures of the various states. Their view prevailed.

Mason, contends Paul Eidelberg, "felt that the states should be left sufficient power to administer local justice. No doubt Mason feared that this power would be swallowed up by the federal government if the states were deprived of a direct voice in the national legislature. He pointed out . . . that the state governments ought to have some means of defending themselves from possible encroachments of the federal government. So, to the mutual restraints between the first and second branches of the national legislature, Mason would add mutual restraint *between* the federal and state governments." (*The Philosophy Of The American Constitution*, New York, Free Press, 1968)

While the Constitution called for the House of Representatives to be elected by popular vote, the Senate was expected to be the more conservative body. As James Madison, Father of the Constitution, put it: "The use of the Senate is to consist in its proceeding with more coolness, with more system, and with more wisdom, than the popular branch." At the Constitutional Convention, five methods of selecting Senators were considered: appointment by the Executive, which was considered too monarchical; by special electors; by Members of the House of Representatives; by state legislatures; and, by popular election. The latter approach, incidentally, had but one vocal proponent.

Among those arguing against a "democratic" Senate were "Delegates from both Massachusetts and South Carolina [*who*] declared that in their respective states the majority of the voters were in favor of paper money as a legal tender, while the legislatures were opposed to it; and both observers attributed this difference to the fact that the legislatures had 'more sense of character and would be restrained by that from injustice.' " (*The Senate Of The United States*, George H. Haynes, New York, Russell & Russell, 1960)

Indeed, only three days were spent by the Constitutional Convention discussing the method of choosing Senators. Later, commenting on the results, Alexander Hamilton opined: "Through the medium of the state legislatures — which are select bodies of men, and which are to appoint the members of the national Senate — there is reason to expect that this branch will generally be composed with peculiar care and judgment." In similar fashion, said John Dickinson: "Let it be remembered that the Senate is to be created by the sovereignties of the several states; that is, by the persons whom the people of each state shall judge to be the most worthy, and who, surely, will be religiously attentive to make a selection in which the interest and honor of their state will be so deeply concerned."

The fact was that the delegates in Philadelphia were well aware of the dangers of unbridled democracy in which no principle or property was safe from pillage by the aroused mob. Commented Lord Acton: "The views of pure democracy . . . were almost entirely unrepresented in that convention." Support for the republican form in which liberty and property would be secure led not only to the adoption of the election of Senators by the state legislatures, but was also the basis for the Electoral College which would choose the President by ballots equal to the total number of representatives of each sovereign state in the House and Senate.

As Gladstone remarked of the original conception of the U.S. Senate, it was a "remarkable body, the most remarkable of all the inventions of modern politics.'' Election of its members by the state legislatures helped diffuse power. And historian George Haynes, himself a critic of the method, acknowledged: ''. . . there is abundant justification for the *Federalist's* statement that in 1787 it was probably 'the most congenial with public opinion.' With rare exceptions, to the progressive thinkers of that period for the filling of important offices no agency seemed more normal, as no agency was more prevalent, than election by state legislatures. It was from current practice, almost as a matter of course, that the framers gave this method their approval. By their legislatures the thirteen colonies made protest against British oppression and prepared to make common resistance.''

Moreover, ''Throughout the war it had been the state legislatures which elected the governors and most other officers, both civil and military. It was by these legislatures that the members of the Continental Congress and the delegates to the Congress of Confederation were elected . . . . In the great majority of the states the judges were elected by the legislatures. Finally, the delegates to this very convention had themselves been elected by the legislatures of their several states.'' (*The Senate Of The United States*)

Yet the Founding Fathers hardly created the Upper Chamber out of force of habit. As Benjamin Franklin put it upon leaving the Constitutional Convention, Americans had carefully been given a Republic. Conservative John Adams marveled at its construction in a letter in 1814:

''Is there a constitution on record more complicated than ours? [*In the first place*] eighteen states and some territories are balanced against the national government . . . . In the second place, the House of Representatives is balanced against the Senate and the Senate against the House. In the third place, the executive authority is in some degree balanced against the legislative. In the fourth place, the judiciary power is balanced against the House, the Senate, the executive power, and the state governments. In the fifth place, the Senate is balanced against the President in all appointment to office and in all treaties . . . . In the sixth place, the people hold in their own hands the balance against their own representatives by biennial which I wish had been annual elections. In the seventh place, the legislatures of the several states are balanced against the Senate by sextennial actions. In the eighth place, the electors are balanced against the people, in the choice of the President. And here is a complication and refinement of balances which for anything I recollect is an invention of our own and peculiar to us.'' (*Clear And Present Dangers*, M. Stanton Evans, New York, Harcourt Brace Jovanovich, 1975)

Which is not to say that Senate elections were without controversy. There was then, as now, more than one case of bribery and corruption, vote deadlocks, and stampeded elections. Some states developed party bosses who determined legislative choices. In other states the move towards a "democratic" Senate led to holding "primary" elections that bound the legislators to a certain choice. Certainly there was no need to destroy the character of the national federation by abandoning the republican form. Senator Elihu Root — who would not always maintain a reputation as a strict constructionist — expressed alarm that direct elections "would discourage the type of senator who accepted membership as a patriotic duty, but would not subject himself to the political campaign necessary for popular election. He said in Congress, 'It is not wise that the people of the United States should contract the habit of amending the Constitution . . . . Reverence for that great instrument, the belief of mankind in its perpetuity, the unwillingness of our people to tamper with it or change it — these, constituting the basis of stability in our government, are the most valuable of all the possessions of the nation that inhabits this rich and fertile land." (*A Biography Of The Constitution Of The United States*)

For a century and a quarter the legislatures of the states had elected U.S. Senators. And "Never in this world," said Senator Root, "has any institution of government wrought out more successful results than the provisions of the American Constitution for the selections of Senators of the United States." The problem, complains Frank Freidel, was that: "State legislatures were occasionally open to bribery, and *much too often they elected conservatives. [Emphasis added.]* ***

"By 1902, the House of Representatives had already five times passed resolutions for a constitutional amendment for direct election of Senators; each time the Senate blocked the amendment. Impatient progressives in various states developed techniques for circumventing the Constitution and providing in effect for direct election. By 1912, twenty-nine states had adopted these devices. In 1911, Governor [*Woodrow*] Wilson of New Jersey gained renown by blocking the legislative election of a party boss. . . . The same year, the Senate ousted one of its members . . . for vote buying. In the wake of public indignation that followed, the Senate in 1912 passed the Seventeenth Amendment, and by 1913 the requisite number of states had ratified it." (*America In The Twentieth Century*, New York, Knopf, 1960)

This tampering with the checks and balances of the Constitution dealt yet another serious blow to the Republic.

Woodrow Wilson's doctoral dissertation was a dirge about the rule of "congressional government" in the United States. He claimed that the President was the "only national voice" and, as such, should be an "irresistible" leader of the country. When he became President, supporters pointed out his well-nigh irresistible influence in the passage of the Federal Reserve Act, often called "the most important piece of domestic legislation in his administration." (*America In The Twentieth Century*)

The alleged purpose of the Act was to stop economic booms and busts, but what it really did was remove the independence of the country's banks and centralize power in order better to create such crises for the benefit of those on the inside. According to Professor Charles Seymour in *The Intimate Papers Of Colonel House*, it was E.M. House — widely known as Wilson's *alter ego* — who was the "unseen guardian" of the Federal Reserve bill as it was pushed through Congress. House, it will be recalled, had cited socialism as dreamed of by Karl Marx as one of his goals. He was himself an agent of the nation's leading bankers and it was he who had chosen Wilson as their candidate to replace Taft. The final bill voted in Congress was like the income tax a derivative — drawn from a plan proposed by Rockefeller agent Nelson Aldrich. And the Aldrich plan, in turn, "was drawn up by Paul M. Warburg, of Kuhn, Loeb & Company, and was cordially endorsed by the American Banker's Association; in brief, it . . . provided for one great central bank . . . . " (*Woodrow Wilson And The Progressive Era*, Arthur S. Link, New York, Harper & Brothers, 1954)

Having the Aldrich name on the bill, coupled with the support of his major financial friends, proved politically too damaging in a Congress suspicious of the financial conspirators. An "alternative" measure was devised under the sponsorship of Representative Carter Glass of Virginia, who solemnly maintained that his proposal had nothing to do with the machinations of Senator Aldrich that had been worked out by the banking insiders in a secret meeting at a Georgia resort.

The situation before passage of the Federal Reserve Act, as described by *proponents* of the legislation, was this: "In 1913, when the Federal Reserve Act was enacted, the economic problems of the world seemed relatively simple and economic systems relatively stable. Economic policies were guided by a few simple maxims: balanced government budgets, gold redemption of currencies, fixed exchange rates, and freedom of trade, capital movements and travel.

"Government intervention in economic life was minimal. In the United States, this took the form mainly of tariff enactments. Tariffs designed to protect industrial products escalated steadily in the post-Civil War period, reaching a peak in the provisions of the Payne-Aldrich enactment of 1909. Agricultural products were sold at competitive prices in world markets. Prior to World War I, the Federal government took little action to mitigate cyclical fluctuations or relieve the hardships of depression." (*Federal*

Reserve System, Benjamin Haggott Beckhart, American Institute of Banking, distributed by Columbia University Press, 1972)

Perhaps it wasn't strictly *laissez faire*, but on the other hand there was little centralized power to be manipulated by the big boys and interfere with the workings of the market. In discussing the Federal Reserve Act, the foresighted Congressman Charles Lindbergh Sr. warned that establishment of the Fed would now mean "depressions will be scientifically created." (See Gary Allen's *None Dare Call It Conspiracy*.) The Glass bill, said Lindbergh, "establishes the most gigantic trust on earth . . . . When the President signs this act the invisible government by the money power, proven to exist by the Money Trust investigation, will be legalized. . . . This is the Aldrich bill in disguise . . . . The new law will create inflation whenever the trusts want inflation."

Indeed, Colonel House even reported by memo on the progress of the Glass bill to his friend Paul Warburg, sent to America by the conspirators of international banking to get the American system under control. Yet the Glass bill, the people were asked to believe, had none of the dangerous features of the Aldrich plan. The conspirators were settling for getting their nose in the tent, just as in the case of the income tax.

Senator Aldrich was meanwhile acting as though the Federal Reserve bill had little to do with his plan for central control of America's money; but somehow he could not stop his allies "from supporting the Glass Bill or from feeling that there was a direct continuity between the two plans. . . . Henry P. Davison, who helped formulate the Aldrich Bill, also thought there was a direct continuity between it and the Federal Reserve Act. Herbert L. Satterlee, Morgan's son-in-law and official biographer, shared this judgment, and many years later an Aldrich descendent, surveying the available evidence, came to the same conclusion." (*The Triumph Of Conservatism*, Gabriel Kolko)

The simplicity of a free market beyond the control of government, which had been the norm before 1913, was not what the insiders of international finance wanted. And, surprisingly, some admitted as much. For example:

" 'I would rather have regulation and control than free competition,' Henry P. Davison, [*J.P.*] Morgan's partner, told Congress in 1912 . . . . And the legislation they obtained, as well as the personnel to administer the Federal Reserve System in Washington and New York, was in essence that which big bankers in New York first articulated and advocated . . . . [*I*]t can be argued that the preconditions for the emergence of Wall Street as the dominant force in banking and finance, with the power to command and be obeyed, depended on the far greater extension of political control over national banking." (*Main Currents In Modern American History*, Gabriel Kolko, New York, Harper & Row, 1976)

The House and Senate versions of the Glass bill were passed in September and December of 1913. Indeed, supported by the full power of the banking conspirators, and with their man Colonel House at his side to plan strategy, Woodrow Wilson "was able to mobilize every single Democratic Senator in support of the Federal Reserve Act, which in view of its controversial nature, was a masterly feat." (*The Development Of The American Constitution*)

President Wilson signed the reconciled version of the Act on December 23, 1913. Within a year nearly half the country's banking resources were under control of the system and its master manipulators, and the Fed controlled eighty percent of these resources by the late Twenties when the conspirators dramatically choked the money supply and bought up the nation's industries for pennies on the dollar.

Yes, America crossed a dangerous threshold in 1913: installing a socialist graduated income tax to finance ever bigger government; ensuring that the U.S. Senate would no longer be the conservative, deliberative, and state-oriented body of old; and, setting up a central machine to create the sticks and carrots of inflation and depression as desired. Thirteen has proved a very unlucky number indeed.

Chapter IX
The Great War

HISTORY, it has been said, rarely records reality. Nietzsche called it "the belief in falsehood," while Henry Ford called it "bunk." Certainly whole libraries of buncombe have been written about the epochal conflict of World War I, fought we were told "to make the world safe for democracy." As is now all too clear, "the war to end all wars" was nothing of the sort.

In fact, it was from the beginning a war for World Government. Writing of the conflict, British Socialist H.G. Wells recorded the propaganda line in 1915: " . . . mankind must succeed within quite a brief period of years now in establishing a world state, a world Government of some sort able to prevent war" or face permanent chaos. "The Warpath or the World State," commented Wells, "that is the choice for mankind." (*The New York Times Current History, The European War*, Volume II)

In similar fashion, the influential Norman Angell was also trying to sell readers on World Government. His 1915 article "America And A New World State," for instance, carried the subtitle: "How the United States may take the lead in the formation of a World Confederation for the prevention of future wars."

One of the foremost proponents of World Government, raising millions to promote it from leading finance capitalists, was a wealthy Machiavellian from Maryland, named Theodore Marburg, who wrote in 1915 of a planned League of Peace (later the League to Enforce Peace): "The police force (army and navy) at the disposition of the League should be a federal force, supported and controlled by the League . . . . It should be overwhelmingly stronger than the military and naval forces of any one member of the League." (*Development Of The League Of Nations Idea*, New York, Macmillan, 1932) The founding of the domestic League to Enforce Peace came in June of 1915; it was headed by former President

William Howard Taft and financed by the Anglophiliac Andrew Carnegie, but Marburg had masterminded the operation and continued to run the show.

Indeed, there is evidence that the war was escalated for the purposes of forming such a league as a means of establishing World Government. Woodrow Wilson's biographer, Jennings C. Wise, confirms concern about this in a reference to British Ambassador Sir Cecil Spring-Rice, observing: "Whether or not Spring-Rice was correct in his belief that Marburg and the Internationalists had brought on the war, certain it is they proposed to 'make hay' out of it." (*Woodrow Wilson: Disciple Of Revolution*)

Several years before the fighting started, some very interesting dialogues were taking place among the World Government planners in the Carnegie Endowment for International Peace. Minutes of their formal conversations were made available to U.S. Government investigators in the 1950s. These records, according to investigators who saw them, show that the Endowment trustees were anxious to promote a general war to create a climate for selling World Government, and considered ways in which the United States could be involved. To facilitate this end, the trustees laid plans for control of the diplomatic machinery of the United States. Subsequently, such Carnegie officers as Elihu Root and Nicholas Murray Butler played a very influential role in U.S. diplomacy.

From 1914 to the time of our entry in 1917, we were "neutral" in name only. The firm of J.P. Morgan and Company was Britain's most valuable financial ally during this period. As Morgan partner Thomas Lamont put it: " . . . our firm had never for one moment been neutral . . . ." (*The Genesis Of The World War*, Harry Elmer Barnes, New York, Knopf, 1927)

The Morgan interests were also farsighted enough during this period to create (and thereby control) their own opposition. It was a Morgan agent, for example, who financed *The New Republic*, a radical magazine where Socialist Walter Lippmann loomed large. Thus were "Big Business" and phony Socialists supposedly fighting for the "little people" joined in the cry for war. Lippmann, for instance, wrote in *The New Republic* for January 31, 1917: "What we must fight for is the common interest of the western world, for the integrity of the Atlantic Powers. We must recognize that we are in fact one great community . . . . Our entrance into it would weight it immeasurably in favor of liberalism, and make the organization of a league for peace an immediately practical object of statesmanship." (*Intervention, 1917: Why America Fought*, edited by Warren I. Cohen, Boston, Heath, 1966)

The shots at Sarajevo, Bosnia, killing Austrian Archduke Franz

Ferdinand are frequently credited as the immediate cause of World War
I. But the crisis between Austria and Serbia that ensued only reflected the
existing tensions of volatile European politics. Another incident would
have suited the war interests as well. In fact, when the assassination took
place it was treated lightly by some Americans; one Philadelphia columnist reported that if Austria lost, the world would say "Servia right."
Yet, before the war was over, almost thirteen million had died from
wounds and disease; another twenty million were wounded; property
worth an estimated four hundred billion dollars had been destroyed; the
empires of Germany, Austria-Hungary, and Russia were crushed; and,
the bells tolled the passing of the Ottoman Empire. The European map
was changed, and the stage set for revolution and further military conflict.

Tension had long existed between France and Germany over the
possession of *Elsass-Lothringen*, acquired by Germany after the 1870 war
with France instigated by Napoleon III (who wrote on March 2, 1871: "I
acknowledge that we were the aggressors"). This territory had been taken
from Germany by Louis XIV. Nevertheless, French Premier (and later
President) Raymond Poincaré, who was from Lorraine, declared he could
see no reason for living if Alsace-Lorraine could not be recovered for
France. And Ferdinand Foch, who was to become Commander-in-Chief
of the Allied Armies, maintained: "From the age of 17, I dreamed of
revenge, after having seen the Germans at Metz." The French idea of
revanche, actively supported by a network of conspiracies dating back to
the French Revolution, was so strong that before Poincaré was elected
President, Georges Clemenceau said: 'If Poincaré gets in, there will be
war." (*The Lamps Went Out In Europe*, Ludwig Reiners, New York,
Pantheon, 1955)

Russia, the French ally, also had designs of conquest: The capture of
Constantinople and the Dardanelles Straits was an ancient Russian dream.
And, it should be noted, much of the French press was in the pay of
Czarist Russia: According to one account, the Russian Embassy in Paris
was each year supplied with the sum of 1,200,000 francs for propaganda.
(*The Franco-Russian Alliance*, Georges Michon, New York, Macmillan,
1929) Russia's Ambassador to Paris, Alexander Izvolski, had taken what
appeared to be a demotion from Foreign Minister in order to be closer to
the action. Ludwig Reiners quotes him as saying when the bloodbath
began: "Congratulate me; now my little war is beginning. It took me only
four years at my post to attain my goal."

Propaganda in the United States was designed to create the idea that
Kaiser Wilhelm wanted to conquer the world. But "Kaiser Bill," dubbed
"The Beast of Berlin" by George Creel's propaganda boys in the U.S.,
was hardly getting fair treatment in the press. The facts were that the

"militarist" German Army in 1914 (806,000) was smaller than that of either France (818,000) or Russia (1,284,000); and Germany's fear of "encirclement" was not all paranoiac. One might far better lay the "militarist" charge on France, which before World War I had been at war more than half the time for over seven hundred years. Indeed, Colonel Edward M. House, Woodrow Wilson's *alter ego* and an agent of Rockefeller, Morgan, and the Rothschilds, wrote the President in May of 1914: "Whenever England consents, France and Russia will close in on Germany and Austria."

With the shooting of the Archduke, Austria desired a local punitive war against Serbia; but conspirators in France and Russia, both hotbeds of intrigue, were promoting a general war. Professor Harry Elmer Barnes tells how it was sold: "Poincaré and Izvolski decided that their joint program — the Russian seizure of the Straits and the French recovery of Alsace-Lorraine — could be realized only by war, and they came to the conclusion that the Balkans were the most favorable area in which to foment or seize upon a crisis suitable for provoking the desired conflict."

The Balkans were indeed astir with trouble; there had been wars in 1912 and 1913 which the Kaiser had dissuaded Austria from entering. But the Austria-Hungary Dual Monarchy was under constant pressure from Servia (Serbia), which wanted to dismember the Hapsburg Empire to form a Great Servia of Southern Slavs. Meanwhile, of the seven kings who ruled Serbia until World War I, not one died a monarch in his bed. Assassination and forced exile were the norm. Serbia, in short, was not the innocent little country that later appeared in Allied war propaganda.

The power behind the throne was the secret "Black Hand" society whose motto was "Union or Death"; this gang of cutthroats was headed by a colonel of the Serbian General Staff named Dragutin Dimitriyevitch, alias Apis, whom Balkan expert Ludwig Reiners called "the foremost European specialist in political murder." In 1903 Apis had King Alexander, his Queen and Ministers, stabbed in the night; he had plotted against Austria's Franz Joseph and the leaders of Montenegro and Bulgaria; he was responsible for a reported five attempts to assassinate the governors of Bosnia and Croatia — usually employing Bosnians living in Belgrade. A master conspirator in the Illuminist tradition, he was definitely not the sort of fellow you would want your sister to marry.

King Peter, the Serbian monarch brought to power by the murder of his predecessor, had appointed the leader of the radical party as premier. And Premier Pashitch said the country's sole purpose was to free the Southern Slav provinces from Austria-Hungary.

Such was the tinderbox into which the fire of assassination fell. But what is ignored is that the assassinated Archduke was actually killed because he intended to *liberalize* policy toward the Slavs in the Empire; the conspirators wanted no such contented subjects. With the death of the heir apparent and his wife, Austria was naturally in a fury — and accordingly sent a list of demands to Serbia, which wasn't even investigating the Black Hand murder. (In fact, the Serbian press was ecstatic.) The Austrian demands for justice do not, in retrospect, seem too harsh — not even the asking of participation by Austrians in the investigation. After all, the Russians then maintained a police bureau in Paris to suppress Russian anarchists.

The Austrians believed (rightly) that the Serbian Government was involved in the conspiracy, and indeed in 1924 one of the Serbian Ministers, Ljuba Jovanovitch, acknowledged that the Cabinet had known of the plot for nearly a month, but had told Austria nothing. Conspirator Dimitriyevitch, alias Apis, boasted when the war came that he was the "organizer of the murder." (*The Lamps Went Out In Europe*) To judge the opinion in Britain before the war censorship settled in, consider that the *Manchester Guardian* declared: "If one could tow Serbia to the edge of the ocean and swamp it, the atmosphere of Europe would be cleared."

Now both Austria and Serbia wanted war, the latter expecting aid from Russia. The Dual Monarchy made invasion plans even before her "ultimatum" was delivered, and the Serbs mobilized (an equivalent, then, to a declaration of war) before replying to the Austrian note in the negative. The decision on whether the war should be localized now lay with Russia, her ally France, and the third member of the Triple Entente (the Allies), Great Britain.

There is even evidence Russia was involved in the Archduke's assassination, with Apis collaborating with the Russian military attaché in Belgrade. In St. Petersburg, French and Russian officials agreed: "This time it is war!" For years their two General Staffs had annually renewed plans for just such an eventuality. Of course the French had virtually given Russia a blank check: If Russia fought, so would her French ally. Russian Foreign Minister Sergei Sazonov proposed mobilization to pressure Vienna. (Later, he said: "If I had not recognized the necessity for this war, it would not have come about." It cost him his country.) Britain's Foreign Secretary Sir Edward Grey — who would later be instrumental in bringing the U.S. into the war — also urged Russian mobilization.[*]

Germany meanwhile urged moderation on her Austrian ally and tried to maintain the neutrality of the French and British. The Czar seemed to oppose entering the war, but his Ministers were both insistent and

---

[*]Russian mobilization when Germany was trying to restrain Austria, says H.C. Peterson, "was discounted as soon as British censorship went into effect." (*Propaganda For War*, Norman, University of Oklahoma Press, 1939)

intentionally misleading. In fact, Sazonov arrested the Czar's aide, General Tatistchev, to prevent his going to Berlin as a mediator.

Furthermore, as revisionist historian Harry Elmer Barnes points out: " . . . France had decided upon war at least sixteen hours before Germany declared war on Russia" — a fact known to the Russian foreign minister who received a telegram to that effect. *"France was, thus,"* says Barnes, *"the first country in the European crisis officially to announce her determination upon war."* (*The Genesis Of The World War*, italics in original) For two days after the Czar ordered mobilization, the Kaiser delayed declaring war; but he failed to convince Nicholas, who was surrounded by intrigue and conspiracy, to suspend the mobilization.

It had long been the German plan, should war come, to strike first at France, hoping to knock her out, then turn to the Eastern Front before Russian mobilization was completed. This plan, with some modification, foresaw a swing through Belgium — which was less fortified than the relatively short frontier between Germany and France. For their part, the French and British military plans of 1911, 1912, and 1913 also contemplated moving through Belgium to Germany. Moreover, in 1914, the Belgian King said he was more fearful of the French than the Germans. The British, who were later to make much of German violation of Belgium's neutrality, had been negotiating with the Belgians to land troops on their shores and had even determined the rate of exchange in February of 1914 for paying British soldiers fighting in Belgium; in fact, Germany proposed to stay out of Belgium if England remained neutral — but Britain wanted to keep her "options" open.

Great Britain had also made a secret naval accord with France in 1912 which, more than Belgian neutrality, bound her to French war efforts. Even before the Germans asked the Belgians for passage on her soil — and well before invasion, after Belgium refused — Sir Edward Grey had told the French Ambassador that England would enter the war on the side of the French. It was only the invasion of Belgium by the Germans that enabled Grey to keep secret the 1912 agreement. As English scholar Frederick Cornwallis Conybeare wrote in 1922: "Grey was doubtless as much a hypocrite in the week before the War as he had been for eight years before that. We attacked Germany for three reasons: (1) to down her navy before it got any larger; (2) to capture her trade; (3) to take her colonies."

In any case, the Allies — England, France, Russia, Belgium, Serbia, Montenegro, and Japan — were now fighting Germany, Austria-Hungary, and the Turks. Eventually twenty-seven nations would be involved. But after the first battles of the Marne and Ypres there was for three years a devastating and bloody stalemate on the Western Front. The Eastern

Front was in time worse for the Allies — Russia was down, troublemaker Serbia and Montenegro out by 1915, and the English were defeated in Churchill's overextended Gallipoli campaign. England, according to some accounts, was to come within six weeks of starvation by the time America was manuevered into the conflict.

People were wondering what the war was about. As the French Ambassador in St. Petersburg noted: "The world is in a welter of blood today for a cause which is primarily Russia's, a cause essentially Slav, a cause of no concern to France or to Britain."

If ever there was a contrived war in which America had no business whatsoever, this was it. Yet, as the distinguished historian Charles Callan Tansill has explained, U.S. Secretary of State William Jennings Bryan was one of the few members of the State Department who stood for true neutrality.* Because his insistence on neutrality was ignored, Bryan eventually resigned and was succeeded by the hawkish Robert Lansing. (His father-in-law had been Secretary of State under President Harrison; Lansing's nephews were Allen and John Foster Dulles.)

According to Tansill: "As the Secretary had anticipated, the large banking interests were deeply interested in the World War because of wide opportunities for large profits. On August 3, 1914, even before the actual clash of arms, the French firm of Rothschilds Frères cabled to Morgan and Company in New York suggesting the floatation of a loan of $100,000,000, a substantial part of which was to be left in the United States to pay for French purchases of American goods." (*America Goes To War*, Boston, Little, Brown, 1938)

The president of the National City Bank, Frank A. Vanderlip, was another conspirator wholeheartedly for the Allies, and "glad to do anything he could for France . . . ." An Establishment insider in the Rockefeller pocket, he later proved to be a major supporter for a Communist Russia. Vanderlip is quoted as declaring: "As a result of the war, a million new springs of wealth will be developed." (*Merchants Of Death*, H.C. Engelbrecht and F.C. Hanighen, New York, Dodd, Mead, 1934)

To be sure, for some, war can be very profitable. Krupp of Germany is said to have provided steel for the World War I navies of France, Great Britain, Italy, Japan, Germany, and the United States. Britain ran into her own mines in the Turkish campaign. The French and Germans — through Switzerland — carried on trade throughout the Great War. Austria-Hungary had helped rearm Russia. Switzerland, we find, was the middle-man

---

*British Ambassador Cecil Spring-Rice confirms: "All the State Department are on our side except Bryan . . . ." (*Road To War: America 1914-1917*, Walter Millis, Boston, Houghton Mifflin, 1935)

for 150,000 tons of lead sent from the Rothschilds' iron mine in Spain to Germany.

There were a number of shady conspirators like the fabled Greek, Basil Zacharias (later Zaharoff), who had arms interests in France, Russia, and England; held stock in Krupp in Germany; and, reorganized the Turkish shipyards and naval ordnance. He also held shares in Austria's Teschen Steel Company, Berghütten Arms factory, and the prominent Skoda works. It has been reported that Allied leaders had to consult him before major attacks, and that Zaharoff had a particularly strong hold on Britain's prime minister, Lloyd George.

Some four billion dollars' worth of munitions were reported bought in the U.S. by the Allies in 1914-1918. Of course trade was not handled equitably: According to Ross Gregory, "Trade with the Allies, which amounted to $825 million in 1914, by 1916 would soar to four times that amount. Trade with the Central Powers, valued in 1914 at some $170 million would dwindle to about one percent of the previous figure." (*The Origins Of American Intervention In The First World War*, New York, Norton, 1971)

The Du Ponts and Morgans did very well indeed by the war; there is even some indication that the latter interests dissuaded the French from peace in 1914. But the bottom line is also important. The authors of *Merchants Of Death*, which dwelled in part on evidence of war-profiteering turned up by a U.S. Senate Committee, noted: "When the armistice was signed in 1918, there were 21,000 new American millionaires, Du Pont stock had gone from $20 to $1,000 a share, and J.P. Morgan was said to have made more money in two years than the elder Morgan made in all his life." When Du Pont supplies forty percent of the powder used by the Allies, powder is nothing to sneeze at.

Meanwhile, President Woodrow Wilson was publicly urging that we must be neutral in thought and action — and that the war's causes were too complex as to ascribe guilt to any party. But the Eastern Establishment was distinctly Anglophiliac.[*] Moreover, the war news in the U.S. was virtually whatever the British censors would allow — for on August 5, 1914, their Navy dredged up and cut the German cables to this country. Thereafter the bulk of the war news was routed through London.

In charge of British propaganda in this country (assisted by A.J. Toynbee) was Sir Gilbert Parker, who acknowledged after the war: "Practically since the day war broke out, I was responsible for American publicity." Parker, according to H.C. Peterson, supplied 360 American

---

[*]The London bureau chief of the influential *New York Times* was an Englishman who had a largely British staff. It has also been charged that a number of U.S. newspapers were early in the war ordered by J.P. Morgan to promote the Allies.

newspapers in the U.S. with English commentary on the war. Peterson's informative book, *Propaganda For War*, also details the mail censorship which eliminated "all references to actions by soldiers of the Allied countries which might be considered uncivilized." Early in 1917, says Mr. Peterson, "there were thirty-seven hundred persons in London alone censoring mail, and fifteen hundred in Liverpool."

The operation, headquartered in Wellington House, was nonetheless so well done that many English officials did not even know there was such a thing as British war propaganda. Among the groups which dealt exclusively with such propaganda, records Peterson, "was the Pilgrim's Society in England, under Harry Brittain. This organization fostered the 'hands-across-the-sea' movement which made a very strong appeal to Americans. The Pilgrims Club was similarly effective and received the commendation of Sir Gilbert Parker." The Pilgrims have long been involved in the conspiracy for World Government, and with the Round Table groups were responsible for the founding of the conspiratorial Council on Foreign Relations.

Like all such conflicts, World War I was not without its share of atrocities — nor without lies about atrocities, a propaganda practice recommended even in ancient China by military strategist Sun Tsu. It was in England, after all, that the story was circulated that Napoleon ate babies. Similarly, in the War Between the States in this country, it was rumored that Southern belles wore necklaces made of lacquered Yankee eyeballs. James Morgan Read has noted that the same eyeball story resurfaced in the Bucharest paper *Dreptatoa* in 1914 . . . about German women, of course. (*Atrocity Propaganda*, New Haven, Yale University Press, 1941)

Another famous tale was that of the German "cadaver conversion plant," where the *Boche* (French slang) supposedly converted the bodies of their own dead soldiers into fertilizer. This concoction of British Intelligence, admitted to be phony by Britain's General Charteris in 1925, was intended for distribution in China, and was given much credit for bringing China into the war on the Allied side; but it also was popular in the United States. Then there was the "crucified Canadian" who some-times appeared in the guise of a Belgian or Frenchman. "An American reporter asked an Englishman if the 'crucified Canadian' story were true," observed H.C. Peterson, "and was told that it wasn't but 'it had an excellent effect on Canadian recruiting.' "

This is not to say there were no atrocities; there were, and on both sides. But it was Allied strategy to make the "Huns" look inhuman. Atrocity pictures taken in Russia in 1905, for instance, were redated 1915 and blamed on Germans. A photograph of a German helping a wounded

Russian soldier was given the title: "German Ghoul Actually Caught in the Act of Robbing a Russian." When the British ship *Lusitania* was sunk, records Professor Carroll Quigley, the *Times* of London reported "four-fifths of her passengers were citizens of the United States," when actually it was about fifteen percent; the French published a photo taken of an enthused Berlin crowd at the beginning of the war, describing it as German "rejoicing" at the sinking. (*Tragedy And Hope*, New York, Macmillan, 1966)

Certainly Germany had her own propaganda machine, but it just could not match that of the English. Berlin's Ambassador to the U.S., Count Bernstorff, admitted as much to the *Wilhelmstrasse*: ". . . our propaganda in this country has, as a result of the *Lusitania* incident, completely collapsed." (*My Three Years In America*, New York, Charles Scribner's Sons, 1920)

In fact, the very week the *Lusitania* went down, the British issued the Bryce Report, named after Lord James Bryce, onetime Ambassador to Washington who was called "the greatest English authority on the United States." The Bryce Committee, or the "German Outrages Inquiry Committee," pieced together rumors of the most vile atrocities imaginable in Belgium; opinions, tales, second- and third-hand information were all included as fact and offered as the final word on the savagery of the Hun. Coming at the height of anti-German feeling over the *Lusitania*, it was very effective propaganda. "Proof," exclaimed the *New York Times*, "now comes to hand." Later, when Lord Bryce was asked about his atrocity report, he answered simply: "Anything goes in wartime!"

Perhaps more than any other single incident leading to our participation in the war was the sinking of the British ship *Lusitania* on May 7, 1915, by a German *unterseeboot*, the U-20. Some twelve hundred lives were lost, including those of 128 U.S. citizens. Coincidentally, that very day, Colonel House was in England discussing with Sir Edward Grey the impact the sinking of such a liner would have. In fact, the King of England asked House — as recorded in the latter's *Intimate Papers* — what would happen if the *Lusitania* were sunk, and the Colonel opined that it would mean the U.S. would enter the war.

No Americans, to be sure, *needed* to sail aboard this munitions-carrying English ship, for the Germans were keeping a sea lane open for American vessels. In fact, two hours after the *Lusitania* left on her journey to the ocean bottom off the Irish coast, the American liner *New York* left port, carrying no munitions. (*Neutrality For The United States*, Edwin Borchard and William Potter Lage, New Haven, Yale University Press, 1937) Nor was the *Lusitania* just a pleasure craft. *The British Naval Pocket Book* for 1914 listed the ship as an "Armed Merchantman"; *The*

Naval Annual, 1914 and *Jane's Fighting Ships*, both issued to German U-boats, listed her as armed as well, though there is still dispute over whether she was actually armed on the fatal trip.

In any event, in this auxiliary cruiser of the British Admiralty, according to the Customs Collector's report to the State Department's Robert Lansing, "practically all her cargo was contraband of some kind," including ammunition to be used against the Central Powers. As William Jennings Bryan said: "England has been using our citizens to protect its munitions." (*Neutrality For The United States*) Furthermore, though the estimate of ammunition seems somewhat high, according to Senator La Follette: ". . . four days before the *Lusitania* sailed, President Wilson was warned in person by Secretary of State Bryan that the *Lusitania* had six million rounds of ammunition aboard, besides explosives . . . ." (*America Goes To War*) During the whitewash investigation that followed the sinking, reports London *Sunday Times* correspondent Colin Simpson, "much of the ammunition became 'metallic packages.' " (*The Lusitania*)

What is now known for certain is that the *Lusitania* was sent without escort and at reduced speed to an area where U-boats were known to be operating. The likelihood that it was a setup is great in the extreme. Certainly Winston Churchill, the First Sea Lord, wanted to involve the U.S. in the war. He wrote in a February 1915 letter to the president of the British Board of Trade: "It is most important to attract neutral shipping to our shores, in the hope especially of embroiling the U.S. with Germany."

Lost in the ensuing controversy were the facts that the English were searching and seizing U.S. officials and ships; intercepting our mail; and even using our flag — actions which had led to war between the two countries in 1812. On an earlier voyage of the *Lusitania*, with Colonel House aboard, the British captain had actually raised an American flag when in submarine waters.

Churchill's sea policy was simply outrageous, and included advocacy of firing on white flags and shooting prisoners when convenient. British merchant vessels were also instructed to ram submarines if they surfaced in a humanitarian effort to allow merchant passengers to disembark. It thus became folly for the German subs to surface, lose the advantage of surprise, and endanger their own crews. In fact, when one U-boat captain did just that — surfaced and allowed passengers to leave a British ship — he was approached by another British ship named *Baralong*, flying the U.S. flag, and sunk. "The *Baralong's* crew then turned on German seamen floundering in the water and brutally shot as many as were within sight." (*The Origins Of American Intervention In The First World War*)

The loss of the non-combatants aboard the *Lusitania* was tragic business. But, the likelihood that it was set up for sinking aside, the British were violating international law in maintaining a blockade which was preventing the U.S. from even trading in foodstuffs with neutral countries — as Wilson looked the other way. As for the English attitude toward non-combatants, consider the words of Churchill: It was policy, he said, to treat "the whole of Germany as if it were a beleaguered fortress, and avowedly sought to starve the whole population — men, women, and children, old and young, wounded and sound — into submission."

Britishers were quoting the late Cecil Rhodes, who once declared: "This war is just because it is useful to my people and will increase my country's power!" Despite the call to patriotism, the war had a far more sinister goal: World Government.

The papers of Theodore Marburg show that he viewed the war as a means to campaign for global domination, about which he was in touch with Lord Bryce. Professor Jennings C. Wise has described their joint formation of the British branch of the League to Enforce Peace, and of course Bryce was also president of the League of Nations Society of England. And both Sir Gilbert Parker and Sir Edward Grey were likewise working with Marburg on the League of Nations concept, now heavily financed by the Rockefellers, Morgans, and Andrew Carnegie. The secret Round table groups were also in action, including among their number in the U.S. such names as Walter Lippmann[*] and Thomas W. Lamont.[†] All were promoting World Government.

In Britain the secretive Lord Milner agreed to share his authority over an insider operation called the "Ginger Group," says Carroll Quigley, "only in the period 1913-1919 when he held regular meetings with some of his close friends to coordinate their activities as a pressure group in the struggle with Wilhelmine Germany." Milner was influential enough, reported Captain Liddell Hart, to intervene in the appointment of the Commander-in-Chief and to dictate some of the victory terms. Director of the London Stock Bank, World Government advocate Lord Milner was an admirer of Karl Marx,[#] who predicted that a general war in Europe would open the door to Socialism.

The Socialists were certainly in on the game. As Rose L. Martin writes:

---

[*]This Socialist was named by Colonel House as executive director of a confidential group to formulate war and postwar aims for President Wilson. Wilson's famous Fourteen Points emanated from the Fabian Socialist Society and Sidney Webb, via House and Lippmann.

[†]Georgetown Professor Carroll Quigley has described the Lamont family as the chief link "between Wall Street and the Left, especially the Communists." Thomas Lamont was also a fan of Mussolini, securing for the Italian Socialist a $100 million loan in 1926.

[#]Professor Antony Sutton quotes Milner: "Marx's great book *Das Kapital* is at once a monument of reasoning and a storehouse of facts." (*Wall Street And The Bolshevik Revolution*)

"It was the outbreak of war in 1914 that offered Fabian Socialism its big opportunity to organize a mass Labour Party on the home front, while the flower of old England was dying on the first traditional, then, red battle lines." That was of course one objective of the conspirators who had maneuvered Britain into the war. And Professor Quigley, who has viewed some records of the One World conspirators, concludes: "The power and influence of this Rhodes-Milner Group in British imperial affairs and in foreign policy since 1889, although not widely recognized, can hardly be exaggerated."

But of course America had to be pushed into the conflict.

As far back as May 30, 1915, Colonel House confided in his diary: "I have concluded that war with Germany is inevitable . . . ," adding that he would persuade Wilson to act. Historian Walter Millis maintains: "The Colonel's sole justification for preparing such a batch of blood for his countrymen was his hope of establishing a new world order of peace and security as a result."

In April of 1915, Woodrow Wilson publicly declared: "If I permitted myself to be a partisan in this present struggle, I would be unworthy to represent you." Yet, according to *The Intimate Papers Of Colonel House* (Charles Seymour, London, Ernest Benn Limited, 1926), that same year the Colonel briefed Wilson on the particulars of the speech he would make when it came time to declare war on Germany.

Meanwhile our Ambassador to Berlin, James W. Gerard, was rabidly anti-German, and "our" man in London, Walter Page, was so pro-British that even Wilson had to restrain him on occasion. Page admitted Britain would have fought even if Germany hadn't attacked Belgium — but that didn't matter to him. Incredibly, it was Page who suggested to Sir Edward Grey that an American vessel with an American crew, the *Dacia*, be seized on the high seas, urging that Grey have the French do the pirating to take the heat off London.

This, remember, is at a time when we were "neutral." One wouldn't know it from the July 1915 memorandum of Secretary of State Robert Lansing, who drew up the guidelines for his foreign policy as follows: ". . . Germany must not be permitted to win this war or to break even, though to prevent it this country is forced to take an active part . . . . American public opinion must be prepared for the time, which may come, when we will have to cast aside our neutrality and become one of the champions of democracy." (*War Memoirs Of Robert Lansing*, Indianapolis, Bobbs-Merrill, 1935) Among these champion democrats, of course, were the Czar of Russia and the Mikado of Japan.

Then came the ultimate in secret covenants secretly arrived at. Ten months before the 1916 election, Colonel House and Sir Edward Grey negotiated our intervention into the war; this secret agreement, made without the knowledge of the Senate, was an act of enormous hypocrisy which certainly violated the spirit of the Constitution. An unreasonable peace would be offered the Germans — now in control on the continent — and when they refused it would bring us in. The Allies now knew they could reject every other peace offer and still count on U.S. intervention.

Then, in April of 1916, the President held the "Sunrise Conference" with leading Democrats in Congress to gather their support for U.S. entry into war. When they refused, Wilson decided to wait until after the election — an election which was run on the theme, "He kept us out of the war." Even in 1916, one of Gilbert Parker's agents reported: "I should say that the bulk of the [*American*] people throughout the country deliberately avoid any serious partisanship as regards the war."

The conspirators of finance capitalism were, however, in control — arranging with Wilson for a Marxian income tax and a captive Federal Reserve System. First, the war would have to be paid for. Second, Britain's line of credit was running out and it was time for the U.S. Treasury to become involved. "The Schiffs, the Warburgs, the Kahns, the Rockefellers, the Morgans put their faith in House. When the Federal Reserve legislation at last assumed definite shape, House was the intermediary between the White House and the financiers." (*The Strangest Friendship In History*, George Sylvester Viereck, New York, Liveright, 1932)

The regulations of the Federal Reserve Board were changed under pressure from House, as H.C. Peterson has revealed. The U.S. Treasury had to bail out the bankers to the tune of $120 million. Business had been good during the "blood-soaked boom," but it was now time for the taxpayers to pick up the tab. After offering his considerable evidence, Mr. Peterson concludes: "It can be seen from the foregoing that the Secretary of the Treasury, the Comptroller of the Currency, the Secretary of State, and the President of the United States were all assisting in the war financing of foreign belligerent governments."

In the Thirties, when the Senate was taking a hard look at our involvement in the World War, Wilson's Secretary of War found it necessary to write *Why We Went To War* for the finance capitalists' Council on Foreign Relations. Our munitions makers and international bankers had nothing to do with it, contended former Secretary Newton Baker. "While I was a member of the Cabinet from 1916-1921, I do not recall having had a conversation with a banker on any subject . . . ." Perhaps Secretary Baker had faulty hearing . . . or a poor memory. A cable from London was sent in March of 1917, from Ambassador Page to President Wilson: "Perhaps our going to war is the only way in which our prominent trade position can be maintained and a panic averted." (*In-tervention, 1917: Why America Fought*) In any case, up to mid-July of 1917, the U.S. had advanced 299 million pounds to the Allies. Minister of Foreign Affairs A.J. Balfour then cabled House: "We seem on the verge of a financial disaster which would be worse than defeat in the field." (*The Real War, 1914-1918*) The loans of J.P. Morgan were to be covered by the U.S. taxpayers.

After the war, Wilson claimed to the Senate Foreign Relations Committee that the U.S. would have gone to war even if Germany had committed no act of war or injustice against us. Our independence and neutrality were gone by the boards. As the authors of *Neutrality For The United States* put it: ". . . Wilson exhibited little awareness that in making his various surrenders he was abandoning the fundamental rights of the United States, and indeed its independence. Such actions no 'vision of a new world order' could justify." There was not supposed to be independence in the New World Order! And that is just what Wilson wanted. As Messrs. Borchard and Lage acknowledged: ". . . President Wilson's aspirations for a new world order had been indicated on several occasions . . . ."

The man the American people would re-elect President said in January of 1916: "No people ever went to war with another people. Governments have gone to war with one another. Peoples, so far as I can remember, have not, and this is a government of the people, and this people is not going to choose war." One year later, Woodrow Wilson would state: "The great fact which stands out above all the rest is that this is a people's war."

Germany, which had curtailed usage of her submarines, was now feeling the effects of the British blockade. Therefore, in 1917, she announced she would resume unrestricted submarine warfare. This was used by Wilson as an excuse to break off diplomatic relations. Supported by the "Zimmermann Note," Wilson now considered the time ripe for war. That note had been intercepted by British Intelligence and kept for weeks for a well-timed airing. All it actually represented was a German request to Mexico for an alliance *if* the U.S. declared war. But headlines like, "Germany Seeks An Alliance Against Us," were commonplace. Ignored was the fact that the Allies had bribed Italy,* Japan, and Romania

---

*The Allies helped bring Mussolini to power. As Richard Collier described it: "Anxious that Italy should enter the war on the Allied side without delay, French government emissaries had paid him [*Mussolini*] a 15,000-franc subsidy (then worth £1,000) via Charles Dumas, Secretary of the Department of War Propaganda — and regular payments of 10,000 francs followed. Other French agents, like Julian Luchaire of Milan's French Institute, weighed in with donations of up to 30,000 lire." (*Duce!*, New York, Viking, 1971)

into the war with territorial promises. Germany, somewhat stupidly, was trying to do likewise with Mexico — should we declare war.

Some of the Wilson posters were still up, reading "He kept us out of war," when Wilson went to Congress in 1917 to demand war with Germany. Preparation had been such that it was deemed virtually treasonous not to agree.

Wilson's official propaganda force, the Creel* Committee, had matters in hand; Mr. Creel became "the greatest propagandist the modern world has known," in the words of one Wilson biographer. An associate propagandist was Sir William Wiseman, head of British Secret Service, who rented an apartment in the residence of Colonel House that became known as the American Number Ten Downing Street.

The timing of all this was beautifully arranged from the point of view of the conspirators. The bloody Russian Revolution had begun simultaneously with delivery of the Zimmermann Note. This was how Wilson phrased descriptions of the subsequent events in his call for war: "Does not every American feel that assurance has been added to our hope for the future peace of the world, by the wonderful and heartening things that have been happening within the last few weeks in Russia? *** Here is a fit partner for a League of Honor."

In short order this "fit partner" would be a Communist toehold in Europe, assured when Woodrow Wilson sent Leon Trotsky to Russia with an American passport. Comrade Trotsky's goal was clear and public: The night before he left New York, Trotsky told Russian and German Reds: "I am going back to Russia to overthrow the provisional government and stop the war with Germany and allow no interference from any outside government." Secretary of State Lansing noted: "They [*Lenin and Trotsky*] indeed plan to destroy civilization by mob violence."

First, however, the Reds needed time to consolidate, and so they signed the Treaty of Brest-Litovsk with Germany, making hundreds of thousands of troops available to kill American soldiers on the Western Front. Germany nonetheless fell back under the Western attack of the Allies. Bulgaria, Turkey, and Austria-Hungary surrendered. With a revolt in Germany, the last resistance broke and an armistice was signed at Compiègne on November 11, 1918. Thirteen million persons lay dead.

Further, the way had been cleared for the Bolsheviks to attempt to gain power in Germany, Hungary, and elsewhere. The vaunted League of Nations became instead a league of victors, demanding vast reparations intended to drive Germany to ruin. As the map was redrawn, it was shown that "the war to end all wars" had made things worse than ever before.

---

*Its head, George Creel, was a contributor to the pro-Bolshevik *Masses*.

For example, the Poles fought the Lithuanians, Ukrainians, Czechs, and Russians; the Russians had their own civil war; Yugoslavia and Italy were in dispute, *etc.* Germany's colonies were taken by the "anti-imperialists," and she was forced to sign the Treaty of Versailles that didn't even stand by the armistice arrangements.

As Count Bernstorff observed: "At Versailles he [*Wilson*] suddenly advanced the theory that the Germans must be punished for their crimes, and not only those among them who were responsible, but also the innocent German people . . . ." The Versailles Treaty would guarantee World War II.

Ironically, however, the horror of foreign wars did for a time prove enlightening. Instead of the American people demanding a League of Nations to prevent "war," they realized that they were being asked to give the warmaking powers of their government to a world body, which could then use American boys to impose "peace" anywhere in the world.

As we have seen, thirteen million had died in this war for World Government . . . and the American people wanted no part of it. Millions were spent by the great foundations to sell the League, but America rejected it overwhelmingly. The Senate refused ratification, but the patient collectivists were hardly defeated. Former Ambassador Bernstorff correctly foresaw, in 1920, "the world of the Peace of Versailles, blooming with starvation, Bolshevism and nationalistic hatred." The World War was to have an interlude.

Chapter X

Versailles Treaty And
The League Of Nations

THE World War that began with a bang at Sarajevo in Bosnia ended with a whimper at Versailles. Five years to the day after the assassination of the Austrian Archduke — on June 28, 1919 — the delegation from the new German Government was conducted to its seats in the *Galerie des Glaces* to sign the Treaty of Versailles. If the Germans had refused to sign, the Commander-in-Chief of the Allies, Marshal Ferdinand Foch, had instructions to occupy their country: The Fifteenth Point was the end of a bayonet. Count Brockdorff-Ratszau, who headed the delegation of the recently resigned Government, declared: "Those who will sign this Treaty will sign the death sentence of many millions of German men, women and children."* (*Woodrow Wilson And The Lost Peace*, Thomas A. Bailey, New York, Macmillan, 1944)

In January 1917, President Woodrow Wilson had declared that a "peace forced upon the loser, a victor's terms imposed upon the vanquished, would be accepted in humiliation, under duress, at an intolerable sacrifice, and would leave a sting, a resentment, a bitter memory upon which terms of peace would rest . . . as upon quicksand." That warning was quickly forgotten — by Wilson as by the others. The President and assorted conspirators in America and abroad had subsequently pushed the United States into the war, and Woodrow Wilson had been made aware of how the game is played.

---

*Certainly millions had already perished because of World War I, and the Count was prophetically accurate about millions of future deaths. The French chose the Palace at Versailles to revenge the 1871 Versailles Treaty that ended the Franco-Prussian War and gave the Germans control of Alsace-Lorraine. In June of 1940 the National Socialist dictator Adolf Hitler would stage another reenactment, this time at Compiègne, site of the 1918 Armistice. In the same railway car used by Marshal Foch (whose statue was nearby), Hitler would accept the French surrender, "and he himself would occupy the chair used by Foch." (*The Life And Death Of Adolf Hitler*, Robert Payne, New York, Praeger, 1973)

According to the enlightened Wilson, we were fighting for "a new international order based . . . on broad principles of right and justice." Those were hollow words. The kind of justice in which we engaged after the Armistice and before the signing of the Treaty is described by historian Thomas A. Bailey. The allied blockade of food, he writes, "was made more severe than it had been during the actual fighting . . . . During this period unaccounted thousands of German men, women and children died of starvation, or were physically and mentally blighted." Wilson, who had arranged passport and passage for Leon Trotsky from New York to Russia, was helping to make it possible for Communist Revolution to be exported (briefly) to Hungary, and (unsuccessfully) to starving Germany as part of his "new international order."*

Winston S. Churchill was another supporter of the German starvation, as he publicly admitted. And later he ably described the stage on which the Paris Conference had been set to lay the foundation for the Versailles Treaty. "Appetites, passions, hopes, revenge, starvation and anarchy ruled the hour; and from this simultaneous and almost universal welter all eyes were turned to Paris. To this immortal city — gay-tragic, haggard-triumphant, scarred and crowned — more than half mankind now looked for satisfaction or deliverance." (*The Aftermath*, New York, Charles Scribner's Sons, 1929)

Germany had agreed to Armistice terms based upon principles announced by President Wilson on February 11, 1918, promising that there shall be "no annexations, no contributions, no punitive damages." (*Peacemaking*, Harold Nicolson, Boston, Houghton Mifflin, 1933) When the Senate Foreign Relations Committee became alarmed by Woodrow Wilson's fanatical insistence upon ratification of the Versailles Treaty to get us in the League of Nations, he denied knowing of any secret treaties under which the Allies had agreed to divide among themselves the wealth and lands of Austria, Hungary, and Germany. Wilson scholar Thomas Bailey (among others) notes: "This, we know, was not the truth. Numerous references in Wilson's private papers, large excerpts from which have been published, . . . relate to the provisions of some of the secret pacts."

British and American conspirators were working very closely. Deals were being made for control of the world. Diplomatic historian Samuel Flagg Bemis reports that Lord Balfour of Britain showed Colonel House "his map with the territories of the secret treaties drawn on it. With the President and House, he went over the same ground." Shortly thereafter,

---

*For their part, the Russian Reds told the Paris Peace Conference the " 'League of Nations' advanced by President Wilson may become a valuable aid to international law" — if it were "democratic" enough. (*Ten Days That Shook The World*, John Reed, New York, Vintage, 1960)

the President promised Balfour 1.5 million troops on the western front by the end of 1918. (*Wilson At Versailles*, edited by Theodore P. Greene, Boston, D.C. Heath, 1957)

Duped into the war, America was not only used by the conspirators to loot and disrupt Central Europe, but she was as a result being pushed into an embryo World Government. Wilson wanted to be President of the World; the conspirators behind him wanted everything. To achieve any of this it was necessary to deceive the American people as long as possible. Consider the peace we were told would involve "no annexations, no contributions, no punitive damages." Germany, alone, was affected as follows:

Militarily: Abolition of the draft and banning of military aircraft, submarines, tanks, and heavy artillery. She was allowed a tiny Navy and an Army of only one hundred thousand men, about one-eighth her pre-war force, with no reserves.

Territorially: Evacuation of all occupied territory and loss of Alsace-Lorraine; the vital coal rights of the Saar valley, estimated to exceed those of all France, were given to the French, with the result that in the Thirties more than ninety percent of the Saar's citizens voted to be ruled by Hitler; the Rhineland was ordered demilitarized; all German overseas colonies were taken, resulting in the loss of some fifteen million subjects; Posen and most of West Prussia were given to Poland; the port of Danzig, overwhelmingly German, was set up as an independent state in the Polish customs union to duck the issue of self-determination while providing Poland with an outlet to the sea. In all, Germany lost one-seventh of her European territory and ten percent of her population, along with seventy-five percent of her iron ore and thirty-three percent of her coal resources.

Financially: When Germany signed the Treaty she had no idea how much it would cost — some publicized claims ran as high as five hundred billion dollars.

Early in the Peace Conference, economist John Maynard Keynes withdrew and wrote a book called *The Economic Consequences Of The Peace*, declaring that "the Peace is outrageous and impossible and can bring nothing but misfortune behind it." He had apparently not yet identified the conspiracy of which he later became an important member. Keynes observed that the German economy depended on overseas commerce; coal and iron-run industries; and, her transport and tariff system. "The treaty," he declared, "aims at the systematic destruction of all three . . . ." An astonished Keynes pointed out in *Everybody's Magazine* in 1920 that Germany's currency had even at that early date been depreciated as a result of this looting "to less than one-seventh of its former value . . . ."

Indeed, Prime Minister David Lloyd George of Britain won the election of 1918 on the slogan: "Hang the Kaiser and make the Germans pay the cost of the war." (*The United States After The War*, James C. Malin, Boston, Ginn, 1930) And a Lloyd George associate promised, amid cries of "Search their pockets," that: "We will get out of her [*Germany*] all you can squeeze out of a lemon and a bit more. I will squeeze her until you can hear the pips squeak." Inflation in Germany, caused by deficit funding of reparations, was harsh: In the spring of 1921, one U.S. dollar equalled sixty-five German marks; by September of 1923, one dollar was worth nine million marks; and, by November of 1923 it took at least 4,200,000,000,000 marks to equal a single U.S. dollar.

Elsewhere, the Hapsburg Empire was destroyed as Austria fell from being the second-largest state in Europe to one smaller than Bulgaria; Serbia and provinces of Austria became Yugoslavia; Poland, as we have noted, was reformed at the expense of Germany; Romania acquired Transylvania from Hungary; Hungary became "independent," then (briefly) Communist under Leninist agent Béla Kun; a heterogeneous Czecho-Slovakia was proclaimed; Italy (with her policy of *sacro egoismo*, or sacred selfishness) was given Trieste and the South Tyrol with its two hundred thousand Austrian Germans (later dealt by Mussolini to Hitler); Russia, of course, was suffering a contrived civil war that would assure her slavery under Communism; and, the Ottoman Empire was broken and stripped of its possessions, including Palestine, Syria, and Iraq.

As Britain's Prime Minister Lloyd George told Lord Riddell on March 30, 1919: "The truth is we have got our way . . . . the German navy has been handed over, German merchant shipping has been handed over, and the German colonies given up. One of our chief trade competitors has been crippled and our Allies are about to become her biggest creditors. That is no small achievement." (*Versailles Twenty Years After*, Paul Birdsall,* New York, Reynal & Hitchcock, 1941)

American blood and treasure had been poured out to reshape the world for the benefit of a vast conspiracy. Wilson gabbled that he had insisted that Germany not be made to pay "war costs," but only reparations. It was more nonsense. Lloyd George claimed that even such items as the pensions of Allied soldiers should be considered "civilian" costs, and therefore reparations. When Americans in Paris rightfully complained, Wilson said: "Logic! Logic! I don't give a damn for logic. I am going to include pensions!" This doubled or tripled what Germany could pay,

---

*Mr. Birdsall calls his book an appraisal of the "struggle between Wilsonian principles of a new world order and the principles of reactionary nationalism."

insuring her destitution and laying the groundwork for what some anticipated would be a Communist revolution. Wilson knew it, but required the
extra burden be carried.

Article 231 of the Versailles Treaty, the so-called "War Guilt Clause,"
was the brainstrom of John Foster Dulles, later Secretary of State under
Dwight Eisenhower. Apologists for Dulles called it a "concession"
providing legal basis for reparations. Historian Paul Birdsall, who is
certainly no critic of either Woodrow Wilson or Versailles, admits of the
backlash to the War Guilt Clause: "Probably no single item of the Treaty
of Versailles has been so useful to Hitler in destroying the morale of his
democratic opponents before attacking them."*

But the major conspiratorial feature of the Treaty was formation of the
League of Nations. It was this which caused the U.S. Senate to refuse to
ratify the package. And for all the war profits and subsequent looting,
merging of the U.S. sovereignty into such a World Government was the
reason we had been pushed into the war. The conspiratorial League to
Enforce Peace had published a book in 1918 called *Win The War For
Permanent Peace*, which was introduced as follows: ". . . The War Must
Be Won by the absolute defeat of Germany, Military Autocracy must be
ended, and to justify the sacrifices of America and her Allies, a Permanent
Peace Must Be Established, guaranteed by a League of Nations." This
volume contains forty-six speeches on that theme by some of the most
prominent men in America.

Theodore Marburg, financed generously by Andrew Carnegie and
other wealthy conspirators, had spent millions to sell the One World
propaganda of his League to Enforce Peace. In fact, just one year after its
formation in 1915, the League to Enforce Peace had branches in almost
every Congressional District. (*The United States And The League Of
Nations*, Denna Frank Fleming, New York, G.P. Putnam's Sons, 1932)
The conspiracy was carefully coordinated. Marburg handled the overt
propaganda. Covert planning was turned over to Colonel House, who
began to work seriously on the scheme in 1915. By July 1918, House
had "hammered out what he called 'A World Constitution.' " (*Unfinished*

---

*As we said, Mr. Birdsall is himself an internationalist. His *Versailles Twenty Years After* compares
1941 with pre-1917, when the League to Enforce Peace, led by conspirator Theodore Marburg and
William Howard Taft, "formed an unofficial association to consider and promote international
institutions for the establishment of a new world order after the war."

In the first instance this led, Birdsall reports, to the League of Nations Covenant. In 1941, he said,
it produced Clarence Streit's *Union Now* (still influential as Atlantic Union), which diagnosed the
"failure of the League as the perpetuation of the principle of national sovereignty, an unrealistic
reliance upon the principle of voluntary cooperation. Nothing will do now [*in 1941*] but a complete
abandonment of those principles." Mr. Birdsall expressly calls for "the complete fusion of the United
States and the British Empire."

Business, Stephen Bonsal,* Garden City, Doubleday, Doran, 1944)

Though Woodrow Wilson's name has been historically attached to the so-called Fourteen Points — plus Four Principles and Five Particulars — he was little more than a spokesman for House and the other One World conspirators. Rose L. Martin has described in *Fabian Freeway* (Santa Monica, Fidelis, 1968) the direct role played by the Socialist Fabian Society, especially through House and Walter Lippmann. Stannard Baker, Wilson's official biographer, acknowledges: "Practically nothing, not a single idea, in the covenants of the League was original with the President. His relation to it was mainly that of editor or compilist, selecting or rejecting or compiling the projects which came in to him from others sources."

Of Wilson's lofty twenty-three "Terms of Peace," only four were incorporated.[†] In *Peacemaking, 1919*, Harold Nicolson of the British delegation at Paris ticked off some of the violations of the public Wilson commitment to idealism:

"Our covenants of peace were not openly arrived at: seldom has such secrecy been maintained in any diplomatic gathering. The freedom of the seas was not secured. So far from free trade being established in Europe, a set of tariff-walls were erected, higher and more numerous than before. National armaments were not reduced. The German colonies were distributed among the victors in a manner which was neither free, nor open-minded, nor impartial. The wishes, to say nothing, of the populations were (as in the Saar, Shantung, and Syria) flagrantly disregarded. Russia was not welcomed into the Society of Nations, nor was she accorded unhampered freedom to develop her own institutions. The frontiers of Italy were not adjusted along the lines of nationality. The Turkish portions of the Ottoman Empire were not assured a secure sovereignty. The territories of Poland include many people who are indisputably not Polish. The League of Nations has not, in practice, been able to assure political independence to great and small nations alike. Provinces and people were, in fact, treated as pawns and chattels in a game. The territorial settlements, in almost every case, were based on mere adjustments and compromises between the claims of rival states. Elements of discord and antagonism were in fact perpetuated. Even the old system of secret treaties was not entirely and universally destroyed."

---

*Wilson called House his "*alter ego*"; House, in turn, called Colonel Bonsal "my *alter ego*." Stephen Bonsal, Gordon Auchincloss (House's private secretary), and Arthur Hugh Frazier of the Foreign Service were the nucleus of the Colonel's "family" at Paris. (*Suitors And Supplicants*, Stephen Bonsal, New York, Prentice-Hall, 1946)

[†]French Premier Georges Clemenceau (The Tiger) observed: "God gave us the Ten Commandments, and we broke them. Wilson gives us the Fourteen Points. We shall see."

Such was the abomination upon which Woodrow Wilson staked his demand for ratification in the United States Senate. In order to form the League of Nations, Colonel House had managed to "satisfy the greedy ones by giving them what they want." But the two had ignored the U.S. Senate that would have to ratify the Treaty. Indeed, Wilson apologist Thomas Bailey contends: "While he [*Wilson*] was concentrating on the colossal task of making a new world order,* the Senate did not seem important." The headstrong Wilson even insisted that he owed nothing to that body.

The snub of the Senate proved to be a major tactical blunder. Wilson included only one nominal Republican on the American Peace Commission, a partisan move that he would have cause to regret. When the Republican Party won the majority in both Houses in November of 1918, Henry Cabot Lodge of Massachusetts became Chairman of the Senate Foreign Relations Committee.

Another cause of resistance was a group called the Inquiry — the President's war and post-war planning staff. Selected by Colonel House, it was made up of radical elitists and headed by House's brother-in-law, Dr. Sidney Mezes, president of the City College of New York. Secretary of the Inquiry was a Socialist named Walter Lippmann, and it included Socialist leader Norman Thomas.

Little wonder that Wilson ran into trouble with his League of Nations. His critics, especially in the Senate, were soon demanding that the Treaty be changed so that the League Covenant would: 1. Specially recognize the Monroe Doctrine; 2. Exclude authority over any of our domestic affairs, such as tariffs and immigration; 3. Recognize our right to withdraw; and, 4. Specify our right to reject League mandates. Eventually, as Wilson tried to play both ends against the middle,† all but the last was included in one way or another. It wasn't enough.

---

*Wilson expected to head the new order, or as Senator Henry Cabot Lodge put it, he "saw himself as a future 'President of the World.' " (*Henry Cabot Lodge*, John A. Garraty, New York, Knopf, 1953) Nor is there any doubt what kind of a world order Wilson desired. Professor Richard Hofstadter quotes him as saying in 1918: "The world is going to change radically, and I am satisfied that governments will have to do many things which are now left to individuals and corporations. I am satisfied for instance that the government will have to take over all the great natural resources . . . all the water power, all the coal mines, all the oil fields, *etc*. They will have to be government-owned.

"If I should say that outside, people would call me a socialist, but I am not a socialist. And it is because I am not a socialist that I believe these things. I think the only way we can prevent communism is by some such action as that . . . ." It is a familiar ruse.

†Mr. Wilson was the first President to visit Europe while in office — a move that left the country without any acting Chief Executive. Criticism of this was such that a Resolution was filed in the Senate to have the office of President vacated. Americans believed in no entangling alliances; in fact, although it may seem a trifle, Wilson was careful officially to list us not as an *Allied* Government, but as an *Associated* Government in the war.

Whenever Wilson found it necessary to appease the Senate, which was concerned about American sovereignty and protecting the U.S. Constitution, our Allies rushed to take advantage. For example, Britain demanded a change in the language creating the League which gave the British Empire six votes to our one. Colonel Bonsal, House's man, noted: ". . . this change helped kill the Covenant and perhaps, as thought by many, prevent[*ed*] America from entering the League." Vocal critics such as Senator William Borah of Idaho denounced the League as "the greatest triumph for English diplomacy in three centuries of English diplomatic life."

The eccentric Senator Borah was perhaps Henry Cabot Lodge's most important ally among the "irreconcilables."* (A colorful figure from Idaho, Borah was so independent he was said to astound observers when he went in the same direction as his horse.) But Borah was an American first and opposed any League whatsoever: "If the Savior of men would revisit the earth and declare for a League of Nations, I would be opposed to it." As Senator Borah saw it: "What we need is the fostering and strengthening of the national spirit." A League is "the first step in internationalism and the sterilization of nationalism." (*The United States After The War*)

The Senator deserves further quotation for his refreshingly direct analysis: ". . . God pity the ideals of this Republic if they shall have no defenders save the scum of the nations organized into a conglomerate international police force, ordered hither and thither by the most heterogeneous and irresponsible body or court that ever confused or confounded the natural instincts and noble passions of a people." (*The United States And The League Of Nations*)

Other Americans dubbed the Wilson body a League of Nations for International Meddling, a League of Fulminations, a League of Notions, and a League of Denationalized Nations. One magazine editor, who became a bitter enemy of Woodrow Wilson and his fellow conspirators, editorialized: "It is the most impudently un-American proposal ever submitted to the American people by an American President."

Yet another "irreconcilable" was Senator James A. Reed, a Missouri Democrat, who made an impassioned speech against the League on the Senate floor—quoting Jefferson, Adams, Clay, and Webster—and pointing out the disasters likely to spring from subjecting our sovereignty to such a World Government. He received an unprecedented five-minute ovation and his fellow Senators crowded about Reed to shake his hand.

---

*All references in this chapter are to Henry Cabot Lodge (1850-1924) and not to his very "Liberal" grandson, Henry Cabot Lodge "Jr.," who was later a Senator from Massachusetts and Ambassador to the anti-American United Nations.

Of course, supporters of the League were well financed, spending millions to sell the idea. Its defenders included Attorney General Palmer, Senator Hitchcock of Nebraska, and former President William Howard Taft, who stumped the nation for the League to Enforce Peace. Wilson's incipient World Government likewise had the support of the radical Federal Council of Churches and Communists and Socialists everywhere. Their frantic lobbying provoked Senator Philander Knox to ask: "Why is there this racing up and down over the face of the whole land by propagandists urging its adoption?"

When in September 1919 the President, himself, went on the road to urge adoption, his steps were dogged by League opponents from the Senate. Henry Cabot Lodge, who had once been in favor of a league, was now among Wilson's most effective opponents and was playing for time. The longer it was debated, the more obvious the flaws of the League of Nations became: It would either be a World Government or laughingly powerless . . . and the Senate wanted to be no party to either. Said Senator Borah, pointing to twenty-three ongoing wars in the world: "Your league will not bring peace. The causes of war cannot be removed by the writing of a covenant. . . ."

Elsewhere, the inestimable Borah declared: "When you think of the fact that they have so lightly wrecked the entire economic system of an entire continent and reduced to starvation millions of people and perhaps prevented the world peace from coming at all in this decade, there is no language too severe for such men . . . . The Treaty in its consequence is a crime born of blind revenge and insatiable greed."

Fate stepped in during September 1919 when, after a pro-League speech in Pueblo, Colorado, Woodrow Wilson suffered a physical collapse. Wilson had, in his absence, bade the Democrats to stand fast and not accept any more of Lodge's reservations, which were largely delaying tactics but aimed in language and intent at protecting U.S. sovereignty. The powerful Colonel House was also ill, and the supporters of the Treaty could not acquire a simple majority — let alone the two-thirds needed for adoption — with or without the Lodge reservations. James C. Malin's analysis of the Senate votes "gives 38 to 41 votes to the supporters of the treaty with the Lodge reservations, from 31 to 41 to the supporters of the administration, and from 12 to 15 to the irreconcilables" who refused to accept the Treaty under any conditions. (*The United States After The War*)

The truth was that America wanted to mind its own business. Our boys had done the job they were sent to do, and it was past time for them to be home. There is, accordingly, much truth in the opinion of Professor Frank Tannenbaum: "What in the end defeated Wilson, and the League of Nations as well, was not just political chicanery, or personal hatreds, or Wilson's stubbornness, but also the bitter disillusionment of the American people when they discovered that they had been misled, not by their enemies, but by their allies." And, more important, by their President himself.

Wilson had gone for broke, but the conspiracy in which he had become engaged was too obvious. The cautious House had been eager to compromise with the Senate, to accept the reservations in order to open the door to the League — but the arrogant Wilson had apparently come to believe his own propaganda about being the savior of the world. There were, of course, still some League backers.* But the 1920 Presidential election was the watershed year for the world body in the United States. Cabot Lodge had indicated he wanted to test the voter opinion as a campaign issue: "There is no room," he said, "for further compromise between Americanism and the supergovernment presented by the League."

As chairman of the Republican National Convention, Senator Henry Cabot Lodge condemned President Wilson as "the man and his associates who have thus endeavored to turn us from the right road into dark and devious ways which with all nations lead to destruction." Woodrow Wilson, he said, "had apparently but one aim — to be the maker of a league of nations of which he should be the head."

That year's Democrat candidate, Governor James Cox (and his running-mate, an obscure fellow named Franklin D. Roosevelt) declared that the League was the supreme issue of the century; it was a vital part of their platform. Republican Warren G. Harding was an old League opponent who said in his 1920 acceptance speech for the G.O.P.: "It will avail nothing to discuss in detail the League Covenant, which was conceived for world super-government . . . ." And, of course, Harding won the election, amassing sixteen million votes to nine million — more than sixty percent of the total. It was a landslide.

All the conniving, conspiracy, and killing had not maneuvered us into the League of Nations. From the ashes of a senseless world war and the vicious "peace" of Versailles would arise no phoenix, but the vultures of Nazism, Fascism, and Communism — strengthening themselves on human misery to tear again at Europe's vitals. In the United States,

---

*John Spencer Bassett lists important individuals as giving "Unofficial Aid to the League," including Establishment insiders Norman Davis, George Wickersham, and Elihu Root. (*The League Of Nations*, New York, Longmans, Green, 1928) Each of the above is also found among Professor Carroll Quigley's grouping of important internationalists in the sphere of the conspiratorial Council on Foreign Relations and/or the J.P. Morgan interests. The Rockefeller Foundation also chipped in with half a million dollars before 1924 to promote the League's "Health Work."

however, the views of Cabot Lodge had carried the day. As the distinguished Senator from Massachusetts put it:

"You may call me selfish if you will, conservative or reactionary, or use any other harsh adjective you see fit to apply; but an American I was born, an American I have remained all my life. I can never be anything else but an American, and I must think of the United States first. And when I think of the United States first in an arrangement like this I am thinking of what is best for the world; for if the United States fails, the best hopes of mankind fail with it. I have never had but one allegiance — I cannot divide it now. I have loved but one flag, and I cannot share that devotion and give affection to the mongrel banner invented for a league. Internationalism, illustrated by the Bolshevik, and by the men to whom all countries are alike provided they can make money out of them, is to me repulsive. National I must remain, and in that way I, like all other Americans, can render the amplest service to the world.

"The United States is the world's best hope, but if you fetter her in the interests and quarrels of other nations, if you tangle her in the intrigues of Europe, you will destroy her power for good and endanger her very existence. Leave her to march freely through the centuries to come as in the years that have gone. Strong, generous, and confident, she has nobly served mankind. Beware how you trifle with your marvelous inheritance, this great land of ordered liberty, for if we stumble and fall, freedom and civilization everywhere will go down in ruin."

It would take the Second World War and twenty-five years of conspiracy and propaganda to push us into a world league called the United Nations, a hydra far more ominous than its predecessor. But the movement to get us out of the United Nations is growing, and will continue to grow. As it does so, we might do very well to remind our fellow Americans of Senator Lodge's advice.

Chapter XI

Enterprise Of
Henry Ford

IN 1978 the Ford Motor Company celebrated its Diamond Jubilee, commemorating the seventy-fifth anniversary of its founding. Yet, in 1903 there was little indication that the first sales of a buggy-like Ford two-seater would lead to anything significant. The capital raised by founder Henry Ford, then age forty, amounted to a modest twenty-eight thousand dollars in cash. But in twenty-three years that had been turned into more than nine hundred million dollars in profits. An early stockholder, the sister of one of Ford's business geniuses, invested one hundred dollars for one share of the new venture. "That one hundred dollars was eventually to bring her $355,000." (*Henry Ford*, William Adams Simonds, Indianapolis, Bobbs-Merrill, 1943)

While fifteen hundred American auto manufacturers tried and failed, Mr. Ford proved he had a better idea.

The great industrialist (1863-1947) also had ideas about peace, prohibition, publishing, and politics that kept him at the center of national attention. He loved the publicity, loved being a public man, though he was anything but a competent speaker. Indeed, Ford was not an easy man to categorize. Charles E. Sorensen, a longtime associate who became Mr. Ford's head of production, has described the founder of the Ford Motor Company as follows:

"He was unorthodox in thought but puritanical in personal conduct.

"He had a restless mind but was capable of prolonged, concentrated work.

"He hated indolence but had to be confronted by a challenging problem before his interest was aroused.

"He was contemptuous of money-making, of money-makers and profit seekers, yet he made more money and greater profits than those he despised.

"He defied accepted economic principles, yet he is the foremost exemplar of American free enterprise.

"He abhorred ostentation and display, yet he reveled in the spotlight of publicity.

"He was ruthless in getting his own way, yet he had a deep sense of public responsibility.

"He demanded efficient production, yet made place in his plant for the physically handicapped, reformed criminals, and human misfits in the American industrial system.

"He couldn't read a blueprint, yet had greater mechanical ability than those who could.

"He would have gone nowhere without his associates, we did the work while he took the bows, yet none of us would have gone far without him.

"He has been described as complex, contradictory, a dreamer, a grownup boy, an intuitive genius, a dictator, yet essentially he was a very simple man." (*My Forty Years With Ford*, New York, Norton, 1956)

That was the "simple man" who determined to produce a "car for the great multitude" and gave America the Model T — the most famous and beloved automobile that was ever built. Within a few years of its introduction in 1908, the Ford Company was producing half of the cars in the world. By the early Twenties, Ford made a full sixty percent of the automobiles manufactured in the United States. More than fifteen million Model Ts, the "universal car," were produced — and the company estimates some one hundred thousand of them are still running today. Moreover, so enthralled did the American public become with Henry Ford's cars that when production of the T was halted in 1927, in order to retool for the Model A, more than four hundred thousand buyers ordered the new model, sight unseen. When that car was introduced in December of 1927, ten percent of the U.S. population stormed showrooms on the first day to get a look at it.

All of this made Henry Ford quite wealthy of course. But Ford "the dreamer" ploughed his profits back into the company to assure maximum growth. This would, he said, "build more and more factories, to give as many people as I can a chance to be prosperous."

Surely the most dramatic proof that he meant what he said was when Ford doubled the pay of his employees, reducing their work hours simultaneously, all without raising the already inexpensive price of his superior product. This introduced the five-dollar day. While such a figure seems insignificant in the greatly inflated money of today, this announcement of a doubling of the minimum wage in Ford plants for every laborer, reaching right down to the sweepers, shook the whole business community in 1914. The Ford publicists predicted it would "inaugurate the greatest revolution in the matter of rewards for its workers ever known to the industrial world.'' That was hardly hyperbole.

This revolutionary increase was to come from profit-sharing of the next year's income, which Ford figured at a minimum of ten million dollars. Even the buyer of Ford cars would share in the benefits: a fifty-dollar rebate would go to each purchaser if enough cars were sold.* And to keep up with expected demand, production hours were to be increased by replacing two nine-hour shifts with three shifts of eight hours each.

Henry Ford, who was not even listed in *Who's Who* of 1913, suddenly became known worldwide. Not everyone was an admirer. The *Wall Street Journal*, for example, declared on January 5, 1914: ''If the newspapers of the day are correctly reporting the latest invention and advertisement of Henry Ford, he has in his social endeavor committed economic blunders if not crimes. They may return to plague him and the industry he represents, as well as organized society . . . .'' If Ford had nothing but contempt for Wall Street, the feeling was mutual.

Predictions of Ford bankruptcy were rampant, but the great industrialist said he would rather keep the families of his fifteen thousand workers happy than please those of thirty millionaires. Moreover, Ford contended: ''This is neither charity nor wages, but profit sharing and efficiency engineering.'' (*Ford: The Times, The Man, The Company*, Allan Nevins with the collaboration of Frank Ernest Hill, New York, Charles Scribner's Sons, 1954) And, as it turned out, the actual distribution of profits was even higher than expected, amounting to twelve million dollars.

Even as far back as 1948 the revolutionary nature of that 1914 five-dollar day needed to be interpreted in terms of the cost of living and the decline in the value of the dollar. ''A generation accustomed to spiraling prices,'' wrote William C. Richards in 1948, ''may not grasp why a good 95 percent of the world reacted to Ford's minimum-wage announcement as if a new holy child had been born, but a worker in manufacturing at the time got 22 cents an hour and weekly earnings averaged $11 though the Ford rate was slightly higher. Ford's program, like his manufacturing methods, was to change the face of the earth.'' (*The Last Billionaire*, New York, Charles Scribner's Sons)

Here was a businessman, a capitalist, who had become an international hero. And for good reason. Ford had brought mobility and productivity to both the urban worker and the farmer. And not with his cars and trucks alone. He called his tractor the Fordson, observing: ''The planning of the tractor really antedated that of the motor car.'' Ever since he had been a boy on the farm it had been a Ford goal ''to lift farm drudgery off flesh

---

*This was not a shabby percentage as the price of the Model T fell as low as $260.

and blood and lay it on steel and motors." When he added to this achievement a labor policy so generous that it literally took firehoses to control the mobs of men flooding into Detroit to work for Ford, his name was one of the most respected in America. "The people admire Ford," said Archibald Henderson in 1930, "from a sense of gratitude." (*Contemporary Immortals*, New York, D. Appleton and Company)

Allan Nevins summarizes in his impressive trilogy on the Ford Company: "To have fought so stubbornly to get an automobile factory started; to have toiled still more stubbornly to devote that factory to just one durable, versatile, and very cheap car [*the Model T*]; to have assembled a staff which pioneered so creatively in mass production; to have welcomed competition, battled in the long Selden [*patent*] suit for full freedom to produce, scorned protective tariffs, fought clear of Wall Street, and remained a man of the people — all of this was impressive enough. But, while doubling the prevalent wage rate, to proclaim that the roughest day laborer could be made worth $5 a day was even more appealing; it touched men's imaginations."

Ford became, in essence, the country's top advocate of both labor and consumers. Profits, he found, could be made by setting low prices for high volume — and the highly productive auto worker could be well paid so he too could afford to buy a Tin Lizzy. At the same time, reports John Chamberlain, the rise in wages at Ford attracted more efficient workers and improved the productivity of those already on the job. It directly increased "the output of given machinery by some twenty percent. The higher wage, by virtue of its 'leverage' on worker attitude, thus paid for itself." (*The Roots Of Capitalism*)

The impact of this was felt worldwide. In France the scholarly Father R.L. Bruckberger exulted that when "Henry Ford put America on wheels, he rescued the farmer from his isolation and brought him within reach of railroads to carry his produce to New York or San Francisco and carry back machines and city goods . . . . Ford created an unlimited national market." How I wish, said Bruckberger, "I could find words to impress the reader with the importance of that decision of the five-dollar day! It means infinitely more than a mere raise in wages." The timing of the decision "cut away the ground from under Marxist revolution." (*Images Of America*, New York, Viking, 1959)

By 1915 the Ford Motor Company was selling four times as many cars as its closest competitor, but Henry Ford had another pressing thought on his mind: the Great War in Europe. Indeed, Mr. Ford was so opposed to American involvement in the war that he declared he would rather burn down his factory than supply war matériel. In the face of constant war propaganda this sentiment was not universally held, even within company management. In fact, treasurer and vice president James Couzens resigned shortly after Henry Ford opined: "To no better purpose can the pages of the 'Ford Times' be given than to voice the mission of peace."

It was this sentiment which produced the expedition of the famous Peace Ship, an enterprise in which Ford led a group hoping to mediate a solution to the European war and keep American men off of the battlefields. Ford obtained an appointment with President Wilson, through the offices of Colonel Edward House, to try to obtain the President's support for the mission of *Oscar II*, a Scandinavian-American liner. He "urged Wilson to appoint a neutral commission, offering to finance it," even offering his steamship to the President. But Woodrow Wilson, who was committed to U.S. involvement in the war, declined. "Ford was only regretful that the President had missed a great opportunity. 'He's a small man,' he said." (*Ford: Expansion And Challenge: 1915-1933*, Allan Nevins and Frank Ernest Hill, New York, Charles Scribner's Sons, 1957)

The mission was hailed by such prominent Americans as Ford's hero and friend, Thomas Edison[*] and resigned Secretary of State William Jennings Bryan, but the criticism from a press dominated by the Eastern bankers was brutal. In *Road To War*, Walter Millis commented that "the Peace Ship was launched, to the undying shame of American journalism, upon one vast wave of ridicule."

Despite Henry Ford's expenditure of some $465,000, the mission was a failure. But the industrialist never publicly expressed regret. Typically he said: "I wanted to see peace. I at least tried to bring it about. Most men did not even try."

As U.S. military involvement became a reality, however, Mr. Ford contributed mightily to the war effort. "I am a pacifist," he explained, "but perhaps militarism can be crushed only by militarism. In that case I am in on it to the finish." Political writers were years later to criticize Ford for making a profit during the war, when he alone had made the unique promise to return all such gain. When his country needed him, Ford was willing and able.

The war record of the Ford Company "in totality," wrote historians Nevins and Hill, "was impressive. As was to have been expected, the

---

[*]Ford had once been chief engineer at the Edison Illuminating Company of Detroit. And he and the inventor became friends, neighbors, and traveling companions. Frequently joining these two were tire magnate Harvey Firestone and the famous, white-bearded naturalist John Burroughs. A no doubt apocryphal story is told of how the four were forced to stop at a small garage for repairs. Was it the piston? asked the mechanic. "No," said one, "I'm Henry Ford, and it isn't due to motor trouble." Perhaps the tires? "No," said another, "I'm Harvey Firestone, and the tires are all right." Well, then, could it be the wiring? "No," said a third voice, "I'm Thomas Edison, and the electric system is working fine." Sure, said the now disbelieving garageman. "Ford! Firestone! Edison! And I suppose you'll tell me that's Santa Claus riding with you!"

Ford factories had supplied a large number of cars, ambulances, and trucks to the American and Allied forces — about 39,000 all told. It had dispatched caissons, helmets, submarine detectors, tubes for use by Allied submarines, shells, armor plate, and helped to develop gas masks. It had produced 3,940 Liberty motors and 415,377 cylinders for such motors. It had built 60 Eagle Boats and developed two types of tanks which it was ready on Armistice Day to produce in quantity . . . . Ford tractors helped to meet the food needs of both Britain and America, while Ford cars, trucks, and ambulances won wide applause for their behavior in battle zones.'' (*Ford: Expansion And Challenge*)

As peace came, Henry Ford once more opted for expansion, only to be sued by two major stockholders — the Dodge brothers — who preferred that the war profits be distributed as dividends to fund their own plant in competition with Ford. Mr. Ford found that his ownership of 58.5 percent of the company was not enough to assure his expansion policy as the case was decided in favor of the Dodges. He resigned as president of Ford Motor Company in 1918, with his son Edsel named to replace him, though he remained on the board of directors. Soon news came that Mr. Ford would start another company. As the *Los Angeles Examiner* reported on March 5, 1919: "His idea is to make a better car than he now turns out and to market it at a lower price, somewhere between $250.00 and $350.00 and to do it through another company than the Ford Motor Company."

Rumors and speculation abounded, but what was happening was that Ford agents were buying out Henry's other stockholders, who were of course now worried about the potential competition of a new Ford company. The outcome was that all Ford Motor Company activities fell into the sole possession of Henry, his wife, and his son. No one man had ever personally controlled such an empire — not even John D. Rockefeller or J.P. Morgan. The man who had constructed the first Ford engine on a kitchen table and in 1896 built his first auto — comprised of a frame on bicycle wheels — owned factories in 1919 worth approximately half a billion dollars.

The name of Henry Ford was by now mentioned frequently in political circles as a potential candidate for President. In 1918 Ford had been narrowly defeated for the U.S. Senate in a race against former Secretary of the Navy Truman Newberry. Ford had been nominated in both Republican and Democrat primaries, finishing second to Newberry in the G.O.P. race, and topping the vote on the Democratic side. The showing was more remarkable in that Ford ran in the November election as a Democrat in a strong Republican state, and with virtually no campaigning.

Though he lost the suit to the Dodge brothers, Henry Ford did win a judgment of six cents in a libel suit against the jingoistic *Chicago Tribune* which erroneously reported that Ford would fire workers mobilized and sent to the Mexican border. The trial embarrassed him when as a witness he seemed to prove the sincerity of his opinion that history is "bunk" by revealing his ignorance of some basic facts about early America. At about this time Ford also became publisher of the *Dearborn Independent*, though virtually all the material attributed to him was ghostwritten. The paper printed a variety of anti-Jewish articles before Ford issued a formal apology and promised he would publish no more such diatribes. He had wondered why his longtime friend and neighbor, Rabbi Franklin, had been cool of late.

Though he had a penchant for putting his foot in his mouth, sometimes roaring ahead on public issues without thinking, he was a businessman and not a politician. He certainly knew what to do when hard times hit during 1920-1921. Despite inflation, Ford ordered a price cut for his automobiles, but demand was still insufficient and a number of Ford plants had to be shut down. Rumor had it that a huge loan was being negotiated. But Ford, who thought New York bankers were nothing short of vultures, was determined not to fall into their hands. Indeed, in his book *My Life And Work* (Garden City, Doubleday, 1923), Ford wrote: "My idea was then and still is that if a man did his work well, the price he would get for that work, the profits and all financial matters, would take care for themselves and that a business ought to start small and build itself up out of its earnings. *** I determined absolutely that never would I join a company in which finance came before the work or in which bankers or financiers had a part."

Ford's view of bankers as predators seemed to be borne out when, with the car market depressed, one after another lined up to offer their "help" in return for his surrender of independence. The game was clear enough to Mr. Ford. One representative of a Morgan-controlled bank in New York came forward with a plan to "save" Ford that involved dictating who would be company treasurer. Charles Sorensen says in *My Forty Years With Ford* that the banker was promptly told to leave and the next day Edsel was instructed to become treasurer as well as president.

Ford saved his company by turning to his dealers, to whom he now shipped his cars collect in spite of the slowness of the market. Some had themselves to go to their bankers, but eventually demand grew, as did sales, and the plants were reopened. The reopening itself "gave a lift to public confidence. So did the fact that he did not borrow. In general, the public saw only that Ford had outwitted the bankers, and applauded him." (*Ford: Expansion And Challenge*) And the credit of the dealers was sufficient, though there were some grumbles. They had made such a good thing out of the Ford franchise for twelve years, observed John Chamberlain, "that virtually none of them cared to risk losing favor with the Dearborn autocrat. And what they lost in 1920-21 they soon recovered in 1922-24, when the Model T sold better than ever." (*The Enterprising Americans: A Business History Of the United States*)

The key to the concept behind automation was "flow," and this flow was desired on an unprecedented scale for the huge new complex on the River Rouge. It meant an uninterrupted supply of raw materials and transportation. Accordingly, the Ford empire was to expand vertically to coal mines, timber, glass manufacture, rubber plantations, aircraft factories that built the Ford trimotor,* and even railroads. Henry Ford acquired the troubled Detroit, Toledo & Ironton line and rebuilt it, upped safety standards, and reduced the labor force while increasing the wage of those who remained. So satisfied were the Ford-era employees that when a nationwide strike hit, D.T.&I. was the only line in the U.S. on which the workers refused to participate. But Henry Ford "found the regulations of the I.C.C. and compliance with Federal law annoying, and in 1928 began negotiations with the Pennroad Corporation (associated with the Pennsylvania), finally selling the D.T.&I. to that company for $36,000,000; more than seven times what he had originally paid for it." (*Ford: Expansion And Challenge*)

Throughout all of this, it was a Ford principle that the workplace should be as pleasant as possible. As a result of this, the open hearth was revolutionized by Henry Ford and transformed from one of the dirtiest work areas to one that was spotless. Visiting steel men razzed Ford, then emulated him. "It cleaned up every steel plant in the country, not only open hearths but rolling mills as well."

Because such innovations kept Ford in the news, he was forever being boomed for President. Ford, said many, is the man to run the country. The death of President Warren Harding, and the subsequent sympathetic support for his successor Calvin Coolidge, cooled the fever. In any case, Henry Ford supported Coolidge, who said the business of America was business.

But the Ford mystique ran deep. "The Nebraska Senate," noted Nevins and Hill in their trilogy, "invited Ford to visit the State to develop its waterpower; a body of Michigan fruitgrowers petitioned the President to buy all the American railroads and hand them over to Ford for really

---

*Despite Ford manufacture of planes and ownership of its own airport, Henry Ford seldom flew. He did take his first flight with Charles Lindbergh in *The Spirit Of St. Louis*. When F.D.R. refused to allow Lindbergh to serve in the military in World War II, Ford gave Lindbergh a job at a bomber plant and hoped later to make him head of the Ford Foundation.

efficient operation; the New York State Waterways Association called on him to persuade Congress to improve the Hudson River; the price of stock in important corporations rose or fell with reports that he would or would not become a director or investor." In Congress, however, the Senate voted to kill Henry Ford's plan privately to develop water power on the Tennessee River — a move Ford thought due in part to the animosity toward him by the politically powerful Eastern bankers. Later, of course, the same body would approve of the socialist Tennessee Valley Authority.

Overseas, Ford Motor Company mushroomed in more than a score of countries — even in Bolshevik Russia, where an estimated eighty-five percent of the trucks and tractors were Ford built. Henry was apparently fooled by the Reds' peace propaganda even though dealings with Amtorg lost the company $578,000 between 1929 and 1935.

Henry Ford was never so shortsighted in the country he knew. Roger Burlingame, the historian of technology, commented that: "It is hard to deny that Henry Ford was ridden by two obsessions: mechanical perfection and the 'common man.' " (*Henry Ford*, New York, Knopf, 1954) Naturally the *New York Times* called him "an industrial fascist — the Mussolini of Detroit." (*Henry Ford*, edited by John B. Rae, Englewood Cliffs, Prentice-Hall, 1969) The head of his so-called Sociological Department reported that Ford "wanted it known his plan is for every family working for him a comfortable home, a bath tub in it, and a yard with a little garden, and ultimately, he wanted to see every employee of his owning an automobile." But not necessarily a Ford, he said. That would be up to the worker.

Mr. Ford was concerned for his employees, but he didn't believe in the philosophy of something for nothing. "I do not believe in charity," he said, "but I do believe in the regenerating power of work in men's lives, when the work they do is given a just reward. I believe that the only charity worthwhile is the kind that helps a man to help himself. And I believe that I can do the world no greater service than to create more work for more men at larger pay."

His immigrant workers were taught American ways by Ford and instructed at his English School; destitute young men continually knocked at the door of the Henry Ford Trade School, which provided them with such skills that graduates were much in demand. An American who wanted to work knew he could find a job with Mr. Ford. "The company continued to treat Negroes with more liberality than any other large corporation, and in 1923 employed about five thousand. It continued to hold an honorable primacy in employing the lame, blind, ailing, and other physically handicapped persons." (*Ford: Expansion And Challenge*)

To reflect on all of this is certainly sad and ironic considering the funding by the Ford Foundation of useless and revolutionary causes after Henry's death. Especially since the great industrialist had declared emphatically: "Endowment is an opiate of imagination, a drug to initiative. One of the greatest curses of the country today is the practice of endowing this and endowing that . . . . No, inertia, smug satisfaction, always follow endowments."

Here was a man who loved America and personally proved the merit of its economic system. Here was a patriotic man who created the historic Michigan Greenfield Village and purchased and renovated the magnificent Wayside Inn in Massachusetts, where Longfellow wrote his famous poem about Paul Revere. Had he lived to see what the Ford Foundation has done to subvert his patriotic and economic principles it would have killed him or he it.

And Ford was a fighter. He went nose to nose with F.D.R.'s New Deal and the unconstitutional National Industrial Recovery Act (N.R.A), which he defied in 1933, the year after introducing the famous Ford V-8. In fact, said Henry Ford, "I am not going to sign away my constitutional rights in recovery's name." (*Henry Ford*, Simonds)

Failure to kowtow, said bureaucratic Washington, could lead to seizure of Ford plants by N.R.A. Administrator General Hugh Johnson — despite the fact that Ford was paying workers *more* than the government code required. Henry Ford's "ability to sense signs of the times and to counteract forces that showed danger signs was almost uncanny," wrote top associate Charles Sorensen. "In the early days of the New Deal he was threatened with all sorts of government reprisal for defying the National Industrial Recovery Act, that the government would take over his company if he didn't sign up and display the Blue Eagle. He replied, 'Go ahead. The government will then be in the automobile business. Let's see if they can manage it better than I can.'

"That stopped General 'Iron Pants' Johnson and President Roosevelt."

Humorist Will Rogers commented: "You can take the rouge from female lips, the cigarettes from the raised hands, the hot dogs from the tourist's greasy paw, but when you start jerking the Fords out from under the traveling public you are monkeying with the very fundamentals of American life."

Death came to the great American capitalist in 1947. Henry Ford left us this message: "Man can do whatever he can imagine . . . ."

Chapter XII

Charles A. Lindbergh, Father And Son

" "WE (that's my ship and I) took off rather suddenly. We had a report somewhere around 4 o'clock in the afternoon before that the weather would be fine, so we thought we would try it." The ship was the *Spirit Of St. Louis*, the man was Charles A. Lindbergh Jr., and the mission was the first non-stop solo flight from New York to Paris. That successful trans-Atlantic run was flown in May of 1927, setting off one of the greatest celebrations in history.

The father of the "Lone Eagle" could not join Charles' mother in earthly tribute, having died three years earlier. Charles A. Lindbergh Sr. (known as C.A.) had been a prominent Congressman from Minnesota, and like his son an authentic American hero. Commenting on a grueling trip that C.A. and his own father had made by foot, the Congressman had remarked in 1914: "I wonder if my boy and his associates would be able to stand up under such a grilling experience. They probably could, but life is so shaped at the present time that they will probably never be put to the test."

The test was put to both the senior and junior Lindbergh, and each made his individualistic mark — the son in the sky and the father representing men of the soil in Congress. The aviator's father, wrote the younger Charles, was rooted in wilderness and soil. "He never severed himself from these roots, for they seemed to him universal . . . . My earliest memories hold stories about my father's Minnesota frontier days, stories of fishing in the lakes and rivers, of hunting in the forests, of breakplowing virgin land. They formed the warp through which an increasingly complicated culture wove — a schoolhouse, a sawmill, a railroad slashing across the territory. His father, August Lindbergh, welcomed that railroad, my father told me, for it moved civilization closer and eased the heavy burdens of frontier life."

And grandfather August, who changed his name to Lindbergh after immigrating to America from Sweden, where he was a member of the Riksdag and a friend of King Charles XV, had borne his burden as well. A St. Cloud newspaper in 1861 reported that when his arm was mangled in a sawmill accident the mill hands claimed his beating heart was visible through the terrible wound.* August recovered to do regular work with a special axe shaped for his remaining arm. That axe once had to be recovered by grandmother Louisa from a band of Sioux who had stolen it while drunk. "My grandmother," wrote Charles Jr., "took time to change her clothes before she ran after those Indians! She put on a silk dress which she had brought from Sweden, and guarded carefully through hard years of frontier life. She knew the importance of dignity in dealing with Indians . . . ." (*The Spirit Of St. Louis*, Charles A. Lindbergh Jr., New York, Charles Scribner's Sons, 1953)

Swift is the passage of history. It was only a little more than fifty years from the necessity of facing down hostile Indians, in the 1860s, through the career of Charles Sr., who was a political ally of Teddy Roosevelt and advised in the construction of the Panama Canal, to the Atlantic crossing of young Lindbergh who later would help America to reach the moon! Meanwhile, the Lindbergh males were expected to be men. Charles Sr., for example, was responsible for seeing that meat was on the family table, having owned his first gun at age six. "Ammunition was so expensive," reports Bruce L. Larson, "that when he missed a bird he tried to get two birds with the next shot. Shots were counted against birds when he returned home, although there were no questions asked when he brought in a deer." (*Lindbergh Of Minnesota*, New York, Harcourt Brace Jovanovich, 1973)

It was appropriate that C.A.'s boy also received a rifle at age six, though "Father thought six was young for a rifle." Nonetheless, remembered Charles, "the next year he gave me a Savage repeater; and the year after that, a Winchester 12-gauge automatic shotgun; and he loaned me the Smith and Wesson revolver that he'd shot a burglar with. He'd let me walk behind him with a loaded gun at seven, use an axe as soon as I had the strength enough to swing it, drive his Ford car anywhere at twelve. Age seemed to make no difference to him. My freedom was complete. All he asked was for responsibility in return . . . ." (*The Spirit Of St. Louis*)

It had been necessary for C.A., himself, to grow up rapidly; that was the way of the Minnesota frontier. As a youth he ran his own successful business marketing game birds, especially in Chicago, until a law was

---

*Charles Jr. would, in telling adventure stories to his own children, relate how grandfather August had reached down and shook hands with his severed arm and wished his "good friend" good-by.

passed prohibiting such out-of-state sales. So C.A. took his profits and departed for law school at the University of Michigan. In his subsequent law practice in the 1880s he specialized in real estate, and he became a local leader in the economic development of the community.

One friend of C.A.'s later recalled that the lawyer could be both a strict businessman and sympathetic neighbor. The friend remembered an instance where C.A. became angry with his partner for accepting from a poor farmer a payment that was thirty-five cents short. He then personally went out and gathered clothing and food from the townspeople to help that same farmer. Said the partner of C.A. Lindbergh: "There you have the man — worried over a missing thirty-five cents in a business deal — but giving time, labor, thought, to a needy man who had no other claim than his need." Apparently C.A. was always a champion of the farmer, since he thought "agriculturists are the fountain-head of the world's energy. All that exists in a social way has grown from the soil and centers upon it. . . ." (*The Lindberghs*, Lynn and Dora B. Haines, New York, Vanguard Press, 1931)

It was the summer of 1906 that C.A. Lindbergh abruptly announced for the U.S. Congress and entered the Republican primary. "He had never meddled in politics," recalled a surprised friend, "nor expressed any desire to hold office." Furthermore, emphasized the Haineses, his personal friends and biographers: "It is well to remember here that Lindbergh had a large law practice, owned many farms and had many income-bearing investments. Financially, it was a sacrifice to go to Congress."

This was a time of bank panic, tight money, and abuses by conspirators who ran the great banks, railroads, and Money Trust. Like the President, C.A. was a "progressive," and he called Theodore Roosevelt "the champion proclaimer and supporter of the will of the people." Which was good politics in Minnesota — where Teddy had in 1904 swept the state by a four-to-one margin. Winning the primary and general election handily, C.A. Lindbergh set off in 1907 for a ten-year career in the Congress.

On his first day in the House, this father and his five-year-old son sat together in the same hall where Charles Jr. would receive the Congressional Medal of Honor twenty-one years later.

Charles Sr. took his rural living habits with him to Washington, where he arose at four each morning and usually was in the office an hour later. "A large part of my father's political career was devoted to the study of money and its misuses," reported Charles Jr. In Minnesota, the new railroads brought in investment interests. "Land values went up, and taxes with them. Farm income was low while bank loans were expensive.

'A man can't pay off a mortgage at twelve percent no matter how hard he works,' my father said. 'Taxes ought not to be raised because of farm improvements.' "

A populist, C.A. asked many of the right questions about monetary chicanery even though he did not always understand the proper solution. The Money Trust was not his only political interest. He also hit out at a related issue, the nearly dictatorial power of House Speaker Joe Cannon, noting: "It is to the interests of the trusts and monopolies to keep the politicians so organized as to create a dominant central power, and bind up a mutuality of interests with it; for, to achieve their ends and prevent legislation for the people, all that is necessary is to reach those in control." Such a "comfortable condition," observed Professor Bruce Larson, "was a virtual conspiracy against the public interest." (*Lindbergh Of Minnesota*)

Then there was the Rockefeller-owned Standard Oil Company, which Lindbergh claimed had undue influence on tariff legislation. The Rockefeller interests, he declared, had "an iron grip on the people's earning, and we now require protection against it rather than for it." At the time the U.S. was purchasing some 1.5 billion gallons of oil from Standard, while the company sold the same amount to England, France and Germany at a reduced price. "The difference," according to Professor Larson, "amounted to an additional tax of more than $30,000,000 on the American people." And the cause was a tariff that protected the Rockefellers from foreign competition only in the domestic market.

President Roosevelt's Panama Canal project had the strong support of C.A. Lindbergh, who was one of a group of Congressmen to visit the site in 1908. He later reported: "Our people have really started a great job — a job that when completed will in no small degree change the transportation and commercial relations of the world. *** The burden is on us and the benefit, commercially, is to all the world equal to us. The government will charge the same toll to all, designed ultimately to cover interest charge and cost of maintenance. In a military sense we will secure an advantage."

One doesn't have to wonder what Lindbergh and his friend Teddy Roosevelt would say, if they could, about the move to give away the Canal to a Marxist satrapy.

Proud of their Representative, the voters of the Sixth District kept sending C.A. back to Washington, where he "was the first congressman to demand a congressional investigation of the Money Trust during the Sixty-second Congress of 1911 and 1912." (*Lindbergh Of Minnesota*) Lindbergh led the unsuccessful fight in the House against the Aldrich-Vreeland Emergency Currency Bill, which provided for creation of the

Aldrich Monetary Commission (named for Senator Nelson Aldrich, maternal grandfather of Nelson Aldrich Rockefeller). Indeed, according to one veteran Capitol Hill reporter at the time, "In all the years I have been in Washington he is the only man I have ever known who had read the entire twenty volumes of the Aldrich Monetary Commission."

Exhaustive study of banking led C.A. to believe there was a powerful conspiracy working to centralize financial control in the hands of a few, and he did his best to expose it. "The remedy for our social evils," he said, "does not so much consist in changing the system of government as it does in increasing the general intelligence of the people so that they may know how to govern. *** If they do not learn how to govern themselves intelligently, Socialism will be the result."

Lindbergh found secret collusion between Southern and English bankers at the time of the Civil War, citing proofs in his 1913 book *Banking And Currency And The Money Trust*. He published there the text of the 1862 "Hazard Circular" which revealed how labor would henceforth be controlled by the amount of currency the bankers permitted in the market, since chattel slavery would be abolished by the war.

Furthermore, C.A. Lindbergh told his colleagues at the time the Glass Currency Bill was before the House:

"In 1877 there was another circular [*issued by the Associated Bankers of New York, Philadelphia, and Boston*] sent out to confidential friends — bankers — that carried the same idea, and it was for the same purpose with the determination that they should control absolutely the currency circulation of this country. And in 1893 another circular [*the famous Panic Circular*] was sent out, that I saw myself, advising the banks of this country, those to whom they dared send it, to bring on a stringency in order to produce a general request on the part of the business men all over the country to appeal to Congress for certain legislation that should favor the bankers."

Lindbergh accused Members of Congress of meeting in secret to determine which currency bill would pass and what type of Federal Reserve System should be established to please the Establishment. "The correct name for a caucus," contended the Congressman, "is 'conspiracy.' The conspiracy here is to usurp the powers of Congress and do as little for the people as it is thought the people will accept. I have been fighting the caucus system and the secret meeting of committees ever since I came to Congress." Time and again the plans of the money manipulators had to be revised because of exposure by Congressman Lindbergh and his associates. Indeed, according to *The Lindberghs*, the Congressman was himself offered a bribe of two million dollars — big money today, but then an astronomical sum — to stop the circulation of his book, *Banking And Currency And The Money Trust.*

A question arises. Why didn't the insiders of the banking establishment, as it is put in *The Lindberghs*, "go out and defeat him? They tried repeatedly. I once asked an Old Guarder why they didn't succeed. His explanation was interesting, and possibly had some significance. 'We spent so much money,' he said, 'trying to lick Lindbergh that the district became too prosperous to care about a change.' "

Discussing the Glass-Owen Bill, now known as the Federal Reserve Act, Representative Lindbergh and a few others noted on December 22, 1913, that it was nothing more than a resurrection of the repudiated Aldrich plan. "This act establishes the most gigantic trust on earth. . . . When the President signs this act the invisible government by the money powers, proven to exist by the Money Trust investigation, will be legalized."

The citation of the Money Trust investigation refers to the inquiries of the Pujo Committee, which many of his colleagues felt should have been headed by Lindbergh. In any event, the Committee found evidence that there was a conspiracy it called the Money Trust: "An established and well-defined identity and community of interest between a few leaders of finance which has been created and is held together through stock holdings, interlocking directorates, and other forms of domination over banks, trust companies, railroads, public service and industrial corporations, and which resulted in a vast and growing concentration of control of money and credit in the hands of a comparatively few men . . . ."

Named as "the most active agents in forwarding and bringing about" this concentration were: J.P. Morgan & Company; First National Bank of New York; National City Bank of New York; Lee, Higginson & Company of Boston and New York; Kidder, Peabody & Company of Boston and New York; and, Kuhn, Loeb & Company.

Lindbergh explained that this "Money Trust caused the 1907 panic, and thereby forced Congress to create a National Monetary Commission, which drew a bill in the interests of the Money Trust, but Congress did not dare to pass the bill as coming from that Commission. The main features of that bill, however, were copied into this [*Glass-Owen*] bill. In 1912 I made a speech predicting that that would be done, and, further, that the Money Trust would cause a money stringency in order to force its bill through Congress. All this has now taken place. This bill is passed by Congress as a Christmas present to the Money Trust."

The invisible government, Lindbergh said, had come up with a new scheme "to make the people believe that the trusts are opposed to the very thing that the trusts favor. It is assumed that the people will favor what the trusts openly claim to be against. Smoothly the Money Trust has played a game of fake opposition . . . ." And Congress obligingly tossed the conspirators into their favorite briar patch.

The bill that created the Federal Reserve System was nothing more than the Aldrich plan in disguise, which Lindbergh opposed because "Wall Street, backed by Morgan, Rockefeller, and others would control the Reserve Association, and those again, backed by all the deposits and disbursements of the United States, and again backed by the deposits of the national banks holding the private funds of the people, which is provided in the Aldrich plan, would be the most wonderful financial machinery that finite beings could invent to take control of the world." In fact, shortly before the end of his congressional career, C.A. Lindbergh formally moved to impeach the members of the Federal Reserve Board and offered a fifteen-count indictment of their conspiracy. The motion was buried in the Judiciary Committee.

Now, according to *The Lindberghs*, there were "detectives shadowing him much of the time, and he was given to understand that it would be safer for him if he was to change his tactics. In speaking of this to a friend, he said: 'They ought to know by this time they can't scare me that way, but they may get me yet.' " In a subsequent campaign, when shots were fired at the Lindbergh car, a companion declared that "C.A. sat up straight" and directed the driver not to drive so fast lest "they will think we are scared."

In the end it was Lindbergh's anti-conspiracy foreign policy that helped the conspirators to "get" him. A proponent of neutrality in World War I, he wondered how America could, on the one hand, follow the Monroe Doctrine and, on the other, involve itself in a foreign war outside our Hemisphere. But he was strongly for military preparedness and certainly no pacifist. "Convinced that an 'inner circle,' composed chiefly of financial interests, was promoting American intervention, Lindbergh became clearly identified as an opponent of war throughout the neutrality period." (*Lindbergh Of Minnesota*) He warned: "It is my belief that we are going in as soon as the country can be sufficiently propagandized into the war mania."

Congressman Lindbergh had never been one to vote the Party Line. Indeed, he came to realize "the plain truth is that neither of these great parties, as at present led and manipulated by an 'invisible government,' is fit to manage the destinies of a great people, and this fact is well understood by all who have had the time and have used it to investigate." Seeking to increase his influence by going directly to the people, Lindbergh announced he was stepping down from Congress. He would never again hold public office, though he later ran for both Governor of

Minnesota and U.S. Senator, the former campaign (in 1918) being one of the dirtiest in American history.

Once the U.S. joined the war, Lindbergh supported the effort: "the thing has been done, and however foolish it has been, we must all be foolish and unwise together, and fight for our country." He offered his services to the Governor and the President, and was asked to serve on the War Industries Board. That is, until his political enemies questioned his loyalty and used war hysteria to force C.A. to resign. One of the points of contention in the 1918 gubernatorial race centered on a little-circulated book Lindbergh published in July of 1917, entitled *Why Is Your Country At War*, written, C.A. said, "to emphasize independence." It was widely, and falsely, labeled as seditious.

A national campaign was launched to destroy C.A. and be rid of his conspiracy theories forever. The Non-Partisan League, with which he was then associated, was frequently denied the right to assembly; and, mobs raged against Lindbergh, who was stoned and hanged in effigy. Plates of his book, and the even more important earlier one on the banking conspiracy, were destroyed. Lindbergh supporters were often arrested without warrants. The *New York Times* called the distinguished C.A. Lindbergh "a sort of Gopher Bolshevik," and the *Duluth Herald* titled one of their typical anti-C.A. editorials "Traitor or Ass."

Judge John F. McGee, chairman of the State Safety Commission, led the Minnesota fight to crush Lindbergh and the Non-Partisan League. McGee was a fanatic who wanted to place the entire country under martial law, and so testified before Congress at the same time declaring that every League "lecturer is a traitor everytime. In other words, no matter what he says or does, a League worker is a traitor. Where we made a mistake was in not establishing a firing squad in the first few days of the war. We should now get busy and have that firing squad working overtime."

Lindbergh, meanwhile, was doing his best on behalf of the Red Cross, the Liberty Loan, and other war efforts. To no avail; the well-funded forces of "loyalty" won.

After the war, C.A. Lindbergh was rightfully critical of the Versailles Treaty, noting that President Wilson "has his pay now for trying to tie us to a world war machine." A losing race for Senator in 1923, running on the Farmer-Labor ticket with young Charles flying him in an airplane, was C.A.'s last campaign. A year later, he was dead. From a plane above the Lindbergh homestead, his son returned the ashes of C.A. Lindbergh's cremated body to the land he loved.

"A great tradition can be inherited," Charles A. Lindbergh Jr. was to write in his *Wartime Journals* during the next World War, "but greatness itself must be won." (New York, Harcourt Brace Jovanovich, 1970) The junior Lindbergh did just that. Having become a barnstorming stunt pilot, he flew the first mail plane from St. Louis to Detroit in 1926, and the next year he winged his way into history.

Recalling that famous New York-to-Paris run in his Pulitzer-winning book *The Spirit Of St. Louis*, young Charles relives the moment the coastline disappeared behind him: "What advantages there are in flying alone! I know now what my father meant when he warned me, years ago, of depending too heavily on others. He used to quote a saying of old settlers in Minnesota: " 'One boy's a boy. Two boys are half a boy. Three boys are no boy at all.' " That had to do with hunting, trapping, and scouting in days when Indians were hostile. But how well it applies to modern life, and to this flight I'm making. *** Now, I can go on or turn back according to the unhampered dictates of my mind and senses. According to that saying of my father's, I'm a full boy — independent — alone."

The Lone Eagle took neither a parachute nor a radio (too heavy) as he set out to try for the Orteig prize of twenty-five thousand dollars in a 220-horsepower monoplane. His own description in *The Spirit Of St. Louis* defies condensation as he recounts the elation, the doubts, the agony of keeping himself awake, and relives the constantly renewing determination of the young hero. "I've *got* to find some way to keep alert. There's no alternative but death and failure. *No alternative but death and failure*, I keep repeating . . . ." It was real enough. Death and failure had been the fate of others who tried.

There is much time for contemplation on a monoplane flight of thirty-three and one-half hours over water without a radio or parachute. "It's hard to be an agnostic up here in the *Spirit Of St. Louis*, aware of the fraility of man's devices, a part of the universe between its earth and stars. If one dies, all this goes on existing in a plan so perfectly balanced, so wonderfully simple, so incredibly complex that it's far beyond our comprehension — worlds and moons revolving; planets orbiting on suns; suns flung with apparent recklessness through space. There's the infinite magnitude of the universe; there's the infinite detail of its matter — the outer star, the inner atom. And man conscious of it all — a worldly audience to what if not to God?"

Memories, hallucinations, and cold all play their part. Then, two hours ahead of schedule, there is the southern tip of Ireland — Valentia and Dingle Bay — and right on course. "People are running out into the streets, looking up and waving. This is earth again, the earth where I've lived and now will live once more. Here are human beings. Here's a human welcome. Not a single detail is wrong. I've never seen such beauty before — fields so green, people so human, a village so attractive, mountains and rocks so mountainous and rocklike. One senses only through change, appreciates only after absence. I haven't been far enough away to know the earth before. For twenty-five years I've lived on it, and yet not seen it till this moment.''

Finally Paris! Le Bourget field at night, and perhaps the biggest traffic jam in the city's history, as the throng — unbeknowst to Lindbergh — has followed his approach by sightings reported over the radio. The reception was so vast and enthusiastic and disorderly that it became almost as much of an ordeal as the flight, with the young pilot being literally dragged from the cockpit upon landing.

"For nearly half an hour I was unable to touch the ground, during which time I was ardently carried around in what seemed to be a very small area, and in every position it is possible to be in. Every one had the best of intentions but no one seemed to know just what they were.

"The French military flyers very resourcefully took the situation in hand. A number of them mingled with the crowd; then, at a given signal, they placed my helmet on an American correspondent and cried: 'Here is Lindbergh!' That helmet on an American was sufficient evidence. The correspondent immediately became the center of attraction, and while he was being taken protestingly to the Reception Committee via a rather devious route, I managed to get inside one of the hangers.'' (*We*, Charles A. Lindbergh, New York, G.P. Putnam's Sons, 1927)

The world all but went wild over this young, modest, and brave American. The sophisticated capitals of Europe rocked with welcome, and America greeted the return of her son even more boisterously. A Congressional Medal of Honor, a Presidential salute of twenty-one guns, a Distinguished Flying Cross, promotion to Colonel in the Officer Reserve Corps, and a New York City parade (with some 4.5 million spectators and eighteen hundred tons of ticker tape) were among the honors received by the pioneer aviator.

"The welcome that Lindbergh was given in New York has never been rivaled,'' reports Brendan Gill. "It lasted for four days and on every day there was an unbroken succession of parades, luncheons, dinners and private and public receptions. *** the New York *Times* devoted its first sixteen pages to Lindbergh; in the eyes of the editors he was plainly the greatest single event in American history.'' (*Lindbergh Alone*, New York, Harcourt Brace Jovanovich, 1977)

The rugged young flyer who arrived in Paris so free of what is called sophistication that he had never even worn (let alone owned) a bathrobe, was inundated with presents. "By this time gifts were flowing in for him from all parts of the world,'' records Leonard Mosely, "from monarchs, presidents, governments, societies, and private individuals. There were tokens of great beauty (such as a pair of lovely silver sixteeth-century globes from William Randolph Hearst, some Orrefors glass from Sweden), some touching curiosa (crocheted egg-warmers, matchsticks, embroidered in silk), and lots of monstrous and expensive junk . . . ." (*Lindbergh*, New York, Doubleday, 1976)

Charles A. Lindbergh Jr. was soon visiting every state in the union in his famous plane on a tour sponsored by the Daniel Guggenheimer Fund for the Promotion of Aeronautics — a tour in which it is estimated that he was physically seen by thirty million Americans. Airmail stamps now bore Lindbergh's image, the first living American so honored. And he was made a "good-will ambassador" to Central and South America. Young Charles even became friends with the legendary Orville Wright, and the Smithsonian wanted the *Spirit Of St. Louis* to place next to the *Kitty Hawk*. It was an American success story without equal.

Nor was the fame fleeting. The former Lone Eagle and his wife, Anne Morrow Lindbergh, whom he married in 1929, became explorers and together pioneered and charted air routes around the world. Anne's father Dwight, ironically, was a J.P. Morgan partner and potential Presidential candidate. Ambassador Morrow counted among his intimate friends such Establishment insiders as Thomas Lamont, also of the House of Morgan, and John D. Rockefeller Jr. The senior Lindbergh would probably not have been pleased about that, though with the press mercilessly hounding the Lindberghs they found what refuge was possible only with such men of great wealth and influence.

Much good resulted. The Guggenheimers, who had befriended Charles, backed at his request the rocketry experiments of Professor Robert Goddard, thus beginning the first move toward travel in outer space. And Charles also involved himself with inner spaces. His idea for a mechanical heart led to the development, along with the work of Dr. Alexis Carrel, of the life-saving perfusion pump, a version of which is still used today. In addition, the pair co-authored an important book called *The Culture Of Organs*.

It was during this period, of course, that the Lindberghs' infant son was kidnapped and murdered, and a frantic press again seemed omnipresent. Biographer Leonard Mosely called it "the biggest story American newspapers have ever had to handle . . . ." And Kenneth S. Davis recreated the scene: " 'There's absolutely no space limit on this story,' said city editors to their reporters. Said the general news manager of the United Press: 'I can't think of any story that would compare with it unless America should enter a war.' " (*The Hero*, Garden City, Doubleday, 1959) Photographers even broke into the morgue, where the body of the murdered child had been placed after its discovery, and tried to pry open the coffin for pictures.

Jon, the Lindbergh's second son, "had to be guarded around the clock from potential kidnappers and murderers — scores of threatening letters were received after his birth — but also from reporters and newsreel and still photographers, who attempted to bribe the servants into taking his picture and who concealed themselves in the backs of moving vans and other portable hiding places in order to spy on him. *** Once, a car in which Jon was being driven to kindergarten was forced up onto the curb by another car; out jumped some photographers, who thrust their cameras full in the face of the frightened child. There were many such incidents, and in 1935 the Lindberghs felt obliged to leave the United States altogether, taking up residence in a secluded house in the English countryside, where (so they had been correctly informed) the press and the public would leave them quite alone." (*Lindbergh Alone*)

Driven into virtual exile, Charles was still perhaps the most admired man in America. Though forced to live abroad, he loved his country and in her behalf became involved in activities his political enemies later used to vilify him during World War II. Many of the streets and landmarks named for the hero of the Twenties would be renamed because of Lindbergh's alleged Nazi "leanings."

It was absurd. Major Truman Smith, the military attaché in Berlin in charge of U.S. Army and Air Intelligence needed help in 1936, and he requested that Lindbergh do his best to gather technical information about the Luftwaffe. The Colonel agreed. There is no doubt that the Nazis did everything they could to try to impress Lindbergh, and as he was literally an espionage agent he responded with politeness. The Colonel was extremely concerned. As he reported after a 1937 visit to Germany: "The growth of German military aviation, I believe, is without parallel in history; and the policies in almost every instance seem laid out with great intelligence and foresight." Lindbergh, reported Professor Wayne S. Cole, "correctly foresaw German actions against Austria, Czechoslovakia, Poland and Russia." (*Charles A. Lindbergh And The Battle Against American Intervention In World War II*, Harcourt Brace Jovanovich, 1974)

Charles Jr., like his father, was no pacifist. As Professor Cole makes clear, "Colonel Lindbergh urged France, England and the United States to speed their military and air preparations."

Doing their best to smear him, wartime critics of Lindbergh later pointed to the medal presented him (in peacetime — on an intelligence mission for the U.S.) by Hermann Göring. It was to honor him for the 1927 flight and was given unexpectedly, with Lindbergh knowing nothing about it in advance. He refused to return it later, noting "if there had been no decoration they would have found something else. I always regarded the fuss about it as a sort of teapot tempest."

Lindbergh had attracted enemies by doing his utmost to keep us out of the coming war in Europe, just as his father had done twenty-odd years earlier. The conniving F.D.R., committed to U.S. involvement, sought to co-opt Lindbergh and keep him from his plan to warn the American people against intervention. To do this he sought unsuccessfully to create a new Cabinet post of Secretary for Air. President Roosevelt, reports Leonard Mosely, "who loved power himself and had no doubt in his mind that Lindberg also nourished political ambitions, despite any protestations to the contrary, decided that the only way was to entice him into the Administration." Charles refused.

And what does that say of F.D.R.? Especially in light of his alleged May 1940 remark to Secretary of the Treasury Henry Morgenthau Jr., as quoted by Wayne Cole: "If I should die tomorrow, I want you to know this. I am absolutely convinced that Lindbergh is a Nazi."

Charles Lindbergh was soon the most popular speaker for the anti-intervention America First Committee . . . and the most controversial. As the Administration was hell-bent on getting us into the war, F.D.R. and his boys did all they could to undermine Lindbergh. Senator Robert Taft (R.-Ohio) hit back at the President's "cowardly" attack on the aviator, saying F.D.R. "lacks the courage to come out openly for a declaration of war, while taking every possible step to accomplish that purpose, and yet threatens those who oppose his policy, as if the country were at war."

Interior Secretary Harold Ickes was meanwhile squeaking away against "this Knight of the German Eagle," a vicious reference to the award given for the 1927 crossing, and went so far as to call Charles a cheerleader for Hitler. Roosevelt, for his part, planted a question with a reporter before a press conference so he could denounce Lindbergh as a traitor, calling him "a copperhead." With that, Colonel Lindbergh resigned his commission in the Army Air Corps. "If I take this insult from Roosevelt, more, and worse, will probably be forthcoming . . . . I would lose something in my character." (*An American First*, Michele Flynn Stenehjem, New Rochelle, Arlington House, 1976)

But Lindbergh, who had learned much from his father about dealing with conspiracy through exposure, would not be silenced. "We have been led toward war by a minority of our people. This minority has power. It has influence. It has a loud voice. But it does not represent the American people." Whereupon, Thomas Lamont of the Wall Street firm of J.P. Morgan, a friend of his wife and a backer (along with his Communist son Corliss) of many a Red cause, wrote to Lindbergh. Who, pray tell, were those "powerful elements"? asked Lamont. In Des Moines, in September of 1941, Lindbergh gave his public answer.

"The three important groups who have been pressing this country toward war are the British, the Jewish, and the Roosevelt Administration. Behind these groups, but of lesser importance, are a number of capitalists, anglophiles, and intellectuals, who believe their future, and the future of mankind depend upon the domination of the British Empire. Add to these the Communistic groups who were opposed to intervention until a few weeks ago, and I believe I have named the major war agitators in this country."

The roof fell in. This was, in fact, the only speech in which Charles Lindbergh mentioned that Jews were pressing for American involvement — as true, and as necessary for their own reasons, as the fact that the British were pushing for American involvement. Nonetheless, Lindbergh was soon being whipped from pillar to post as anti-Semite. He had expected this, and written in a first draft of the speech (which part was undelivered): "I realize that in speaking this frankly I am entering where Angels fear to tread. I realize that tomorrow morning's headlines will say 'Lindbergh attacks Jews.' The ugly cry of Anti-Semitism will be eagerly joyfully pounded upon and waved about my name." Just so.

Former President Hoover, at lunch with Charles, was among those who told him his speech was a blunder. "Lindbergh insisted that what he had said was true, and was depressed when Hoover replied 'that when you have been in politics long enough you learned not to say things just because they are true.' " (*Lindbergh*)

Pearl Harbor stopped the debate. But when Charles Lindbergh — the world's most famous pilot — offered his services to the military he was rebuffed on the direct orders of Roosevelt. Unless he recanted his previous position and, in essence, groveled before the President, Lindbergh would be informed he was unfit to fight for his country. Charles Lindbergh would not grovel. After all, he said, we were fighting for freedom "and one's right to express his own political view, aren't we?" Lindbergh knew better. And so did F.D.R.

Eventually, at age forty-two, Charles Lindbergh arranged through friends to fly to the South Pacific in a *civilian* capacity, helping train American pilots. He personally took part in fifty combat missions and shot down at least one Japanese plane. As a civilian, had he been captured, Lindbergh would have been immediately beheaded.

Two years after the war's end, Charles pointed to the result he had predicted: "western civilization greatly weakened in a world full of famine, hatred and despair. We have destroyed Nazi Germany only to find that in doing so we have strengthened Communist Russia, behind whose 'iron curtain' lies a record of bloodshed and oppression never equalled.'' And he was well aware of Establishment objectives. He feared, Lindbergh wrote the next year, that in a world of underdeveloped nations ''for Americans the doctrine of universal equality is a doctrine of death.'' We could, he worried, be pushed toward World Government. And ''it is unlikely that a world government in which Asia cast one billion votes would maintain taxes, regulations, and freedom of action which would permit our American standards to go on.''

Having seen political conspirators smear the reputations of both his father and himself, Lindbergh now left the fight against the conspiracy to other hands. Still, he was to remain active — as advisor for the Berlin Airlift, for example. And he was finally permitted to rejoin the Air Force and named a general in 1954. Space flight and an increased interest in conservation were other Lindbergh preoccupations in later years. And it must be said that death held no fear for him when in 1974 it came at last to General Charles A. Lindbergh. The Lone Eagle was off on one final flight, and somehow we feel sure he made it.

Chapter XIII
Fascism And National Socialism

Permit us to begin here by introducing two leading players. The first was highly praised by no less a dramatic critic than George Bernard Shaw, who called his movement most "progressive." Mahatma Gandhi, the diapered champion of staged non-violence, called our protagonist a "superman." According to the then Archbishop of Canterbury, our first player was "the one great figure in Europe." And Winston S. Churchill also heaped critical accolade on this performer, informing him that if they were countrymen "I am sure I would have been with you from beginning to end . . . ," and pointing to his "gentle and simple bearing and his calm, detached poise." The world, declared prominent banker Otto Kahn of this leading player, "owes him a debt of gratitude."

Our second character, in the words of French intellectual André Gide, "behaves like a genius. I particularly admire the diversity of his methods. . . . Soon even those he vanquishes will feel compelled, while cursing him, to admire him." "Liberal" historian Arnold Toynbee was sure this was a man of peace. And the president of Hunter College declared in 1934 that this leading man was "destined to go down to history as a cross between Hotspur and Uncle Toby and to be as immortal as either."

Well, now. The fact is that, like Hotspur, both of these dramatic figures are now food for worms. Thus, as the Prince said of Hotspur, "Ill-weaved ambition, how much art thou shrunk!" For the two luminaries here described were, respectively, Benito Mussolini and Adolf Hitler.

For years, of course, our commentators have excoriated Fascism as the worst of all possible worlds. But "Liberal" accounts stop with the anti-Semitism, book-burnings, concentration camps, and wartime atrocities of the Axis powers. Ignored is the collectivist ideology that made such outrages possible if not inevitable.

The truth is that Fascism springs from a conspiratorial appeal for power to the lower and middle classes — via handouts — permitting elitists at the top to call the shots while themselves remaining protected from the resultant confiscations. And that description now hits very close to home.

We are not mimicking the radicals and Reds who universally brand their enemies as "Fascists" to distract attention from their own style of totalitarianism. Nor are we saying the United States has become a Fascist country. Rather, we are pointing with concern to the trend in that direction and the similarities to what happened in Italy and Germany earlier in this century.

Mussolini chose as the symbol for his Blackshirts the *fasces* — a bundle of rods bound together with a protruding blade, which had been used as a symbol of authority under the ancient Romans. The fasces appears, in fact, on the U.S. ten-cent piece, and it also was on the coat of arms of the French Republicans. So much for the origin of the name.

Of more interest is the fact that the supposedly "rightwing" Mussolini was nothing of the sort.[*] He was for years an orthodox Marxist who, like most Italian Socialists, opposed entry into World War I. In this he had differed from other European Marxists and, fearing waning popularity, gratefully accepted what amounted to a French bribe and abruptly began propagandizing for the war. It was to be a war to destroy the old order and establish Communism. And, as Ludwig von Mises noted in *Planned Chaos* (Irvington-on-Hudson, Foundation for Economic Education, 1947): "More than anybody else Mussolini was instrumental in achieving Italy's entry into the first World War."

That war gave the Communists a base in Russia and the Reds attempted to take power in Hungary, Germany, and Italy as well. They failed in Italy in 1920 after occupying factories in the North, but provided Mussolini with the opening he needed. In 1921, he founded the Fascist Party and many of the Reds of 1920 became Blackshirts. A takeover by any name was just as sweet. As Comrade Benito declared, "Our program is simple: we wish to govern Italy. They ask us for programs but there are already too many. It is not programs that are wanting for the salvation of Italy, but men and will power." In other words, trust me.

Eugene H. Methvin called the difference between Lenin and Mussolini "ephemeral; the similarities are fundamental." For Il Duce "considered himself a good socialist and revolutionary until a short three years before his 'March on Rome.' He always referred to his seizure of power as 'the fascist revolution' much as a Russian Bolshevik might refer to 'the Soviet revolution.' And to Italians the word 'fasci' meant about the same as

---

[*]In 1904, for example, Mussolini spoke at the anniversary of the Paris Commune before an audience of Italians, Germans, French, and Russians.

'soviet' to the Russians.'' (*The Rise of Radicalism*) All power to the *Fasci di combattimento*!

Like Hitler a decade later, however, Mussolini came to power by "constitutional" means. After Rome was occupied by his bands, Il Duce received a telegram declaring: "His Majesty the King asks you to come immediately to Rome for he wishes to offer you the responsibility of forming a Ministry." The conspiring bankers and industrialists who had supported his March would likewise support consolidation of a Corporate State. Thus "big industrialists were able to remain fairly free from the state," writes Christopher Leeds. "They bought their freedom [*sic*] by generous gifts to Fascist Party Funds." (*Italy Under Mussolini*, London, Wayland, 1972)

The Fascists, like all collectivists, had a peculiar notion of freedom and liberty. One of their leading "philosophers," Giovanni Gentile, maintained: ". . . the maximum of liberty coincides with the maximum of state force." He was certainly a Blackshirt suited for the Occupational Safety and Health Administration. Mussolini preferred to make Gentile his Minister of Education.

Benito Mussolini's own thesis was no less absurd: "If historic fact exists it is this, that all of the history of men's civilization, from the caves to civilized or so-called civilized man, is a progressive limitation of liberty." (*Comparative Economic Systems*, William N. Loucks and J. Weldon Hoot, New York, Harper & Brothers, 1948) And remember, claimed the Duce in his Grand Fascist Report for 1929: "We were the first to assert that . . . the more complicated the forms assumed by civilization, the more restricted the freedom of the individual must become." (*The Fascist*, E.B. Ashton, New York, Morrow, 1937)

Mussolini was soon being greatly honored in collectivist circles of America. Thomas W. Lamont, the international banker who was probably the most influential partner in the House of Morgan, wrote a glowing preface to a 1927 book* praising the economic wonders of Italian Fascism. The Chairman of the U.S. House Foreign Relations Committee told his colleagues in 1926: "He is something new and vital in the sluggish old veins of European politics. It will be a great thing not only for Italy but for all of us if he succeeds." Herbert Matthews, the peripatetic *New York Times*man who would later be instrumental in bringing Castro to power in Cuba, acknowledged that he was "an enthusiastic admirer of fascism." And Dr. Nicholas Murray Butler, the socialist president of Columbia, boasted of his friendship with Il Duce,

---

*Lamont had secured a $100 million loan for the Duce the previous year. The banker had similar admiration for the Bolsheviks — indeed he sired one named Corliss Lamont who supports the Red fascists of today.

calling Fascism "a form of government of the first order of excellence" and maintaining "we should look to Italy to show us what its experience and insight have to teach in the crisis confronting the twentieth century." (*As We Go Marching*, John T. Flynn, New York, Free Life, 1944)

What was this Twentieth Century Caesar doing that earned him such praise? The Duce's plan was a variant of the medieval guild system redubbed *corporativism*. "But there was no question of the *corporazione's* self-government," wrote economist Ludwig von Mises. "The Fascist cabinet did not tolerate anybody's interference with its absolute authoritarian control of production." Such control is the essence of Fascism. Fascist law, as defined by E.B. Ashton, "is a means of regulating the people's function of serving the state." Production in a free market is supposed to be the American way "while Communism and Fascism both consider it a communal interest — with the Communist state taking its operation into its own hands, while the Fascist one 'contracts' it out to individual businessmen."

A pretense of Free Enterprise in Italy was nonetheless written into the Fascist Labor Charter of 1926, which declared in Article VIII: "The corporate state considers that private enterprise in the sphere of production is the most effective and useful instrument in the interest of the nation." Fine . . . but there's a catch. Article IX, you see, read: "State intervention in economic production arises only when private initiative is lacking or insufficient, or when the political interests of the state are involved. This intervention may take the form of control, assistance or direct management." Perhaps you thought that today's "Liberals" invented the doubletalk that produces their doublethink. Not so.

The economics of Fascist Italy were soon being imported into this country by President Franklin D. Roosevelt, whose C.C.C., W.P.A., P.W.A., and other Depression-era schemes proved so damaging. Indeed, in his *Memoirs* former President Herbert Hoover* told it as it was: "Among the early Roosevelt fascist measures was the National Industry Recovery Act (NRA) of June 16, 1933 . . . . [*These ideas*] were adopted by the United States Chamber of Commerce. During the campaign of 1932, Henry I. Harriman, president of that body, urged that I agree to support these proposals, informing me that Mr. Roosevelt had agreed to do so. I tried to show him that this stuff was pure fascism; that it was a remaking of Mussolini's 'corporate state' and refused to agree to any of

---

*Hoover was not exactly unblemished. Which is why, *before* his election, F.D.R. tossed barbs not only at regimentation by trade association, but also "when it is done by the government of the United States itself." Hoover was hit, with what then seemed a justifiable fervor, for "fostering regimentation without stint or limit." And F.D.R. — who would soon give us the Brain Trust — decried his predecessor's "doctrine of regulation and legislation by 'master minds.' "

it. He informed me that in view of my attitude, the business world would support Roosevelt with money and influence. That for the most part proved true.''*

Eventually the N.R.A. and another Fascist plan called the Agricultural Adjustment Administration (A.A.A.) were declared unconstitutional by the Supreme Court. Though another A.A.A. passed in 1938, Roosevelt had been making his own appointments to the Supreme Court and it stuck, with the result that current federal agricultural acts are amendments to that 1938 Fascist decree. There were so many such schemes patterned after the Fascist "experiment" that F.D.R. doubled the National Debt in six years and the lure of formal national planning beckoned evilly.† The "Liberals," as John T. Flynn observed, "called it the Planned Economy. But it was and is fascism by whatever name it is known." (*The Roosevelt Myth*, New York, Devin-Adair, 1956)

Meanwhile, in Italy, the situation was not so rosy as powerful U.S. collectivists were describing it. The Fascist bands took to heart Mussolini's dictum: "Everything for the State, nothing outside the State, nothing above the State." The Chamber of Deputies was replaced by the Chamber of Fasces and Corporations. Italian children in the government schools prayed: "I believe in the supreme Duce, creator of the Blackshirts, and in Jesus Christ, his sole protector."

Lower living standards were passed off as "a preparation for tomorrow by the renunciations of today." Said the supreme Duce in 1934: "We are probably moving toward a period of humanity resting on a lower standard of living. Humanity is capable of ascetism such as we perhaps have no conception of." Hairshirts, you see, were fashionable even before Ralph Nader.

Professors Loucks and Hoot write of Fascist Italy in the Thirties. Consider what they have to say and identify what you can of "contemporary" proposals and solutions: "The problem of 'overproduction' was tackled by encouraging and forcing competing concerns into "consortia" — production and marketing concerns similar to German cartels. In many instances government licences were required to establish new plants or expand old capacity. In addition to the above forms of economic intervention the government accelerated the public works programs, shortened the work-week to spread employment, and increased its expenditures for military purposes. One result of these measures was a public budget heavily unbalanced . . . ." (*Comparative Economic Systems*)

Despite claims to the contrary, Mussolini never had a balanced budget. His subterfuge, as described by John Flynn, reminds one of today's "off-Budget" legerdemain. Mussolini, writes Flynn, "would make a contract with a private firm to build certain roads or buildings. He would pay no money but sign an agreement to pay for the work on a yearly installment plan. No money was paid out by the government. And hence nothing showed up in the budget. *** If these sums were added to the national debt as revealed in the Treasury admissions, the actual debt was staggering ten years after Mussolini's ascent to power on a promise to balance the budget. According to Dr. [*Gaetano*] Salvemini's calculations, the debt of 93 billion lire, when Mussolini took office, had grown to 148,646,000,000 lire in 1934." (*As We Go Marching*)

Like F.D.R., like so many of today's "Liberals," Mussolini favored "public-works" spending as a cure for unemployment. "Huge sums of money were spent by the Fascists," writes Christopher Leeds, a graduate of the London School of Economics, "on building roads, government buildings, Party headquarters, and housing projects."

Naturally the Dictator had to be on guard to prevent graft, to see that the people got their lira's worth, and to deal with the terrible crime problem. So he set up his own national police force and corps of special agents. "Known as OVRA (*Organizzazione di Vigilanza e Repressione dell' Antifascismo*, Organization for the Surveillance and Stamping-out of Anti-Fascism)," records Richard Collier, "they bugged telephones, reported on all who received mail from abroad, and even filed reports on the *graffiti* in public lavatories." (*Duce!*, New York, Viking, 1971)

The establishment of law and order; setting of population policy; balancing of the currency and Debt management; building of bridges, roads, and canals; and, even the waging of the "Battle of the Wheat" — all these and more were credited to Il Duce. "No other Italian ruler, the propagandists blared, had ever taken thought of his people from cradle to grave. Who but Mussolini had set up 1700 mountain and seaside summer camps for city children? What other man paid out £1,600,000 to pre-natal clinics each year, or £3,500,000 in family allowances? Who gave the Italians the eight-hour day and codified insurance benefits for the old, the unemployed and the disabled? Only Mussolini, who proclaimed on every hoarding that his one ambition was to make the Italians 'strong, prosperous, great and free,' had achieved that.'' (*Duce!*)

And, by the mid-Thirties, the supreme Duce was spending like a madman. "In Italy," wrote Albert Jay Nock, "the State now absorbs fifty percent of the total national income." (*Our Enemy, The State*, New York, Free Life, 1935) Indeed, in the United States during the Carter years the figure was forty-three percent. The federal Budget *alone* under Ronald Reagan is at a modern high — twenty-five percent of the Gross National Product, three points higher than the Carter average. Which may be reason enough for our own Duces to remember that in the end Mussolini was slaughtered by the Communists and hung from his heels like a carcass of dressed meat.

Hitlerism, similarly, did not spring full-blown from the brow of some aberrant German Zeus. Indeed, as Ludwig von Mises has observed: "For more than seventy years the German professors of political science, history, law, geography and philosophy eagerly imbued their disciples with a hysterical hatred of capitalism and preached the war of 'Liberation' against the capitalistic West." They were, said Mises, the " 'socialists of the chair,' much admired in all foreign countries . . . ."

Also setting the stage for the arrival of a dictator was the contrived inflation that followed the World War, wiping out the savings of the conservative and frugal German middle class and throwing it, destitute and enraged, into the hands of Hitler. According to economist Henry Hazlitt, by November of 1921 the circulation of money had increased eighteen times over that of 1913 and wholesale prices thirty-four times. "By November 1922 circulation had increased 127 times and wholesale prices 1,154 times, and by November 1923 circulation had increased 245 *billion* times and prices 1,380 *billion* times." The value of the mark, reports Frederic V. Grunfeld, "deteriorated to the point where it reached 136,000,000,000 to the dollar." (*The Hitler File*, New York, Random House, 1974)

Hitler thought his time had come and he launched his unsuccessful Beer Hall Putsch. In failure he became a national figure, and during his short stay in prison the future despot dictated his plans in *Mein Kampf* for all who cared to read what he intended to do. "There must be no majority decisions," he declared, "but only responsible persons, and the word 'council' must be restored to its original meaning. Surely every man will have advisers by his side, but *the decision will be made by one man*."

Within a decade that one man would be Adolf Hitler. In the meantime, he vowed to destroy the Weimar Republic "with the weapons of democracy."

Hitler, like Marx and Engels, was influenced by the thought of Hegel.

And, as he admitted in *Mein Kampf,* he also "studied Bismarck's Socialist legislation in its intention, struggle, and success." Remember, this is a man "Liberals" are still falsely trying to identify as a creature of the Right.

Years after taking over in Germany, Hitler remarked of a 1922 street fight: ". . . the Reds we had beaten up became our best supporters . . . . Wasn't my party at the time of which I'm speaking composed of 90 percent of left-wing elements? I needed men who could fight." (*The Rise Of Radicalism*) Indeed, in the mid-Twenties, top Nazi Joseph Goebbels published an open letter to a Communist leader "assuring him that Nazism and Communism were really the same thing. 'You and I,' he declared, 'are fighting one another, but we are not really enemies.' " (*The Rise And Fall Of The Third Reich*, William L. Shirer, Greenwich, Fawcett Crest, 1959)

Supporters of dictatorship are interchangeable. Consider S.A. Captain Ernst Roem, later killed on orders of the Führer, who boasted he could turn the Reddest Communist into a Nazi in four weeks. (*The True Believer*, Eric Hoffer, New York, Harper & Row, 1951) Hitler openly acknowledged that he copied the Communists and declared: "I have always . . . given orders that former Communists are to be admitted to the party at once." (*The Rise Of Radicalism*) These were known as the "Beefsteak Nazis" — brown on the outside, Red on the inside.

As late as February 1941, according to Nobel laureate Friedrich A. Hayek, Hitler declared that "basically National Socialism and Marxism are the same." (*The Road To Serfdom*, Chicago, University of Chicago Press, 1944) Which may be why, decades after the defeat of Nazi Germany, it was disclosed that hundreds of former Nazis held key jobs in Communist East Germany.

As with Benito Mussolini, Adolf Hitler came to power with the support of well-placed conspirators in the Establishment. Powerful leaders among industrial magnates, landed nobility, and the large bankers literally commissioned him, much as Karl Marx was commissioned to write the *Communist Manifesto.* In 1932, a year before he became Chancellor, the future dictator was introduced by Fritz Thyssen (a leading steelman who later wrote *I Paid Hitler*) to some six hundred major industrialists at Düsseldorf's Manufacturers Club. "The Krupp [*arms*] and Thyssen concerns were among the earliest financial supporters of the Nazis. As Alfred Krupp stated in 1946: 'We are realists, we . . . put our efforts behind the man who made our work secure.' " (*A Sign For Cain*, Fredric Wertham, New York, Warner, 1966) Hitler's press chief, Otto Dietrich, admitted that a year earlier — Socialist rhetoric notwithstanding — the Führer had "suddenly decided to concentrate systematically on cultivating the influential industrial magnates.'' Certain conspirators among them were eager to be cultivated.

William Keppler, a Hitler financial advisor, "brought in a number of South German industrialists," writes William Shirer, "and also formed a peculiar society of businessmen devoted to the S.S. Chief, Himmler, called Friends of the Economy (Freundeskreis der Wirtschaft), which later became known as the Circle of Friends of the Reichsfuehrer S.S. who was Himmler, and which raised millions of marks for this particular gangster to pursue his 'researches' into Aryan origins.'' Officials of Krupp, I.G. Farben, and the United Steel Works were among the biggest contributors to this arcane fund.

In an important exposé too detailed to be reviewed here, Professor Antony Sutton has documented the considerable aid given Hitler by the Chase and Manhattan banks, General Electric, Standard Oil, I.T.T., Henry Ford, American I.G. Farben, and other top U.S. corporate interests. (*Wall Street And The Rise Of Hitler*, Seal Beach, California, '76 Press, 1976) Certain directors of Standard Oil of New Jersey, for example, "had not only strategic wartime affiliations to I.G. Farben, but also had other links to Hitler's Germany — even to the extent of contributing, through German subsidiary companies, to Heinrich Himmler's personal fund and with membership in Himmler's Circle of Friends as late as 1944.''

A full eleven years earlier, according to American Ambassador to Germany William Dodd, Rockefeller public-relations man Ivy Lee "showed himself at once a capitalist and an advocate of Fascism.'' At the same time such powerful industrial insiders as G.E.'s Gerald Swope — who backed the Fascist R.N.A. scheme — were supporting F.D.R.'s New Deal as vigorously as Hitler's New Order.

Once in power, a key Hitler move involved passage of the so-called Enabling Act of 1933, officially the "Law for Removing the Distress of People and Reich,'' placing all power in the hands of the Cabinet and thence the Führer. As he had promised in *Mein Kampf*, all authority now belonged to "one man.''

Likewise, just as he had vowed while in prison, "within a fortnight of receiving full powers from the Reichstag, Hitler had achieved what Bismarck, Wilhelm II, and the Weimar Republic had never dared to attempt: He had abolished the separate powers of the historic states and made them subject to the central authority of the Reich, which was in his hands. He had, for the first time in German history, really unified the Reich by destroying its federal character.'' (*The Rise And Fall Of The Third Reich*)

Conspirators in Germany long before Hitler had been working toward increased collectivism, central control, and government regulation. He took advantage of their work, and the result was "in part an effort to use existing forms of economic organization in the new 'economic order.' " (*Comparative Economic Systems*) As in Italy there would be "private property," but only subject to the needs of the state. One young Nazi put it this way just before World War II: "We Germans are so happy. We are free from freedom." (*The True Believer*, quoting the *Reader's Digest*, May 1948)

The erasure of state lines and federal control of even the city governments — just as with regional and metro government here in the United States, "came under the heading of 'Gleichschaltung' or 'uniformization.' " (*The Hitler File*) Then came that key to every dictatorship, a national police. "On June 16, 1936, for the first time in German history, a unified police was established for the whole of the Reich — previously the police had been organized separately by each of the states — and Himmler was put in charge as Chief of German Police. This was tantamount to putting the police in the hands of the S.S. . . ." (*The Rise And Fall Of The Third Reich*)

The Führer was fast establishing "der totale Staat"; there was forced unionization, the Hitler Youth, price-fixing, myriad Welfare programs, and a federal takeover of education. Credit expansion and "public works" programs helped to create the myth of full employment. Hitler organized that current "Liberal" panacea, a national health service, in which care was "centralized, and the Department was given surprisingly wide powers. It looked after the health of children and workers; it controlled the training of doctors and midwives and dentists and chemists; it had charge of genealogical research; it made investigations into measures that would increase the population; and, it had a variety of duties ranging from water supplies to serology, from means of securing fertility to disposal of corpses." (*The House That Hitler Built*, Stephen H. Roberts, New York, Harper & Brothers, 1938)

Health care, or employment, that could be given by the state could be taken away by the state. After September of 1939, "no German worker could change his job without obtaining permission, while if he absented himself from work without proper excuse he was liable to imprisonment." (*The Social Policy Of Nazi Germany*, C.W. Guillebaud, London, Cambridge University Press, 1941) Earlier, just as Mussolini had done — and as some union leaders and others today suggest — the work-week was officially reduced to "spread" employment.

National Socialist medicine also soon ran its logical course. A government that could save your life, or job, could take it away. Before Hitler made overt moves in the direction of "euthanasia," bureaucratic forms went out to state hospitals to be marked plus or minus as to whether various mental patients, epileptics, the handicapped, and others in the care of the National Socialist state should be permitted to live. Yes, there was a "right-to-die" in Nazi Germany, and the Nazis determined that right. There developed a special bureacracy for the "euthanasia" of children called the Reich Commission for the Scientific Registration of Hereditary and Constitutional Severe Disorders. According to Dr. Fredric Wertham: "The children slated for death were sent to special 'children's divisions,' first Goerden, then Eichberg, Idstein, Steinhof (near Vienna), and Eglfing. They were killed mostly by increasing doses of Luminal or other drugs either spoon-fed as medicine or mixed with their food. Their dying lasted for days, sometimes for weeks. In actual practice, the indications for killing eventually became wider. Included were children who had 'badly modeled ears,' who were bed wetters, or who were perfectly healthy but designated as 'difficult to educate.' The children coming under the authority of the Reich Commission were originally mostly infants. The age then increased from three years to seventeen years. Later, in 1944 and 1945, the work of the commission also included adults." (*A Sign For Cain*)

Abortion, on the other hand, was not sanctioned in Nazi Germany because the National Socialists wanted to increase the German population. Had they wanted to decrease it, as our national socialists do here, they might have done as well as the city of Washington, D.C., where as long ago as 1976 there were more abortions than live births, with eighty-five percent of these killings being subsidized by the federal government.

Of course day-care facilities of the kind to be proposed years later by then-U.S. Senator Fritz Mondale were available from the start through an institution called *Mutter und Kind*, or Mother and Child. "Recuperation homes are made available for mothers after child-birth, nurseries and kindergartens have been provided, in particular in the country districts, for looking after the young children when the mothers are in the fields. . . ." (*The Social Policy Of Nazi Germany*)

And there was the Winter Relief. The above source describes this Welfare program provided by the benevolent Nazis: "Every winter an army of collectors appears on the streets selling badges; apart from this, on one Sunday in the month there is an obligatory one-course midday meal throughout Germany, the saving resulting from which has to be contributed to the Winter Relief Fund; further, every worker in employment pays a graded sum . . . ." They cared, you see. Oh, like all socialists, the Nazis cared.

Bread and Circuses? To be sure. There was *Kraft durch Freunde*, or

Strength Through Joy, which "sponsored hundreds of concerts, theatrical performances, sports events, adult education lectures . . . , package holidays, and guided tours of National Socialist shrines." (*The Hitler File*) It seems the Nazis also had their own Endowment for the Arts.

The state promised husbands for the girls; promised everyone would have a Volkswagen; it determined who could own a weapon; and, it even had a beautification program — called Beauty of Labor — of which Lady Bird Johnson could be proud. "First we persuaded [*sic*] factory owners to modernize their offices and to have some flowers about," reminisced nature lover Albert Speer, who was also Hitler's Minister of Armaments and War Production. "But we did not stop there. Lawn was to take the place of asphalt. What had been wasteland was to be turned into little parks where the workers could sit during breaks." (*Inside The Third Reich*, New York, Macmillan, 1970)

All this benevolence cost a bit, to be sure. According to William Shirer: "In the mid-Thirties it was estimated that taxes and contributions took from 15 to 35 percent of a worker's gross wage." Which is *less* than in the United States today. And, to give the Nazis their due, apparently in some places they were "equal opportunity" employers.

For example, there was the health spa, officially described as "an educational institution for all those of any race, faith or social position who are not willing to grasp the fact that the Third Reich has definitely and irrefutably dawned," where they would be kept until "our gallant SS men have instilled in them, as in all others, a feeling for discipline and order, neatness and comradeship."

We know that "health spa" as Dachau.

As we have seen, both Mussolini and Hitler pioneered in numerous domestic programs with which today's Left could feel comfortable. These include federal Welfare, national health care, loopholes for inside interests, gun control, federal control of education, youth indoctrination and day-care, national economic "planning," and massive deficit spending. In fact, as long ago as 1969, the administrator of the U.S. Law Enforcement Assistance Administration predicted that, if crime continues to grow, the American people will demand and get a national police force — just as in Nazi Germany and Fascist Italy.

Meanwhile the corporate state grows. In the U.S. we already have reached one government employee for every four employed in private industry. We are spending ourselves into national socialism. It took 163 years — from 1789 to 1952 — for U.S. domestic expenditures to reach thirty-four billion dollars; yet, in the next twenty-five years of growing national socialism such spending leaped to nearly three hundred billion dollars. If this rate were to be continued, said economist Roger A.

Freeman in 1975, "domestic public expenditures would, within less than forty years, account for all the GNP."

Continued? It's escalating: The Fiscal 1985 Budget is in the range of $925 billion — with a planned deficit of some $180 billion. According to the Grace Commission Report to President Reagan, if federal spending is not cut the National Debt in just sixteen years will be *thirteen trillion dollars* with annual interest of $1.5 trillion.

What is America doing about it? Not long ago, American economist Milton Friedman was given a Nobel Prize in economics. Yet his warnings against disruptive and counter-productive interference by the state in our daily lives, catalogued in his 1962 book *Capitalism And Freedom*, go unheeded. Mr. Friedman showed how we were crippling ourselves with radical adventures — emulating the national socialists, as we have demonstrated — by instituting price controls, volumes of needless regulations, mandatory Social Security, control of the freedom of the airwaves by the Federal Communications Commission, public housing, and all the rest.

As Friedman observed: "The central defect of these measures is that they seek through government to force people to act against their own immediate interests in order to promote a supposedly general interest." The Nazis' economic slogan, one remembers, was *Gemeinnutz geht vor Eigennutz* — the commonweal ranks above private profits. Or, as the Fascists of Italy put it: ". . . the maximum of liberty coincides with the maximum of state force."

A warning of this general theme, with emphasis on growing collectivism in the United States, is ably developed in Charlotte Twight's scholarly *America's Emerging Fascist Economy* (New Rochelle, Arlington House, 1975), which we recommend for its wealth of research. Twight points to Fascist pretense about property rights, which are in turn abrogated by licensure, regulation, limiting of competition, rule by Executive Order, agriculture marketing orders, economic "stabilization," price supports, and the like. "To sustain its power and achieve its economic ends," she writes, "fascism seeks to make its people economically and psychologically dependent on the government. Such dependence both enhances the government's tangible control over its citizens' economic activities and stimulates that intangible psychological support so crucial to maintaining a viable fascist state."

In short, if you are concerned about Fascism in America, don't look for jackboots and swastikas but for powerful Establishment insiders promoting encroachments by government on your property rights and civil liberties. To stop them, we must be willing to fight for liberty even harder than our would-be masters are prepared to fight to impose their tyranny.

Chapter XIV

A Brief On Populism

Just the other day we were at a local library, in the history section, and ran across a copy of *The Americans*, by one Harold Coy, published by Little, Brown & Company in 1958. It was dedicated to "young readers who are curious to know more about an inventive, freedom-loving people." Mr. Coy's book is typical of the sort of thing pushed at young readers by the "Liberal" Establishment for a quarter of a century.

Here we read of the amalgam that in the 1890s became the Farmer's Alliance. "A People's Party grew out of the Alliance Movement," Coy tells his readers. "The Populists, as they were called, wanted the government to regulate railroad rates, make loans to farmers, and put more money into circulation. They favored popular election of United States senators, parcel post and rural free delivery, and an income tax. All of these ideas seemed outlandish at the time, and all of them are now law of the land." Doubtless Little, Brown would have been happy to emboss the word *Hallelujah*! in gold between every line.

This sort of thing is to be expected from a "Liberal" source. But recently some respected Conservatives were urging a coalition with populists. And *Spotlight*, the umbratile Washington tabloid, has long been calling Populism "America's authentic political heritage . . ." and carrying short mythomaniacal biographies of Populist heroes. That series has now been published in book form as *Profiles In Populism*, an amazing adventure in political charlatanry in which editor Willis Carto reflects:

"Populism, you see, is man's one hope for the future. Thus, this book is one of the most important books published in the past half-century. The need for Americans to understand the past as it really was, free from the purposeful propaganda of rapacious minority plunder groups [*presumably Negroes and Jews*], is not only central to our survival and to our future but to the future of the world. Populism and nationalism set forth the only 'new' political philosophy of this turbulent century, a desperately needed understanding of political and economic and monetary facts as they really exist, and our hope for years to come.''

Hmmm. Who were these Populists whose heritage Mr. Carto calls ''man's one hope for the future''? Their leaders, says sympathetic historian Foster Rhea Dulles, ''believed that government action was necessary to satisfy their well-founded grievances against the existing economic system, and they were prepared to organize the power of the agricultural community to force Congress to meet their demands. This was the beginning of what was to become the Populist movement — the emphatic political expression of agrarian revolt — that dominated the political scene through the 1890's. It was to challenge the whole concept of a laissez faire economy, for a time split the country asunder as it had not been divided since the Civil War, and came to an exciting climax in the bitterly fought election of 1896.'' (*The United States Since 1865*, Ann Arbor, University of Michigan Press, 1959)

If centralized power was (or is) the problem, more government isn't the answer. As Dr. George Roche has reflected: ''The Populists forgot that the very plutocracy that they so much feared had grown strong precisely *because of* its connection with government. Thus the underlying cause of farmer and worker discontent in the late nineteenth century, that is, strong centralized government, was now thought to be the means of salvation from the same discontents.'' (*The Bewildered Society*)

Nevertheless, as the disparate Populist groups grew into one party, their common demand was for ever more government. ''In the South,'' records James Truslow Adams, ''the Alliance worked through the only white man's party in that section, the Democratic, but in the West the various new parties worked independently, such as the People's Party in Kansas, the Industrial Party in Michigan, or the Independent Party in South Dakota, and in the elections of 1890 they managed to send two senators and eight representatives to Congress. Their success was not to be wondered at. In the South the price of corn was steadily declining, and in the West the prices of wheat and corn were fast falling to the point at which, in 1893, they were less per bushel than the cost of production. In four years, over 11,000 farms in Kansas alone were taken from their owners under foreclosure of mortgages. 'Ten cent corn and ten per cent interest' were driving the West to despair. The sources of the Populist movement, which was so to frighten the conservative [*sic*] East, were not hard to discover . . . .'' (*The March Of Democracy*, Volume IV, New York, Charles Scribner's Sons, 1968, first copyright 1933)

What had happened in Kansas, for example, was a land boom of such magnitude that, on average, mortgages were carried by every second adult. Then came deflation and weather so dry that the oversettled western part of the state lost its crops. Between 1887 and 1891, half the new citizens of the state had left. Often in wagons bearing signs such as: "In God we Trusted, in Kansas we Busted." As eventually happens where there is wild speculation, there were plenty of losers. And the arid land became fertile ground for Populists such as the imposing Mrs. Mary E. Lease, the "Kansas Pythoness," who exhorted farmers to "raise less corn and more hell." (*The Oxford History Of The American People*)

The mainstream parties soon adapted to embrace the new discontent. One remembers how more recently the Socialist Party leader Norman Thomas, who ran for President in every election between 1928 and 1948, often remarked of his Democratic and Republican opponents that they stole his planks. "The American people will never knowingly adopt socialism," he said, "but under the name of liberalism they will adopt every fragment of the socialist program until one day America will be a socialist nation without knowing how it happened."

So it was also, with rare exceptions, for the Populists. While they were swinging battering rams at the front door, their programs were slipped in the back door by the major parties. By asking for more federal government they simply played into the hands of the would-be monopolists. As Albert Jay Nock observed: "The simple truth is that our businessmen do not want a government that will let business alone. They want a government that they can use."

Gabriel Kolko's mistitled book, *The Triumph Of Conservatism*, reminds us: "The dominant fact of American political life at the beginning of the century was that big business led the struggle for federal regulation of the economy. If economic rationalization could not be attained by mergers and voluntary economic methods, a growing number of important businessmen reasoned, perhaps political means might succeed. At the same time, it was increasingly obvious that change was inevitable in a political democracy where Grangers, Populists, and trade unionists had significant and disturbing followings and might tap a socially dangerous grievance at some future time and threaten the entire fabric of the status quo, and that the best way to thwart change was to channelize it."

Big business, comments Professor Kolko, "has no vested interest in pure, irrational market conditions, and grew to hate the dangerous consequences in such situations. Moreover, the history of the relationship between business and government until 1900 was one that could only inspire confidence in the minds of all too many businessmen. The first federal regulatory effort, the Interstate Commerce Commission, had [*for the special interests*] been cooperative and fruitful; indeed, the railroads themselves had been the leading advocates of extended federal regulation after 1887."

After organizing formally in 1891, the People's Party met in convention at Omaha the summer of the next year. Drafting of a platform was largely the work of Minnesota's Ignatius Donnelly, also known as "The Prince of Cranks" and "The Great Apostle of Protest." Donnelly had been a "Liberal" Republican, a Granger, a Greenbacker, editor of the *Anti-Monopolist*, as well as Lieutenant Governor, U.S. Congressman, and state senator. Historian Foster Rhea Dulles reports:

"There was almost no reform that Donnelly had not sponsored at one time or another, and among his literary effusions were a colorful account of *Atlantis: the Antediluvian World*, and a discursive elaboration of the Baconian theory, entitled *The Great Cryptogram*, in which he once and for all settled, at least to his own satisfaction, the question of Shakespearian authorship. Ready to take up any cause with an enthusiasm that nothing could dampen, he threw himself heart and soul into Populism." (*The United States Since 1865*)

The party's platform preamble shook with indignation: "We have witnessed for more than a quarter of a century the struggles of the two great political parties for power and plunder, while grievous wrongs have been inflicted upon the suffering people. We charge that the controlling influences dominating both these parties have permitted the existing dreadful conditions to develop without serious effort to prevent or restrain them. Neither do they now promise us any substantial reform. They have agreed together to ignore, in the coming campaign, every issue but one. They propose to drown the outcries of a plundered people with the uproar of a sham battle over the tariff, so that capitalists, corporations, national banks, rings, trusts, watered stock, the demonetization of silver and the oppressions of the usurers may all be lost sight of. They propose to sacrifice our homes, lives, and children on the altar of mammon; they destroy the multitude in order to secure corruption funds from the millionaires." (*Living Ideas In America*, edited by Henry Steele Commager, New York, Harper & Row, 1964)

The convention resolved, among other things, to call for shorter work hours; direct election of U.S. Senators (which would go a long way toward destroying the Republican form of government); and, an initiative and referendum system. In order to favor the debtor over the creditor, Populists believed inflation should be encouraged. Hence these three planks: "We demand free and unlimited coinage of silver and gold at the present legal ratio of 16 to 1." And, "We demand that the amount of circulating medium be speedily increased to not less than $50 per capita." Also, "We demand a graduated income tax." Radical historian Henry Commager gloats: "Though regarded as wildly socialistic at the time, almost every plank in this platform was later incorporated into law in one form or another." Which, of course, is part of the problem. As Dr. George Roche has noted, the Populist platform "contained demands for most of the measures previously urged by European socialists."

Nominated for President on the People's Party ticket was Iowa's General James B. Weaver, a former nominee of the Greenbackers, who had in large numbers turned Populist. But in 1892 Grover Cleveland, the Democrat, was returned to the White House with a narrow plurality over the man who had beaten him four years earlier, Benjamin Harrison. Cleveland carried seven Northern states and the Solid South, but General Weaver carried four states for the People's Party.

"The Democrats," one reads in *Home Of The Brave*, "made deals with the Populists in several Midwestern states, agreeing to withdraw their local candidates in favor of the Populists in the belief that if Cleveland did not win outright, the Populist vote would throw the election into the House of Representatives, where the Democrats had a majority. But Cleveland easily carried the election, getting a plurality of 381,000 votes over Harrison and an electoral-college margin of 277 to 145. The great surprise of the race was Weaver, the Populist, who received more than a million popular votes and twenty-two electoral votes. Clearly, the Populist Party had made a creditable showing in its first national race.

"Cleveland's second term proved even more conservative than had his first. On the money question he stood for gold with the fervor of a Republican, so much that some liberal Democrats talked of joining the Populists."

The contrived monetary panic of 1893 and the Pullman Strike of 1894 in Illinois brought more converts to the Populist cause. In the latter case, when federal troops were called out against the strike led by Eugene V. Debs, President Cleveland was quoted as saying: "If it takes every dollar in the Treasury and every soldier in the United States to deliver a postal card in Chicago, that postal card should be delivered." The strike was broken; the Supreme Court ruled the use of federal power was legitimate; and, Debs went to prison, a socialist hero of the Populists.

Confrontation politics is nothing new. Consider the remarks of Populist and former South Carolina Governor "Pitchfork Ben" Tillman, who acquired his nickname while running for the U.S. Senate when he shouted against Grover Cleveland: "Send me to Washington, and I'll stick my pitchfork into his old ribs."

The Populists got their income tax, but it was soon struck down by the Supreme Court in an 1895 decision. Opposing the tax — a flat *two* percent of income over four thousand dollars a year — was the famous attorney Joseph H. Choate, who had prosecuted New York's Tweed Ring and later became U.S. Ambassador to Great Britain. The principles of the income tax, argued Choate, were "communistic, socialistic — what shall I call them? — as populistic as ever have been addressed to any political assembly in the world." Those were the days!

Demagogic Populists meanwhile fanned the emotions of the crowds. Concerning congressional elections of the period, journalist William Allen White later recalled: "Sacred hymns were torn from their pious tunes to give place to words which deified the cause and made gold — and all its symbols, capital, wealth, plutocracy — diabolical . . . . Far into the night the voices rose — women's voices, children's voices, the voices of old men, of youths and maidens, rose on the ebbing prairie breezes, as the crusaders of the revolution rode home, praising the people's will as though it were God's will and cursing wealth for its iniquity."

Kansas, says Foster Rhea Dulles, "furnished Populism with more leaders than any other state," including "Sockless Jerry" Simpson and Senator William Peffer, once characterized as a "well-meaning, pin-headed, anarchistic crank." In 1896 William Allen White was not the "Liberal" he became in later years, and he remembered in his autobiography being stopped in the street by a gaggle of Populists during that year's election campaign. "They ganged me — hooting, jeering, nagging me about some utterances I had made." The result was a famous editorial in the *Emporia Gazette* which read in part:

"What's the matter with Kansas? We all know; yet here we are at it again. We have an old mossback Jacksonian who snorts and howls because there is a bathtub in the state house; we are running that old jay for Governor. We have another shabby, wild-eyed, rattle-brained fanatic who has said openly in a dozen speeches that 'the rights of the user are paramount to the rights of the owner'; we are running him for Chief Justice so that capital will come tumbling over itself to get into the state. We have raked the old ash heap of failure in the state and found an old human hoop-skirt who has failed as a businessman, who has failed as a preacher, and we are going to run him for Congressman-at-Large. He will help the looks of the Kansas delegation at Washington. Then we have discovered a kid without a law practice and have decided to run him for Attorney General. Then, for fear some hint that the state had become respectable might percolate through the civilized portions of the nation, we have decided to send three or four harpies out lecturing, telling the people that Kansas is raising hell and letting the corn go to weeds.***

"That's the stuff! Give the prosperous man the dickens! Legislate the thriftless man into ease, whack the stuffings out of the creditors and tell debtors who borrowed the money five years ago when money 'per capita' was greater than it is now, that the contraction of capital gives him a right to repudiate. Whoop it up for the ragged trousers; put the lazy, greasy fizzle, who can't pay his debts, on an altar, and bow and worship him. Let the state ideal be high. What we need is not the respect of our fellow men, but the chance to get something for nothing." (*Great Issues In American History*, edited by Richard Hofstadter, New York, Vintage, 1958)

Meanwhile, organized labor had lost several major strikes and was looking to unite with the farmer under the Populist flag. After all, the People's Party had in 1894 increased its representation in Congress by fifty percent. As the elections of 1896 neared, Congressman William McKinley of Ohio, author of the McKinley Tariff, became the Presidential candidate of the G.O.P. on a tide of big money and the political skill of Mark Hanna. The Democrats, whose convention was held three weeks later in Chicago, debated the case against gold and for free silver. Especially a 36-year-old Nebraskan called the "Boy Orator of the Platte," who gave what many considered to be the most effective convention speech in history. An impassioned William Jennings Bryan told the throng:

"We do not come as aggressors. Our war is not a war of conquest; we are fighting in the defense of our homes, our families, and posterity. We have petitioned, and our petitions have been scorned; we have entreated, and our entreaties have been disregarded; we have begged, and they have mocked when calamity came. We beg no longer, we entreat no longer; we petition no more. We defy them! . . .

"And now, my friends, let me come to the paramount issue. If they ask us why it is that we say more on the money question than we say upon the tariff question, I reply that if protection has slain its thousands, the gold standard has slain its tens of thousands. If they ask us why we do not embody in our platforms all the things that we believe in, we reply that when we have restored the money of the Constitution, all other necessary reform then can be accomplished . . . .

"You come to us and tell us that the great cities are in favor of the gold standard; we reply that the great cities rest upon our broad and fertile prairies. Burn down your cities and leave our farms, and your cities will spring up again as if by magic; but destroy our farms, and the grass will grow in the streets of every city in the country . . . .

"Having behind us the producing masses of this nation and the world, supported by the commercial interests, the laboring interests, and the toilers everywhere, we will answer their demands for a gold standard by saying to them: You shall not press down upon the brow of labor this crown of thorns; you shall not crucify mankind upon a cross of gold."

At first stunned, the twenty thousand in the hall promptly went wild, marching raucously for an hour. And the next day they nominated young William Jennings Bryan for President of the United States. So did the

Populists. And even Eugene V. Debs campaigned for the Nebraskan orator before he formed his own Socialist Party. (*The Rise of Radicalism*) Bryan stumped across the country while McKinley sat on his front porch as his backers outspent the Democrats and Populists by a huge margin.

Here is a summary of the 1896 election from *The Oxford History Of The American People*: "Radical only on the coinage issue, strictly orthodox in matters of morality and religion, Bryan was an honest, emotional crusader for humanity with the forensic fervor and political shrewdness that would have made him a good state leader in the age of Jackson. His object was merely to reform the government and curb privilege; but he was accused of 'proposing to transfer the rewards of industry to the lap of indolence.' In the hundreds of speeches that he delivered during a whirlwind tour of 13,000 miles, there was no appeal to class hatred. But his followers were full of it, and 'Pitchfork Ben' Tillman of South Carolina called upon the people to throw off their bondage to a money power more insolent than the slave power. On the other side, Mark Hanna assessed metropolitan banks, insurance companies, and railroad corporations for colossal campaign contributions, which even the silver-mining interests could not match for Bryan. Employees were ordered to vote for McKinley on pain of dismissal, and their fears were aroused by the prospect of receiving wages in depreciated dollars. On Wall Street there was even talk of a secession of New York City from the Union if Bryan should win. The Democratic ticket carried the late Confederacy and most of the Far West; but the heavy electoral votes of the East and Middle West gave McKinley an emphatic victory."

The loss delivered a deathblow to the People's Party, which had placed all of its eggs in the Bryan basket. But it did not mean the end of "populism." As we noted earlier, even today radical publications like *Spotlight* hoot ignorantly that their examination of history reveals "populism's superiority to late 20th-century 'conservatism,'" as well as the reasons why only populism offers salvation to the U.S." As examples, *Spotlight* and its man Willis Carto cite such radicals or fools as William Henry "Alfalfa Bill" Murray, Governor of Oklahoma (1931-1935), who as it happens is best known for sending out the National Guard to close down all the state's oil wells, supposedly to "stabilize" prices. Then they cite Georgia's Thomas E. Watson, called a "great populist leader" by the tabloid. Tom was apparently their kind of guy, specializing as he did in turning class against class and fomenting strife between rural and urban interests. Watson, says *The Oxford History Of The United States*, was elected "to Congress as a Populist in 1890 by the votes of both black and white, [*but*] he was defeated for a second term. He then adopted the poor-white point of view. That class simply would not vote for a biracial party. As Watson wrote, 'No matter what direction progress would like to take in the South, she is held back by the never failing cry of "nigger." ' So, after ten years of ruminating, writing bad history, and worse biography, Tom decided to hunt with the hounds. From 1906, when he became the most popular leader in the South, he outdid every other white demagogue in Negro-baiting; he lauded lynching, described Booker T. Washington as 'bestial as a gorilla,' and bracketed Catholics, Socialists, and Jews with Negroes in his catalogue of hate.''

Mr. Carto's hero Thomas Watson, notes V.O. Key, did not hold public office between 1892 and 1920, when he was elected to the U.S. Senate. Nevertheless, though "he became a national figure, he continued active participation in Georgia politics. Watson never let the self-awareness of the farmer fade. He addressed himself to the 'men of the country' and pitted them against their iniquitous, slick brothers in the cities. He appealed, viciously in his later years, to sectional, race, class prejudices. Through his hold on underprivileged white farmers he was able to exert powerful and sometimes decisive influence in state primaries until his death in 1922.'' (*Southern Politics*, New York, Vintage Books, 1949)

Yet another hero in the *Spotlight* propaganda series was Montana Senator Burton K. Wheeler, who during his Senate career (1923-1947) was long a New Deal backer and only belatedly an "isolationist." He was in fact endorsed for his original election by the Communist front known as the Conference for Progressive Political Action. So was another Willis Carto idol, Robert M. La Follette Sr. of Wisconsin, who along with his sons, was responsible for radicalizing the Badger State. (See *Reds In America*, R.M. Whitney, Boston, Western Islands, 1970.)

Mr. Wheeler was long a champion of the radicals. In his 1925 book *The Red Web*, Blair Coán pointed out: "The paramount issues of the campaign of Wheeler for the Senate were 'free speech' for seditionists and revolutionary agitators, the termination of 'persecution' of red radicals by the Department of Justice, and the 'Get Daugherty' [*U.S. Attorney General Harry Daugherty was a bane of the Bolsheviks*] slogan born of the Department's prosecution of the railroad strike injunction suit in the federal courts. 'I'll get Daugherty. I'll drive him from the Cabinet,' Wheeler told the Montana radicals in speeches he delivered in his own behalf as a candidate for the Senate.'' And he did his worst.

The Progressives, notably Wisconsin's "Fighting Bob" La Follette Sr., polished the act of the Populists. "With the turn of the century," reports *The United States Since 1865*, "the seemingly radical ideas of the Populists were to become the programs of the Progressives. The latter's broader appeal for popular support, enlisting the middle class in their ranks rather than solely embattled farmers and workers, was to win a measure of success that had evaded the Populists but for which they had prepared the way.''

As Wisconsin's Governor and Senator, ''Fighting Bob'' brought prairie radicalism from the farms to the cities. ''The average member of the American middle class,'' observed Dr. George Roche, ''had been bitterly opposed to the 'radicalism' of Populism. The same ideas, couched in a slightly different setting, offered at a slightly later point in time, and labeled Progressivism, were to sweep the middle class off their feet and lead them down essentially the same road that the Populists had urged a few years before. With Progressivism, large-scale government intervention in the life of the American citizen came to be viewed not only as necessary, but desirable.''

Such is ''America's authentic political heritage'' of Populism and Progressivism, a legacy of demagogues and rogues, panderers and mountebanks, national socialists and hate mongers. And those who preach that message today either are ignorant of American history or are applicants for a sinister legacy.

Chapter XV

The Progressive Deal
Of Herbert Hoover

HERBERT CLARK HOOVER (1874-1964) was orphaned at age eight, raised by a series of Quaker relatives, worked his way through Stanford as a member of its first class, and became an internationally respected mining engineer. In the heady two decades before World War I, engineering was the fastest growing American profession; and, as Hoover wrote in his *Memoirs*, it had within his lifetime "been transformed from a trade to a profession." (New York, Macmillan, 1951)

Young Hoover toured the world in responsible jobs for the years between 1897 and 1917, did not vote for a Presidential candidate until he became a candidate himself, and was a millionaire by age forty. Not bad for a young man who left Stanford in a depression year with a bachelor's degree in geology, forty dollars in his wallet, and a two-dollar-a-day job pushing a mine cart. Historian Gene Smith recounts:

"Hoover became the richest engineer of his time. He sought gold, lead, zinc, copper, tin. He went to India, New Zealand, the Hawaiian Islands, Egypt, Korea, Russia, France, Ceylon, crossing the Pacific ten times and the Atlantic twenty-five or more. Mrs. Hoover gave him two boys, both born in London . . . ." (*The Shattered Dream*, New York, William Morrow, 1970)

Indeed, Herbert Hoover was in London in 1914 as Commissioner of the forthcoming San Francisco Panama-Pacific Exposition when the Germans conquered Belgium on their way toward Paris. The U.S. Ambassador in the British capital asked him to organize passage for some one hundred twenty thousand Americans trapped by the outbreak of yet another European war. Thus began the public life of Herbert Clark Hoover. Treating the evacuation with the skills of an efficient engineer, he seemed a miracle worker. Eugene Lyons reports:

"Along with the organizational efficiency there was great faith. With a few friends whom he drew into his gamble, Hoover induced one bank in London to cash any kind of American paper, on his personal pledge to make good any losses. Obviously there was neither the time nor the machinery for checking credit ratings. Before the exodus was completed, over $1,500,000 had been cashed. That was the extent of the gamble. But faith was vindicated: less than three hundred dollars was lost in the big transaction." (*Herbert Hoover: A Biography*, Garden City, Doubleday, 1964)

The rules of war did not require the Germans to feed a conquered Belgium, nor did they intend to do so. The trouble was that the Allies proposed to starve Germany into submission, and this now included Belgium, which imported most of its food. Hoover arranged with the belligerents to feed the Belgians through the Commission for Relief in Belgium. But not without making enemies including Winston Churchill, who called Mr. Hoover a "son of a bitch" for feeding the hungry Belgians and freeing the Germans of the responsibility. Hoover was to call the effort "turning barren neutrality into something positive . . . ." But on the home front some Americans wondered how Herbert Hoover was escaping what seemed a clear violation of the Logan Act, since private citizen Hoover now flew his own flag and was making treaties in all but name. Though Massachusetts Senator Henry Cabot Lodge investigated, nothing came of the charges.

The Belgian relief committee, ostensibly set up as a private charity, received seventy-eight percent of its funds over the course of the war from various government sources. No "other business in the world ever rose so far or so fast as did that of the relief of Belgium," claimed Hooverite Herbert Corey. (*The Truth About Hoover*, Boston, Houghton Mifflin, 1932) The committee took in some $1.3 billion and delivered more than five million tons of food.

Herbert Hoover despised the Germans and in early February of 1917 he sent a long memorandum to President Woodrow Wilson's alter ego, Colonel Edward M. House, advising Wilson "to provide the Allies with munitions, money, and food." This at a time when the U.S. was officially neutral. Hoover, who anticipated American involvement in the war, declared: "I am no extreme pacifist." The Quaker in him only went so far. (*Herbert Hoover: A Public Life*, David Burner, New York, Knopf, 1979)

Mr. Hoover made himself more than available to his friend Woodrow Wilson as the wartime U.S. Food Administrator, becoming known as the "Food Dictator" and the "Food Czar." It began with a letter from London dated April 3, 1917, "just three days before America entered World War I," in which Herbert Hoover "described his qualifications to Colonel Edward House, who on European trips had used Hoover as a listening post on the war." (*Herbert Hoover: A Public Life*) The next month President Wilson directed Congress to create the position of Food Administrator.

"Food Will Win The War," rang the slogan of Administrator Hoover. The market no longer set its own price; Herbert Hoover did. As Missouri Senator James Reed put it during Hearings before the Senate Committee on Manufacturers, Hoover's war powers were "such as no Caesar ever employed over a conquered province in the bloodiest days of Rome's bloody despotism." It was intoxicating stuff.

The domestic Food Administrator was now also directed to head relief efforts in Europe. By the war's end he not only directed the American Relief Administration but also the United States Grain Corporation, the Sugar Equalization Board, and the Belgian Relief Commission; was a member of the War Trade Council; was alternating chairman of the Inter-Allied Food Council; and, was head of the European Coal Council, European Children's Fund, and the Supreme Economic Council. He advised President Wilson on peace negotiations, and it was noted by British economist John Maynard Keynes that: "Mr. Hoover was the only man who emerged from the ordeal of Paris with an enhanced reputation. . . ." Meanwhile, as General John Pershing expressed it: "Mr. Hoover is the food regulator of the world." (*Herbert Hoover: American Quaker*, David Hinshaw, New York, Farrar, Straus, 1950)

Hoover was later to say that in certain places he had "absolute dictatorship over economic forces." He used that dictatorship. David Burner found that in Hungary administrator Hoover's "most blatant employment for political purposes of his food distribution was in fact for the displacement" of Archduke Joseph. When Communist tyrant Béla Kun came to power there it was another matter. Food was to be sent to Kun's Budapest, said Hoover, "so long as no excesses are committed by the Government . . . ."

Excessive is a polite term for the tyranny of Kun. "The régime had carried out hundreds of political executions; Kun had purchased munitions and artillery from Italy; his armies threatened to link up with Russia's Red Army through Galicia; he had doubled his troops beyond Armistice terms; above all, the Hungarian revolutionaries had turned to violence and threatened to overflow their borders . . . ." (*Herbert Hoover: A Public Life*) For a while the A.R.A. boss is said to have favored use of French troops against the Hungarian Reds, but if so he quickly reversed himself and argued otherwise. In time Kun was forced to flee to the Soviet Union.

Hoover returned to the United States in 1919, but the work of the American Relief Administration continued under his direction . . . even feeding Bolshevik-held Moscow. Hoover thought we should be moderate toward the Bolsheviks — though he knew they had "resorted to terror, bloodshed, murder to a degree long since abandoned even amongst reactionary tyrannies." Incredibly, the A.R.A. chief advised President Wilson that we should not tell others how to work out their "internal social problems." He opposed dislodging the embryonic Bolsheviks and said he "did not like the looks" of a White Russian campaign against Petrograd. Mr. Hoover claimed to deplore Red atrocities against refugees in Odessa, but callously declared that they brought it upon themselves by living too well. So food from the West continued to be sent to prop up the Communists, despite the advice of the French Foreign Minister that such action was "a moral and material reinforcement of the iniquitous Bolshevik government."

At the time, Herbert Hoover contended he thought such aid would expose the weakness of Bolshevism. What it did in fact was insure Communist rule. Indeed, Lenin wrote that without aid from abroad "the government will perish." That was in 1921, and such aid continues to this day. "If anything," writes Joan Hoff Wilson, "American relief served instead to stabilize Bolshevik rule during the crucial civil war years of the early 1920s. Hoover himself later admitted to reporter Henry C. Wolfe that through his Russian relief activities 'we may have helped to set the Soviet Government up in business,' but that saving lives was worth such a political risk." (*Herbert Hoover: Forgotten Progressive*, Boston, Little, Brown, 1975)

Accordingly, the Hoover mission sent some one hundred fifty shiploads of food and supplies to the Communist Government in Russia, for the alleged purpose of implanting "the love of the American flag in the hearts of millions." (*Herbert Hoover: American Quaker*) Consider the "Russian Red Cross" and how it treated aid from abroad. It was members of this body, wrote R.M. Whitney in 1924, "in the famine districts of Russia, under the direction of the Soviet government, who gather small children, suffering from hunger, into rooms decorated with the old symbols of their Russian religion, and commanded these starving children to pray to their ikons for food. When no food appeared in answer to their prayers they were told to pray to the Soviets for food. The children did so and the doors flew open as if in answer to their prayers and plentiful food appeared." (*Reds In America*)

Even George Kennan admitted in his 1960 book *Russia And The West Under Stalin* that the A.R.A. under Hoover "importantly aided" the Bolshevik regime, "not just in its economic undertakings, but in its political prestige and capacity for survival." Not that the Reds were thankful. In fact, they turned relief into a hustle as soon as they could.

Benjamin Gitlow, one of the founders of the Communist Party of America and a onetime Comintern member, explained in *The Whole Of Their Lives*:

"For actual relief the Bolsheviks depended on the help supplied by the Hoover Relief Mission. The Comintern therefore decided that the relief organization dominated by the communists should be tied together into an international relief organization. The communist international relief set-up opened a central bureau in Paris. To this bureau were sent all relief monies collected by the communist relief organizations, not squandered in the home countries. The Paris bureau issued receipts for the same to prove that the monies were legitimately handled. Afterwards the monies received by the Paris bureau were allocated to the communist parties in Europe and America to help finance communist activities."

In the meantime, Herbert Hoover was in the political limelight. According to Louis Brandeis, he was "the biggest figure injected into Washington by the war." So it was no surprise when Brandeis supported Hoover for President in 1920, as did such other prominent "progressives" as Heywood Broun, Walter Lippmann, William Allen White, and Jane Addams. Since Hoover's party affiliation was not clear (he had worked for Democrat Wilson, belonged to a Republican club, and financially supported Teddy Roosevelt's Bull Moose Party), even Franklin D. Roosevelt wrote at the time: "He is certainly a wonder, and I wish we could make him President. There couldn't be a better one."

Endorsements came from the radical staff of the *New Republic* as well as "George Lorimer of the *Saturday Evening Post*, Norman Hapgood of *World's Work*, Harford Powell of *Collier's*, Frank Cobb of the *New York World*, and Edward Bok of the *Ladies Home Journal*. Even Democratic progressives [*sic*] such as . . . businessman Edward A. Filene, Wilson's personal adviser Col. Edward M. House, Senator James D. Phelan, and former secretary of the Democratic National Committee Robert Jackson pushed Hoover for president until he cleared up the matter of his party affiliation." (*Herbert Hoover: Forgotten Progressive*) In 1919, when Mr. Hoover returned to the U.S. for the first time in thirteen years, his "most insistent advocacy was of a Federal Employment Service, a Department of Public Works, and a Home Loan Bank." (*Herbert Hoover: A Public Life*) This was assuredly not the rock-ribbed Conservative of later legend.

After declaring himself a Republican, however, Hoover received but thirteen votes in the 1920 G.O.P. Convention. Nonetheless President Warren Harding named him Secretary of Commerce, a position he continued to hold under Calvin Coolidge until 1928. As Secretary, Hoover initiated government supervision of the radio airwaves as well as commercial aviation, and set in motion initiatives that led to the St.

Lawrence Seaway and the Boulder (later Hoover) Dam. Businessmen, he said, could not themselves conquer inefficiency, but needed "national guidance and a national plan."

As head of the American Engineering Council, Herbert Hoover called for "abandonment of the unrestricted capitalism of Adam Smith . . . , for a new economic system based neither on the capitalism of Adam Smith nor upon the socialism of Karl Marx." He was a social engineer arguing that Big Brother could best assure the future. As Commerce Secretary, Hoover wrote that "laissez faire had been 'dead in America for generations,' except in the recalcitrant hearts of 'some reactionary souls.' It had died, he claimed, when 'we adopted the ideal of equality of opportunity.' "(*Herbert Hoover: Forgotten Progressive*) If Free Enterprise was dead, Herbert Hoover was not a mourner.

Indeed, the man who by ability and hard work in a free market had gone from a two-dollar-a-day laborer to a millionaire complained that in the Twenties some people were simply making too much money — "far beyond the needs of stimulation to initiative." Undoubtedly the man did not consider himself a socialist; what he wanted was to "balance" socialism and capitalism somehow, as if the economic life of a nation could long be half-free. The country was passing, Hoover told the U.S. Chamber of Commerce in 1924, "from a period of extreme individualistic action into a period of associational activities." His own individual action had made him wealthy enough to be generous with the future of others.

For decades the "Liberals" ran for office against the failure of Hoover's alleged Conservative economics. Yet Hoover opposed open competition and favored economic planning and an expansion of public works, with government as arbiter of what should be done. An internationalist, he not only backed the League of Nations but favored a "commercial league of nations" for multinational corporations. His Commerce Department, reports David Burner, "added a variety of new agencies and programs, recognized and expanded its existing bureaus, pushed its influence into nearly all of federal economic policy, and proceeded to link public with private action through a series of important cooperative conferences. One small-town California editor insisted in the mid-1920s that he had received a piece of Hoover's Commerce Department publicity every day for several years; they were like flakes of snow in a heavy storm. Commerce became the epitome of 'progressive government' . . . ."

Herbert Hoover was the "progressive" who not only saved the Bolsheviks in the early Twenties through the American Relief Administration but also helped them in other important ways as well. Antony Sutton, formerly of the Hoover Institution at Stanford, has noted that in 1922

Secretary Hoover worked with the State Department to make partners of the State Bank in Moscow and Guaranty Trust in New York. Professor Sutton comments:

"This scheme, wrote Herbert Hoover, 'would not be objectionable if a stipulation were made that all monies coming into their possession should be used for the purchase of civilian commodities in the United States'; and after asserting that such relations appeared to be in line with general policy, Hoover added, 'It might be advantageous to have these transactions organized in such a manner that we know what the movement is instead of disintegrated operations now current.'

"Of course, such 'disintegrated operations' are consistent with the operations of a free market, but this approach Herbert Hoover rejected in favor of channeling the exchange through specified and controlled sources in New York. Secretary of State Charles E. Hughes expressed dislike of the Hoover-Guaranty Trust scheme, which he thought could be regarded as de facto recognition of the Soviets while foreign credit acquired might be used to the disadvantage of the United States. A non-committal reply was sent by State to Guaranty Trust. However, Guaranty went ahead (with Herbert Hoover's support), participated in formation of the first Soviet international bank, and Max May of Guaranty Trust [*a vice president, who was associated with both German espionage during World War I and the Bolshevik Revolution*] became head of the foreign department of the new Ruskombank [*Russian Commercial Bank*]." (*Wall Street And The Bolshevik Revolution*)

This was at a time when Herbert Hoover was advocating a soak-the-rich program and railing that too much American wealth was caused by "the ruthlessness of individualism." While many latter-day historians call Hoover an exponent of "rugged individualism," that is hardly the case. Nor was Hoover damaged by the Watergate-style press crusade against President Harding's alleged misdemeanors, allowing him to continue under Coolidge as Commerce Secretary. After President Coolidge announced his intention not to run for President in 1928, he had harsh words (unusual for him) about Hoover. Records Joan Hoff Wilson: "Coolidge resented what he called the 'Wonder Boy's' spendthrift programs and finally in 1928 said: 'That man offered me unsolicited advice for six years, all of it bad.' "

The truth is that the Wonder Boy, despite his later criticism of Franklin Roosevelt's imitations of fascism, was anything but an advocate of vigorous competition in the marketplace. Indeed, as Professor Sutton noted in *Wall Street And FDR*:

"The American Construction Council, formed in May 1922, was the first of the numerous trade organizations created in the 1920s, devices used to raise prices and reduce output. The original proposal and the drive for the council came from Secretary of Commerce Herbert Hoover, and the council operated under the leadership of Franklin D. Roosevelt, then just beginning his Wall Street career following his service as Assistant Secretary of the Navy. The stated public objectives of the A.C.C. were a 'code of ethics' (a euphemism for restraint of trade), efficiency, and standardization of production. Most importantly, but less publicized, the A.C.C. was to provide the industry with an opportunity to fix its own price and production levels without fear of antitrust prosecutions by the government.''

Hoover was not in the least as he has been painted. For instance, this man whom propagandists later smeared as an enemy of federal relief was in fact an early supporter of just such action. After the 1927 Mississippi flood, for instance, Mr. Hoover "established a precedent of federal responsibility for floods. Hoover exercised plenary authority as in war-time.'' (*Herbert Hoover: A Public Life*) And as usual he milked the disaster for publicity. So popular did he become by such grandstanding that in 1928 he was selected the Republican nominee for President with 837 of the 1,089 votes on the first ballot. Accepting the nomination, Mr. Hoover declared: "We in America today are nearer to the final triumph over poverty than ever before in the history of any land. The poorhouse is vanishing from among us . . . . We shall soon with the help of God be in sight of the day when poverty will be banished from this nation.''

The 1928 Democrat nominee, Al Smith, was not only a Roman Catholic in a predominantly Protestant country but was burdened with New York's reputation for urban corruption and viewed as an enemy of Prohibition. Hence: "Rum, Romanism and Rebellion.'' But it was Smith, not Hoover, who was the Conservative. Ironically, when one considers what followed, Democrat Franklin Roosevelt was bemoaning that: "Mr. Hoover has always shown a most disquieting desire to investigate everything and to appoint commissions and send out statistical inquiries on every conceivable subject under Heaven. He has also shown in his own Department a most alarming desire to issue regulations and to tell businessmen generally how to conduct their affairs.''

Some folks seemed to know what kind of President that man Hoover would make. For example, prominent "social worker'' Jane Addams of Chicago — a secret member of the Communist Party as of 1928 (see *Return To My Father's House*, Maurice Malkin, New Rochelle, Arlington House, 1972) — had opted for the Socialist Eugene Debs in 1920, the Progressive Robert La Follette in 1924, but supported Hoover in 1928. Hoover was elected in a landslide, with the then second-largest percentage of the popular vote ever recorded, and 444 electoral votes to Al Smith's 87. Hoover was even endorsed by the militant Women's Party.

As subsequently with Jimmy Carter, a show of simplicity was immediately arranged. Hoover put the Presidential yacht into dry dock and closed the White House stables. And during his first week in office President Hoover maintained that "excessive fortunes are a menace to true liberty by the accumulation and inheritance of economic power." As Chief Justice William Howard Taft observed: "The truth is that Hoover is a progressive." Indeed, social welfare was to be a prime concern of the new Administration. And though it took until Dwight Eisenhower's day to become a reality, creation of a Cabinet-level Department of Health, Education and Welfare was a Hoover goal. Another Presidential recommendation was that the federal parole board establish what would today be called an Affirmative Action program for blacks and women.

"During the summer months of 1929," recounts "Liberal" historian Joan Hoff Wilson, "he refused to give any government backing to proposed 'red hunts' against suspected communists, and later in the year he refused to take action" when Communists marched to gates of the White House itself.* Not that such action appeased the Reds. To Hoover's credit he did refuse to promise to implement the cartel takeover proposed by industrialist Gerard Swope, rightfully called fascist and unconstitutional. When F.D.R. said he had no such compunctions the Wall Street money switched to Roosevelt for the 1932 election. Meanwhile the Reds also screamed for Hoover's head on a pike. As former Communist leader Benjamin Gitlow reported in *The Whole Of Their Lives*:

"Hoover served as the target of a venomous mud-slinging campaign. He was pictured as a lyncher of Negroes, as a policeman with a club mashing in the brains of workers. Hoover was the arch imperialist, the fascist, the agent of Wall Street, plotting wars of aggression. The communists were determined to make Hoover the scapegoat of the world's economic crisis, the leader of world reaction, a man to be hated by the people. In a large measure they succeeded."

The world was now in an economic crisis which came to be called the Great Depression. The Federal Reserve System was playing boom-and-bust with the American economy and Mr. Hoover was well aware of how the game was played. As early as November of 1925, for example, he wrote: "As to the effects of the Reserve policies upon the United States, it means inflation with inevitable collapse which will bring the greatest

---

*In 1950, when asked by Harry Truman to head an investigating committee on subversion, Hoover declined, saying: "I doubt if there are any consequential card-carrying Communists in the Government." He was assuredly wrong.

calamities upon our farmers, our workers and legitimate business . . . ."
(*The Hoover Administration*, William Starr Myers and Walter H. Newton,
New York, Charles Scribner's Sons, 1936) In the past, depressions were
left to run their course and were quickly corrected by the marketplace. But
not under Hoover — and with tragic results. As Myers and Newton report:
"President Hoover was the first President in history to offer Federal
leadership in mobilizing the economic resources of the people . . . ." The
result was prolonged disaster.

Certainly Hoover did not put much stock in the potential results of such
leadership. In April of 1929 he formally "instructed his own financial
agent, his friend Edgar Rickard, to liquidate certain of his personal
holdings 'as possible hard times coming.' By May, when car sales dipped
and building slackened, he was switching to 'gilt-edged bonds.' "
(*Herbert Hoover: A Public Life*)

After the stock market crashed, President Hoover made a show of
meeting with business leaders and urging them to "cooperate" with the
government and pretend that all was business as usual. "Instead of
anticipating trouble, they were to behave as if conditions were normal.
And by pledging to maintain wages, prices, and employment they would
minimize rather than augment the potential deflationary impact of the
market collapse. 'It was,' as Walter Lippmann remarked, 'an open
conspiracy not to deflate.' " (*The Poverty Of Abundance*, Albert U.
Romasco, London, Oxford University Press, 1965)

Public-works spending had traditionally been decreased during depressions, but under Hoover it was increased by some $700 million in two
years. The President would boast in his *Memoirs* that his Administration
spent more on public works than in the previous thirty years. But with the
Federal Reserve contracting the money supply it didn't work.

Meanwhile the Agricultural Marketing Act gave even more power to
the Federal Farm Board, Hoover's first relief agency, which was in fact
headed by a man who believed in communally consolidating all farms
under three hundred acres. Even Bernard Baruch called this power grab
the "most socialistic legislation this country has ever seen." Thinking of
earlier criticism from Republicans about plans to manipulate agriculture,
Hoover enemy George Peek commented: "It makes me smile . . . ," for
the "Farm Board is in business, is in effect fixing prices, and the
government is assuming all the risk."

None of this helped the Republicans. In the elections of 1930 the
G.O.P. "suffered a net loss of five governors, eight senators and over
fifty congressmen. The Democrats would organize the House of Representatives." (*The Hoover Presidency*, edited by Martin L. Fausold and
George T. Mazuzan, Albany, State University of New York, 1974) By

August of 1931 the Hoover Administration had moved dramatically to the Left. David Burner reports that the Farm Board surprised "Southern governors with a telegram that urged the plowing under of every third row of standing cotton. Hoover initially favored the scheme (and wanted to kill off little pigs as well). The *New York Times* called it 'one of the maddest things that ever came from an official body,' and the farmers ignored it. Yet the destruction of crops — subsidized directly by Washington and, in most cases, accepted by vote of the farmers concerned — became an essential part of the Agricultural Adjustment Act of 1933."

There really was a Hoover New Deal. Indeed, Thomas Dewey later commented to Hoover: "I have a suspicion that you would have signed practically all the legislation that F.D.R. signed." And Hoover responded: "I think I would have." As Roosevelt Brain Truster Rexford Tugwell confirmed in 1974: "We didn't admit it at the time, but practically the whole New Deal was extrapolated from programs that Hoover started." (*Herbert Hoover: Forgotten Progressive*)

Another member of the so-called F.D.R. Brain Trust, Raymond Moley, acknowledged in *Newsweek* as early as 1948: "When we all burst into Washington . . . we found every essential idea enacted in the 100-day Congress in the Hoover administration itself. The essentials of the NRA, the PWA, the emergency relief setup were all there. Even the AAA was known to the Department of Agriculture . . . . The RFC, probably the greatest recovery agency, was of course a Hoover measure, passed long before the inauguration."

The Reconstruction Finance Corporation (R.F.C.) was modeled after the War Finance Corporation and heavily lobbied for by Eugene Meyer, Governor of the Federal Reserve Board who once ran the W.F.C. Hoover agreed to Meyer's wishes. "*Thus, the ill-fated Hoover administration became the first in American history to use the power of the federal government to intervene directly in the economy in time of peace.*" (Emphasis in original, *Herbert Hoover: Forgotten Progressive*)

And it is hard to argue that it was not all planned that way. The Federal Reserve, which had wildly inflated during the Twenties, had simply pulled the plug and shrunk the money supply by about a third. Protectionism around the world was exacerbated when Hoover embraced that false panacea. "The stock market," notes economist Murray Rothbard, "broke sharply on the day that Hoover agreed to sign the Smoot-Hawley [*tariff*] Bill." (*America's Great Depression*, Los Angeles, Nash, 1963)

Real income and production fell as more taxation on individuals and business alike was imposed to fund deficit spending by government. In 1931, for example, government expenditures increased forty-two percent. In short, writes Murray Rothbard, "in the midst of a great depression when people needed desperately to be relieved of government burdens, the dead weight of government rose from 16.4 percent to 21.5 percent of the gross private product (from 18.2 percent to 24.3 percent of the net private product). From a modest surplus in 1930, the Federal government [*still*] ran up a huge $2.2 billion deficit in 1931.''

In the midst of all of this came the much ballyhooed Bonus Army March, which was taken over by the Communists. According to one Red leader who later turned American, a top Party agitator ''told me that Moscow regarded this bonus march as a real propaganda opportunity to bring about a revolt and hatred against President Hoover.'' Violence was instigated against the Washington, D.C., police and two men were killed. Finally, President Hoover called out the troops under General Douglas MacArthur. As David Hinshaw reports: ''The federal troops *restored order without firing a shot or otherwise injuring a single individual.''* (*Herbert Hoover: American Quaker*, his emphasis) But the propaganda damage was done. Indeed, when F.D.R. heard of the eviction from Washington of the Bonus Army, he is said to have turned to Felix Frankfurter and smiled: ''Well, Felix, this will elect me.'' Forcing Hoover to call out Army Chief of Staff MacArthur, recalled Benjamin Gitlow, ''was just what the communists wanted. It was what they had conspired to bring about. Now they could brand Hoover as a murderer of hungry unemployed veterans.'' And never mind that the troublemakers among the ''veterans'' had turned out to be subversives and ex-convicts.

By 1932, industrial production was half the level of three years before, and a quarter of the labor force was out of work. Franklin Roosevelt and running-mate John Nance Garner came to power vowing to ''accomplish a saving of not less than 25 percent in the cost of federal government,'' promising ''real economy,'' and accusing the Hoover Administration of ''being the greatest spending administration in peacetime in all our history.''

The very same Democrats who had in large numbers supported Hoover's onerous tax increases put their man in the White House by calling on voters to ''throw the spenders out.''

President Hoover's final tax bill was signed on June 6, 1932. Former *Wall Street Journal* editor Jude Wanniski writes: ''The retroactivity feature of the tax boost was Hoover's last gift to Roosevelt. As the March 15, 1933, deadline approached for payment of 1932 tax liabilities, taxpayers throughout the nation had to withdraw funds from the banks. The bank panic of 1933 was the result. Roosevelt's 'bank holiday,' announced as soon as he was inaugurated March 4, 1933, merely enabled the Federal Reserve to reflow tax receipts to the banking system.'' (*The Way The World Works*)

Democratic leader Charles Michelson, who led the slander and smear campaign against Herbert Hoover, reports that F.D.R. told him as President-elect ''that the bank crisis was due to culminate just about inauguration day.'' And that's exactly what happened. Little wonder that as Mr. Hoover left the White House he termed it an ''emancipation from a sort of peonage.'' But, for his fellow Americans, it was no emancipation at all. Herbert Clark Hoover had initiated principles of social engineering that would for decades be applied by his successors with disastrous consequences.

Chapter XVI
The Great Depression

W HAT WE NEED, television's Archie Bunker said for years, is a President like Herbert Hoover. It's some New York "Liberal's" idea of a joke, you see, for Bunker is so oafish that he yearns for a return to Free Enterprise — a policy that under Hoover, as every New York "Liberal" knows, brought on the Great Depression. That was the depression so bad that, as *everyone* knows, it could only have been cured by the progressive policies of Franklin Delano Roosevelt. For decades the collectivist idolaters of Roosevelt have pointed to the Hoover years as threadbare proof of why *laissez-faire* can never again be trusted in American economic policy.

The truth is that the Great Depression was possible only because of an interventionist and inflationary government. And, to the extent that Mr. Hoover was guilty of counter-productive policies, he was more than matched by Mr. Roosevelt, whose economic meddling kept our economy seriously depressed until the outbreak of World War II.

The cycles of boom-and-bust started well before Mr. Hoover took office. But they are so much more useful — for the favored few on the inside — when the timing of such economic adjustments can be controlled by credit and monetary inflation and depression. After all, as Proctor W. Hansl indicated in 1935: "In times of depression many choice plums fall into the hands of banking or other money interests. In such times the foundations of great fortunes are laid by those who are shrewd enough or far-seeing enough to take advantage of those who are less fortunate or less equipped with foresight or financial resources. It was under such conditions that Rockefeller was enabled to gather in the units that entered into the Standard Oil Company and, at a later day, following the depression of the Nineties, J.P. Morgan brought about the reorganization of the railroad system of the country with enormous profit to himself and his associates. And so it has become axiomatic that the banker profits by the distress of the community as a whole and if he can anticipate or control the swing of the pendulum his position is one of great advantage." (*Years Of Plunder*, New York, Harrison Smith and Robert Haas, 1935)

Control of that pendulum is what creation of the Federal Reserve was all about. Hansl continues: "Under the existing order the key to inflation is credit and in this country the key to credit is the Federal Reserve System . . . . Led by Benjamin Strong [*later a member of the conspiratorial Council on Foreign Relations and head of the New York Federal Reserve Bank — which came to dominate the System*] of the Bankers Trust Company, and with the active support of the Morgan interests, a determined effort had been put forth, even prior to the adoption of the [*Federal Reserve*] act, to divert the control of the System to Wall Street."

The Fed had been created in 1913 by banking insiders to manipulate booms and busts. It was largely the work of Paul Warburg, a partner of Kuhn, Loeb & Company, brother of Germany's central banker Max Warburg, and Chairman of the Board of the International Acceptance Bank — which greatly benefitted from the subsidized and completely artificial rates paid for the credit-producing bills "bought" by the Fed. Incestuous? You bet. Those Federal Reserve bills, reports the distinguished economist Murray Rothbard, "led the inflationary parade of Reserve credit in 1921 and 1922" and were even "more important than securities in the 1924 inflationary spurt, and equally important in the 1927 spurt. Furthermore, bills bought alone continued the inflationary stimulus in the fatal last half of 1928." (*America's Great Depression*)

The United States, to be sure, had suffered earlier depressions at the hands of the Federal Reserve manipulators. Indeed, after World War I there was an eighteen-month slump in 1920-1921. But, as economist Howard Kershner has pointed out, in that short-lived depression the U.S. had a flexible wage and price structure; the dollar was sound and convertible to gold; and, both the populace and federal government emphasized thrift instead of large-scale deficit spending. In 1929 and thereafter, notes Dr. Kershner, we reversed "the policies that had proved so effective in 1920-21, [*and*] the Great Depression was fastened upon us permanently. The severe maladjustments were not corrected . . . ." (*Dividing The Wealth*, Old Greenwich, Devin-Adair, 1971)

To maximize the looting in a bust there must be a boom — and the conspirators back of the Federal Reserve saw to that in the Twenties with a deliberate inflationary policy. It was this policy, reports Professor Hans Sennholz, that "generated a boom through easy money and credit, which was soon followed by the inevitable bust . . . . The spectacular crash of

1929 followed five years of reckless credit expansion by the Federal Reserve System . . . ." (*The Freeman*, October 1969) That fatal expansion, incidentally, was less than the inflation to which we were subjected under Jimmy Carter. Dr. Rothbard places inflation of the money supply between 1921 and 1929 at 61.8 percent, or 7.7 percent per year. Given double-digit figures not long ago, this doesn't seem so bad. It was brutal. Britisher Antony Fisher recalls the purpose of the conspirators responsible for it:

"To meet a decline in business in 1924, the Reserve Bank suddenly created some $500 million of new money which led inevitably to a bank credit expansion of over $4,000 million in less than one year. The immediate effect was a temporarily agreeable economic boom. Predictably, when the threat of inflation loomed up, the authorities provoked the worst world slump ever by equally suddenly reducing [*deflating or depressing*] the supply of money and raising protective tariffs [*such as Hawley-Smoot*], which invited retaliation from other countries and all but throttled international trade. Even such a classic case of government folly, however, has not prevented the legend that the world slump was caused by the failure of the free market!" (*Must History Repeat Itself?*, Levittown, New York, Transatlantic Arts, 1974)

But it wasn't "folly" from the point of view of the looters who were responsible. The point to keep in mind is that the super-rich bankers were well aware that the artificial boom of the Roaring Twenties was bound to result in bust because the Fed's reckless credit expansion encouraged bad investment in unprofitable fields. No one knows better than a banker that poor investments can not be kept afloat forever. Inflation of money and credit by the Federal Reserve meant that the fall, when it came, would be a hard one. To paraphrase Herbert Spencer: To shield men from the effects of their folly is to fill the world with fools. In this case, poor fools.

The Fed pumped up the money and credit balloon, for example, by easing the reserve-ratio requirements for banks and by setting itself up as the lender of last resort. Professor Rothbard estimates that this "combined to inflate the monetary potential of the American banking system six-fold. . . ." The inflation of the Twenties, explains Rothbard, "distorted the production structure and led to the ensuing depression-adjustment period. It also prevented the whole populace from enjoying the fruits of progress in lower prices and insured that only those enjoying higher monetary wages and incomes could benefit from the increased productivity." (*America's Great Depression*)

Whereas inflation is the expansion of available money and credit, producing boom, depression is a reduction in available money and credit, producing recession or bust. In a free market a recession is the correction the market makes until production, wages, and prices "clear" by reverting to where they should have been without the aforementioned inflation. If this correction is hindered by government, the economic depression turns to bust and will continue. The yanking of a tooth may hurt, in other words, but it is better than letting the abcess spread and poison the patient. Eminent Austrian economist Ludwig von Mises, in fact, argues that even the terms boom and bust are misleading. The boom, says Mises, is actually "retrogression and the [*recession*] progress. The boom squanders through malinvestment scarce factors of production and reduces stock available through overconsumption; its alleged blessings are paid for by impoverishment. The [*recession*], on the other hand, is the way back to a state of affairs in which all factors of production are employed for the best possible satisfaction of the most urgent needs of the consumers." (*Human Action*, Third Revised Edition, Chicago, Regnery, 1966)

But remember that the extremism of inflation and depression are created by government (or via government through the banks). And the U.S. was not operating in an economic vacuum after World War I. We had acquired more than half the world's supply of gold, and foreign bankers who noted this certainly played a part in encouraging inflation of our gold-backed money supply. Wall Street, commented Proctor Hansl, "was international-minded and could see no hope for the world or profit for itself save through a distribution of our stock of gold or the credit that made it possible through international channels. To effect this purpose, however, required the subservience of the Federal Reserve System, and this was readily obtained through the underground connections that ran between Wall Street and Washington . . . . [*The bankers*] proceeded to carry out their [*inflationary*] policies of world rehabilitation without regard to consequences so far as this nation was concerned." (*Years Of Plunder*)

In essence, it was decided that since Britain was losing her gold, and her unions refused to allow reductions in wages to make her products competitive with ours, the answer to reduced profits for Britain's Establishment insiders would be *American* inflation. Secret conferences were arranged between, for example, Montagu Norman — head of the Bank of England — and Benjamin Strong — Governor of the Federal Reserve Bank of New York, who worked closely with the House of Morgan and Paul Warburg. In 1920, Montagu Norman "began taking annual trips to America to visit Strong, and Strong took periodic trips to visit Europe. All these consultations were kept highly secret and were always camouflaged as 'visiting with friends,' 'taking a vacation,' and 'courtesy visits.' The Bank of England gave Strong a desk and a private secretary for these occasions, as did the Bank of France and the German Reichsbank." (*America's Great Depression*)

Secretary of Commerce Herbert Hoover referred to Governor Strong as a "mental annex to Europe."*

In 1925, reports John Chamberlain, "Britain went back on the gold standard at the unrealistic prewar parity of $4.86 to the pound. As a result exports suffered, imports increased and London found itself with great difficulties. Accordingly, the Bank of England pleaded with Governor Benjamin Strong . . . to ease the situation by a money policy that would divert short-term funds from New York to London." (*The Enterprising Americans: A Business History Of The United States*) In the spring of 1927, the Governor of the Bank of England, the Governor of the Reichbank, and the Deputy Governor of the Bank of France "came to the United States to urge an easy money policy. (They had previously pled with success for a roughly similar policy in 1925.) The Federal Reserve obliged." (*The Great Crash, 1929*, Third Edition, John Kenneth Galbraith, Boston, Houghton Mifflin, 1972)

This despite the fact that the United States was already hemorrhaging gold. Said a dissenting member of the Federal Reserve Board, this was "the greatest and boldest operation ever undertaken by the Federal Reserve System, and . . . [it] resulted in one of the most costly errors [sic] committed by it or any other banking system in the last 75 years!" (*The Great Depression*, Lionel Robbins, New York, Macmillan, 1934) On the other hand, Fabian conspirator John Maynard Keynes exulted in the Fed's "triumph" of bringing about "the successful management of the dollar . . . from 1923 to 1928." It depends on your point of view, and Keynes was British.

After all the U.S. inflation supposedly to help Great Britain back to gold, and at our expense, Britannia's bankers pulled her off the gold standard precipitously in 1931 without even a by-your-leave, escalating the chaos then rampant in the international market and putting American gold up for grabs.

---

*Strong died in 1928, before the bursting of what Hoover called the "Mississippi Bubble of 1927-1929." All his cryptic dealing was explained away on humanitarian grounds. Strong, wrote an assistant in a private memo, "was obliged to consider the viewpoint of the American public, which had decided to keep the country out of the League of Nations to avoid interferences by other nations in its domestic affairs, and which would be just as opposed to having the heads of its central banking system attend some conference or organization of the world banks of issue." The same explanations are made to cover the dealings of today's Bilderbergers and Trilateralists, who believe national patriotism is parochial. Governor Strong, concluded his staffer, "said that very few people indeed realized that we were now paying for the decision which was reached early in 1924 to help the rest of the world . . . ." (*Benjamin Strong, Central Banker*, Lester V. Chandler, Washington, D.C., Brookings Institution,1958)

There were those who saw a stock market crash coming. There was, for instance, Paul M. Warburg, father of the private bankers' little hustle called the Federal Reserve System, who became so favored by the Fed's treatment of his International Acceptance Bank. The master conspirator Warburg was described by a gushing biographer in *Century* magazine in 1915 as "probably the mildest-mannered man that ever personally conducted a revolution. It was a bloodless revolution: he did not attempt to rouse the populace to arms. He stepped forth armed simply with an idea. And he conquered. This is the amazing thing. A shy, sensitive man, he imposed his idea on a nation of a hundred million people." This mild-mannered man's warnings, really signals to his fellow conspirators, naturally failed to slow the general speculation in the stock market where he predicted, in 1929, there would be a collapse which would "bring about a general depression involving the entire country." (*The Great Crash, 1929*) Those who are not on the inside never believe that sort of thing in the middle of a boom market.

Heeding the warning of their co-conspirator, of course, "John D. Rockefeller, Bernard Baruch, and other substantial holders had withdrawn from the market before the Crash . . . ." (*The Invisible Scar*, Caroline Bird, New York, McKay, 1966) The Crash did not cause the Great Depression but resulted from it. The inflation of the Twenties had actually ended in 1928 and it took the economy a short time to reflect the malinvestments which the boom had created. "For the first time since June 1921," comments Murray Rothbard, "the money supply stopped increasing, and remained virtually constant. The great boom of the 1920s was over, and the Great Depression had begun. The country, however, did not really discover the change until the stock market finally crashed in October." (*America's Great Depression*)

In August of 1928, when Herbert Hoover accepted the G.O.P. nomination for the Presidency, he declared: "We have not yet reached the goal, but given a chance to go forward with the policies of the last eight years, and we shall soon, with the help of God, be within sight of the day when poverty will be banished from the nation." And so it must have appeared to those who trusted, say, the *New York Times* industrial averages as an indicator of a healthy economy. In three months of 1929, in the normally slower summer season, the industrials gained one hundred ten points, more than the entire previous boom year. But on just one day in October, the same averages would drop so sharply as to cancel all of the gains of the year before. (*The Great Crash, 1929*) When the boom busted, reports Robert L. Heilbroner:

". . . it was as if an enormous dam had suddenly crumbled. All the frenzy that had stretched out over two years in sending stocks up was concentrated in a few incredible weeks beating them down. On Tuesday, October 29, 1929 an avalanche of selling crushed the exchanges. On occasion there were *no* offers to buy stock at all — just to sell it. Goldman Sachs, a much sought-after investment trust, lost almost half its quoted value on this single day. By the end of the trading session (the ticker, lagging behind, stretched out the agony two-and-a-half hours longer than the actual market transactions) 16,410,000 shares of stock had been dumped. In a single day, the rise in values of the entire preceding year had been wiped out. A few weeks later, 3 billion dollars of 'wealth' had vanished in thin air. Millions who counted their paper gains and thought themselves well off discovered they were poor." (*The Making Of Economic Society*, Englewood Cliffs, Prentice-Hall, 1962)

Previous busts had been left to bottom out, and this is what Secretary of the Treasury Andrew Mellon recommended: "Liquidate labor, liquidate stocks, liquidate the farmers, liquidate real estate." Though this is brutal, it would have been much kinder in the long run. But President Hoover "disagreed with this uncompromising *laissez-faire* viewpoint." Above all else, Hoover now sought to "require 'the co-ordination of business and governmental agencies in concerted action . . . .' This last suggestion was the very heart of this program." (*The Poverty Of Abundance*)

Hoover, to reiterate, did not look for a Free Market solution. His admirers praise him for this. For example, biographers William Starr Meyers and Walter H. Newton are quoted as follows:

"President Hoover was the first President in our history to offer Federal leadership in mobilizing the economic resources of the people, and in calling upon individual initiative to accept definite responsibility for meeting the problem of depression . . . . The depressions that arose in the Van Buren, Buchanan, Grant, Cleveland, Theodore Roosevelt, or Wilson Administrations were practically ignored by the government in any official action." (*The Hoover Presidency*)

After the stock market crashed, the government, leading financiers, labor unions, and big business agreed to act as though there were no depression. As we pointed out in Chapter XV, rather than allow the market to reach its own level, there were well-publicized White House conferences with business and labor to "reassure" one and all in the economy. "And by pledging to maintain wages, prices, and employment they would minimize rather than augment the potential deflationary impact of the market collapse. 'It was,' as Walter Lippmann remarked, 'an open conspiracy not to deflate.' " (*The Poverty Of Abundance*)

Unfortunately there was no one to protect the country from the protectors. Harry Browne emphasizes the point: "The 1929 depression evoked the ultimate in government interference. Herbert Hoover has been characterized so often as a 'do nothing' President and the symbol of the 'rugged individualist.' But that isn't true. He reacted to the depression by calling for a fantastic program to keep wages and prices high, and to prevent the liquidation of mistakes. He vowed to reverse all previous government policies in fighting this depression. And he did. In the process, he succeeded in keeping the economy immobilized.'' (*How You Can Profit From The Coming Devaluation*, New Rochelle, Arlington House, 1970)

Professor Murray Rothbard has enumerated the ways to interface with recovery from an economic bust: **1.** Prevent or delay liquidation, such as by granting loans to faltering businesses; **2.** Further inflate by "easy money" credit expansion; **3.** Maintain artificially high wage *rates*, so that when business demand slackens, unemployment is aggravated; **4.** Keep prices above the level of a free market so surpluses are created; **5.** Stimulate consumption through Food Stamp programs, relief payments and other increased government efforts, while discouraging savings through income, corporate, and estate tax increases; and, **6.** Subsidize unemployment so workers are encouraged not to shift to the available fields of work. These measures, he noted, ''are the time-honored favorites of government policy, and . . . they were the policies adopted in the 1929-1933 depression, by a government known to many historians as a 'laissez-faire' Administration.'' Hoover himself called it a ''program unparalleled in the history of depressions in any country and in any time.'' Just so. Alas.

Between 1929 and 1933 the Gross National Product fell by almost one-half. (*After The Crash*, John Rublowsky, New York, Crowell-Collier, 1970) Yet federal spending had increased by forty-two percent in 1930-1931 alone. Because of White House pressure, wage *rates* were not at first reduced, forcing unemployment. Then hours-worked decreased — and, finally, the rates also dropped. Average weekly earnings fell by more than forty percent between 1929 and 1933. Moreover, in 1932, the people and their economy were subjected to one of the largest tax increases in peacetime history. To quote *America's Great Depression*:

''The range of tax increases was enormous: many wartime excise taxes were revived, sales taxes were imposed on gasoline, tires, autos, electric energy, malt, toiletries, furs, jewelry, and other articles; admission and stock transfer taxes were increased; new taxes were levied on bank checks, bond transfers, telephone, telegraph, and radio messages; and the personal income tax was raised drastically as follows: the normal rate was increased from a range of 1½ percent-5 percent, to 4 percent-8 percent; personal exemptions were sharply reduced, and an earned credit of 25 percent eliminated; and surtaxes were raised enormously, from a maximum of 25 percent to 63 percent on the highest incomes. Furthermore, the corporate income tax was increased from 12 percent to 13¾ percent, and an exemption for small corporations eliminated; the estate tax was doubled, and the exemption floor halved; and the gift tax, which had been eliminated, was restored, and graduated up to 33⅓ percent.''

It was the surest way imaginable to choke a free economy to its knees, and government was doing the choking. But more mischief was afoot. The Federal Reserve System which had supposedly been "active, vigorous, self-confident in the 1920s was followed by a passive, defensive, hesitant policy from 1929 to 1933 . . . .'' The total stock of money — defined as the seasonally adjusted sum of currency and deposits at commercial banks held by the public — "fell by over one-third from 1929 to 1933; commercial bank deposits fell by over 42 percent . . . .'' (*The Great Contraction: 1929-1933*, Milton Friedman and Anna Jacobson Schwartz, Princeton, National Bureau of Economic Research, 1963) Professor Rothbard notes that what was a 7.7 percent annual inflation rate in the Twenties (totaling 61.8 percent over eight years) was turned into a 16 percent total monetary contraction (depression) between June of 1929 and the end of 1933. And amid the alleged economic panaceas came this gem from the top economist at *Business Week*: "Just as we saved our way into depression, we must squander our way out of it.'' Banker Franklin Roosevelt was to accept this advice.

This *Business Week* "wisdom'' was aired before a Chamber of Commerce crowd. And it is to Mr. Hoover's credit that he resisted what came to be known as "Chamber of Commerce fascism,'' exemplified by the Swope Plan — named for the Establishment insider who was president of General Electric. This was the collectivist interventionism (see Chapters XIII and XIX) implemented in F.D.R.'s New Deal. As Mr. Hoover later recalled:

"Among the early Roosevelt fascist measures was the National Industry Recovery Act (NRA) of June 16, 1933. The origins of this scheme are worth repeating. These ideas were first suggested by Gerard Swope (of the General Electric Company) at a meeting of the electrical industry in the winter of 1932. Following this, they were adopted by the United States Chamber of Commerce. During the campaign of 1932, Henry I. Harriman, president of that body, urged that I agree to support these proposals, informing me that Mr. Roosevelt had agreed to do so. I tried to show him that this stuff was pure fascism; that it was merely a remaking of Mussolini's 'corporate state' and refused to agree to any of it. He informed me that in view of my attitude, the business world would support Roosevelt with money and influence. That, for the most part, proved true.'' (*The Memoirs Of Herbert Hoover*)

And F.D.R. was elected, calling Hoover "the greatest spender in history" and a man who refused to cut taxes and balance the Budget. "Stop the deficits!" cried candidate Roosevelt. (*The Roosevelt Myth*, John T. Flynn) Where Hoover's deficits resulted from an unanticipated lack of revenue, F.D.R. would *plan* deficits. (*As We Go Marching*) As President Hoover left office, his Administration had seen the G.N.P. fall by almost half, unemployment was at twenty-five percent of the labor force, and "hardest hit was investment, especially business construction, the latter falling from about $8.7 billion in 1929 to $1.4 billion in 1933." (*America's Great Depression*) Investment was, and is, the key to jobs.

The Establishment Left, including C.F.R. founder Colonel House and F.D.R. himself — who had been close to Hoover in the Wilson Administration — had once promoted Hoover for the Presidency. But his Administration was now made an object of ridicule as Roosevelt came to power. Yet even Walter Lippmann, another C.F.R. founder, would admit that "most of President Roosevelt's recovery program is an evolution from President Hoover's." (*After The Crash*)

The new President opined that "too often liberal governments have been wrecked on the rocks of loose fiscal policy." But as John Chamberlain, among others, has noted: " . . . there was no 'economy' as such in the Agricultural Adjustment Act, in the Civilian Conservation Corps, in the Works Progress Administration, in the Ickes program of Public Works, or in the Tennessee Valley Authority. All of these involved spending by the state in order to expand the market. The NRA, on the other hand, presupposed a conscious limitation of markets, of competition, of the number of firms permitted to do business in a given field." (*The Roots Of Capitalism*)

Boondoggling was the term that came to be identified with the W.P.A., for example. "In Cleveland, $179 thousand was spent counting the same trees a private contractor was willing to count for $5 thousand. A rat extermination project in New Orleans ended up costing $2.97 a rat. Twenty-one thousand dollars was spent placing two thousand street signs in Montgomery, Alabama, and $78,000 to repair a ditch in Denver, Colorado. After a 5 million-word history of New York City was written under the supervision of the WPA-sponsored Federal Arts Program, one critic pointed out that 'the story of creation was written in 700 words, but not at government expense.' " Nevertheless, said F.D.R.: "If we can boondoggle ourselves out of the Depression, that word is going to be enshrined in the hearts of people for many years to come." (*The*

Prosperity And Depression Decades, Thomas J. Ladenburg and Samuel Hugh Brockunier, New York, Hayden, 1971)

And, after taxing ouselves blue to squander our way out of the Depression, there were more people unemployed in 1938 than in 1932. (*The Bewildered Society*, George C. Roche)

Some profited by the Great Depression of course. Some politically and some financially. One prominent Socialist was quoted some months before the Crash as saying: "Within the next ten years we are going to have a change such as we have not had in the last forty." (*Fabian Freeway*, Rose L. Martin) And the Communist Party gained also; because, as Eugene Lyons noted, in such a climate even "the most inept fishermen could make a good haul." (*The Red Decade*, New Rochelle, Arlington House, 1971) Which is exactly what the Reds did. By 1939, reports even the frenetically "Liberal" Caroline Bird, "Communists controlled the Maritime Federation of the Pacific; United Electrical, Radio and Machinists; State, County and Municipal workers; International Longshoremen and Warehousemen; Mine, Mill and Smelter; Fur Workers; American Communications Association; United Cannery, Agriculture, Packing and Allied Workers. Communist factions plus fellow workers dominated Mike Quill's transport workers, the Newspaper Guild, the teachers' union, and the furniture workers." (*The Invisible Scar*)

Nor did all business suffer equally. Overall, of course, industry stagnated in the Great Depression, but "some of the great empires managed to expand: U.S. Steel, Western Electric, Du Pont, Standard Oil, Gulf Oil, Shell Oil, Armour, Monsanto Chemical, General Motors. When stock market values fell, the giant corporations bought up more properties at bargain prices." (*Brother, Can You Spare A Dime?*, Milton Meltzer, New York, Knopf, 1969) Individuals who profited included such manipulators of government as the elder Joseph Kennedy, who reportedly parlayed four million dollars into one hundred million between 1929 and 1935; oil operator J. Paul Getty; and, Hunt foods magnate Norton Simon, who bought a bankrupt canning company in 1931 for seven thousand dollars, and, with access to credit, turned it into an empire. (*The Invisible Scar*)

Not until after the war year of 1941, a dozen years later, did the dollar value of U.S. production return to that of the year the stock market crashed. The economic and political consequences were devastating. But surely this great disaster, created by banking conspirators through the boom-and-bust meddling of the Fed, and perpetuated by federal interference in the economy, could never be repeated. One can hope so. But we will let the acknowledged socialist John Kenneth Galbraith have the next-to-the-last word on that here: "The powers of the Federal Reserve

Board — now styled the Board of Governors, the Federal Reserve System — have been *strengthened* both in relation to the individual Reserve banks and the member banks.'' What is past, it is said, is prologue.

Chapter XVII
Hitler-Stalin Pact

"Stalin and i," said Adolf Hitler to his generals in 1939, "are the only ones that see only the future. So I shall shake hands with Stalin within a few weeks on the common German-Russian border and undertake with him a new distribution of the world . . . . My pact with Poland was only meant to stall for time . . . . After Stalin's death . . . we shall crush the Soviet Union." (*Battles Lost And Won*, Hanson Baldwin, New York, Harper & Row, 1966)

So it was that, virtually overnight, these socialist archenemies became allies feasting on the corpse of Poland — a fact that promoters of today's publicized Sino-Soviet split would do well to remember. For it was the Nazi-Soviet Pact, signed on August 23, 1939, that made World War II a certainty.

Adolf Hitler had long had his eye on Poland, which had been promised military aid by France and Britain if attacked, but he wanted to avoid a two-front conflict of the kind that had contributed to German defeat in World War I. Offering Stalin a share of the booty, he made a deal. The Communist Party line changed abruptly, to the point that Soviet secret police chief Lavrenti Beria ordered guards in the Gulag Archipelago to stop referring to political prisoners as fascists. Comrade Hitler, after all, might be offended.

Since the Party Line was later changed again, and Stalin is no longer in favor, it is permissible for a Soviet Communist like Roy A. Medvedev to review the domestic impact of the Nazi-Russian agreement. "Stalin did not merely stop antifascist propaganda in the Soviet Union," writes Medvedev. "In plain violation of the resolutions of the VIIth Comintern Congress, he sent a directive to all Communist parties demanding curtailment of the struggle against German fascism, naming Anglo-French imperialism as the basic aggressive force, which was to become the main target of Communist propaganda. This sudden about-face caught the

Western Communist parties by surprise. One result was the paralysis of the Rumanian Communist Party, which had been making great progress, as shown by the massive May Day demonstrations of 1939 in Bucharest. The Communists in other European countries were also thrown into complete disarray. At that time they were considered sections of the Comintern, obliged to submit to discipline. Thus the Comintern's declaration that France and Great Britain were the aggressors, while Germany wanted peace, put the French and British Communists in an especially difficult position. The logic of the directive required Communists in those countries to take a defeatist stand, or at least to refuse support to the military efforts of their bourgeois governments." (*Let History Judge*, New York, Knopf, 1972)

French Communists were soon distributing anti-war propaganda, committing sabotage in military factories, and hailing the Soviet-German pact as "making a new and invaluable contribution to the preservation of peace." (*The Great Wall of France*, Vivian Rowe, New York, G.P. Putnam's Sons, 1959) The Communist Party, U.S.A., and its Fronts also obediently supported Stalin's new pro-Nazi policy. As Eugene Lyons recalls in the preface to his 1971 edition of *The Red Decade*: "Overnight they turned militantly 'pacifist' and neutralist on the Axis side — worldwide and especially American support against the Allies was for Hitler a valuable part of his bargain with Stalin. The years of shrill anti-Nazi and anti-fascist fervor quite forgotten, the comrades now assumed a substantial role in the debate between advocates of isolationism and interventionism . . . . Their strong position in the labor movement enabled them to sabotage defense production and slow up arms shipments to Britain."

Anticipating the Nazi pact with the U.S.S.R., and seeking to tighten discipline through fear, Stalin had initiated a devastating purge of the Army and of the Party in general. "Prisoners were predicting the Nazi-Soviet Pact in 1938," remarks Russian historian Robert Conquest, "on the basis of the categories being arrested — in particular the foreign Communists. When the Pact came in August 1939, the effects of years of hard organizational work and propaganda work in the Comintern became visible. All over the world, with negligible and temporary exceptions, the Communist Parties accepted the switch and began to explain its necessity — sometimes in the later editions of papers which the same day had been urging a fight to the last against Nazism." (*The Great Terror*, New York, Collier, revised 1973)

Though the announcement of the German-Russian non-aggression pact caught the world at large by surprise, Stalin had been putting out feelers since at least 1936. Indeed, the U.S.S.R.'s top military man, Marshal

Tukhacevski, had told friendly Germans before the pact that ". . . if Germany adopted a different position, nothing need stand in the way of further Soviet-German collaboration — if both countries enjoyed their friendship and political relations as in the past, they could dictate peace to the world."

The Marshal was one of millions who did not survive the purges, but his removal had more to do with the discipline of fear than with any disagreement with Stalin over policy. The purge of the military has been cited by some Stalin apologists as excusing the Soviet dictator's deal with Hitler — the excuse being that the Red Army was too weak for Stalin to do otherwise. But of course it was Stalin who had decimated his officer corps, a point which suggests that citing the military purge as mitigation is akin to the boy who murdered his parents and then begged for mercy on the ground he was an orphan. Indeed, Stalin made orphans of many.

Only two of five "Marshals of the Soviet Union" survived purging, reports historian Alan Clark. "Out of eighty members of the 1934 Military Soviet only five were left in September 1938. All eleven Deputy Commissars for Defence were eliminated. Every commander of a military district (including replacements of the first 'casualties') had been executed by the summer of 1938. Thirteen out of fifteen army commanders, fifty-seven out of eighty-five corps commanders, 110 out of 195 divisional commanders, 220 out of 406 brigade commanders, were executed. But the greatest numerical loss was borne in the Soviet officer corps from the rank of colonel downward and extending to company commander level." (*Barbarossa: The Russian-German Conflict*, New York, Morrow, 1965) A year later, Stalin made his deal with Hitler that started the war.

That Hitler and Stalin had so little trouble making common cause was no bolt out of the blue to anyone who had compared their methods. Hitler, for example, admired the work of Communist propagandists and readily admitted to following their example. Indeed, there was an overwhelming number of Reds who became Nazis in Germany. They were said to be "Beefsteak Nazis" — brown on the outside, Red on the inside. Hitler gave strict orders that "former Communists are to be admitted to the party at once." And, vice versa, former Nazis are even now operating throughout the Communist regime of East Germany. (See *The Rise of Radicalism: The Social Psychology Of Messianic Extremism*, Eugene H. Methvin.)

The Führer, reports General Reinhard Gehlen, former head of German military espionage on the Russian front, "nurtured something like a love-hate relationship with Joseph Stalin. When he was in difficulties, Hitler sometimes asked himself out loud, 'What would Stalin do in a situation like this?' It was perhaps in emulation of Stalin that Hitler instituted the arrest of the relatives of certain conspirators in the assassination plot of

July 20, 1944.'' (*The Service: The Memoirs Of General Reinhard Gehlen*, translated by David Irving, New York, World, 1972) The dictator of Nazi Germany, reiterates historian John Toland, "had long admired Stalin, regarding him as 'one of the extraordinary figures in world history.' " (*Adolf Hitler*, Volume II, Garden City, Doubleday, 1976) He especially admired Stalin's ruthlessness.

At the same time, both dictators were certain of the cowardice of the West. After all, England and France had done nothing to stop Hitler as he instituted the military draft, occupied the Rhineland, took Austria and the Sudetenland, and then occupied all of Czecho-Slovakia. Despite the promises of London and Paris to the Poles, the dictators expected continued appeasement. These were "little worms," in Hitler's words, who had backed down at Munich and would do so again.

The day before Germany invaded Poland, Molotov made the following remarks before the Supreme Soviet:

"We all know that since the Nazis came to power, relations between the Soviet Union and Germany have been strained. But we need not dwell on these differences; they are sufficiently familiar to you anyway, Comrade Deputies. But, as Comrade Stalin said on March 10, 'we are in favor of business relations with all nations'; and it seems that, in Germany, they understood Comrade Stalin's statement correctly, and drew the right conclusions.

"August 23 [*the day of the signing of the Hitler-Stalin Pact*] must be regarded as a date of great historic importance. It is a turning point in the history of Europe, and not only Europe.

"Only recently the German Nazis conducted a foreign policy which was essentially hostile to the Soviet Union. Yes, until recently, in the realm of foreign policy, the Soviet Union and Germany were enemies. The situation has now changed, and we have stopped being enemies . . . .

"The Soviet-German agreement has been violently attacked in the Anglo-French and American press, and especially in some 'socialist' papers . . . . Particularly violent in their denunciations of the agreement are some of the French and British socialist leaders . . . . These people are determined that the Soviet Union should fight against Germany on the side of Britain and France. One may well wonder whether these war-mongers haven't gone off their heads. [*Laughter*]

"Under the Soviet-German Agreement, the Soviet Union is not obliged to fight either on the British or the German side. The U.S.S.R. is pursuing her own policy, which is determined by the interests of the peoples of the U.S.S.R., and by nobody else. [*Loud cheers*] If these gentlemen have such an irresistible desire to go to war, well then — let them go to war by themselves, without the Soviet Union. [*Laughter and cheers*] We'll

see what kind of warriors they will make. [*Loud laughter and cheers*]"
(*Russia At War*, Alexander Werth, New York, E.P. Dutton, 1964)

German Foreign Minister von Ribbentrop, Molotov's counterpart, was
more concise in his braggadocio: "Our treaty with Stalin keeps our rear
covered and insures us against a war on two fronts such as brought disaster
to Germany once before. I regard this alliance as the crowning achievement of my foreign policy." (*Hitler Moves East: 1941-1943*, Paul Carell,
Boston, Little, Brown, 1964)

The Alliance was arranged, reports Dr. Barton Whaley, "at Stalin's
initiative and with eager response from Hitler . . . . The pact, scheduled
to run for five years, guaranteed mutual non-aggression. The attached
'Secret Additional Protocol' [*not disclosed until after the conclusion of
World War II*] assigned to the Russian sphere of influence Finland,
Estonia, Latvia, the Bessarabian section of eastern Rumania, and, most
important, eastern Poland. Nine days later Hitler invaded Poland, and
Britain and France declared war. When Warsaw fell the next week, Stalin
telephoned his congratulations to the German ambassador in Moscow.
Nine days later the Red Army moved in to occupy its share of Poland."
(*Codeword Barbarossa*, Cambridge, M.I.T. Press, 1973)

But France and Britain declared war only on Germany. In the Anglo-
Polish Treaty there was also a "secret additional protocol," which stated
that the "European Power" from which the countries were mutually to
protect one another was Germany. This was used as an excuse to avoid
declaring war on the Soviets when they also invaded Poland.

Military specialist Hanson W. Baldwin reports that the Nazi blitz had
already taken its toll when, on September 17, 1939, "in a surprise blow
to all but Hitler, Stalin and their entourage, thirty-five Red Army divisions and nine tank brigades invaded Poland from the east. This was a
coup de grâce to a nation already vanquished. The Russians marched
against minor Polish resistance, for the Polish Army had already been
concentrated in the west against Germany, and there were elements of
only two infantry divisions and two cavalry brigades to meet the Soviet
advance to the Bug and San rivers. Moscow's jackal-like snatch surprised
even some of the German troops; there were sporadic shooting incidents
between the suspicious soldiers of Poland's two traditional enemies as the
Russian and German armies stood face to face." (*The Crucial Years:
1939-1941*, New York, Harper & Row, 1976)

Just as Hitler had predicted, the two former adversaries now sat on a
common border and could undertake "a new distribution of the world."
For the Russians, it had been easy. As they crossed all along the thousand
mile border stretching from Latvia in the north to Romania in the south
they met only token opposition by the Polish Frontier Corps. Nicholas

Bethell cites an eyewitness report of this treachery: "It was dawn, and morning mist covered the flat countryside as the sparse Polish patrols stood manning their unwieldy eastern border. Suddenly they saw shapes looming towards them through the mist — a few tanks but mostly horse-drawn carts full of Red Army soldiers. 'Don't shoot!' they shouted at the Poles, 'we've come to help you against the Germans.' White flags fluttered from many of the vehicles. This thoroughly confused the defenders, and in many cases the invaders were simply allowed to pass. A Soviet colonel writes that the Red Army advanced about sixty miles during the first day, suffering only insignificant losses. They were greeted by the population without much hostility, but with a sense of puzzlement." (*The War Hitler Won*, New York, Holt, Rinehart and Winston, 1973)

The Hammer and Sickle had thus supported the Swastika to stab Poland in the back, but England and France made only weak diplomatic protests to Moscow. Russian reaction was typified by a gloating Foreign Minister Molotov, who berated the quality of the betrayed Polish Army and whose remarks have been bowdlerized as follows: "A short blow at Poland from the German Army, followed by one from the Red Army, was enough to annihilate this monster child of the Treaty of Versailles."

The dictators Hitler and Stalin had begun World War II. Yet the question remains whether it was their intention to do so. German historians Hermann Mau and Helmut Krausnick argue in their part of *The Outbreak Of The Second World War: Design Or Blunder?* that the ". . . Russians seemed to have given much more serious thought to the conclusion of their pact with Hitler. Their official argument, that they merely wanted peace, is refuted by the Additional Protocol, which contained the draft for the partition of Poland. The truth is that by making the pact with Hitler, Stalin made the war possible. For a treaty between Russia and the Western Powers would have been the one means — at least at this stage — of preventing Hitler from setting the world alight. But faced with the alternative of a pact with the West or a pact with Hitler, Stalin chose the latter. Hitler had more to offer: a chance for the Soviet Union to extend its influence in the East European states which the Treaty of Versailles had established in Russia's absence as an anti-Soviet *cordon sanitaire*. The pact with the West would have obliged the Soviet Union to defend these states." (Edited by John L. Snell, Boston, D.C. Heath, 1962)

The official Soviet history of the period is quoted by Nicholas Bethell. It is devoted to justifying Russian aggression in the west, and falsely declares that "the workers of Western Byelorussia and Western Ukraine welcomed the Red Army ecstatically," while the peasants allegedly "came out with bread and salt," traditionally a sign of welcome and respect. Bethell notes that the history states, incorrectly, that "the Soviet move took place 'after the flight of the Polish Government into Rumania and the collapse of the Polish State. The Red Army was only fulfilling its international duty, affording the only assistance possible in the given circumstances to its neighbouring people. It was a campaign aimed at forestalling the capture of the Western Ukraine and Western Byelorussia by the German fascist forces.' The history does not explain, nor has any Soviet printed work, that the German-Soviet partition of Poland was agreed, and the Red Army advance into Poland was envisaged, in a document signed by Molotov and Ribbentrop." (*The War Hitler Won*)

With Poland crushed, von Ribbentrop again traveled to the Kremlin and received Stalin's offer to exchange all of the highly populated area of Poland east of the Vistula in return for Lithuania. Germany agreed, and then ordered the withdrawal of all of the German population from the Baltic States, knowing Stalin's repression of the people there would be brutal. Ribbentrop was told in Moscow, reports Trumbell Higgins, "that the Soviets demanded all the Polish oil fields (despite their own vast, and the Reich's negligible, resources in this respect) but also that they intended a military occupation of selected Latvian and Estonian bases in the immediate future." (*Hitler And Russia*, New York, Macmillan, 1966)

So Lithuania, Latvia, and Estonia went to Stalin, as did key sections of Poland, and the map of Eastern Europe was remade between the dictators by agreement. William L. Shirer has described the making of the butchers' agreement in Moscow:

"Dividing up Eastern Europe took quite a bit of intricate drawing of maps, and after three and a half more hours of negotiations on the afternoon of September 28, followed by a state banquet at the Kremlin, Stalin and Molotov excused themselves in order to confer with a Latvian delegation they had summoned to Moscow. Ribbentrop dashed off to the opera house to take in an act of *Swan Lake*, returning to the Kremlin at midnight for further consultations about maps and other things. At 5 A.M. Molotov and Ribbentrop put their signatures to a new pact officially called the 'German-Soviet Boundary and Friendship Treaty' while Stalin once more beamed on, as a German official later reported, 'with obvious satisfaction.' He had reason to." (*The Rise And Fall Of The Third Reich*)

The Kremlin was in high spirits. Hitler aide Albert Speer reports in his memoirs that when Ribbentrop returned from Moscow with the pact containing the partition of Poland he sat at Hitler's table and "recounted that he had never felt so much at ease as among Stalin's associates: 'As if I were among old party comrades of ours, *mein Führer!*' " (*Inside The Third Reich*)

The Führer and the Vozhd were dividing spoils. The Russians now had only to move formally on Estonia, Latvia, Lithuania . . . and Finland. On the very day that Poland was partitioned, reflects historian Louis Snyder, "the Soviet Union, in flat violation of previous pledges, forced Estonia to sign a treaty permitting the U.S.S.R. to establish military garrisons and naval and air bases on Estonian soil. Shortly afterward came similar treaties with Latvia (October 5) and Lithuania (October 10) . . . . No one doubted that these were but preliminary steps to outright annexation." (*The War, A Concise History*, New York, Messner, 1960) Nevertheless Molotov contended: "We stand for scrupulous and punctilious observance of the pacts on the basis of complete reciprocity and we declare that all nonsense about Sovietizing the Baltic countries is only to the interest of our common enemy of anti-Soviet provocateurs." That was in October of 1939; Lithuania, Latvia, and Estonia were formally annexed the next summer.

Hitler was soon to show what his word was worth also. Exactly three months after the signing of the Nazi-Soviet agreement, the Führer told his senior officers he would attack the U.S.S.R. as soon as he could after dealing with Western Europe. Meanwhile the Führer was content to keep his backside covered, even to the point of making what seemed like enormous concessions to Stalin. As William Shirer puts it: "Hitler fought and won the war in Poland, but the greater winner was Stalin, whose troops scarcely fired a shot. The Soviet Union got nearly half of Poland and a stranglehold on the Baltic States. It blocked Germany more solidly than ever from two of its main longterm objectives: Ukrainian wheat and Rumanian oil, both badly needed if Germany was to survive the British blockade. Even Poland's oil region of Borislav-Drogobycz, which Hitler desired, was claimed successfully by Stalin, who graciously agreed to sell the Germans the equivalent of the area's annual production." (*The Rise And Fall Of The Third Reich*)

Finland was also on the Soviet Union's hit list, as we have noted, and as early as October of 1939 the Russians were putting pressure on the Finns to surrender a part of the Karelian Isthmus north of Leningrad and to grant them a naval base on the Finnish mainland, among other concessions. With the Russian demands, writes Louis Snyder, "as if by push-button control, the press in the U.S.S.R. and the Communist parrot-newspapers throughout the world opened a campaign of abuse against the Finns. How could the Finns be so obstinate in the face of reasonable, just, and fair demands? Were not the Finns aware, hinted *Pravda*, the official Soviet organ, that they might meet the fate of Poland? Headlines in the Russian newspapers screamed that the Finns were preparing to attack the Communist mainland. Since Moscow had caught cold, the New York *Daily Worker* promptly sneezed in sympathy." (*The War*)

But when negotiations broke down, and the Reds attacked little Finland in late 1939, they met with military catastrophe in what came to be called the Winter War. The world was inspired and amazed by the ferocious fighting of the invaded Finns, and the U.S.S.R. was even expelled from the League of Nations. But inevitably — facing Soviet forces outnumbering their own by fifty to one — Finland was forced to sue for peace in March of 1940, with Moscow then extracting even more than Stalin's previous demands. Perhaps twenty-five thousand Finns had been killed, but the Russians had lost as many as two hundred thousand dead and had been made to look both brutal and weak in the eyes of the world.

During the Winter War, on February 11, 1940, a Soviet-German economic agreement was signed, with the Russians thankful that the Nazis had remained "neutral on their side" in the conflict. This new deal would prove very helpful, said *Pravda*: "Present-day Germany is a highly-developed power requiring many raw materials; and these the Soviet Union can largely supply. We also are a great industrial power; nevertheless, we can do with certain forms of imported industrial equipment . . . . Our trade with Britain and France has dwindled, and the increase in our trade with Germany is only to be welcomed." *Pravda* for February 18, 1940, quoted a Hitler speech stating that after conquest of Poland there was "more to come." (*Russia At War*) Indeed there was.

While Stalin digested the other three Baltic States, Hitler moved against Denmark and Norway, then swept across the Low Countries, and allowed the Allies to evacuate from Dunkirk. Italy entered the war, with Mussolini aping Russia by stabbing the French in the back. By June of 1940, France had surrendered. Stalin, meanwhile, grabbed off parts of Romania for the U.S.S.R. But the partners Hitler and Stalin were still cautious of one another.

Communist spy chief Leopold Trepper, who was head of the ring known as the Red Orchestra (*Die Rote Kapelle*), was in 1940 on the continent obtaining firsthand knowledge of Hitler's military strategy. "He sped toward Dunkirk," writes Gilles Perrault, "with Forner's Panzer company and was an eyewitness to the fall of the town. In his pocket was a notebook crammed with facts and figures. He took particular interest in the Wehrmacht's method of bringing up reinforcements, in the part played by the Stukas, and in the tactics used by the Panzers to knock out the enemy's antitank defenses . . . . [T]he Big Chief sent an eighty-page report to Moscow, giving a detailed account of the new strategy which Hitler had devised and carried out: the Blitzkrieg." (*The Red Orchestra*, New York, Simon and Schuster, 1967) But the Communists were only being their usual suspicious selves, and Molotov heartily congratulated Hitler on the "splendid success achieved by the Wehrmacht" — the brilliantly led Army that would soon turn on Mother Russia.

After the French surrender the Moscow press boasted of Germany's peaceful Eastern Front, a result of the Nazi-Soviet Pact. Josef Stalin now worked even harder to please his ally Hitler and share in the spoils of conquest. As Comrade Roy Medvedev notes, "Stalin did not stop at 'friendship' with Hitler. In 1940 he entered negotiations concerning spheres of influence after the presumed defeat of Great Britian. These negotiations were begun on Hitler's initiative, since he wanted to divert Stalin's attention from German preparations for war against the U.S.S.R. And Stalin, to a certain extent, took the bait. He even agreed to negotiations concerning adherence of the U.S.S.R. to the Tripartite (Anti-Comintern) Pact. These negotiations were interrupted, though not by Stalin; Hitler simply stopped answering Stalin's letters on the subject." (*Let History Judge*)

Even as Nazi Germany made preparations to strike at the U.S.S.R., the Reds continued to supply Hitler. Between February 10, 1940, and June 22, 1941 — when the attack came — "Stalin had delivered to Hitler 1,500,000 tons of grain. The Soviet Union was thus Germany's principal supplier of grain. But not only rye, oats, and wheat had been sent across the bridges over the Bug. During the sixteen months of friendship Stalin had sent Germany, strictly according to their contract, nearly 1,000,000 tons of mineral oil, 2700 kilograms of platinum, and large quantities of manganese ore, chrome, and cotton." (*Hitler Moves East*) For his part, Hitler ordered on March 30, 1940, "that the deliveries of war materials to Russia receive top priority, over that of the Wehrmacht itself, which he knew to be on the eve of its assaults on Denmark, Norway, Holland, Belgium and France." (*Codeword Barbarossa*) So much for trade bringing peace, as today's Left is wont to suppose.

In fact, between the signing of the Nazi-Soviet Pact and June 22, 1941, the international Left was declaring with full voice that resistance to Hitler was an imperialist war and not a people's conflict. The Red Front known before the pact as the Hollywood Anti-Nazi League quickly evolved into the Hollywood League for Democratic Action. When Stalin was attacked the American Peace Mobilization, which was run by the Reds, was quickly changed into the American People's Mobilization. (See *The Fellow-Travellers*, David Caute.) The Communists in France, who had received permission from the invading Germans to continue publishing their journal *Le Humanité*, were not permitted to resist the invader until June 22, 1941, when *Russia* was attacked and the war was no longer "imperialist." As Sisley Huddleston put it in *France: The Tragic Years*, the attack on the Soviet Union marked "the date on which the Communists, or sympathizers with Communism, found themselves released from an equivocal position. They were free to serve Russia while incidentally serving France." (New York, Devin-Adair, 1955)

The Communists and fellow-travelers among American authors also found themselves with egg on their face. As Eugene Lyons recorded of one post-Pact congress: "Ignoring the 'capitalist lies' about Comrade Hitler's aggressive intentions against Führer Stalin, the muddled literati went all out in support of Moscow's 'peace' policy for the U.S.A. They passed resolutions condemning our 'war mongering' aid to Hitler's victims, supporting outlaw strikers in our defense plants and glorifying Stalin's genius in keeping out of the unsavory imperialist squabble. They indicated their adherence to the 'peace vigil' picket line maintained by the American Peace Mobilization around the White House . . . . But a fortnight later Hitler invaded Russia; Stalin's 'peace' diplomacy appeared in its true light as a ghastly and futile super-appeasement; and the party line on war was switched again!" (*The Red Decade*)

Harrison Salisbury reports that in the Kremlin "the Nazi attack sent Stalin into a state of psychic collapse which verged on nervous breakdown. He was confined to his room, unable or unwilling to participate."

It was clearly a time to let the Nazis and Communists — erstwhile partners in slaughter — claw one another to the death. But now it was Communist Russia that needed help, and that was a different matter! As Wisconsin Senator Robert La Follette predicted: "The American people will be told to forget the purges in Russia by the OGPU, the confiscation of property, the persecution of religion, the invasion of Finland, and the vulture role Stalin played in seizing half of prostrate Poland, all of Latvia, Estonia and Lithuania. These will be made to seem the acts of a 'democracy' preparing to fight Nazism." Former President Herbert Hoover warned that if we entered the conflict and were victorious over Hitler we would only win "for Stalin the grip of Communism on Russia and more opportunity for it to extend over the world." But we nonetheless did just that. The pro-Soviet propaganda was massive. And we even covered up the systematic butchery by the Reds of some fifteen thousand Poles in the Katyn Forest, including the execution of the cream of the Polish officer corps.

History has since shown that what Stalin couldn't get from Hitler, he got through concessions and negotiations with the West. Yet the fact remains that it was Stalin who made the war possible in 1939. And, as the post-war map indicated all too clearly, it was the Soviet Union for which the war was fought and won.

Chapter XVIII
Betraying Poland

STRATEGICALLY sited between Moscow and Berlin, Poland has over its long history been frequently partitioned. Though in the Fifteenth Century it reached from the Baltic to the Black Sea, it has been independent in this century for only the two decades preceding 1939. Of course, Poland has lately been much in the news, just as it was in 1939 when invasion by Nazi Germany and the Soviet Union ignited World War II. One recent dispute was said to be about how much "freedom" was to be allowed a labor group known as Solidarity, which was eventually outlawed. But Poland's problems result from yet another time in which dictators determined its fate as the Free World callously looked the other way.

The 1939 Hitler-Stalin Pact was not an agreement made in a hurry, as we pointed out in the previous chapter. Indeed, Paul Blackstock pointed out in his narrative *The Secret Road To World War Two*: "By the fall of 1936 Stalin had decided to make a deal with Hitler and began to speed up the purge of all internal *political* opposition. By December the *Yezhovschchina* (the 'time of Yezhov,' the Grand Inquisitor of the Great Purge) was well under way. The next step was to set in motion a covert operation which would justify the killing of his top *military* leadership, which in Stalin's sick delusional world might also conceivably stand in the way of his contemplated settlement with Hitler. This would be a most delicate piece of surgery requiring instruments that could cut both ways and injure the hands of the surgeon." (Chicago, Quadrangle Books, 1969)

In time, backed by the productive might of America, "surgeon" Stalin cut his pound of flesh. The U.S.S.R., reported Professor Louis L. Snyder, "emerged from the war with a gain of 262,533 square miles of territory and 22,162,000 more people. In Eastern Europe, where she had been sealed off by buffer states after World War I, the Soviet Union set up a series of satellite states dominated from Moscow — Poland, East Germany, Lithuania, Latvia, Estonia, Rumania, Bulgaria,

Czechoslovakia, and Albania, an area totaling 433,504 square miles with a population of 90,874,358.'' (*The War*)

The first step was for Stalin and Hitler to enter into a partnership and divide Europe, the Balkans, and the Middle East into spheres of influence. If this necessitated liquidation of onetime Bolshevik comrades, show trials, or even world war, so be it. The negotiating of the Nazi-Soviet agreement was, however, kept very private — even from the Soviet Commissariat of Foreign Affairs. As Walter Krivitsky commented in his 1939 book, *I Was Stalin's Agent*: "Since Stalin was executing his Old Bolshevik comrades as Nazi spies at the same time that he was himself conducting these secret negotiations with Hitler, they obviously could not be made widely known."

On September 29, 1939, after Poland had been attacked, German Foreign Minister Joachim von Ribbentrop "returned from his second Moscow conference with a German-Soviet frontier and friendship treaty which was to seal the fourth partition of Poland. At Hitler's table he recounted that he had never felt so much at ease as among Stalin's associates: 'As if I were among old party comrades of ours, *mein Führer!*' " (*Inside The Third Reich*) It had taken but eight days after the signing of the pact, on September 1, 1939, for the Nazis to attack Poland, and they were just outside Warsaw in a week's time. Molotov said that "Russia would move militarily 'within the next few days.' Earlier . . . the Soviet Foreign Commissar had officially congratulated the Germans 'on the entry of German troops into Warsaw.' " (*The Rise And Fall Of The Third Reich*) Moscow invaded from the east on September seventeenth, and Poland was pronounced dead on the twenty-eighth.

"A month later," reported a subsequent Prime Minister of Poland, "Molotov crowed over our downfall. Speaking before the Supreme Council of the U.S.S.R. on October 31, 1939, this vehement man hailed the united operations of his country and Germany that had conquered Poland and exclaimed: 'Nothing is left of that monstrous bastard of the Versailles Treaty.' " (*The Rape Of Poland*, Stanislaw Mikolajczyk, New York, Whittlesey House, 1948)

After the Nazis attacked the Soviet Union in 1941 a military agreement was reached between Moscow and Poland's Government in Exile; the Ribbentrop-Molotov line in Poland was announced dissolved; a Polish army was organized in the Soviet Union, though Poles were already fighting elsewhere; and, "amnesty" was announced for loyal Poles who had resisted Moscow in Soviet-occupied territory. "It now plainly became the task of Poland to aid to the best of its ability the same Red forces that had stabbed at our back in 1939, consumed the eastern half of our country, packed off about 250,000 of our troops to Russian prisoner-of-war camps and deported 1,500,000 Polish civilians to Russian slave camps." (*The Rape Of Poland*)

Oh yes, and Molotov now signed the Atlantic Charter which had been prepared by Winston Churchill and Franklin Roosevelt. Its First Point declared that signatories "seek no aggrandizement, territorial or other." This by a nation that had annexed the Baltic states, divided up Poland, and was thrown out of the League of Nations for invading Finland! "It would have been no more a mockery had Adolf Hitler, for a prize of fifty thousand tanks and twenty-five thousand airplanes, scribbled his signature on a paper saying he was dedicated to the sacred Judaic laws of the Talmud." (*Roosevelt's Road To Russia*, George N. Crocker, Chicago, Regnery, 1959)

After the Nazis turned on their former Soviet partners, Moscow allowed Poland's Government in Exile at London to communicate with and aid Poles in the U.S.S.R. But in late 1942, "as Poland stubbornly refused to cede territory [*to the Soviets*], such activities were progressively harassed. Poles in Russia were subjected to widespread persecution. Some who had been forcibly deported from their own homes were imprisoned because they could not show legal entry papers. Others were charged with spying and various other crimes. In November 1942, sixteen welfare delegates of the Polish embassy in Moscow were even being held on charges of spying for [*Allied*] Great Britain and the United States." (*'Twas A Famous Victory*, Benjamin Colby, New Rochelle, Arlington House, 1974)

The Poles even had to protest to the U.S. State Department about the tone of the broadcasts into Poland by the U.S. Office of War Information. "Such broadcasts, which we carefully monitored in London might well have emanated from Moscow itself." (*The Rape Of Poland*) You see, top Reds were running the show in Washington also. For example, Soviet agent Alger Hiss. Indeed, Hiss was later to comment on the Allied conference which sealed Poland's fate that "it is an accurate and not immodest statement to say that I helped formulate the Yalta agreement to some extent." Which helps to explain why it resulted in what has been described as the largest uprooting of persons in human history.

Roosevelt, however, had reassured Poland's exiled Prime Minister Mikolajczyk that he shouldn't worry. "Stalin doesn't intend to take freedom from Poland. He wouldn't dare do that because he knows that the United States government stands solidly behind you. I will see to it that Poland does not come out of this war injured." What F.D.R. did, without even consulting Polish leaders, was to agree to let the Reds take seventy thousand square miles of Polish territory. Indeed Roosevelt had told the Polish Premier that he *knew* "Stalin doesn't want to annihilate Poland.

Stalin knows that Poland has a strong position in the Allied camp, especially with the United States. I will see to it that Poland will not be hurt in this war and will emerge strongly independent.'' That was assuredly a lie.

And F.D.R. knew it. Just as he knew about the butchery by the Soviets of Poland's captive officer corps at the Katyn Forest in a deliberate genocide. President Roosevelt, reports George Crocker, ''was familiar with the outrages already committed. From Ciechanowski, Mikolajczyk, General Sikorski and others, he received unimpeachable evidence of what was taking place and being planned in eastern Europe. The gruesome facts of the Katyn massacre, which had wiped out fifteen thousand Polish officers who had been taken prisoner by the Russians in 1939 and whose whereabouts had been shrouded in mystery, had been laid on his desk; he was silent when the Kremlin angrily broke off relations with the Polish government in April, 1943, because the latter had appealed to the International Red Cross to investigate the Katyn murders. *** When a special intelligence report and documents and pictures attesting Russian guilt in the cold-blooded atrocity were brought to Roosevelt in the White House, he reacted with anger, not to the Russian murderers, but at those who had collected the facts, and he clamped the lid down tight.'' (*Roosevelt's Road To Russia*)

When former Pennsylvania Governor George Earle repeatedly laid the truth about the massacre before President Roosevelt, F.D.R. took advantage of the fact that Earle had a Naval commission, forbade him to mention the facts publicly, and ordered George Earle to Samoa. F.D.R. claimed it was only German propaganda.

In ironic fact, the horrible atrocity made excellent Axis propaganda. For instance, Polish troops fighting bravely in Italy were told by radio, ''Your land has been delivered into Stalin's hands . . . . You've been sold out to Moscow.'' Just so. Almost half of Poland's territory and a third of her population had been ceded secretly to the Kremlin by Roosevelt and Churchill. Having the western border moved into German territory was of little consolation.

Poland was to be split along the so-called Curzon line, very similar to the division drawn by Ribbentrop and Molotov. All under a secret deal whereby Stalin was actually given an even better arrangement from the Allies than he had gotten from Hitler in 1939! Polish Premier Mikolajczyk discovered this, to his horror, when he visited Moscow in 1944. He relates:

'' 'But all this was settled at Teheran!' he [*Molotov*] barked. He looked from Churchill to [*Averell*] Harriman, who were silent. I asked for details of Teheran. And then he added, still with his eyes on Churchill and the American Ambassador:

" 'If your memories fail you, let me recall the facts to you. We all agreed at Teheran that the Curzon line must divide Poland. You will recall that President Roosevelt agreed to this solution and strongly endorsed the line. And then we agreed that it would be best not to issue a public declaration about our agreement.'

"Shocked, and remembering the earnest assurances I had personally had from Roosevelt at the White House, I look at Churchill and Harriman silently begging them to call this damnable deal a lie. Harriman looked down at the rug. Churchill looked straight back at me.

" 'I confirm this,' he said quietly." (*The Rape Of Poland*)

The Soviets had but to keep this arrangement silent for three more weeks; or, as F.D.R. said, "for the time being," until the 1944 elections were over. (*The Roosevelt Myth*) Not only were there many American voters of Latvian, Lithuanian, and Estonian extraction to worry about, the President had told Stalin, "there were in the United States from six to seven million Americans of Polish extraction, and, as a practical man, he did not wish to lose their vote." (*'Twas A Famous Victory*)

At Teheran, Roosevelt had totally agreed to Stalin's demands, later formalized at Yalta and other conferences. In the meantime there was that fourth term to be won. In October 1944, Franklin D. Roosevelt finally had to receive a delegation of the American Polish Congress. Benjamin Colby reports that the President did this "before a large map of Poland showing boundaries as of before the war, which was taken by some as promising restoration of the old Poland. But Roosevelt's actual words were only glowing generalities. Rumblings of Polish-American disillusionment became so loud that the President was impelled to seek a second meeting with the spokesman of the White House conference, Charles Rozmarek, head of the Polish National Council. It was held in the President's private car, in Chicago, on an election trip in later October. According to Rozmarek, the President was more specific this time, saying he would uphold the principles of the Atlantic Charter and that these principles included the integrity of Poland. Rozmarek thereupon gave his pledge of support in the election, which was immediately publicized by the Democratic National Committee, and widely quoted in Polish language newspapers and the press just before the election." It apparently worked.

Roosevelt, of course, won that race. Prime Minister Churchill, on the other hand, was soon turned out of office. Churchill spoke with far more candor than F.D.R. Later, in his memoirs, he notes the haughty manner of the disposal of the historic city of Lvov, with its Fourteenth Century cathedrals, into the hands of dictator Stalin. "I was not prepared to make a great squawk about Lvov," recorded Churchill. Then there was Königsberg (now Kaliningrad), the capital of East Prussia, the ancient city where Immanuel Kant once taught. Writing of the conference at Teheran, Churchill reports, "Stalin then said that the Russians would like to have the warm-water port of Königsberg, and he sketched a possible line on the map." (*Closing The Ring*, Boston, Houghton Mifflin, 1951) What Stalin wanted, he got. When Polish Premier Mikolajczyk argued about acquiesence to this by the Moscow-appointed Lublin gang, Mr. Churchill ignored the fact that the World War was brought on by an attack on Poland and huffed that he "was not going to wreck the peace [*sic*] of Europe because of a quarrel between Poles." (*Defeat In Victory*, Jan Ciechanoswki, New York, Doubleday, 1947)

The redoubtable Churchill later wrote that after Hitler attacked the Poles in 1939: "The guarantee to Poland was supported by the leaders of all parties and groups in the [*British*] House. 'God helping, we can do no other,' was what I said." (*The Gathering Storm*, Boston, Houghton Mifflin, 1948) But by the time of the Potsdam conference in 1945, "when Churchill's turn came actually to meet with the Poles, he was appalled. 'I'm sick of the bloody Poles,' the Prime Minister said. 'I don't want to see them.' ✳✳✳ Just to add a final touch of cruelty, the Poles had no idea that the fate of Poland had already been settled in broad outline. . . ." (*Meeting At Potsdam*, Charles L. Mee Jr., New York, M. Evans & Company, 1975)

The earlier agreement at Yalta had broken Poland's back. Ambassador William C. Bullitt said of that Yalta agreement: " . . . no more unnecessary, disgraceful, and potentially disastrous document has ever been signed by a President of the United States." Arthur Bliss Lane, who served as the U.S. Ambassador to Poland from 1944 through 1947, called the Yalta agreement "a capitulation on the part of the United States and Great Britain to the views of the Soviet Union on the frontiers of Poland and the composition of the Polish Provisional Government of National Unity." (*I Saw Poland Betrayed*, Bobbs-Merrill, Indianapolis, 1948)

Even Churchill later called the consequences of Yalta a "tragedy on a prodigious scale." Yalta advisor Charles E. Bohlen, however, went so far in defense of this betrayal as to contend: "I do not presume to know what was going on in Roosevelt's mind, but from what he said at Yalta and from his actions there, I feel that he did everything he could to help the Poles." (*Witness To History: 1929-1969*, New York, Norton, 1973)

A more truthful Yalta observer, Admiral William Leahy, called the Polish arrangement at Yalta a "phony." This is, he said, "so elastic that the Russians can stretch it all the way from Yalta to Washington without technically breaking it.'' Even F.D.R. concurred.

The Soviets had already set up a phony Government under the Polish Communists. It was called the Lublin Committee or the Polish Committee of National Liberation. Anxious that the Lublin gang not be opposed, Moscow called for an uprising by the underground in Warsaw, which was still occupied by the Nazis. For four months, as the brave Poles fought the Nazis in the capital, the Soviets waited on the outskirts of the city, across the Vistula, to allow Hitler's troops to kill the best of the non-Communist resistance.* Finally, when the crushed Home Army was at last forced to surrender, Moscow denounced them as ''traitors.''

Franz Borkenau summarized in *European Communism*: ''From the beginning Stalin had fought a battle of extermination against any conceivable non-Communist Polish leadership; a battle starting with the extermination of many thousand captured Polish officers in 1941 (in Katyn and other camps), continuing . . . to the prompting and subsequent sabotage of the Warsaw rising in July 1944 (which led to the extermination of the best Polish forces, as was Stalin's intention), and to the kidnapping of all available Polish underground leaders in March 1945. . . . Between the Lublin committee and the Polish government-in-exile which enjoyed the loyalty of an overwhelming majority of Poles, there ensued a fierce struggle. Wherever the NKVD went, it exterminated the Home Army forces within its reach, *while simultaneously Roosevelt preached to the Polish leaders in exile the virtues of Stalin's Russia . . . .* Thus the men of Lublin became the rulers of Poland.'' (New York, Harper, 1953)

The top Red in the Lublin gang was one Boleslaw Bierut, who was in 1936 made head of the Polish Department of Moscow's secret police, and who had been responsible for sending scores of thousands of his countrymen to Siberia. After he became ''President,'' Bierut explained to Churchill, ''his Government did not want to stop people expressing political views, but they were anxious to avoid a lot of small parties . . . . Elections in Poland would be even more democratic than English ones and home politics would develop more and more harmoniously.'' (*Triumph And Tragedy*, Boston, Houghton Mifflin, 1953) What happened instead was that the heroic leaders of the anti-Nazi Underground, virtually all anti-Communists, were taken under false pretenses for trial in Moscow because of their alleged ''diversionary tactics in the rear of the Red Army.''

---

*Waiting with these troops was the present Polish dictator, Wojciech Jaruzelski.

Such was the treatment the Reds handed to their political adversaries in Poland that U.S. Ambassador Lane reported: "Despite the suffering which the Poles had endured under the Nazi occupation and especially in Warsaw, many of the Poles with whom we spoke amazingly admitted that they preferred Nazi occupation to their present plight. Under the Nazis, they said, there were great brutality, complete deprivation of liberty, and even murders, but at least the Nazis had matters well organized. If a Pole was arrested for political reasons, his family generally knew in what town, prison and cell he was confined. They knew that food could be sent to him on such and such a day, and when it was possible for him to receive visitors. Under the NKVD system, however, a person disappeared, usually clandestinely. If he was heard of again it was a stroke of good luck. In most cases there was no word from Russian or Polish authorities confirming the arrest of the unfortunate person or his fate. He might have been temporarily detained in a Polish prison; he might have been sent to a Siberian slave camp; or he might have been 'liquidated.' ✳✳✳

"In addition to the terror created in Poland by the returning Red Army, the newly formed Polish Security Police — Urzad Bezpieczenstwa, colloquially known as 'U.B.' — was making itself unpleasantly known. Like the NKVD, the Russian counterpart, the members of the U.B. were distinguished by blue collar tabs and hatbands. Many an arrest by these uniformed agents was witnessed by members of the American Embassy on the streets of Warsaw during those early days. Later, more subtle and terrifying methods were employed, such as arrests in the middle of the night; and the person arrested generally was not permitted to communicate with the outside world, perhaps for months, perhaps for all time." (*I Saw Poland Betrayed*)

And this was the Communist Government that was now given ninety million dollars in American aid at the insistence of the U.S. Department of State! The Red reaction was to become even more brutal. "In the Wroclaw region all members of the Polish Peasant Party's executive committee were arrested; some were tortured. In Bochnia the Security Police station became a house of horrors. Bartkowicz, commander of the station, who had worked closely with the Gestapo during the occupation and who had an unsavory record as a gangster before that, became the most feared of despots. On September 8, 1945, he murdered Jozef Kolokziej, of Bogucice; Wojciech Kaczmarczyk, underground hero and local chairman of our Peasant Party's youth movement *Wici*; Wladyslaw Kukiel, manager of a local dairy; and Stanislaw Mariasz, a Peasant party executive.

"Soon after, Bartkowicz tortured the mayor of Lapanow, Jan Jarotek, to pitilessly slow death in full view of the victim's son. He then ordered his torturers to seize Jozef Szydlowski, the Peasant Party's local executive committee member, whose tongue was cut out, fingernails ripped off, and eyes seared with a hot poker before he was finally shot." (*The Rape Of Poland*)

The "free and unfettered" elections promised for Poles were of course postponed until the Reds could fully consolidate their power. To do this the Communists "legalized the formation of a 'voluntary' citizen militia called 'ORMO,' which permitted them eventually to arm 120,000 hand-picked thugs and ex-convicts, who helped to expand and make more efficient the work of the Security Police." (*The Rape Of Poland*) Those "policemen" attacked students in Cracow who dared so much as to gather on Poland's National Day. Mr. Mikolajczyk reports that in Katowice the Security Police, "angered by the success of the meeting we had held a few days earlier, broke up a National Day parade, trampled our banners, and destroyed a tapestry of the Blessed Virgin. There were similar actions in Gliwice, Wloclawak, Inowroclaw, and Lublin."

The Soviets were not only staking a claim to Poland but to virtually the whole of central Europe. Yet the new U.S. President, Harry Truman, "felt that 'a good deal' of the new Russian claims were 'bluffs,' and he would not let them get away with such claims." For the most part, however, he did. When the so-called "Truman Doctrine" was finally announced, congressional critics pointed out that there was "no sense in giving aid to [*Communist-threatened*] Greece and Turkey while at the same time aid was being given to Poland, Hungary and other Russian-dominated countries. If communism was such a real threat to freedom, then why had Roosevelt and Truman made Russia an ally at Teheran, Yalta and Potsdam? Why had there been so many concessions? Why was the U.S. helping Russia and its satellites and at the same time Greece?" (*Harry S Truman And The Russians: 1945-1953*, Herbert Druks, New York, Speller, 1966)

The takeover in Poland now proceeded openly. The Reds ran the election commission and had one hundred thousand members of the Peasant Party arrested before balloting; children circulating campaign literature for candidates not approved by the Communists were beaten; censorship of the press was heavy; and, even former Nazis were used to help crush opposition to the Reds. When many Poles refused to sign a manifesto supporting the Communists, their housing and jobs were threatened. Indeed, reported Ambassador Lane, the secret police " . . . went further than merely threatening. Many cases of physical torture were reported to the Embassy. The Reds were not far behind the Gestapo in inventing refined brutalities. We learned of persons forced to remain during that unusually cold winter in icy water for two or three whole days in attempts to drive them to sign the manifesto. An unfortunate man stood this torture for seventy-two hours rather than agree to support the government ticket. Gangrene set in. Both feet were amputated.''

Soviet dictator Stalin had given his word, records Benjamin Colby, that the ''Communist Polish government would later hold 'free elections.' . . . [*Yet when*] the Yalta-promised elections were finally held in 1947, any remaining non-Communist influence had been extinguished by terrorism and murder.''

American Ambassador Arthur Bliss Lane resigned in 1947 to tell Poland's story to a world that did not want to hear it; and former Prime Minister Mikolajczyk escaped the same year to relate his account. It was the same story that is again being repeated today: that of a Communist jackboot crushing the face of the Polish people.

Millions and millions of Poles, noted former Premier Mikolajczyk, who ''underwent fantastic hardship while remaining in the Allied camp during the war, and who were promised freedom, are now wholly enslaved by what amounts to not even five percent of the population. The Poles sought to vote that yoke off their backs, and the vote was stolen. They looked to the Big Three to carry out the solemn promises made to what President Roosevelt once called 'the inspiration of the nations — Poland.' But those pacts have been callously broken by Russia with only 'paper protests' from the remaining parties to the pledges . . . .''

There was, and unfortunately still is, an undeniable pattern of betrayal by the West. What does a captive people have to do to earn our support? Whatever it is, millions of captive peoples the world over are watching to see how we respond. Given reason to believe that we will assist their liberation with more than words, there are not enough troops in the Warsaw Pact to keep them from throwing off their chains and destroying their Communist masters.

Chapter XIX

First Two Terms Of
Franklin D. Roosevelt

PROMISES, say the latter-day incarnations of Franklin Delano Roosevelt, are what America is all about — which should remind us of the value of a Roosevelt pledge.

One recalls with irony the promises of the 1932 Democratic Party Platform upon which F.D.R. was elected. At its heart, it solemnly committed the candidate to:

"1. An immediate and drastic reduction of governmental expenditures by abolishing useless commissions and offices, consolidating departments and bureaus and eliminating extravagance, to accomplish a saving of not less than 25 percent in the cost of the Federal Government; and we call upon the Democratic party in the States to make a zealous effort to achieve a proportionate result.

"2. Maintenance of national credit by a federal budget annually balanced on the basis of accurate executive estimates within revenues, raised by a system of taxation levied on a principle of ability to pay."

One need not be a meticulous student of history to know that this platform was soon chopped up into firewood as Franklin Roosevelt set out, in the words of his aide Harry Hopkins, to "spend and spend, tax and tax, and elect and elect." (*Memoirs*, Arthur Krock, New York, Funk & Wagnalls, 1968)

It now seems incredible that F.D.R. was sold in 1932 as a Conservative nationalist. The "isolationist sentiment in the Democratic Party became so strong that in 1932," recalls Barnard College Professor Basil Rauch, "it was politically expedient for Roosevelt as a presidential candidate to reject United States entry in the League [*of Nations*], and this he did before he was nominated." (*Roosevelt From Munich To Pearl Harbor*, New York, Creative Age Press, 1950)

The object was, at all subsequent cost to credibility, to get elected. It was recognized that Roosevelt's predecessor, Herbert Hoover, was perceived as a "Liberal" and an internationalist; Roosevelt placed himself at the other pole. He promised to help the farmer, for instance, without it costing "the Government any money," declaring that unlike Mr. Hoover, he would not "keep the Government in business." The Democrat candidate sounded just like the populists of today.

Biographer William E. Leuchtenburg notes that F.D.R. promised to "increase aid to the unemployed, but he would slash federal spending. On this one point he was specific; he would cut government spending 25 percent. At Sioux City, Iowa, in September [*1932*], Governor Roosevelt stated: 'I accuse the present Administration of being the greatest spending Administration in peace time in all our history. It is an Administration that has piled bureau on bureau, commission on commission, and has failed to anticipate the dire needs and the reduced earning power of the people.' In Pittsburgh the next month, he declared: 'I regard reduction in Federal spending as one of the most important issues of this campaign. In my opinion, it is the most direct and effective contribution that Government can make to business.' " (*Franklin D. Roosevelt And The New Deal*, New York, Harper & Row, 1963)

Candidate Roosevelt explained that he opposed massive public spending as well as government borrowing because "a government, like any family, can for a year spend a little more than it earns, but you and I know that a continuation of that means the poorhouse." America "cannot sugar-coat the pill," F.D.R. preached, for the U.S. must "have the courage to stop borrowing and meet the continuing deficits." Nor would public works "relieve the distress," for they can be only "a stopgap." (*Public Papers And Addresses Of Franklin D. Roosevelt, 1928-36*, New York, Random House, 1938)

This is not to say that before he was elected F.D.R. was any sort of Conservative, for if he had been he would not have received the influential backing needed to win the Democratic nomination. The rhetoric was strictly bait for the Depression-wracked electorate. Here was Governor Roosevelt blistering Herbert Hoover for the very things he would himself escalate, including "fostering regimentation without stint or limit." As far back as March of 1930, this subsequent father of the Brain Trust proclaimed:

"The doctrine of regulation and legislation by 'master minds' in whose judgment and will all the people may gladly and quietly acquiesce has been too glaringly apparent at Washington these last ten years. Were it possible to find master minds so unselfish, so willing to decide unhesitatingly against their own personal interests or private prejudices, men almost Godlike in their ability to hold the scales of justice with an even hand, such a government might be in the interest of the country. But there are none such on our political horizon, and we cannot expect a complete reversal of all the teachings of history.''

History has since taught that with Franklin D. Roosevelt the United States got more of the same. Much more.

And Roosevelt knew exactly what he was doing. One remembers that this man who campaigned against Wall Street in 1932 was himself a creature of Wall Street — a banker and speculator who directed eleven corporations, held two law partnerships, and was president of a giant trade association. Thus it was not from idle speculation that shortly after becoming President he wrote to ''Colonel'' Edward Mandell House, the conspirator who was influential in founding the Council on Foreign Relations: ''The real truth of the matter is, as you and I know, that a financial element in the larger centers has owned the Government ever since the days of Andrew Jackson — and I am not wholly excepting the Administration of W.W. [*Woodrow Wilson, House's "alter ego"*]. The country is going through a repetition of Jackson's fight with the Bank of the United States — only on a far bigger and broader basis.'' (*The Coming Of The New Deal*, Arthur M. Schlesinger Jr., Boston, Houghton Mifflin, 1958)

The fact is, however, that F.D.R. was himself a creation and partisan of this ''financial element,'' for it helped re-elect him Governor of New York in 1930 and started him on the road to the White House. It included William Woodin (later F.D.R.'s Secretary of the Treasury, then of the Federal Reserve Bank of New York), Colonel House, Henry Morganthau, the Lehman family, and Joseph P. Kennedy (later Ambassador to the Court of St. James's).

So Franklin Roosevelt was hardly an enemy of the Establishment. Indeed, as one Roosevelt biographer assures us, F.D.R. had ''personal confidence in the banking community.'' For example, explains Frank Freidel: ''Herbert Lehman was one of the soundest as well as politically liberal of Wall Street bankers; in banking matters Roosevelt seems to have followed Lehman's lead, and that was to cooperate as far as possible with the banking titans.'' (*The Triumph*, Boston, Little, Brown, 1956) Others to whom Roosevelt looked solicitously were General Motors' vice president John J. Raskob and the legendary millionaire Bernard Baruch. Whereupon, observes Arthur Schlesinger, ''they naturally expected influence in shaping the party's organization and policy.'' (*The Crisis Of The Old Order*, Boston, Houghton Mifflin, 1958) Naturally.

In fact F.D.R. could not have been elected without Baruch's aid. One of the wealthy Wall Streeter's former associates, General Hugh ''Ironpants'' Johnson — who was head of the fascist-like National Recovery Administration (N.R.A.) — cited the millionaire's ''effective role'' in his book *The Blue Eagle From Egg To Earth*, reporting: "Headquarters just didn't have any money. Sometimes they couldn't even pay the radio bill for the candidate's speeches. They had practically nothing to carry on the campaign in the critical state of Maine. Every time a crisis came, [*Baruch*] either gave the necessary money, or went out and got it." (New York, Doubleday, 1935)

There were a number of ironies from the start. For instance, a deadlock of the 1932 Democratic Convention had threatened, raising the possibility of a compromise being made and the prize going to Al Smith or Newton Baker. Key delegations were controlled by California's William G. McAdoo, former Secretary of the Treasury and a close friend of Bernard Baruch, and House Speaker John Nance Garner of Texas. Hoping to break the logjam, F.D.R.'s floor strategist James Farley telephoned William Randolph Hearst at San Simeon to warn him that Smith might be nominated and to work out a deal. Smith was a Conservative in most respects, but he was a backer of the League of Nations and thus anathema to Hearst. F.D.R. idolater John Gunther innocuously remarks: Hearst "didn't like Roosevelt but he hated Smith. Exactly what Hearst said to Farley — and to others who got through to him on the telephone — has never been revealed fully." (*Roosevelt In Retrospect*, New York, Harper & Brothers, 1950) The upshot was that at Hearst's insistence Roosevelt was thus nominated to block a presumed internationalist. McAdoo turned California to F.D.R. and Garner released Texas. McAdoo was offered a Cabinet post, which he refused; and Garner was nominated for Vice President.

It was the end for Al Smith, an honorable man of Conservative principles, and his supporters were none too happy. The galleries, observes William Manchester, "packed with Smith men, erupted in rage. Smith's delegates refused to make the party choice unanimous; instead they ran around tearing up Roosevelt posters. Will Rogers said, 'Ah! They was Democrats today. They fought, they fit, they split and adjourned in a dandy wave of dissension. That's the old Democratic spirit.' " (*The Glory And The Dream*, Volume I, Boston, Little, Brown, 1974)

In such a climate Roosevelt might still have been stopped except for a gang of Big Business insiders who were enemies of Free Enterprise. H.I. Harriman, president of the U.S. Chamber of Commerce, was their spokesman in 1931 when he said: "A freedom of action which might have been justified in the relatively simple life of the last century cannot be tolerated today, because the unwise action of one individual may adversely affect the lives of thousands. We have left the period of extreme individualism and are living in a period in which the national economy must be recognized as a controlling factor." (*As We Go Marching*) Business prosperity and employment, claimed Harriman, "will be best maintained by an intelligently planned business structure." And any dissenting businessman would be "treated like any maverick . . . . They'll be roped, and branded, and made to run with the herd." Such super-rich collectivists viewed the mass of men as dumb animals, which is why the economist for the National Industrial Conference Board was on target when he said big business was ready for an "economic Mussolini."

It certainly got one in philosophy as well as style. The latter was as phony as the former. In his inaugural speech, F.D.R. plagiarized Henry David Thoreau ("Nothing is so much to be feared as fear"); the very term "New Deal" was taken without credit from Stuart Chase's book of the same name; and, even the reference to "the forgotten man" was plagiarized from the great William Graham Sumner. But it was Mussolini who was the man of the hour, and Roosevelt was moving in the direction of fascism. The New Deal's centerpiece was "borrowed" from Mussolini's own medieval models as recently proposed in such forms as the Swope Plan, named after General Electric boss Gerard Swope, calling for cartel rule which openly imitated fascism.

While it was from the genesis of the Swope Plan that the Blue Eagle of the N.R.A. was hatched, such collectivist ideas had first been introduced into our own country in the Twenties. According to Murray N. Rothbard in *America's Great Depression*, it was economic interventionism and manipulation of the money supply that had brought on the Depression which propelled Roosevelt to the White House.

Professor Rothbard reports that one of "the most important supporters of the cartellization idea was Bernard M. Baruch, Wall Street financier. Baruch was influential not only in the Democratic Party, but in the Republican as well, as witness the high posts the Hoover Administration accorded to Baruch's protégés, Alexander Legge and Eugene Meyer Jr. As early as 1925, Baruch, inspired by his stint as chief economic mobilizer in World War I, conceived of an economy of trusts, regulated and run by a Federal Commission, and in the spring of 1930, Baruch proposed to the Boston Chamber of Commerce a 'Supreme Court of Industry.' [*As it happens, on May Day.*] McAdoo was Baruch's oldest friend in government; and Swope's younger brother, Herbert Bayard Swope, was Baruch's closest confidant."

These insiders sought to fix prices and avoid competition. Friendly commentators attribute altruism to such men. Gerard Swope, one observer reminds us, had worked with Jane Addams at Hull House. Miss Addams, not so coincidentally, has since been identified as a secret member of the Communist Party by Maurice Malkin, a charter member of that body. The fact is that these collectivists were conspirators who "shared a common revulsion against the workings of a competitive, individualistic, laissez-faire economy." (*Franklin D. Roosevelt And The New Deal*)

Herbert Hoover had his faults, to be sure, but he would not buy the conspirators' Swope Plan, so Wall Street switched its support to F.D.R. in 1932. Nor was Hoover exaggerating when he called the Son of Swope — which is what the N.R.A. was — a "fascist" program. In fact, when Baruch's friend General Johnson took over N.R.A. he presented each Cabinet member with a copy of a book by an Italian Fascist. Secretary of Labor Frances Perkins, for example, received a Fascist handbook from the General entitled *The Corporate State*. And when General Johnson left N.R.A. "he invoked what he called the 'shining name' of Mussolini. . . ." (*The Coming Of The New Deal*)

As F.D.R.'s predecessor pointed out in his memoirs, referred to earlier, during the 1932 Presidential campaign H.I. Harriman of the Chamber of Commerce "urged that I agree to support these proposals, informing me that Mr. Roosevelt had agreed to do so. I tried to show him that this stuff was pure fascism; that it was merely a remaking of Mussolini's 'corporate state' and refused to agree to any of it. He informed me that in view of my attitude, the business world would support Roosevelt with money and influence. That for the most part, proved true."

When Hoover lost in a landslide, Roosevelt refused to do anything during the interregnum to stop the growing banking crisis — being advised to take over the Presidency when things were at their worst. The President-elect and the outgoing President looked at things differently, observed John T. Flynn in his definitive and critical political biography: "Hoover was talking about saving the banks and the people's savings in them. Roosevelt was thinking of the political advantage in a complete banking disaster under Hoover. Actually, on February 25, Hoover received a message from James Rand that [*F.D.R. Brain Truster*] Rexford Tugwell had said the *banks would collapse in a couple of days and that is what they wanted*."

Banks in most states were closed when F.D.R. took over the Presidency and declared a banking "holiday." This was the beginning of the historic Hundred Days which set the mood of the New Deal, and during which fifteen far-reaching laws were rushed through an obedient Congress. These measures included: the Emergency Banking Act, involving the printing of two million dollars in new currency; the Economy Act, calling for cutting of federal expenses by twenty-five percent, shortly negated by the N.R.A. and a $3,300,000,000 deficit; the creation of the Civilian Conservation Corps, paying one million persons a dollar a day to do such things as plant trees; abandonment of the gold standard as well as abrogation of the gold clause in public and private contracts; creation of a national Welfare system under the Federal Emergency Relief Act; establishment of the Agricultural Adjustment Administration, which in a hungry nation would pay farmers not to grow food and would slaughter millions of young pigs as "surplus"; a move by the federal government into the power business through the Tennessee Valley Authority Act; establishment of federal regulation of Wall Street to the great benefit of Roosevelt's friends; refinancing of mortgages of homes and farms; establishment of a federal Coordinator of Transportation; federal guarantee of small bank deposits; and, institution of fascist "chartering" of business under the N.R.A. Oh yes, and beer was legalized. Thanks, one might say, we needed that.

In June the President signed the largest peacetime appropriations bill ever passed, saying more history was being made that day than in any "one day of our national life." To which Oklahoma Senator Thomas Gore added: "During all time." In One Hundred Days, F.D.R. ran up a larger deficit than the "spendthrift" Hoover had produced in two years. All by design. "It is simply inevitable," F.D.R. wrote to Colonel House, "that we must inflate." He wrote the radical Farmers' Union: "I am just as anxious as you are to give the dollar less purchasing power." (*The Coming Of The New Deal*)

Candidate Roosevelt had only a few months before cried: "Stop the deficits! Stop the deficits!" But as John Flynn recorded: "That deadly thing, the deficit, which, as he had said was at the bottom of all our woes and which stemmed from big government and extravagant government, was not slain as Roosevelt had proposed. Instead it was adopted and fed and fattened until it grew to such proportions that Hoover began to look like a niggard. The theory that relief should be carried on by the states was abandoned and all forms of relief were carried on by public loans, adding to the national debt. The idea of useful public works was abandoned in favor of hurriedly devised 'make-work' which was nothing more than a disguised dole.

"The 'spendthrift' Hoover had increased his expenditures by 50 per cent in four years over the 1927 level. In four years Mr. Roosevelt increased his 300 per cent over the 1927 level to 100 per cent over Hoover's." The deficit was not reduced as promised, of course, but stood at the end of his first term at fifteen billion dollars.

General Johnson, meanwhile, was hurrying to subject our nation's industries to the claws of his Blue Eagle "Codes." We have gone, he admitted, "to extreme measures to get them under it . . . ." First comes an "agreement," then "the phase of disciplining these people begins," he said. Those who wouldn't go along with federal dictates would "get a sock right on the nose." Literally. Take, for example, the tactics of Sidney Hillman, a union leader later exposed as a Communist by Maurice Malkin.* Sidney ran N.R.A. enforcement police in the garment industry with federal blessing.

And how he did run things. "They roamed through the garment district like storm troopers," recalled early New Deal supporter John Flynn. "They could enter a man's factory, send him out, line up his employees, subject them to minute interrogation, take over his books on the instant. Night work was forbidden. Flying squadrons of these private coat-and-suit police went through the district at night, battering down doors with axes looking for men who were committing the crime of sewing together a pair of pants at night."

This report is not hyperbolic. General Hugh Johnson snarled, "May God have mercy on the man or group of men who attempt to trifle with this bird" — the Blue Eagle of the N.R.A. A New Jersey tailor became famous when he was arrested, tried, fined and jailed because he had pressed a suit for thirty-five cents, undercutting the N.R.A. Code price of forty cents. The Codes attempted to cover everything . . . even ecdysiasts. Yes, Code 348 for the Burlesque Theatrical Industry restricted (to four) the number of stripteases that might be performed per production.

The top aides to General Johnson in all this dangerous nonsense were bigwigs from Standard Oil of New Jersey, General Electric, and Filene's of Boston. Or as Antony C. Sutton has summarized: "The peak of the Roosevelt National Recovery Administration consisted of the president of the largest electrical corporation, the chairman of the largest oil company, and the representative of the most prominent financial speculator in the United States." (*Wall Street And FDR*)

Then there was the radical Agricultural Adjustment Act (A.A.A.), so structured that a Representative from Massachusetts feared: "We are on our way to Moscow." Another Congressman, from Illinois, declared: "The bill before the House is more bolshevistic than any law or regulation existing in Soviet Russia." Which wasn't far off. Administration of the Agriculture Department was being manipulated by the notorious Harold Ware cell, including such Communists as Lee Pressman, John Abt, Nathan Witt, Nathaniel Weyl, and Alger Hiss. They were not the only Reds now making policy by a long shot. But they cranked out schemes that had us killing pigs while importing lard; both burning and importing

---

*Hillman in time became the second most important figure in American politics as F.D.R. said "Clear it with Sidney." It was he who cleared the choice of Harry Truman as F.D.R.'s 1944 running-mate.

oats; and, paying for the reduction of corn production while importing thirty million bushels of that commodity.

Eventually the N.R.A., the A.A.A., and a number of other creatures of radical legislation were found by the Supreme Court to be unconstitutional, though enough of the New Deal remained that one Justice warned that the U.S. Constitution was now "gone." (*Roosevelt: The Lion And The Fox*, James MacGregor Burns, New York, Harcourt, Brace, 1956) The President's response was to attempt to retire Justices of the High Court who respected the Constitution and to appoint new ones willing to let him do as he pleased. It was a blatant attempt to pack the Supreme Court he now contemptuously referred to as the Nine Old Men. The arrogant President had gone too far, and even his sycophants in the Congress would not go along.

Unfortunately, within "two and a half years after the rejection of the Court measure, Roosevelt had named five of his own appointees to the nine-man bench: [*Hugo*] Black, Stanley Reed, Felix Frankfurter, William O. Douglas, and Frank Murphy. The new Court — the 'Roosevelt Court' as it was called — greatly extended the area of permissible national regulation of the economy . . . ." (*Franklin D. Roosevelt And The New Deal*)

But instead of stimulating the economy, the New Deal prolonged the agony. The 1934 national income was even ten billion dollars less than in the Depression year of 1931. "Most ominous of all," admits F.D.R. admirer Arthur Schlesinger, "while the number of unemployed had declined fairly steadily from 1933, nearly 10 million persons — almost one-fifth of the labor force — were still out of jobs. 'It seems to me,' Henry Morgenthau, Jr., the Secretary of the Treasury, said in 1935, 'that we are not making any headway and the number of unemployed is staying more or less static.' No one knew this any better than Franklin Roosevelt. 'The unemployment problem' he wrote an English friend in February 1935, 'is solved no more here than it is with you.' " (*The Politics Of Upheaval*) There were fluctuations, but when the war started in Europe the number of unemployed in the United States was still virtually the same as when F.D.R. took office.

The people were terrified. The Congress they sent to Washington in 1934 was even more radical than its predecessor, and the President was able to get approval of five more far-reaching bills in the so-called Second Hundred Days, including the Wagner Labor Relations Act; a modified A.A.A.; the Social Security Act; and, a controversial tax bill that established inheritance taxes, gift taxes, and graduated provisions for corporate taxation. With a radical majority in the Congress, analyzed James M. Burns, Roosevelt's fanaticism had "resulted in an even more important array of measures than those of the first Hundred Days." More important if you are building socialism.

As the Socialist Party leader Norman Thomas was to complain: "What cut the ground pretty completely from under us . . . was Roosevelt in a word. You don't need anything more." In any event, thanks largely to his brilliant use of radio, the popularity of the President remained high. His adulteries, well known to the press, were kept under wraps. And many Americans did not even realize he was crippled, as there was a virtual ban on films or photos showing him being carried about and propped up to make his speeches. "Many a hapless cameraman, who knew nothing of the ban," recalled veteran *Chicago Tribune* journalist Walter Trohan, "had his box smashed by alert Secret Service men when he attempted to take a picture of the President being lifted from his limousine." (*Political Animals*, New York, Doubleday, 1975)

Meanwhile, F.D.R. rode roughshod over the civil liberties of his opponents and critics. As his son John admitted during the Watergate hubbub: "I can't understand all the commotion in this case. Hell, my father just about invented bugging. Had them spread all over, and thought nothing of it."

In 1936, despite the continuing economic disaster, F.D.R. carried every state but Maine and Vermont. Playing a growing role (including contribution of a million 1936 dollars) was the Communist-infested C.I.O. The Communists had been ordered to infiltrate the labor movement and work against F.D.R.'s enemies. Roosevelt was now very friendly with Moscow, having arranged diplomatic recognition of the Soviet dictatorship with Maxim Litvinov in 1933. Those who had led him to this unpopular move were old friends among the Establishment insiders. At a farewell dinner for Litvinov at the Waldorf-Astoria, "executives of the House of Morgan, the Pennsylvania Railroad, the Chase Manhattan Bank, and other firms feted the Soviet emissary. Thomas Watson, president of International Business Machines, asked every American, in the interest of good relations, to 'refrain from making any criticism of the present form of Government adopted by Russia.' " (*Franklin D. Roosevelt And The New Deal*)

The Communists now saw Roosevelt as a useful friend. Previously the Communist Party, U.S.A., had systematically attacked F.D.R. as a "fascist . . . financial dictator," given to "shameless demagogy." Then Party boss Earl Browder was called to Moscow and told to change his tune, whereupon Comrade Browder announced that F.D.R. was a savior "keeping our country on the path of progressive and diplomatic development . . . ." (*The Red Decade*, Eugene Lyons) Such hosannas were sung until the Nazi-Soviet Pact of 1939. Indeed the Reds and fellow-travelers were seen by F.D.R.'s strategists as important to his re-election in 1936, acting not only through their bases in organized labor but through the so-called Non-Partisan League and the American Labor Party in New York.

During this period the President turned a deaf ear to complaints about Reds in his Administration — after all, he told Congressmen Martin Dies, some of them were his best friends. For instance there was young Alger Hiss — who F.D.R. was reliably informed in 1938 was a Soviet spy. The President did not want to hear about such things, explains Maurice Malkin, "perhaps because there were leftists and Communists among his advisors and cabinet: Harry Hopkins, Albert R. William, Harold Ickes, Lauchlin Currie, Nathan Gregory Silvermaster, Harry Dexter White — not to mention his chiefs in the WPA, where Communists were in charge or control of the most important projects . . . . [M]ost national projects were under Communist supervisors. During the international crisis FDR was too busy with his leftist advisors, building up his reputation as the 'savior of our country,' to notice that the Communists had infiltrated most Departments, including the National Labor Relations Board, the Justice Department, the State Department, the Treasury Department and even the Army, Navy and Defense Departments. The First Lady of the Land, Eleanor Roosevelt, was busy sponsoring Communist agents . . . ." (*Return To My Father's House*) In fact Eleanor's young radical friend, Joe Lash, was sleeping in the White House . . . in Abraham Lincoln's bed.

By 1938 the economy was worse. The public Debt of twenty-two billion dollars in 1932 had grown to thirty-seven billion. Taxes had meanwhile doubled, and the President was trying to "purge" the Conservative Democrats who opposed his radical programs as disasters. He would brook no opposition. Harry Hopkins "had pulled together a council of liberals, including Corcoran, Ickes, and the President's son and secretary, James Roosevelt, to explore the possibility of purging the party of its conservatives. Dubbed the 'elimination committee,' they wished not only to discipline party irregularity but to assure liberal control of the 1940 Democratic convention." (*Franklin D. Roosevelt And The New Deal*)

That wasn't the half of it. House Rules Committee Chairman John J. O'Connor told the Senate Judiciary Committee that, during 1938 and 1939, Communist Party boss Earl Browder was a frequent guest in, and had immediate access to, the White House. "In fact, during the President's 'purge' of 1938, Browder directed purge operations from the White House, from which he telephoned instructions, from time to time."

The purge failed. In the Democratic primaries the Conservatives defeated the "Liberals" in all but one election in which the President had been involved. And the G.O.P. was making a comeback. (*Roosevelt From Munich To Pearl Harbor*) The Roosevelt magic was sinking in the wake of the lingering Depression. At this point it seemed all but certain that nothing could assure F.D.R.'s re-election for a third term. Nothing, that is, short of war.

Chapter XX

F.D.R. At War

THE OUTBREAK of World War II assured the salvation of the New Deal and virtually guaranteed the re-election of Franklin Delano Roosevelt. The President's "purge" of Conservative Democrats had failed; at least ten million Americans were unemployed; and, in his own state of New York, a National League to Oppose the Third Term for President had been incorporated. In December of 1938, a Gallup poll found seven out of ten voters opposed to returning F.D.R. to the White House. (*Never Again: A President Runs For A Third Term*, Herbert S. Parmat and Marie B. Hecht, New York, Macmillan, 1968) Three out of ten did favor the President's re-election, of course. One of them was H.L. Mencken, who opined that Roosevelt "ought to be made to bury his own dead horse."

The President was to keep his cards close to his vest throughout 1939, but when the shooting started in Europe it became even more likely he would seek another term. Before Poland was dismembered by Hitler and Stalin, Roosevelt had reconciled himself to choosing his successor, though he never publicly admitted this lest he reduce his political leverage. Mrs. Roosevelt's intimate friend, Joseph P. Lash, has noted that the President was reluctant to run because of "his conviction that he would have more trouble with Congress in a third term than he had had in his second term. He so advised Sen. George Norris, the Nebraska progressive known as the father of TVA and an enthusiastic advocate of a third term. FDR told Tom Corcoran while working on his annual message to Congress that he felt he had 'probably gone as far as he can on domestic questions.' " (*Roosevelt And Churchill: 1939-1941*, New York, Norton, 1976)

"If the war had not begun in Europe," agrees historian T.R. Fehrenbach, "it is very doubtful if Franklin Roosevelt would, or could, have run for a tradition-breaking third term. There was no groundswell of sentiment for such a term before September 1939. Actually, there was enormous opposition to it in the Democratic Party." (*F.D.R's Un-declared War: 1939 To 1941*, New York, David McKay Company, 1967) But the shooting changed all that. The President would be re-elected because he promised to keep us out of the war and the people believed him.

The Anglophile Roosevelt was anything but neutral, however, and he soon found it would take some doing to drag the country into the conflict. The people were not reacting as he had predicted hopefully to King George in June of 1939, when he said: "If London was bombed, U.S.A. will come in."

Not everyone was duped by the President's ruses. In September of 1939, Roosevelt declared: "This Nation will remain a neutral nation." And *The Nation* magazine, at the time against intervention because Stalin had made an ally of Hitler, observed: "Is the Roosevelt Administration neutral? Certainly not. Is there any chance of the United States to stay out of another world war? Practically none. Will the Roosevelt program of liberal reform go on in the event of a general war? It will not. Would the outbreak of war mean a third term for President Roosevelt? Probably." Irresistible!

There was still the Democratic Convention to keep in mind, and the problem of how he would aid the Allies when less than eight percent of the country in the summer of 1940 thought we should join the conflict. Fancy footwork was required. An admiring Joseph Lash remarks: "Roose-velt, in the winter and spring of 1940, was walking not one but two tightropes. In one ring he sought to keep the politicians guessing about his ultimate presidential intentions while maneuvering, usually behind the scenes, to ensure that the convention and platform would be controlled by the liberal forces in the Democratic party. And, as if that were not a sufficiently intimidating balancing act, in another ring he had to educate a resistant and wishful-thinking American public in the Allied cause. It took events — catastrophies, unhappily — to place him on firmer ground." (*Roosevelt And Churchill*)

As Hitler and Stalin grabbed off country after country in Europe, the American people feared war and began to look hopefully to the President who swore he would avoid intervention. In August of 1939, only forty percent favored a third term; by June of 1940 the figure had risen to fifty-seven percent. (*Never Again*) As if setting up a coalition Government to deal with the crisis, F.D.R. added two Republicans to his Cabinet on the eve of the G.O.P. Convention. They were Henry Stimson, who had served on the Cabinet under Taft and Hoover, and Chicago newspaper publisher Frank Knox, a former Rough Rider and Alf Landon's running-mate in 1936. (*Roosevelt: The Lion And The Fox*) Both were selected because they were hawks. Knox became Secretary of the Navy, and Stimson took over the War Department.

Frederic R. Sanborn explained: "On June 20, 1940, Mr. [*Henry*] Woodring was ousted as Secretary of War because he had refused to strip the nation of its defenses in order to aid the Allies; he was replaced by Mr. Stimson, a confirmed interventionist and an advocate of peacetime conscription. On that same day the draft act was introduced in the Senate, because, if enlistments in the Army are any criterion of public opinion, the country was overwhelmingly opposed to Mr. Roosevelt's policies. The Army's recruiting was a failure; only nine thousand men had enlisted after a six weeks' drive." (*Perpetual War For Perpetual Peace*, edited by Harry Elmer Barnes, Caldwell, Idaho, Caxton, 1953)

Just two days prior to Stimson's being named as Secretary of War he had made a radio speech calling for universal military training, repeal of the Neutrality Act, opening of U.S. ports to British and French ships, and speeding up arms shipments to the Allies — "sending them if necessary in our own ships and under convoy." In short, Stimson was for everything but declaring war. When offered the job of War Secretary, he "asked Roosevelt over the telephone whether the latter had seen the text of his radio address and whether this would be embarrassing. The President replied that he had read the speech and was in full accord with it. There could hardly be a more complete acknowledgement, in advance, of the insincerity of his subsequent campaign peace assurances." (*America's Second Crusade*, William Henry Chamberlain, Chicago, Henry Regnery, 1950)

But first came the Convention at which F.D.R. was to be "drafted" for a third term. The delegates were sent into an early frenzy by a cute trick in which a microphone was illicitly set up in the basement of the Convention Hall and Mayor Ed Kelly's commissioner of sewers, Big Tom McBarry, waited with a gang of toughs for the prearranged signal to patch into the sound system on the floor. The tricksters read a self-serving message from F.D.R., claiming he did not want to run again, but . . . .

At this point, reports Finis Farr, "the loudspeakers began bellowing again, the hooligans in the aisles revealed their signs reading 'ROOSEVELT AND HUMANITY,' and Mayor Ed Kelly began yelling and capering on the platform. Farley called it 'a machine-made tumult.'* Nevertheless, the convention nominated Roosevelt by almost a thousand votes on the first ballot and Farley, himself, moved to make it unanimous.

---

*James Farley and F.D.R. had broken over the third-term issue. *Chicago Tribune* reporter Walter Trohan recalled that Mayor Kelly's "voice from the sewer" had thus repaid F.D.R. "for getting him off the income-tax hook arrears that ran into six figures, even though it meant cutting the political throat of the man who arranged the tax deal, Farley." (*Political Animals*)

It was hard for the delegates to accept the President's choice of Henry A. Wallace as running mate, but they do so, for Roosevelt's word was law in Chicago, as Harry Hopkins passed it on." (*FDR*, New Rochelle, Arlington House, 1972) It would be the "third-term candidate" versus Wendell Willkie, the One Worlder.

In the meantime, Roosevelt attempted to change the Neutrality Act and eliminate the arms embargo, saying this would be a move toward peace. But Senator William Borah of Idaho recalled that Secretary of State Cordell Hull had once said the purpose of the Neutrality Act, itself, was to keep us out of war. Borah declared: "If the purpose of the Embargo Act then was to keep us out of war, what is the purpose of repealing it: to get us into it?" Of course not. At least not until after the election.

Scare stories were sent out from the White House that "we were next on Hitler's list." Omaha might be bombed, F.D.R. said, so do not worry if we send aid to the Allies "short of war." This was coupled with his promise that America would not go to war. In fact, Roosevelt had us well on the way. "Having changed the Neutrality Act," recalled John T. Flynn, "given a million army rifles to England and increased the army to 1,500,000 [*which number the Army said could only be needed for overseas operations*], the President took the next step — he handed over to Britain 50 destroyers belonging to the American navy without authority of Congress. Those men and women who formed the various committees to induce this country to go into the war approved these moves. They were honest about it and logical, because they were saying openly we should give every aid, even at the expense of war. But the President was saying he was opposed to going to war and that he was doing these things to stay out of war." (*The Roosevelt Myth*) Of course, what he said in public and planned in secret were very different things. When he warned, for instance, that "convoys mean shooting and shooting means war," he was at the same time starting to convoy. Very soon American and British ships were hunting German submarines in the Atlantic. It was undeclared war.

But more time was needed before F.D.R. could move openly into the conflict. The electorate first had to be deceived into granting him another term. In late October of 1940, at Madison Square Garden, even Roosevelt admirer Robert Sherwood noted his "speech was one of the most equivocal of Roosevelt's career . . . . Here Roosevelt went to the length or depth of taking credit for the Neutrality Law and other measures which he had thoroughly disapproved and had fought to repeal and had contrived to circumspect." (*Roosevelt And Hopkins*, New York, Harper & Brothers, 1948) This was done because Willkie was gaining strength by claiming F.D.R. was a warmonger. There seemed to be, said Sherwood, a "fear-of-war hysteria."

The idea was to pose as a determined neutral while moving toward war. The distinguished historian Charles A. Beard has pointed out that: "In supplementing the pledges of the Democratic platform, President Roosevelt had been unequivocal in his personal declarations. At Philadelphia, October 23, 1940, he had branded as false a Republican charge that 'this Administration wishes to lead this country into war,' and proclaimed that he was 'following the road to peace.' At Boston on October 30, he was even more emphatic, for there he declared: 'I have said this before, but I shall say it again and again and again: Your boys are not going to be sent into any foreign wars . . . . The purpose of our defense is defense.' At Buffalo, November 2, his vow was short and unqualified: 'Your President says this country is not going to war.' " (*President Roosevelt And The Coming Of The War*, New Haven, Yale University Press, 1948)

Goebbels had no monopoly on the Big Lie. Indeed, said the disaffected New Dealer Hugh Johnson: "I know of no well informed Washington observer who isn't convinced that if Mr. Roosevelt is elected he will drag us into war at the first opportunity, and that if none presents itself he will make one." In truth, Willkie was also committed against neutrality in the war in Europe, but on the stump he was effective as he emphasized: "If his promise to keep our boys out of foreign wars is no better than his promise to balance the budget, they're already almost on the transports." Bypassing Congress on the destroyer deal for Britain, Willkie charged, was "the most dictatorial and arbitrary act of any President in the history of the United States."

Of course Wendell Willkie approved of the destroyer deal, claiming to disapprove only of the method. The brilliant historical analyst Charles Callan Tansill explained: "From the viewpoint of international law the destroyer deal was definitely illegal. As Professor Herbert Briggs correctly remarks: 'The supplying of these vessels by the United States Government to a belligerent is a violation of our neutral status, a violation of our national law, and a violation of international law.' Professor Edwin Borchard expressed a similar opinion: 'To the writer there is no possibility of reconciling the destroyer deal with neutrality, with the United States statutes, or with international law.' The whole matter was correctly described by the *St. Louis Post-Dispatch* in a pertinent headline: 'Dictator Roosevelt Commits an Act of War.' " (*Back Door To War*, Chicago, Regnery, 1952)

Posing as a peace-maker, Roosevelt won by nearly five million popular votes. Yet, "Willkie had gained five million more votes than Landon had in 1936; Roosevelt's plurality was the smallest of any winning candidate since 1916 [*when Wilson was also re-elected as an equally phony "peace" candidate*]. The President's margin in New York — about

225,000 — was his lowest since his hair-breadth victory for governor in 1928." (*Roosevelt: The Lion And The Fox*) Indeed it was estimated that a switch of 250,000 voters in pivotal states would have changed the results of the election in Willkie's favor. Ah, the power of the lie! Before the election F.D.R. even promised that if given a third term he would not seek a fourth. (*Design For War,* Frederic R. Sanborn, New York, Devin-Adair, 1951)

The people had put F.D.R. back in charge. As Roosevelt aide Harry Hopkins said in 1941: "The people are too ***damn dumb to understand." But British Prime Minister Winston Churchill understood exactly what Franklin Roosevelt — the peace candidate — had in mind. Harry Hopkins was sent to make it all clear. In January of 1941, Churchill was visited by Hopkins in England, and the P.M. saw that "here was an envoy from the President of supreme importance to our life. With gleaming eye and quiet, constrained passion he said: 'The President is determined that we shall win the war together. Make no mistake about it. He has sent me here to tell you that at all costs and by all means he will carry you through, no matter what happens to him — there is nothing he will not do so far as he has human power.' " (*The Grand Alliance*, Winston S. Churchill)

Meanwhile, F.D.R.'s war program was euphemistically called a defense program. And the President's "neutrality" was becoming very expensive by the standards of the Forties. "It was already anticipated that the eleven billion dollars authorized for 1940, and already spent, would be followed by an equal amount in 1941, and even more in 1942. By 1942 the Treasury was planning on being on a full mobilization or war footing. Withholding taxes — something new and revolutionary — went into the planning stage in early 1941." (*F.D.R.'s Undeclared War*)

Then came the Lend-Lease Act, symbolically labeled H.R. 1776, making us in F.D.R.'s words "the arsenal of democracy." All this because England was said in 1941 to be faced with imminent invasion. In fact, Winston Churchill himself dismissed that vaunted threat to the island nation, saying in *The Grand Alliance*: "I did not regard invasion as a serious danger in April, 1941, since proper preparations had been made against it." But Roosevelt built up the alleged threat, saying that when Britain fell "all of us in the Americas would be living at the point of a gun."

Already Churchill and Roosevelt were living in sin, or as F.D.R.'s biographer Robert Sherwood put it: They had a "common-law marriage" certainly " 'not recognized' in such 'jurisdictions' as the Congress, and if the isolationists [*let alone the American public at large*] had known the full extent of it their demands for the impeachment of President Roosevelt would have been a great deal louder." (*Roosevelt And Hopkins*)

Sherwood went even further in discussions with the man called IN-TREPID. He was Sir William Stephenson, whose biographer later confirmed that there was indeed a secret alliance between Roosevelt and Churchill. This, of course, was an impeachable offense. And it was exactly what the so-called isolationists suspected. For example, Senator Burton K. Wheeler asked in January of 1941: "If it is our war, how can we justify lending them stuff and asking them to pay us back? If it is our war, we ought to have the courage to go over and fight it, but it is not our war." Shortly thereafter Senator Wheeler referred to the destruction wrought by the agricultural agency, A.A.A., commenting that Lend-Lease was "the New Deal's 'triple A' foreign policy — to plow under every fourth American boy." The President called this the "rottenest thing that has been said in public life in my generation." (*Back Door To War*) Indeed it would have been had it not been true.

The aforementioned Sir William Stephenson was even now operating out of Rockefeller Plaza as chief of British Security Coordination. It was a replay of World War I. Stephenson reportedly met personally with the President with a proposal "so confidential, so shattering in its implications, that nothing could be placed on the record without the risk of political chain reaction." (*A Man Called Intrepid*, William Stevenson, New York, Harcourt Brace Jovanovich, 1976) Reporting back home the British secret agent told Prime Minister Churchill, among other things: "The President has laid down the secret ruling for the closest possible marriage between the FBI and British Intelligence."[*]

Apologists for Roosevelt have argued, indeed continue to argue, that the President did not lie us into the Second World War. (See, for example, the judicious editing by Francis L. Loewenheim, Harold D. Langley, and Manfred Jonas in *Roosevelt And Churchill: Their Secret Wartime Correspondence*, New York, E.P. Dutton, Saturday Review Press, 1975.) Yet even Robert Sherwood informed the head of British intelligence in this country: "If the isolationists had known the full extent of the secret alliance between the United States and Britain, their demands for the President's impeachment would have rumbled like thunder through the land."

---

[*]How times change. Or do they? Reports war opponent Walter Trohan of the *Chicago Tribune*: "My home phones were tapped — I had two lines — and the *Tribune's* office phones were also tapped. I had a Washington police lieutenant, an expert on bugging, check the phones; he came from an examination of the lead box to my home, saying he had never seen such a setup, that I had taps on my taps. He found that my telephones were being monitored by the FBI, military intelligence, naval intelligence and the Anti-Defamation League. This didn't concern me or my colleagues, although I made it known widely. Most of my colleagues felt it served me right for my opposition to the war. Today bugging seems to be the crime of crimes." (*Political Animals*)

Military cooperation was complete, including furtive liaison between the British and our "neutral" Army Chief of Staff and Chief of Naval Operations. "American-British staff talks opened in Washington in January 1941 with warnings from General George C. Marshall and Admiral Harold R. Stark that utmost secrecy must prevail. If their plans had fallen into Axis hands, no great harm would have resulted. Had they leaked to the press and Congress, American preparation for war might have been wrecked. 'Utmost secrecy' meant preventing disclosure to the American public. 'Roosevelt never overlooked the fact that his actions might lead to his immediate or eventual impeachment,' Sherwood was to say . . . . ''
(*A Man Called Intrepid*)

In fact, for more than a year before Pearl Harbor was attacked, Hitler was doing everything possible to keep us out of the conflict. Roosevelt would have none of it, brazenly occupying Iceland to replace the British troops there. Even such F.D.R. supporters as James MacGregor Burns admit: "If there was a point when Roosevelt knowingly crossed some threshold between aiding Britain in order to stay out of war and aiding Britain by joining the war, July 1941 was probably the time. Others including Morgenthau and Ickes had crossed this threshold earlier, and more decisively. If Roosevelt was still waiting on events, he was now nudging them in a direction that would deepen the cold war in the Atlantic and produce a crisis.'' (*Roosevelt: The Soldier Of Fortune*, New York, Harcourt Brace Jovanovich, 1970)

For his own reasons, Hitler made things difficult for Roosevelt by forbidding attacks on U.S. ships unless the Americans attacked first. Indeed, Grand Admiral Karl Doenitz was later to testify that Hitler ordered him "to avoid conflict with the United States.'' In fact, the Admiral added, "When American destroyers in the summer of 1941 were ordered to attack German submarines, I was forbidden to fight back.''
(*Design For War*) But, regardless of his election pledge of neutrality and peace, F.D.R. was trying to get us into the conflict by every means at hand. Even Joe Lash acknowledges that "Roosevelt, with Churchill's concurrence, was looking for an incident ('everything was to be done to force an incident,' he had advised Churchill), one that would permit him to wage war in the Atlantic without declaring it.'' (*Roosevelt And Churchill*) Six months before Pearl Harbor, Secretary of the Navy Knox declared that the "time to use our Navy to clear the Atlantic of the German menace is at hand.'' Top Naval officers considered themselves to be at war. (*Design For War*)

When Germany attacked the Soviet Union, the cautious American response might have been to let the dictators fight it out. Senator Harry S Truman put it this way: "If we see Germany winning we ought to help

Russia and if we see Russia winning we ought to help Germany, and in that way let them kill as many as possible, although I wouldn't want to see Hitler victorious under any circumstances. Neither of them think [*sic*] anything of their pledged word.''

The history of World War I, as F.D.R. acknowledged, had repeated itself. We were now to fight England's war and save the Bolsheviks. This time, however, every effort would be made to prevent exposure of those behind the scheming. The revisionist authorities have been few and far between, never to be found up front at your public library and seldom referred to at prestigious universities. And for good reason. As Professor C.A. Beard observed as far back as 1953:

"The Rockefeller Foundation and the Council on Foreign Relations . . . intend to prevent, if they can, a repetition of what they call in the vernacular 'the debunking journalistic campaign following World War I.' Translated into precise English, this means that the Foundation and the Council do not want journalists or any other persons to examine too closely and criticize too freely the official propaganda and official statements relative to 'our basic aims and activities' during World War II. In short, they hope that, among other things, the policies and measures of Franklin D. Roosevelt will escape in the coming years the critical analysis, evaluation and exposition that befell the policies and measures of Woodrow Wilson and the Entente Allies after World War I.'' (*Perpetual War For Perpetual Peace*)

For the most part the conspirators have been successful. Anti-Nazi movies and books still appear regularly some forty years after that menace has been destroyed — while the Communists, our former allies, are all but ignored even though they conquered at least one-third of the world. The propaganda imbalance was planned that way. To appease Stalin in World War II we were to, in the words of Averell Harriman: "Give and give and give, with no expectation of any return, with no thought of a *quid pro quo*.'' American propagandists spoke of Stalin as a man of "kindness and gentle simplicity.'' Revisionist Frederic Sanborn reiterated that "when Mr. Hopkins went to Russia 'in return for the offer of such aid he asked nothing.' Fulfillment of the Russian demands was given a first priority by Mr. Roosevelt over everything else, and materials and equipment were diverted to Russia in late 1941 over the opposition and in spite of strong protests from the Armed Forces.'' (*Perpetual War For Perpetual Peace*)

After BARBAROSSA, the Hitler attack on his Soviet ally, the decks had been cleared for action. As we read in *A Man Called Intrepid*: '' 'The President now fully accepted the concept of *offensive* intelligence,' Stephenson said later. The attack on Russia made it politically possible for him to declare Bill Donovan his Coordinator of Information 'to collect and analyze all information and data which may bear on the national security.' The Executive Order of July 11, 1941, made official a situation that was fundamentally irregular. 'As much as six months before Pearl Harbor,' the BSC [British Security Coordination] Papers recorded, 'we had secured full American participation and collaboration in secret activities directed against the enemy throughout the world.' "

In the Atlantic we had repealed the arms embargo; given away our destroyers; enacted Lend-Lease; instituted convoys that F.D.R. called "patrols"; blocked German credits; occupied Iceland; given orders that U.S. vessels shoot Axis ships at sight; and, armed and sent merchant ships into war zones — all while officially at peace. And to no avail.

So F.D.R. turned to the Pacific. The tactic was simple. As Secretary of War Harry Stimson recorded in his diary: "The question was how we should maneuver them [the Japanese] into firing the first shot without allowing too much danger to ourselves." (America's Second Crusade) Or as Japanese Ambassador Nomura put it: "I understand the British believe that if they could only have a Japanese-American war started at the back door, there would be a good prospect of getting the United States to participate in the European war." (Design For War)

Japanese assets were frozen as a provocation; a visit to the President from the Japanese Prime Minister was rejected; a warning from our Ambassador in Tokyo of a Pearl Harbor attack was ignored; a knowingly impossible and humiliating ultimatum to Tokyo was issued; while embargoing Japan, we steamed through her waters with oil for the Soviet Union; and, the necessary defensive responses to our intercepted messages from Japanese diplomatic traffic, pointing to the attack on American bases in Hawaii, were sabotaged in Washington. The result was the disaster at Pearl Harbor — culpability for which Chief of Staff George Marshall implored Thomas Dewey, F.D.R.'s opponent in 1944, not to mention.* Franklin Roosevelt had his war at last.

As the Italian Foreign Minister, Count Ciano, recorded in his diaries: "Now that Roosevelt has succeeded in his maneuver, not being able to enter the war directly, he has succeeded by an indirect route — forcing the Japanese to attack him." Hitler and Mussolini met their treaty commitments by declaring war, as Roosevelt knew they would, and once again the globe became a single battleground.

Ostensibly the war in Europe was begun for the rights of Poland; while in the Pacific the foremost issue was said to have been the sovereignty of

---

*Pearl Harbor was a setup. Jonathan Daniels, F.D.R.'s administrative assistant, later said: "The blow was heavier than he had hoped it would necessarily be . . . . But the risks paid off; even the loss was worth the price . . . . " (Perpetual War For Perpetual Peace) The families of the thousands who were wounded or died at Pearl as sitting ducks would no doubt have thought otherwise.

Nationalist China. At the war's end, both were maneuvered into the grasp of Communist dictators. Another result was that those who kept quiet or were deceitful about betrayal of Pearl Harbor were paid off. Among others, the list included General Marshall, Colonel Bedell Smith, Senator Barkley, and Senate Majority Leader Lucas. (For details, see "The Pearl Harbor Investigations," by Percy L. Greaves Jr., in *Perpetual War For Perpetual Peace*.) Others were scapegoated, and the truth about the attack on Hawaii was submerged as far as possible. (A notable exception was publication of *The Final Secret Of Pearl Harbor*, by Rear Admiral Robert A. Theobald, Old Greenwich, Connecticut, Devin-Adair, 1954; more confirmation came later from John Toland — though that author was then attacked by the Establishment — in *Infamy: Pearl Harbor And Its Aftermath*, New York, Doubleday, 1982.)

In 1944, of course, a dying F.D.R. was re-elected in the closest of his victories and went off to Yalta to deal with a tough Stalin who was demanding, among other things, sixteen votes in the post-war United Nations organization. "Uncle Joe," as he was called by Churchill and Roosevelt, allowed himself to be "compromised" to three votes. Poland was betrayed and Communist rule was accepted over most of Eastern and Central Europe; China's rights in Manchuria were secretly signed away; the West approved slave labor for the conquered Germans; and, only belatedly, Roosevelt stopped just short of agreeing to destroy German industry forever in the Communist-inspired Morgenthau Plan.

"The coming of the war in Europe," reports historian William Henry Chamberlain, "accomplished what all the experimentation of the New Deal had failed to achieve. It created the swollen demand for American munitions, equipment, supplies of all kinds, foodstuffs — which started the national economy on the road to full production and full employment." (*America's Second Crusade*) But at what a price!

Not only were there more than a million American casualties, but such Red aides to the President as Alger Hiss, Harry Dexter White, and Owen Lattimore (among others) saw to it that the Communists were the ultimate beneficiaries of World War II. Roosevelt, and later Truman, agreed to domination by the Comrades of some two-thirds of Europe and Asia. Stalin, who said he didn't want one additional inch, "added to his empire some *725 million people*, which with the 193 million in Russia gave him dominion over *918 million human beings* in Russia and 16 other European and Asiatic countries." (*The Roosevelt Myth*)

In April of 1945, Franklin Delano Roosevelt died. His wife Eleanor said: "I am more sorry for the people of the country and the world than I am for us." She was, for once, very much on target.

Chapter XXI

An Inquiry Concerning Churchill

IF Winston L.S. Churchill had died in 1939, at age sixty-five, posterity would have remembered him, if at all, as an eccentric British politician, author, and military adventurer. The historical footnote might have pointed out that he was in and out of political office as he crossed the aisle in the House of Commons from Conservative to Liberal and back; that, though not a striking physical specimen, he had seen military action in Cuba, India, The Sudan, and South Africa; and, that he had published voluminously, if self-servingly, assorted works on himself and his family, including the Duke of Marlborough and his own father, Lord Randolph Churchill, who died insane of syphilis at age forty-five. Mr. Churchill's career as Chancellor of the Exchequer would no doubt have been mentioned, and perhaps a listing of his Ministry posts. Most certainly his World War I role as First Lord of the Admiralty would be recalled, and his subsequent dismissal as a result of the disaster arising from his campaign to force the Dardanelles.

And that would be that. Distinguished but not great.

Yet because of World War II, when Churchill became the Prime Minister of Britain, the popular impression of the man is that of a fiery orator and great leader who rallied his people against Hitler's blitz, personified the indomitable spirit of British resistance, and gave blood, sweat, toil, and tears to make surrender unthinkable and defeat of the Hun inevitable.[*] V for Victory. Justice triumphs.

A balanced view of Churchill is possible only as his contribution to the Battle of Britain is viewed in perspective, say as compared to the loss of the Empire which he swore he would not permit, even as he made it

---

[*]"One of his old liberal colleagues was still at the age of 94 going through his great speeches for phrases borrowed from others. Thus Clemenceau had inspired 'We shall fight them on the beaches,' and Byron 'Blood, sweat and tears.' " (*Winston Churchill: The Yankee Marlborough*, R.W. Thompson, Garden City, Doubleday, 1963)

inevitable and agreed to the surrender of vast areas of the globe to the Communists. It is not without meaning that Winston Churchill, the historian, acknowledged: "I have achieved a great deal to achieve nothing in the end." (*The Great Man*, Robert Payne, New York, Coward, McCann & Geoghegan, 1974) In one of his six volumes on the Second World War, it was a despondent Churchill who admitted: "The human tragedy reaches its climax in the fact that after all the exertions and sacrifices of hundreds of millions of people and of the victories of the Righteous Cause, we have still not found Peace or Security, and that we lie in the grip of even worse perils than those we have surmounted."

However impressive the mythology wrapped around his deeds of 1940, it is clear that they tell us very little of the real Winston Spencer Churchill. For the supposedly brilliant anti-totalitarian was in fact a poor student who had publicly admired Hitler, Mussolini, and Stalin. The great Conservative orator was a longtime advocate of the Welfare State, whose speaking ability, unfortunately marred by a lisp and stammer, was notable chiefly because of a stolid commitment to spending up to six weeks preparing one address.

Is there any wonder that Churchill was plagued by a melancholia so grave that he called it the "Black Dog"? Indeed, as biographer Robert Payne reports: "A strain of madness ran through his family and he needed to search himself continually to be sure he was untouched by it." David Lloyd George and others openly questioned Winston's sanity, and not without cause.

Winston Churchill suffered fits of arrogance as well as depression. He wanted to become a super-general in World War II, for instance, apparently because he felt qualified as a result of having attended Sandhurst after his undistinguished years at Harrow. By all accounts, he was personally a self-centered, ill-tempered, and insolent man. Historian R.W. Thompson writes in *The Yankee Marlborough* that "Churchill provoked intense dislike in almost everyone who had the misfortune to serve with him, and it has remained a source of some astonishment to many that his behavior was tolerated." Winston was notorious for refusing to admit that he had ever been wrong, and his apparently manic impulsiveness terrified even his closest friends.

From the Conservative Party he turned not only to the Liberals, but in 1903 to the Radicals, finding the Left an attractive vehicle for advancement. Early in his career, Winston Churchill was close to Fabian Socialist founders Beatrice and Sidney Webb.* Not always hewing to the party line

---

*Robert Payne recalls that Lenin was also a Webb-ster, translating "one of their books on social reform; Churchill put their ideas into practice. For a very brief period Churchill became the darling of the Socialists."

he made enemies; but in his book, *Liberalism And The Social Problem*, Churchill cited as the greatest threat to Britain "the unnatural gap between rich and poor," a Fabian line if ever there was one. (*Churchill*, edited by Martin Gilbert, Englewood Cliffs, Prentice-Hall, 1967)

Winston also fantasized about Marxist panaceas, reporting that while visiting Uganda he had found the perfect place for State Socialism. Churchill surely believed in state intervention in the economy, and helped initiate such Socialist projects as the National Insurance Act, the Labor Exchanges, minimum wage, maximum working hours, and similar Fabian favorites. Randolph S. Churchill, Winston's son, proudly called his father one of "the architects of the modern Welfare State." (*Churchill: A Study In Failure, 1900-1939*, Robert Rhodes James, New York, World, 1970) No, this man was no Conservative.

On the other hand, Winston Churchill earned lifelong foes among Labourites for alleged heavy-handedness against strikers when he served as Chancellor of the Exchequer. As Freda Utley reminisced: " . . . I still remember the passionate anger I felt in 1926 against the 'capitalist government' and its most ruthless member, Winston Churchill, who was responsible for the show of armed force and was prepared to have the workers shot at if the strike went on." (*Odyssey Of A Liberal*, Washington, D.C., Washington National Press, 1970) Even his sometime friend Lloyd George referred to Winston as "the Minister of Civil Slaughter."

His icy brutality was amazing to behold. As First Lord of the Admiralty in World War I, Winston Churchill helped impose a blockade on the continent, including neutral countries, in the hopes of starving the Germans into submission. The suffering of the non-combatant women and children was something he overlooked, and the blockade was continued after the Armistice, producing widespread hunger and misery. Churchill even laughed at the respect his officers sought to show for the rules of the sea, personally directing the misuse of truce flags, ordering the flying of the flags of neutral nations, and even authorizing the killing of prisoners. Churchill wrote: "Survivors should be taken prisoner or shot — whichever is the most [*sic*] convenient." (*The Lusitania*, Colin Simpson)

There now appears to be more than enough evidence to convict Woodrow Wilson and Winston Churchill of collusion in arranging the sinking by a German submarine of the British ship *Lusitania*, which the First Lord called "another 45,000 tons of livebait." The object was to create a *cause célèbre* for pushing the United States into the war.*

---

*The courier between F.D.R. and Churchill, code-named INTREPID, has written that Roosevelt paid close attention to President Wilson's secret files on the incident while he was maneuvering us into the Second World War. (*A Man Called Intrepid*)

It was the tragic episode at the Dardanelles Straits, however, that proved Churchill's undoing in the Great War, although there was more than enough blame to be shared by others. The objective of his impetuous Gallipoli campaign was to take Constantinople and relieve the Russians for action on the stalemated Western front. One of his colleagues told Winston: "You are simply eaten up with the Dardanelles and cannot think of anything else. Damn the Dardanelles. They will be our grave!" (*From The Jaws Of Victory*, Charles Fair, New York, Simon and Schuster, 1971) As it turned out, there were so many graves that the extent of the losses at Gallipoli had to be kept a secret throughout the war.

Posterity, said an enraged Admiral Wemyss, would see Churchill as one "who undertook an operation of whose requirements he was entirely ignorant." The King called his First Lord of the Admiralty "impossible,"* and Admiral Jellicoe said Winston had become "a public danger to the Empire." When he was removed, Admiral Beatty declared that the "Navy breathes freer now it is rid of the succubus Churchill." (*Churchill Revised*, A.J.P. Taylor, *et al.*, New York, Dial, 1969)

As Major Churchill, Winston sought to regain what he could of his reputation by taking a tour of the trenches with the Grenadiers; as it happened, he was only thirty miles away from a young soldier named Adolf Hitler, who was to be awarded the Iron Cross, first class, at the recommendation of a Jewish officer. Winston and Adolf did not meet. But, in July of 1918, President Wilson's Assistant Secretary of the Navy, F.D. Roosevelt, and the then-Minister of State for Air and War, W.S. Churchill, were introduced in London.

Churchill had met another interesting American a year earlier, when he had made a friendly contact with Establishment insider Bernard Baruch, boss of the American War Production Board, and perhaps the second most powerful man in the United States. Winston later learned some inside lessons in finance from Baruch, being in New York with him on "Black Thursday" in 1929 when the plug was pulled on Wall Street.[†] Said Churchill in amazement: "The whole wealth so swiftly gathered in the paper values of previous years vanished. The prosperity of millions of

---

*Another Churchill failure was his inability, despite repeated attempts, to prod the King into naming a battleship after Oliver Cromwell, one of Winston's heroes. The monarch was reluctant to honor the man who, in addition to other outrages, had beheaded King Charles I.

†Winston's knowledge of the machinations of international finance, developed during his stint as Chancellor of the Exchequer, was obvious in the subsequent war. " 'We need Rockefellers and Rothschilds,' grumbled Churchill 'We need gold. Do you know we have *none*.' " Secret agent INTREPID then acknowledged (in 1940): "I can find the Rockefellers and they'll support us. We can offer our secret intelligence in return for help. It has to be done at the President's level. There have been intelligence breakthroughs in the United States that would advance our own efforts." And it was to British agent INTREPID that F.D.R. confided: "I'm your biggest undercover agent." (*A Man Called Intrepid*)

American homes, grown upon a gigantic structure of inflated credit, now suddenly proved phantom.''

The Twenties were a low point for Churchill. Scorned alike by Conservative, Labour, and Liberals, he had acquired a reputation as an anti-Bolshevik, but also organized the withdrawal of the British forces supporting the anti-Communist White Russian forces. Robert Rhodes James notes that the Lloyd George coalition he served "attempted, and failed, to rule Ireland by force." When Churchill was Colonial Minister, in fact, they "succeeded in alienating virtually every sizable interest or section of the nation." (*Churchill Revised*)

Nor is his reputation as a sentinel of preparedness justified. While War and Air Minister between 1918 and 1921, Churchill ordered the Air Staff to reduce its plans for 154 R.A.F. squadrons to a sparse 24. He had never understood the importance of air power, and even *The Times* commented: "He [*Churchill*] leaves the body of British flying well nigh at that last gasp when a military funeral would be all that would be left for it." Furthermore, every year he was Chancellor of the Exchequer between 1924 and 1929, the "Army Estimates were pared down," with particular detriment to the development of the tank, said Basil Liddell Hart, the century's foremost military strategist. Later Churchill would claim responsibility for tank development when in fact he had been a disarmament fanatic who had choked the military budget to just this side of royal purple.

In fact, it was Churchill's "ten-year-rule," formally established by the British Cabinet in 1928, under which all plans for defense were made on the presumption there could be no war for ten years. The disarmament of which Churchill was to complain in the Thirties was, for the most part, of his own doing.

Another popular misconception is that only the brave Winston Churchill had dared speak out against the rise of Fascism. This is so far from the truth as to be laughable. In 1926, Churchill visited Italy to tell the Duce, "if I had been an Italian I am sure that I should have been wholeheartedly with you from start to finish . . . ." Benny was a "really great man," Winnie confided in 1935. Even after the invasion of Ethiopia, Churchill pointed in 1937 to "the enduring position in world history which Mussolini will hold; or the amazing qualities of courage, comprehension, self-control and perseverance which he exemplifies." (*A Study In Failure*)

Churchill assured Mussolini he would himself "don the Fascist black shirt" were he Italian, and declared that he ranked the Italian dictator above George Washington and his own favorite historical dictator Oliver Cromwell. (*As We Go Marching*, John T. Flynn) "Even when the issue of the war became certain," wrote Churchill, "Mussolini would have been welcomed by the Allies." Benito Mussolini defended, he declared, "the honor and stability of civilized society." And, as late as 1940, Winston Churchill proclaimed: "I do not deny that he is a very great man. But he became a criminal when he attacked England."*

His attitude toward Hitler was much the same. Churchill wrote in 1937 of the Führer's "patriotic achievement. If our country were defeated, I hope we should find a champion as indomitable to restore our courage and lead us back to our place among the nations." That same year Winston denounced any reservations he may have had about Hitler as "alarmist," predicting "a major war is not imminent, and I still believe there is a good chance of no major war taking place in our lifetime." (*Churchill Revised*) Hitlerism was fading, said Churchill in 1937; "judged by every standard, Germany is bankrupt." Still, he said, "I will not pretend that, if I had to choose between Communism and Nazism, I would choose Communism." (*The Yankee Marlborough*)

This is not to insinuate that Churchill personally favored either system, but merely to establish that he was anything but a Cassandra warning the world about the rise of totalitarianism. Indeed, in 1936, Winston Churchill blamed America for the troubles in Europe, telling the editor of the *New York Enquirer*:

"America's entrance into the war was disastrous not only for your country but for the Allies as well, because had you stayed at home and minded your business we would have made peace with the Central Powers in the spring of 1917, and then there would have been no collapse in Russia followed by communism; no break-down in Italy, followed by fascism; and nazi-ism would not at present be enthroned in Germany. If America had stayed out of the war and minded her own business, none of these 'isms' would today be sweeping the continent of Europe and breaking down parliamentary government."

He did not mention that America's entry into that war was stage-managed from London as well as New York and Washington, and that a prime conspirator in hooking us in was First Lord of the Admiralty Winston S. Churchill. Nor did any of this preclude his efforts to draw us into yet another world war. As early as 1940, Churchill's secret envoy, INTREPID, was setting up headquarters for British Security Coordination in New York City. Other plans were also in the works, as reported by revisionist historian Benjamin Colby:

---

*When informed four years later that the "very great man" had been murdered by Communists and hung up by his heels in the street, Churchill exulted: "The bloody beast is dead." (*Duce!*, Richard Collier)

"Americans did not know that less than two weeks before Pearl Harbor President Roosevelt had discussed with his advisers the problem of maneuvering Japan 'into the position of firing the first shot.' Nor did they know that Roosevelt had told Churchill the United States would probably go to war against Japan even if not attacked. As to Germany, they did not know that the President had issued orders . . . in August for American naval vessels to seek incidents on the Atlantic which would justify war; that Roosevelt — as the British cabinet papers have now documented — was 'determined' to go to war against Germany." (*'Twas A Famous Victory*)

England acquiesced in Hitler's taking of the Rhineland, Austria, and Czecho-Slovakia. But when Hitler demanded Danzig from Poland and prepared to enforce it, France and England declared war. The sad French forces, which the year before Churchill had called "the most perfectly trained and faithful mobile forces in Europe," fell quickly. To make things worse, First Lord of the Admiralty Churchill was inviting losses by telegraphing potential counterpunches. As Captain B.L. Hart observes: Churchill "labored under the delusion that 'we have more to gain than lose by a German attack upon Norway and Sweden.' " War documents show Hitler preferred to maintain neutrality in Norway, but struck after a British destroyer entered Norwegian waters. By the time First Lord of the Admiralty Churchill moved to Norway's aid it was too late and the debacle resulted in the fall of the Chamberlain Government. Hart comments: "It was the irony, or fatality, of history that Churchill should have gained his opportunity of supreme power as a result of a fiasco to which he had been the main contributor." (*Churchill Revised*)

Winston himself wondered about his ascension to Premier after the demoralizing Norwegian evacuation: "Considering the prominent part I played in these events . . . it was a marvel that I survived." (*Churchill In Power*, Brian Gardner, Boston, Houghton Mifflin, 1970) But Churchill had roared about appeasement, the blame was reflected on Prime Minister Chamberlain, and Winston Churchill was given his job.

This was to be "their finest hour" if the British Empire were to last a thousand years, and Churchill was embraced by the people. London could indeed take it. The British rallied behind rhetoric promising only "blood, toil, tears and sweat."*

But now the icy brutality which had permitted the shooting of enemy sailors helpless in the water during World War I again surfaced in Churchill, and it was he who initiated the bombing of cities and civilians

---

*After that memorable speech, the new Prime Minister left the chambers, only to look up at a friend and grin: "That got the sods, didn't it." The term, of course, is British slang for Sodomite.

outside of battle zones. His objective was to force the Nazis to retaliate in kind and relieve pressure on the British airfields which, as legitimate war targets, were being badly hit. "Actually the bombing of German cities," reports Benjamin Colby, "as attested by official British histories, began nearly four months before any bombs fell on London, and the blitz itself was deliberately encouraged by Prime Minister Churchill." (*'Twas A Famous Victory*)

Chilling are the decisions of wartime. Yet, one stands in horror at the callousness with which Churchill invited the suffering of the British people. For example, the second great fire-bombing of London and the disastrous losses at Coventry were permitted despite the breaking of the German code, providing foreknowledge of the raids. F.W. Winterbotham tried to explain away the failure to act by claiming that "if Churchill decided to evacuate Coventry, the press, and indeed everybody would know we had pre-knowledge of the raid . . . ." (*The Ultra Secret*, New York, Dell, 1974)

Which is utter and complete nonsense. There are many channels of intelligence, and many more potential leaks, and there was heavy press censorship. The Americans had broken essentially the same Enigma code in the Pacific, enabling them to ambush, attack, and kill Admiral Yamamoto, Commander-in-Chief of the Japanese Navy and Japan's greatest war hero. Admiral Bull Halsey simply ordered details withheld from the press. "Japanese communications officers never suspected their code had been broken. To the end of the war they were convinced it was 'unbreakable.' " (*The Rising Sun*, John Toland, New York, Random House, 1970)

Churchill, who had long discounted the importance of air power, sought an excuse for his extension of the definition of "military objectives" in Germany beyond the meaning accepted for more than two hundred years by civilized nations at war. And his War Cabinet, revealed F.J.P. Veale, accepted the plan "by which 'top priority' as an objective for air attack was in the future to be given to 'working-class houses in densely populated residential areas.' " (*Advance To Barbarism*, New York, Devin-Adair, revised 1968)

None of this was reported at the time. While the bombing of Coventry, specializing in the manufacture of cars and cycles, was described as wanton destruction of hospitals, little homes, and churches, the bombing of German cities which had provoked the reprisals was invariably presented as hitting military targets only. "Prime Minister Churchill was a strong proponent of bombing people as people," observes Benjamin Colby. "In July 1941, the RAF historians wrote, he was an 'enthusiast . . . for the mass bombardment of German towns,' and in August 'repeatedly' urged it. In January 1941, when oil installations were named as the principal target, he 'regretted that oil plants were for the most part far removed from centers of population.' The 'increasing insistence' of the Prime Minister and of members of his government on a 'more ruthless' bombing policy is noted by the official historians.''

Disasters were mounting for the British. The largest warship in the world, *H.M.S. Hood*, was sunk with several important aircraft carriers. Campaigns had failed in Norway, France, Greece, Crete, Libya, Hong Kong, Singapore, and Burma. Tobruk fell. Churchill was by now ranting about the need for courts-martial and firing squads to deal with his troops. When a British general in Somaliland, facing overwhelming odds, fought a bold rearguard action and inflicted some six times the casualties on the enemy, Churchill was infuriated at the relatively light British losses and demanded the general's dismissal.

Churchill became daily more callous. In Greece, for example, when the defenders had driven out the Italians, insufficient British forces had been sent by Churchill from Egypt, as supposed reinforcements, despite Greek warnings. ''It was utterly useless and unwanted, the Greeks fearing the British 'help' might call down upon them the full vengeance of the enemy.'' (*Generalissimo Churchill*, R.W. Thompson, New York, Scribner's, 1973) It did, followed by the Greek tragedy of a ''second Dunkirk'' and yet another in Crete. It cost the loss of thirty thousand men, equipment for more than four divisions, and nine warships. ''The magnificent New Zealand division was sacrificed. 'Never, never again,' protested the New Zealand Prime Minister, Fraser, 'must New Zealanders be allowed to fight without air cover.' And Rommel's Afrika Korps was given the opportunity to establish itself in Tripolitania.'' (*Vote Of Censure*, George Malcolm Thomson, New York, Stein and Day, 1968)

Mr. Churchill, who throughout the war insisted that he be allowed to hold both the post of Prime Minister *and* Minister of Defense, was proving a bloody burden to the British military. General Sir Alan Brooke, an admirer of the P.M. who was Chief of the Imperial General Staff, commented: ''the more you tell that man about the war, the more you hinder the winning of it.'' Winston regularly tried to intervene with the commanders in the field who knew their own capabilities and were short of troops and supplies. As R.W. Thompson put it: ''Churchill never understood, nor wished to understand, the problems of administration, maintenance and supply in such an area. He had no idea what it meant to keep aircraft in the air, or armour and infantry in the field.'' (*Generalissimo Churchill*)

Apparently ignorant of logistics, Churchill was actually elated at the news of the attack on Pearl Harbor. He knew that F.D.R. now had his incident and, as the Prime Minister had predicted, the new world would save the old . . . temporarily. Three days after Pearl Harbor the sitting-duck *Prince Of Wales* and *Repulse* were sunk off the Malay Peninsula and the Japanese attack on British territory in the Far East — which Churchill had refused to consider — began. The Prime Minister had sent in the ships as a "vague warning" with no air cover and over the objections of the military. The area was woefully unprotected. But Russia was nonetheless being sent 250 airplanes a month from England, while Singapore sat virtually naked.

Singapore was supposed to be the "Gibraltar of the East" and "the most impregnable barrier in the waters of the world." But attacking Singapore from the land side was another matter and the British knew it. In fact: "the [*British*] exercise of 1938 accurately prefigured the Japanese attack assault four years later. So much for the legend that nobody had ever supposed Singapore would be attacked from the rear." (*Vote Of Censure*) Naturally Churchill supported the myth, however, expressing amazement to his Chiefs of Staff that the great guns of Singapore could only face the sea. "It never occurred to me for a moment," he bellowed.

Biographer Robert Payne correctly assesses: "Much of the blame for the fall of Singapore lies with Churchill. He had never understood the problem, and never, until it was too late, looked at a map of the island." Winston was Minister of Defense, remember, and Singapore was a vitally strategic base but four years old that had cost twenty million pounds.

Now the arrogant Churchill, caught up in a disastrous blunder of his own making, declared that the untenable position of British forces in Singapore must be "defended to the death. No surrender can be contemplated." (*The Rising Sun*) He demanded of his Supreme Commander in the Far East: "There must at this stage be no thought of saving the troops or sparing the population. The battle must be fought to the bitter end at all costs . . . . Commanders and senior officers should die with their troops. The honour of the British Empire is at stake."

Be that as it may, the "most important British settlement in Asia had been captured," wrote George Malcolm Thomson, "and the greatest number of soldiers had capitulated in the whole of British history." As a result of Winston's arrogance, some 130,000 troops who might have been saved were captured, half of them to die in Japanese captivity. General Yamashita, at the cost of less than ten thousand casualties, earned "the greatest land victory in Japanese history." (*The Rising Sun*)

At home, Churchill was in deep trouble politically, but he still refused to relinquish his Defense post. General Brooke wrote of Winston in his diary: "Planned strategy was not his strong card. He preferred to work by intuition and by impulse . . . . He was never good at looking at all the implications of any course he favored. In fact, he frequently refused to look at them.''

But now America was in the war openly, and American boys could help with the dying. Also Churchill could be blunt in his demands on the United States, as he told one of his Chiefs of Staff who noted his change in tone: "Oh! That is the way we talked to her [*the U.S.*] while we were still wooing her; now that she is in the harem, we woo her quite another way." (*Winston Churchill On America And Britain,* edited by Kay Halle, New York, Walker, 1970) Talk was now all of a *United Nations* effort. Even a common citizenship was urged by Churchill, who frequently played on his Anglo-American lineage.

To quell discomfort over the alliance with the dictator Stalin, Churchill told the House of Commons that "profound changes" had occurred in the U.S.S.R. with the destruction of "the Trotskyite form of communism" and a "wonderful rebirth" of religion. Although Churchill knew better (and himself had no religious convictions) such propaganda was used to help assure a twenty-year Anglo-Soviet Pact. Churchill's hypocrisy in these matters carried over into his secret messages to F.D.R., including a number of warm references to good old "Uncle Joe" Stalin and blasphemous invocation of God's blessings on their mutual undertakings.*

For their part, the Soviets were already acting like haughty victors, with *Pravda* carrying vicious cartoons even in 1942 charging the British with cowardice and Nazi collaboration. General Brooke, who went to the Kremlin with Churchill, observed in his diary: "Winston appealed to sentiments in Stalin which do not, I think, exist. Altogether, I felt we were not gaining much ground. Personally, I feel our policy with the Russians has been wrong from the very start . . . . [W]e have bowed and scraped to them, done all we could do for them, and never asked them for a single fact or figure concerning their production, strength, disposition, *etc.* As a result, they despise us and have no use for us except for what they can get out of us."

What the Soviets got was considerable. In 1944, Stalin and Churchill even worked out a schedule dividing spheres of influence in the Balkans, an agreement Churchill preferred to tear up so as not to appear crass to future historians, but which "Uncle Joe" insisted that he retain. The U.S.S.R. was to get ninety percent predominance in Romania (within

---

*The P.M. was quite familiar with "Uncle Joe's" substantial undertaking business. Over a suckling-pig dinner in Moscow, the two chatted about the deaths of the kulaks who resisted the collective farms. "Uncle Joe" put the number killed at ten million. Churchill rationalized in *The Hinge Of Fate*: "With the World War going on round us it seemed vain to moralize aloud." This, remember, from the man who told the boys at Harrow to never give in, "in nothing, great or small, large or petty — never give in except to convictions of honour and good sense."

months, the Soviet Deputy Foreign Minister led a *coup* in Bucharest); ten percent in Greece; a fifty-fifty split in Yugoslavia and Hungary; and, seventy-five percent predominance in Bulgaria. According to Professor Carroll Quigley: "At Stalin's insistence, the gist of the arrangement had already been sent to Washington, where Roosevelt initialed it . . . ."(*Tragedy And Hope*)

Churchill even covered up the slaughter by the Russians in Katyn Forest of almost fifteen thousand Polish officers and intellectuals, and pressured the Government-in-Exile to withdraw demands for investigation. Throughout the war, the Nazis were blamed for the Katyn massacre, though the Polish Prime Minister had presented Churchill with a "wealth of evidence" of Russian responsibility. While it was allegedly for the independence of Poland that Britain declared war, thirty years after the fact a small item appeared on page sixteen of the *New York Times* for August 5, 1973, revealing: "Wartime papers of Sir Winston Churchill made public this week show that he agreed in 1944 to Soviet domination of Poland in exchange for Stalin's support of British interests in the Far East and the Mediterranean."

Winston Churchill may have explained it himself with the assertion: "I do not care much for Poles myself." (*The Great Man*) Churchill, in fact, grew angry with the free Poles in London who refused to be ruled by the Kremlin's Lublin gang. He "was not going to wreck the peace of Europe," he roared, "because of a quarrel between Poles." John T. Flynn sadly reflected on the birthday party held for Churchill at the Teheran Conference:

"Czechoslovakia's disappearance in 1939 into the darkness of Hitler's tyranny had called forth doleful eloquence from Mr. Churchill. Now the disappearance of Poland and the four little Baltic states behind the dark iron curtain of Stalin's tyranny was made to the flowing beakers of vodka and the merry shouts of the happy chieftains who were arranging the affairs of the brave new world."

It was agreed that the deal would remain secret so that Roosevelt would not lose the votes of "from six to seven million Americans of Polish extraction . . . ." That was the kind of politics "Uncle Joe" understood.

At Teheran, Stalin played with Churchill as a dog plays with a bone — sometimes threatening, sometimes jovial. Shortly thereafter, U.S. General Albert C. Wedemeyer stayed at the villa in Marrakech where Churchill had just spent a month. "He [*Churchill*] let it be known he was suffering from a bad cold, but actually, I was told he did not want to return to London and face a hostile Commons after having his nose twisted by Stalin at Teheran." (*Wedemeyer Reports!*, New York, Holt, 1958)

Stalin always seemed to have little trouble getting what he wanted from the British Prime Minister. For instance, it was Churchill who urged the sellout of General Draža Mihailovic and his brave Chetniks in favor of Tito's Yugoslavian Communists. W.S.C. wired F.D.R. in 1944 to urge that he cease even communicating with Mihailovic. Roosevelt complied and the general was later executed by Josíp Broz Tito. Churchill assured the British that Comrade Tito had "largely sunk his Communist aspect in his character as a Yugoslav patriotic leader." Winston called him an "outstanding leader, glorious in the fight for freedom." Around this time, when one of Churchill's pro-Tito associates offered some slight worry about a post-war Yugoslavia under the Communists, Churchill challenged him by inquiring whether he intended to live there after the war. No sir, was the reply. "Neither do I," Churchill said. "And, that being so, the less you and I worry about the form of Government they set up, the better." (*War In The Shadows*, Robert B. Asprey, Garden City, Doubleday, 1975)

For the postwar world, Churchill foresaw and approved a greatly expanded Welfare State in Britain and proposed a United States of Europe which would mean an end to the British Empire. But first German industry and productivity must be destroyed forever.

Churchill agreed with Roosevelt to implement the infamous Morgenthau-White Plan for Germany. This plan, blocked by fear of public outrage, would have turned all Germany into a Communist satellite. Which is hardly surprising since it was the work of Morgenthau's assistant Treasury secretary Harry Dexter White, a secret Communist agent. "Under this plan," noted English lawyer F.J.P. Veale, "Germany was to be transformed into a pastoral country by the simple process of blowing up the mines and demolishing the factories. With regard to the existing population, numbering some seventy millions, most relying on industry for support, reliance was placed on starvation reducing their number to a level which could be supported by agricultural and pastoral pursuits."

Then there was the hideous fire-bombing of the refugees in Dresden. The deputy commander of the British Bomber Command ordered to make the attack was so horrified at the time that he formally queried the Prime Minister about this plan for killing thousands of civilians and rubbling one of the great cities of Europe which, nonetheless, had no strategic importance. The "message was forwarded to Churchill at Yalta, and the reply was instructions to bomb Dresden at the first suitable opportunity." (*'Twas A Famous Victory*)

Then there was the massive forced repatriation after the war. This surrender of millions to immediate execution, or worse in Stalin's death camps, was not even part of the Yalta accords, says "Liberal" Ambassador Charles E. Bohlen. Nothing "in this agreement . . . required the forcible repatriation of unwilling Soviet citizens to the Soviet Union. Yet this is exactly what happened in Germany . . . . The execution of the repatriation was entirely determined by the American and British military." (*Witness To History, 1929-1969*) The villain in this piece was primarily Dwight D. Eisenhower. But where was the eloquent Churchill, lover of freedom, scourge of tyrants? He was off painting pictures and pouting about in his special imported silk underwear. His Government had been voted out of office by the Labour Party and Winnie was depressed. Siberia wasn't a very jolly place either.

Yet the sulking Churchill gave no warning of Soviet plans known to him well before the famous "Iron Curtain" speech of 1946. For example, former German spymaster Reinhard Gehlen describes in his memoirs a copy of a Churchill intelligence analysis, received in 1943, "that was entirely accurate in its picture of Soviet potential and intentions." Britain "had few illusions about the future development of Poland and the Balkan countries, including Hungary, into Soviet satellites." (*The Service*) No indeed, in fact Churchill agreed to it.

British Intelligence was now riddled with such creatures as Soviet agent Kim Philby, working hard to make certain that Churchill did not renege on the sellout. Onetime British secret agent Malcolm Muggeridge recalls the times he spent with another such agent, whose *nom de guerre* was Adrian. "At one end of the scale, Adrian insisted, Roosevelt and Churchill did everything in their power to ensure that, when Germany finally collapsed, Stalin easily occupied and dominated the countries adjoining his frontiers, and, at the other, our young spy-masters showed a like determination so to arrange matters that, in countries further away, he was presented with a well-armed, well-financed and well-organized underground army." (*Chronicles Of Wasted Time: The Infernal Grove*, New York, Morrow, 1974)

Winston S. Churchill was to return to office as Prime Minister between 1951 and 1955, and finally to die at age ninety in 1965. By then the British Empire was no more. Stalin and his successors and surrogates had placed more than one billion people in a Communist hell.

But one Churchill prediction had certainly come true. It was his 1945 secret message to F.D.R. quoted in *Triumph And Tragedy*, which read: "I think the end of this war may well prove to be more disappointing than was the last."

Ah, Winston Churchill, the master of understatement.

Chapter XXII
The Truth About Truman

DISCOVERED at age thirty-eight by the boss of a corrupt big-city machine; elected by that same machine twelve years later to the U.S. Senate with tens of thousands of "ghost" votes; nominated as candidate for Vice President after being "cleared" by a top Communist operative; rising to the Presidency upon the intervention of death; elected in his own right by the slimmest of margins; then, leaving the White House when it got too hot in the kitchen. That, in capsule, was the political career of Harry S Truman (1884-1972), thirty-third President of the United States — a man who in the 1976 election was cited by candidates of *both* major political parties as an exemplary Chief Executive.

"And thus the whirligig of time," said the Bard's clown, "brings in his revenge."

The passage of time and a widespread and deliberate misrepresentation of the Truman Administration have left a distorted portrait of Harry Truman and his political career. Consider the fabled rise of the humble but oh-so-honest Man from Independence. Before being picked up by the Tom Pendergast machine of Kansas City, Truman ran a haberdashery that failed. The official legend has it — see *Webster's American Biographies*, for one example — that Truman "refused to declare himself a bankrupt and eventually paid back every penny." It is a nice story, but those with reason to know say it is utter fabrication; that Harry ran out on his debts and never paid a penny until, as President, he was fearful of being exposed.

William Bradford Huie, in 1951 the editor of *The American Mercury*, quoted the lawyer who represented the President's brother, Vivian, in the mortgage foreclosure on the President's mother's farm.* As the lawyer put it: "Harry Truman is a deadbeat and has been all his life. Vivian is a splendid citizen, honest and responsible; Harry is the bad apple in that barrel. He has escaped his responsibilities simply by slopping at the public trough . . . . Even after he became President his brother had to run around here with other people's money trying to settle — not *pay*, but *settle* — judgments against him at ten cents on the dollar. As a person Harry Truman is a liar and a deadbeat; and as a willing tool of Tom Pendergast he was the enemy of every decent citizen in this community."

Which is the true account? Well, President Truman flew into one of his well-known rages over the *Mercury* report, and editor Huie noted in the August 1951 issue that "the Truman water boys activated at least sixteen government lawyers who began flying around at Lord knows how much government expense; and our telephone lines in both Maryland and New York suddenly had enough taps on them to give us stage fright were we not accustomed to addressing large audiences." The President certainly wasn't behaving like an innocent man.

Harry Truman claimed repeatedly: "Tom Pendergast never asked me to do a dishonest thing." But then old Tom never *asked* his kept politicians to do a thing — he *told* them what to do. Tom had to do that to run the only open city between Houston and Chicago, where gangsters walked the streets without fear and gambling and prostitution were protected industries. In any case, Harry had a great capacity for rationalizing away dishonesty, to the point that he once actually spoke endearingly of Jesse James on the floor of the U.S. Senate. Some of the Truman land, you see, had been bought from the notorious Younger brothers who ran with the James Gang. (*Give 'Em Hell Harry*, Eldorous L. Dayton, New York, Devin-Adair, 1956)

Of course the Pendergast Gang had put Harry in the Senate in the first place. The year was 1934, and in Kansas City it was known as the "Bloody Election," involving an estimated one hundred thousand felonies, two hundred assaults, and four murders. By 1936, Tom Pendergast was under federal investigation, and Harry Truman took the Senate floor to demand that the U.S. Attorney investigating old Tom not be reappointed, saying that "a Jackson County, Missouri, Democrat has as

---

*In 1938, Senator Truman obtained — through Pendergast Gang connections — an unsound, illegal, non-bankable loan of $35,000 on his mother's already-mortgaged farm, for which he apparently repaid not one cent. Despite the rapid rise in land values because of World War II, reported the *Mercury*, "the county finally had to foreclose the mortgage when Republicans gained the power to do so. Truman's mother had begun borrowing the money originally for him; and, on the bitterest day of her life, he allowed her to be dispossessed and sent to the little house in Grandview where she died." Harry's federal wages were not garnishable, and he kept no funds in any bank. According to a Kansas City banker: "He either kept money in his pocket or in Old Tom's safe."

much chance of a fair trial in the Federal District of Western Missouri as a Jew would have in a Hitler Court . . . ." Whereupon U.S. District Court Judge Albert Reeves called the Truman tirade the "speech of a man nominated by 'ghost' votes, elected with 'ghost' votes, and whose speech was probably written by 'ghost' writers."

U.S. Attorney Maurice Milligan "eventually secured 283 convictions for vote frauds and revealed that 86,000 phony names had been added to the registration rolls" to elect Truman, reported Robert S. Allen and William V. Shannon. "Concerning these scandals, Truman remarked, 'Those things were due to the over-zealousness of Tom's boys. They were too anxious to make a good showing for the boss, and they took the easiest way. Tom didn't know anything about it — he has never been involved in that sort of thing.'

"Milligan soon proved that the sort of thing Tom was personally involved in was equally fraudulent. Pendergast was bundled off to Leavenworth for taking a bribe in an insurance-settlement case."* (*The Truman Merry-Go-Round*, New York, Vanguard, 1950)

In fact he took bribes from the whole insurance industry.

There was enough of the Pendergast strength remaining in 1940 to renominate Truman by a scant seven thousand votes. Harry did not forget the gang boss who made him Senator, and as Vice President of the United States he attended the funeral of Kansas City's answer to Al Capone.[†] After Roosevelt's death, Truman immediately replaced Pendergast prosecutor Milligan with one Sam Wear. Sam had been chairman of Missouri's Democratic State Committee. "He pardoned fifteen of the Pendergast people who had been in prison for the vote frauds. On December 7, 1945, the President wrote to Jim Pendergast, Tom Pendergast's nephew who was the heir to the Pendergast machine: 'Dear Jim: I am enclosing you a check for $6 in payment of my Jackson Democratic Club dues. I hope the outfit is still going good. Sincerely yours, Harry.' On the wall of Jim Pendergast's office hung a White House portrait of Harry Truman with the autograph 'To James M. Pendergast — friend, comrade, and adviser.' " (*The Truman Scandals*, Jules Abels, Chicago, Regnery, 1956)

One gets some idea of the continuing effort to whitewash Truman from the fact that not too many years ago ABC Television broadcast a

---

*In 1946 yet another vote-fraud scandal was uncovered in Kansas City. Prosecution was avoided when a safe containing the evidence for scores of indictments of Truman cronies was cracked even as the President was only blocks away. The crooks took only ballot boxes and registration books. Naturally the President said he had "no comment" and the cases against his friends were dropped.
†In fact, Truman compared Old Tom to Old Joe Stalin, for whom he had high praise as late as 1948. When President Truman first met the Soviet dictator at Potsdam, he exclaimed: "Stalin is as near like Tom Pendergast as any man I know." (*Give 'Em Hell Harry*)

"documentary" on Harry Truman that presented him as a *courageous opponent* of the Pendergast Gang!

Truman's rise to the White House is one of the most bizarre in America's political history. In 1944, political insiders knew that in nominating a Democratic Vice President they were probably choosing the next President. Franklin Roosevelt was dying. And F.D.R. placed the nomination of his Vice President in the hands of the notorious Moscovite labor leader Sidney Hillman, saying "Clear it with Sidney." Hillman picked Truman. As a Senator, Harry had once urged us to support Hitler against Stalin, and *vice versa*, while they fought it out. He was now back in line.

To Middle America, of course, Truman seemed preferable to the screwball Henry Wallace. But now and again embarrassing rumors crept out about Truman's onetime membership in the Ku Klux Klan. A witness reported that he and Harry had joined the Klan on the same day, and boasted that he had been the man who introduced his fellow Klansman to Tom Pendergast. It was not an uncorroborated report. "Late in the [*1944*] campaign, the Hearst newspapers carried a charge that Truman had been a member of the Ku Klux Klan . . . ." (*Beyond The New Deal: Harry S. Truman And American Liberalism*, Alonzo L. Hamby, New York, Columbia University Press, 1973) But, says Hamby, "the senator's swift and convincing denial doubtless carried weight with most liberals." In any case, the denial let "Liberals" off the hook — just as they got off the hook with such former Klansmen as longtime Supreme Court Justice Hugo Black and the current Senate Minority Leader, Robert Byrd.

Klansman or not, Harry came to know the impact of the allegation. He later falsely charged the patriotic John Birch Society with being "nothing but the Ku Klux Klan without the $16 nightshirts." A fanatical partisan to the end, he even alleged that Birchers were "not fighting Communism. It's a camouflage with them, and they don't mean it. They are trying to set up a police state." Sadly for Mr. Truman that was in 1961, before his friends began to explain away his growing vituperation by noting that he was suffering advanced senility.

E.L. Dayton comments that Harry Truman "of course gets furious whenever the Klan is brought up, and it keeps popping up, its most determined appearance being in 1944. The reason it does keep coming up is that there seems to be some basis for the story. At least enough to make political foes believe he applied for membership and offered to pay his dues, but withdrew when he found he would have to give promises to give no more political jobs to Catholics" in the vital Italian wards controlled by Pendergast. (*Give 'Em Hell Harry*) The most charitable thing that can be said is that graft and patronage were more important to Mr. Truman than bigotry.

As Vice President, Truman knew little of what went on at Yalta, nor was he briefed on development of the atomic bomb — two matters with which he soon had to deal. The Yalta Agreement, which divided Germany; gave the Soviets hegemony over much of Eastern and Central Europe; and allowed belated Soviet entry into the war with Japan, was actually believed by Vice President Truman to be a godsend. Thanks to Yalta, he said, "We are going to look forward to the most glorious period of history in the world." (*No Wonder We Are Losing*, Robert Morris, Plano, Texas, University of Plano Press, 1958)

Our betrayal of Chiang Kai-shek by surrendering Manchuria to the Reds, and our arming of the Communists in the East, were both decided at Yalta — but they were commitments to which Truman acceded at Potsdam. Never mind that our ally Nationalist China was trying to hold off a Communist insurgency while fighting the Japanese. And never mind that, three months before Potsdam, Truman was advised by fifty top Army intelligence officers through General George C. Marshall:

"The entry of Soviet Russia into the Asiatic war would be a political event of world-shaking importance, the ill effects of which would be felt for decades to come . . . . [*It*] would destroy America's position in Asia quite as effectively as our position is now destroyed east of the Elbe and beyond the Adriatic.

"If Russia enters the Asiatic war, China will certainly lose her independence, to become the Poland of Asia; Korea, the Asiatic Rumania; Manchukuo, the Soviet Bulgaria. Whether more than a nominal China will exist after the impact of the Russian armies is felt is very doubtful. Chiang may have to depart and a Chinese Soviet government may be installed in Nanking which we would have to recognize.

"To take a line of action which would save few lives now, and only a little time — at an unpredictable cost in lives, treasure, and honor in the future — and simultaneously destroy our ally China, would be an act of treachery that would make the Atlantic Charter and our hopes for peace a tragic farce.

"Under no circumstances should we pay the Soviet Union to destroy China. This would certainly injure the material and moral position of the United States in Asia." (*McCarthyism: The Fight For America*, Joseph R. McCarthy, New York, Devin-Adair, 1952)

Ignoring the wise advice of his intelligence team, Truman went off to deal with an unyielding Stalin at Potsdam. After all, he had been fully briefed a mere two days before departure by Owen Lattimore, who presented the President with what amounted to a blueprint for U.S. policy toward China after the war. The trouble, alas, was that it was a Communist blueprint, and Lattimore was a conscious agent of the Soviet conspiracy. When Truman announced the Japanese surrender it was reported that one of the two books on the President's desk was Lattimore's *Solution In Asia*.

The Atomic Age was upon us, and with it the move for a New World Order that involved Soviet manipulation of U.S. foreign policy. Among Stalin's lawyers in this country even before the U.S.S.R. was recognized by Washington was Dean Acheson, a man later to be U.S. Secretary of State under Truman. Which makes the following gushing hyperbole of editor Jack Stuart more understandable: "When Dean Acheson proclaimed that he had been 'present at the creation' of a new world order, he identified the proper basis for evaluating the Truman presidency." (*Succession Or Repudiation? Realities Of The Truman Presidency*, edited by Jack Stuart, New York, Simon and Schuster, 1975) This is not the place to debate the issue, but it is instructive to recall that Truman's Chief of Staff, Admiral William D. Leahy, didn't think the atom bomb needed to be dropped. And the fact is that the Japanese were suing for peace *before the bombings* on virtually the same terms demanded after Hiroshima and Nagasaki were obliterated.

As the war ended, the scene shifted dramatically to China. The Communist agents in our government had Truman's ear as well as Acheson's. For example, among the Communists and subversives advising Dean Acheson on China were Alger Hiss, Owen Lattimore, Lauchlin Currie, John Stewart Service, John Carter Vincent, John P. Davies, and Edmund Oliver Clubb. Mao and Stalin had quite a team throwing subversive advice at Truman — with more Reds than a Cincinnati baseball club. And, as John T. Flynn of the *New York Times* observed, "there is little doubt that the conspirators got to the mind of President Truman — for from that day to this he has been the most ferocious defender" of all the ugly consequences. (*The Lattimore Story*, New York, Devin-Adair, 1953)

Accordingly, Truman is himself most responsible of those Who Lost China. Indeed, in 1946 the Nationalists had the Communists on the run, but Truman sent General Marshall to China and Marshall forced Chiang to agree to a cease-fire and to let the Reds hold their gains in Manchuria.

"In the interval that followed," recorded Freda Utley, "General Marshall and President Truman took steps to prevent the Nationalist forces from obtaining arms and ammunition. At the end of July 1946 General Marshall clamped an embargo on the sale of arms and ammunition to China. For almost a year thereafter the Chinese Government was prevented from *buying*, and definitely *not given*, a single round of ammunition. On August 18, 1946, President Truman issued an executive order saying that China was not to be allowed any 'surplus' American weapons 'which could be used in fighting a civil war,' meaning a war with the Communists.'' (*The China Story*, Chicago, Regnery, 1951) The Soviets, meanwhile, were turning over to Mao the vast stores of U.S. military supplies Truman had provided Stalin for the assault on Japan.

Little wonder that Senator Robert Taft (R.-Ohio) declared ''that the Democrats 'at Teheran, at Yalta, at Potsdam, and at Moscow pursued a policy of appeasing Russia, a policy which has sacrificed throughout Eastern Europe and Asia the freedom of many nations and millions of people.' Truman, he continued, wanted Communist support in the elections and a Congress 'dominated by a policy of appeasing the Russians abroad and of fostering Communism at home.' The senator depicted the Democratic party as being 'so divided between Communism and Americanism that its foreign policy can only be futile and contradictory.' '' (*Conflict And Crisis*, Robert J. Donovan, New York, Norton, 1977)

In those 1946 elections, the Republicans won both Houses on Capitol Hill for the first time since 1928.

The Communist issue was meanwhile capturing the attention of concerned Americans. And in March of 1947 the United States agreed to take over the commitments of the hard-pressed British in the Red-threatened countries of Greece and Turkey. This resulted from the so-called Truman Doctrine, the work of U.S. Secretary of Defense James Forrestal, who was determined to save those beleaguered nations from the Communists. That was very different from the ballyhooed Marshall Plan, which offered to aid even the Soviet Union and her satellites, but not anti-Communist Spain. ''What Marshall did,'' said Senator Joseph McCarthy, ''to borrow the facetious language of some opponents of his plan, was to put Europe on the WPA.''[*]

On March 12, 1947, while turning a deaf ear to our Chinese allies, ''Mr. Truman took his case to Congress, laying the Greece-Turkey crisis before a special joint session. He called for American assistance to 'support free people who are resisting attempted subjugation.' And he asked Congress for an initial grant of $400,000,000 in economic and armed aid, the bulk of it for Greece.

''The President's program, and his statement of what became known as the 'Truman Doctrine,' brought a decidedly mixed reaction from Congress and the country. Americans sensed a radical new departure in foreign policy, and one with perhaps untold implications for the future.

---

[*]With all due respect to McCarthy, it wasn't Marshall's plan but was created by the infamous Council on Foreign Relations.

Some called it the most significant development in American relations since the Monroe Doctrine. Critics on the left declared that the program was imperialist in nature and would find the United States 'bailing out' an outdated and unpopular monarchy in Greece. Critics on the right, including some newly-elected Republican senators, held that it meant unlimited expenditures and that the nation was 'bailing out' the responsibilities of the British Labor Government.'' (*The Private Papers Of Senator Vandenberg*, edited by Arthur H. Vandenberg Jr., Boston, Houghton Mifflin, 1952) There was some truth in all of this, but the Congress was nearly as anti-Communist as the American people and welcomed the President's apparent change in course.

Harry Truman was anything but consistent. Reporters Allen and Shannon comment: ''Within a period of nine months, Truman oscillated violently between endorsing the 'iron curtain' speech of Winston Churchill at Fulton, Missouri, and endorsing the 'let's-mind-our-own-business' speech of Henry Wallace at Madison Square Garden in New York.'' (*The Truman Merry-Go-Round*)

Harry was playing domestic politics with U.S. foreign policy, something he also did in the case of Israel. On one occasion Truman declared himself very much ''put out'' with the Jews, and said ''Jesus Christ couldn't please them when he was here on earth, so how could anyone expect that I would have any luck?'' (*It Didn't Start With Watergate*, Victor Lasky) According to then-Commerce Secretary Henry Wallace: ''Truman said he had no use for them [*Jews*] and didn't care what happened to them.'' Nevertheless, he immediately approved the founding of Israel. As did the Soviet Union, by the way.

Truman explained to the U.S. diplomats working with the Arab states: ''I'm sorry, gentlemen, but I have to answer to hundreds of thousands who are anxious for the success of Zionism; I do not have hundreds of thousands of Arabs among my constituents.'' (*Conflict And Crisis*)

Maybe Truman thought there were more Maoists among his constituents than there were Americans faithful to our ally Chiang Kai-shek. Either that or his Communist advisors had him completely spellbound; for, as Truman's man George Marshall was to boast in withholding arms from Chiang: ''As Chief-of-Staff I armed 39 anti-Communist divisions. Now with a stroke of a pen I disarm them.'' (*America's Retreat From Victory*, Joseph R. McCarthy, New York, Devin-Adair, 1951)

We have reaped the whirlwind of the Truman sellout of the Republic of China, and now others labor to betray the R.O.C. on Taiwan. Frazier Hunt reported of the first betrayal that Lieutenant General Albert Wedemeyer ''did everything in his power to offset the working of the unfair embargo that denied aid to the Nationalist government while Russia armed the Communist elements. Even after the embargo was formally lifted in May 1947, the State Department managed to keep all real military help from reaching the Nationalists by simply holding up shipping permits. Marshall, then Secretary of State, eventually ordered Wedemeyer to make a full investigation of both the Chinese and Korean situations. The report Wedemeyer delivered was an extraordinarily wise and far-seeing analysis, but neither its findings nor its solemn warnings were followed. Instead, its suggestions concerning the formation of a strong defense organization in South Korea were pigeonholed by order of Secretary of State Marshall, who ordered General Wedemeyer to step out of the picture." (*The Untold Story Of Douglas MacArthur*, New York, Manor Books, 1977) In fact, Marshall wrote to Truman of the Wedemeyer Report that "I think this should be suppressed." The President noted on the letter, "I agree — H.T."

When the deteriorating situation in China became a concern before the 1948 elections, even a Kansas City ward heeler knew enough to make a show of expediting Chiang's orders for weapons. But by the time they were sent — November of 1948 — most of China had fallen to the Reds. And while Greece and Turkey, among others, were permitted to buy our "surplus" weapons at ten percent of list price, the Chinese discovered that they were "required to pay more than double published prices, and an average of *50 per cent in excess of current commercial quotations for new manufactures.* There was no possibility of obtaining the arms or ammunition from any private sources." (*The China Story*)

But you see, claimed Truman in May 1949, Chiang's Government was just a bunch of "grafters and crooks" who had stolen at least a billion dollars in American aid and had no interest in the masses of hungry Chinese.* In *Beyond The New Deal*, Alonzo Hamby noted that Harry Truman actually professed to believe that the "insurgents were not real Communists — 'Joe Stalin says that people of North China will never be Communists and he's about right.' Truman clearly hoped that the United States could have a working relationship with the new regime. 'The dragon is going to turn over,' he told [*David*] Lilienthal, 'and after that perhaps some advances can be made . . . .' In August, the administration

---

*The charge was bitterly ironic coming from a Truman Administration that was itself far more corrupt than it claimed of Chiang — especially in the Reconstruction Finance Corporation and the Internal Revenue Bureau. After offering more than three hundred pages of detailed evidence, Jules Abels concluded that the amount of money lost through the Truman wholesale tax frauds "must have run into the billions. *** The Teague committee of the Democratic 82nd Congress estimated the loss in the graft-ridden G.I. educational programs in the 'hundreds of millions.' In the Section 608 swindles under FHA, profits of 20,000 per cent were not uncommon, as we have seen, and one financing company netted $26,000,000." Corruption, found Mr. Abels, "was so rampant and so widespread, and officials within the Administration acted so often in concert, that the shape of a general conspiracy to obstruct justice is indicated." (*The Truman Scandals*)

released a 'White Paper' which strongly indicted the Chinese Nationalists and defended the administration's refusal to become more deeply involved in the Chinese conflict.''

Indeed, after the Nationalist Government had retreated to Taiwan, President Truman declared in 1950 that no aid or defense would be provided to the island. Of seventy-five million dollars in aid voted to Chiang by the Congress, Harry Truman said off-the-record: ''I have still got that $75 million locked up in the drawer of my desk, and it is going to stay there.'' (*Beyond The New Deal*) Moreover, said Truman, Taiwan should be ''returned'' to the Mainland regime under the Cairo agreement made during World War II. (*No Wonder We Are Losing*)

Not only Taiwan, added Dean Acheson, but South Korea too was outside of ''our defense perimeter.'' In other words, the Truman Administration would follow the advice of Owen Lattimore to let Korea fall to the Reds but not to let it look like we pushed her. In large part this was to be accomplished by withholding arms from the South Korean ''police force'' as North Korea mobilized for war — all the time suppressing the Wedemeyer Report which predicted what this would mean. The China betrayal was to be repeated in Korea. ''The Korean Aid Bill of February 14, 1950, afforded only economic aid, and the $10.5 million of arms aid voted the previous October had not actually been given nine months later when the war began. As in the case of the 1948 China Aid Act, the Administration succeeded in thwarting the intent of Congress by not delivering the munitions.'' (*The China Story*)

Meanwhile, of course, the President had been elected in his own right in 1948, despite the growing concern over the Alger Hiss spy case, which Truman repeatedly called a ''red herring'' in the course of the campaign. After all, as far as the public knew, it was still the word of Hiss against that of Whittaker Chambers. The F.B.I. knew better, of course, and so did Truman. The President campaigned against *the Congress*, and called it the worst in history. Truman went so far as to declare: ''Personally, I like old Joe Stalin, but he's a prisoner of the Politburo, which is like our 80th Congress.'' A frothing Truman bellowed that: ''Powerful forces, like those that created European Fascists, are working through the Republican Party [*to*] undermine . . . American democracy.'' (*McCarthy And His Enemies*, William F. Buckley Jr. and L. Brent Bozell, Chicago, Regnery, 1954)

That 1948 election, which delivered a Truman victory over Thomas E. Dewey, was anything but a match between ''Liberal'' and Conservative. Truman won ''the farm states' votes that elected him,'' explained Arthur Krock of the *New York Times*, ''by successfully blaming the Republicans in Congress for a shortage of farm storage facilities, whereas the blame actually lay at the door of his own Secretary of Agriculture. He struck at Dewey's jugular which had been foolishly exposed by his attempts to out-promise the Democratic liberals." (*Memoirs*) The "me-too" Republican lost the White House by refusing to take the offensive.

Meanwhile it was gradually dawning on the American people that the world was rapidly falling, and being pushed, into Communist hands. Even Truman's own National Security Council issued a document (NSC-7), dated March 30, 1948, which observed: "Today Stalin has come close to achieving what Hitler attempted in vain. The Soviet world extends from the Elbe River and the Adriatic on the west to Manchuria on the east, and embraces one fifth of the land surface of the world." (*Conflict And Crisis*) And that was before the fall of Mainland China and the attack on South Korea.[*]

After Senator Joseph McCarthy's famous 1950 speech in Wheeling, West Virginia, the President again indicated what he thought of a strict anti-Communist line. The day after that speech, commented Senator McCarthy, "I wired President Truman and suggested that he call in Secretary of State Acheson and ask for the names of the 205 who were kept in the State Department despite the fact that Truman's own security officers had declared them unfit to serve. I urged him to have Acheson tell him how many of the 205 were still in the State Department and why. I told the President that I had the names of 57. I offered those names to the President. The offer was never accepted. The wire was never answered." (*McCarthyism: The Fight For America*)

Similarly, and typically, Truman also ignored the Report of a Senate Subcommittee that refused to approve Philip Jessup, Truman's nominee as a U.S. delegate to the U.N. The Subcommittee found that, at the very least, Jessup had an "affinity for Communist causes." Truman responded by appointing him to an interim position at the United Nations — and Comrade Jessup appeared as a character witness at both of Alger Hiss's trials. Harry Truman was likewise repeatedly informed by the F.B.I. that Assistant Treasury Secretary Harry Dexter White was a Soviet spy, and White was not only kept in office but promoted to become U.S. Director of the International Monetary Fund.

As Attorney General Herbert A. Brownell reported in 1953: "Harry Dexter White was known to be a Communist spy by the very people who appointed him to the most sensitive and important position he held in Government service. The F.B.I. became aware of White's espionage

---

[*]For a review of President Truman's role in the Korean War, see Chapter XXIII. Suffice it to say that Truman's response to General Douglas MacArthur's assertion that "There is no substitute for victory" was to relieve our foremost military genius of command while continuing to grant the enemy sanctuary.

activities at an early point in his Government career and from the beginning made reports on these activities to the appropriate officials in authority. But these reports did not impede White's advancement in the Administration . . . .

"But I can now announce officially for the first time in public, that the records in my department show that White's spying activities for the Soviet Government were reported in detail by the F.B.I. to the White House by means of a report delivered to President Truman through his military aide, Brig. Gen. Harry H. Vaughan, in December of 1945."

Oh yes, General Vaughan of the famous deep-freeze and mink-coat scandals. Vaughan was vigorously involved in lining his own pockets and those of his friends as a tool of "certain lobbyists who came to be known as the 'five percenters' because of the fee they exacted for their influence on behalf of the War Assets Administration and elsewhere. [*Vaughan was*] Truman's oldest, closest buddy from the Argonne . . . ." (*Harry S Truman*, Joseph Gies, Garden City, Doubleday & Company, 1968) Like his mentor, old Tom Pendergast, the President who scourged corruption in Nationalist China sheltered those crooks among his buddies that he could. And there were many.

All of this was too much for the electorate. Especially after Truman showed his contempt for the Constitution by attempting to seize the steel industry in 1952, having refused to invoke the Taft-Hartley Act which had been approved over his veto, and began to hint of a communications takeover. *That* was too much even for a Supreme Court whose members had all been appointed by Roosevelt and Truman.

In March of 1952, aware that he couldn't be re-elected, Truman announced his decision not to run again for the Presidency. He had been caught covering up for the "five-percenters," for his Pendergast cronies, and for Communists and security risks; he had delivered Eastern Europe to the Reds and then Mainland China; our atomic secrets were reported stolen and the people were alarmed; the Wedemeyer Report had been suppressed and Truman's fumbling had brought on the Korean War; when General MacArthur tried to win it, Truman sacked him; the Administration's hand was caught in the till again and again, so that between January 1951 and April of 1952 at least one hundred seventy-seven officials of the Internal Revenue Bureau had to be "separated" from their jobs; and, Alger Hiss had proved not to be a "red herring" after all. Truman couldn't have been re-elected in a race against a cross-eyed polecat with halitosis, and he knew it. His reputation would now have to be left to friendly "Liberal" historians — who would be more than glad to oblige.

For his own part, according to a favorable biography, Harry Truman asked only that Americans remember him in terms of his favorite epitaph from Tombstone, Arizona, which declared in part: "HE DONE HIS DAMNDEST." Just so.

Chapter XXIII

Police Action In Korea

IN WORLD WAR II we won on the battlefield — then lost the peace. But President Truman wouldn't even admit we were at war in Korea — a war in which we were forbidden to win and forced to settle for stalemate. The precedent having been set, victory was out of bounds in Vietnam as well, only this time we were defeated. This led to President Carter's willingness to surrender the American Canal and U.S. Canal Zone in Central America without even a fight.

In the middle of the Korean War, General MacArthur said there was no substitute for victory. Today's "Liberal" leaders accept three substitutes — retreat, defeat, and even surrender.

A journey begins with a single step, and that step was taken in Korea even before our policymakers foreswore victory. Roosevelt, Churchill, and Chiang Kai-shek had agreed at the Cairo Conference in 1943 that all of Korea — then occupied by Japan — would at the end of the war become "free and independent." But, at Potsdam two years later, Truman, Churchill, and Stalin hit upon a joint occupation of the country. Dean Rusk, who later recommended Manchurian sanctuary for the Red Chinese during the Korean War, and who as Secretary of State managed the subsequent no-win war in Indochina, was a top staffer involved in choosing the 38th Parallel as the "temporary" division of Korea. For one week of war against his longtime Japanese ally, Stalin was to receive control of North Korea.

The puppet People's Democratic Republic of Korea (N.K.) was set up in the north under thirty-six Soviet-trained Koreans led by Kim Sung Chu — a young fanatic who soon adopted the name of a celebrated anti-Japanese guerrilla leader, Kim Il Sung. The feeble United Nations called for national elections; but the Reds, armed to the teeth by Stalin, refused. The Republic of Korea (R.O.K.) assumed control in the south, elected an Assembly, and chose the great Korean patriot Syngman Rhee as

President. Rhee had for decades headed the Korean Government-in-Exile; held degrees from George Washington, Harvard, and Princeton; was a committed Christian; and, as General James Van Fleet later observed, was certainly "one of the greatest statesmen who ever lived."

After heavily fortifying N.K., the Soviets demanded that all foreign occupation forces be withdrawn. The United States not only agreed to comply, but Secretary of State Dean Acheson pointedly excluded the R.O.K. from our military defense commitments. (*Retreat From Victory*, Drew Middleton, New York, Hawthorn, 1973) In fact Senator Tom Connally, Chairman of the Senate Foreign Relations Committee, "said that Russia could seize South Korea without U.S. intervention because Korea was not 'very greatly important.' " (*Conflict*, Robert Leckie, New York, G.P. Putnam's Sons, 1962)

Moreover, as Major General Courtney Whitney observed, "the State Department made its unilateral decision to limit South Korea's defensive force to light weapons and to organize the defenders along constabulary lines. The excuse given for this decision was that it was necessary to prevent the South Koreans from attacking North Korea — curiously myopic reasoning that of course opened the way for the North Korean attack. It simply provided too much of a temptation for the Communists to resist." (*MacArthur: His Rendezvous With History*, New York, Knopf, 1956)

During the first half of 1950, notes General S.L.A. Marshall, "the NK Army doubled in size. It numbered 170,000 troops with 15 infantry and 2 armored divisions. Russia supplied its main heavy weapons — 150 sturdy T-34 tanks and 200 Yak (propeller-driven) fighter planes — without which there would have been no aggression. South Korea had no tanks, no military planes." (*The Military History Of The Korean War*, New York, Franklin Watts, 1963) In June of 1950, the Reds attacked in force, ripping through the 65,000 lightly armed R.O.K. combat troops in a six-pronged assault intended to sweep the entire peninsula.

The United Nations Security Council, which was being boycotted by the U.S.S.R., quickly voted that North Korea should stop fighting and go home. Seoul fell. American Naval and Air Force units were ordered from Japan by President Truman, and finally authority was granted for the U.S. Army to enter the action . . . under the flag of the United Nations. With the R.O.K.s in disarray, the battle lines shrank rapidly around Pusan at the tip of the peninsula. The U.S. forces, necessarily introduced piece-meal as they became available, were ordered to trade space for time until reinforcements could arrive.

Incredibly, President Truman turned down the offer of 33,000 seasoned troops from the Republic of China, whose government was like ours a member of the U.N. Security Council, and ordered the Seventh Fleet into the waters between Formosa and the mainland to keep Chiang from acting against the Chinese Communists. Everything seemed to be going according to the plan laid down at the State Department by Owen Lattimore, who had in 1949 recommended: "The thing to do is let South Korea fall, but not to let it look as if we pushed it."

The Communists were now aware that we would insure them sanctuary even as our own men were under fire with their backs to the sea. Isolating Chiang, as Frazier Hunt observed, gave Peiping's "war plans a tremendous impetus, because Red China could now enter the Korean war at any time she chose without fear of being attacked on her flank and rear by the Nationalist troops on Formosa. What seemed to the muddled public to be a far-sighted move by the President to save Chiang Kai-shek from invasion was actually nullifying all use for the present of the large Nationalist Army on Formosa as a fighting force against Red China. In one significant gesture it banged the door shut in Chiang's face, and it opened the door into Korea for the Chinese Communists. Possibly as many as a million Red Chinese could now be released from the mainland opposite Formosa and made available for future assignment in Manchuria." (*The Untold Story of Douglas MacArthur*)

But there was still Douglas MacArthur to contend with, now Commander-in-Chief of the U.N. forces. Here was a great soldier who believed in victory. With Seoul in enemy hands, the five-star general flew from Japan to Korea, telling his staff: "Let's go to the front and have a look." He did exactly that, selecting as his observation post a hill only a mile from the occupied former capital of the Republic. "MacArthur had stood on this hill only about an hour. But in that short time he had sketched out in his mind the outline of a strategy that would not only rescue the South Koreans but would defeat the North Koreans as well." (*MacArthur*) This was a plan to invade the port of Inchon, half-way up the peninsula near Seoul, thrusting into the enemy's rear and cutting off his supplies. Such a surprise would allow General Walton Walker to burst out of the Pusan Perimeter at the toe of the peninsula and crush the N.K. forces between them.*

MacArthur planned to strike with X Corps — comprised of the 7th Infantry and 1st Marine Divisions — under his chief of staff, Major General Ned Almond. The Marines would take the port and capture Seoul, while the infantry blocked the enemy from the south. But the Chairman of the Joint Chiefs of Staff, General Omar Bradley, opposed

---

*General Walker had been forced to stabilize his defense lines by ordering: "There must be no further yielding under pressure of the enemy. From now on let every man stand or die."

General MacArthur's plan. As it happens, Bradley had publicly testified in 1949 that he doubted a large amphibious assault would ever again be made. Moreover, General Bradley was critical of the Marine Corps which would lead such an effort. As was Harry Truman, who got into Dutch when he claimed the Marines "have a propaganda machine that is almost equal to Stalin's." But then Harry had liked Uncle Joe.

To be sure, Inchon had huge tides and could be invaded only on a very limited number of days. A sea wall, mud flats, and a garrison island in the harbor were great problems. These and scores of other difficulties were pointed to by Army Chief of Staff General J. Lawton Collins and Chief of Naval Operations Admiral Forrest Sherman — who went to Tokyo to try to dissuade MacArthur from his strategy. Said Admiral Sherman: "If every possible geographical and naval handicap were listed — Inchon has 'em all." (*Reminiscences*, Douglas MacArthur, New York, McGraw-Hill, 1964)

But MacArthur contended that it was exactly these difficulties which would lead the enemy to believe such an attack to be impossible — causing the Reds to commit the sort of military miscalculation that had permitted Wolfe to surprise Montcalm at Quebec and end the French and Indian War.

Virtually all of MacArthur's overseers were skeptical of the Inchon invasion except Defense Secretary Louis Johnson, who was shortly replaced in the post by General George C. Marshall. Even with the whole of the military establishment against him, however, MacArthur remained determined. "The only alternative," he said, "to a stroke such as I propose will be the continuation of the savage sacrifice we are making at Pusan, with no hope of relief in sight. Are you content to let our troops stay in that bloody perimeter like beef cattle in the slaughterhouse? Who will take the responsibility for such a tragedy? Certainly, I will not."

Inchon in our hands, MacArthur explained, would become the anvil upon which General Walker could hammer the retreating enemy, a foe with his supply line cut. "If my estimate is inaccurate and should I run into a defense with which I cannot cope, I will be there personally and will immediately withdraw our forces before they are committed to a bloody set-back. The only loss then will be to my professional reputation. But Inchon will not fail. Inchon will succeed. And it will save 100,000 lives." (*War In Peacetime*, J. Lawton Collins, Boston, Houghton Mifflin, 1969)

The operation was one of the great triumphs of military history. Even to the point that Navy Lieutenant Eugene Clark was able to infiltrate and turn on a lighthouse to guide the ships into the channel. It took but one day to capture Inchon and move on toward Seoul. As Fleet Admiral

"Bull" Halsey put it, Inchon was "the most masterly and audacious strategic stroke in all history."

Seoul was liberated within two weeks, and the Kimpo Airfield taken as well. Only three days after the lightning strike, the enemy's weakness was noticed at Pusan — and General Walker's men, who had been forced to choose between making a bitter stand or dying, now attacked. The Reds "abandoned their arms and equipment; tanks, artillery, trucks and small arms littered the highways all over South Korea. The total of enemy prisoners rose to 130,000. In one brilliant strike — and against the advice of all his superiors — MacArthur had turned defeat into victory and virtually recaptured South Korea." (*MacArthur*)

General MacArthur had vowed: "I shall crush them." And that is what he did. The Hammer and Sickle was hauled down, and everywhere Old Glory was raised in its place. What was all this flag-raising by the Marines? critics asked. And Leatherneck Colonel "Chesty" Puller growled: "A man with a flag in his pack and the desire to run it up on an enemy strongpoint isn't likely to bug out." (*Victory at High Tide*, Robert D. Heinl Jr., Philadelphia, J.B. Lippincott, 1968)

The President and Joint Chiefs now authorized MacArthur to cross the 38th Parallel. "My mission," the general later testified before a Congressional Hearing, "was to clear out all North Korea, to unify it and to liberalize it." But, without MacArthur knowing, the fix was in.

The clearing of the south soon revealed the terrible nature of the intended Red conquest. In Seoul and throughout the country the Reds simply liquidated their opposition. Robert Leckie reports: "At Sachon the North Koreans burned the jail and the 280 South Korean police, government officials and landowners who were inside it. At Anui, at Mokpo, at Kongju, and at Hamyang and Chonju, United Nations soldiers uncovered trenches stuffed with the bodies of hundreds of executed civilians, many of them women and children. Near Taejon airstrip 500 ROK soldiers lay with their hands bound behind their backs and bullet holes in their brains." (*Conflict*)

President Truman was meanwhile telling the American people: "We are not at war." It was, he said, a "police action" against a "bunch of North Korean bandits." (*Douglas MacArthur*, Clark Lee and Richard Henschel, New York, Holt, 1952) But Truman was not above flying to Wake Island in mid-October of 1950 as MacArthur's victorious forces rolled north. The United States was facing congressional elections, and it would not be harmful to be photographed with the heroes of the "police action." At Wake Island, General of the Army MacArthur told President Truman that he did not believe the Russians or Red Chinese would intervene — because our vast air power, which included a virtual monopoly on atomic weapons, could cut their supply lines and guarantee their destruction. MacArthur had no idea he would be forbidden the use of these forces.

The critical betrayal occurred when the Red Chinese were given sanctuary in Manchuria without fear of counterattack. This limitation, read a staff commentary, ''upon available military force to repel an enemy attack would have no precedent either in our own history or the history of the world. That the Red Chinese commander apparently knew such a decision would be forthcoming while General MacArthur did not, represents one of the blackest pages ever recorded.'' (*MacArthur: 1941-1951*, Charles A. Willoughby and John Chamberlain, New York, McGraw-Hill, 1954)

Our British allies maintained diplomatic relations with Red China, and there is little doubt that the British informed Peiping that the sanctuary policy would not be breached. In any case, Russian spies Donald Maclean and Guy Burgess, who fled to the Kremlin in 1951, were Red agents with access to such information. As was Kim Philby — the head of British intelligence in Washington maintaining liaison with the State Department, Central Intelligence Agency, Federal Bureau of Investigation . . . and Moscow, for whom he really worked. Veteran reporter Willard Edwards of the *Chicago Tribune* told part of the story in 1968:

''In a private interview, not published until after his death, MacArthur said that every message he sent to Washington during the Korean War was turned over by the State Department to the British, who, in turn, leaked it to Moscow.

''He also charged, in another statement, that President Truman refused to investigate his warnings about such leaks because they came 'after the Alger Hiss and Harry Dexter White spy scandals' and therefore 'caused the deepest resentment.' Truman fired MacArthur on April 11, 1951.

''A former CIA officer told the *Chicago Tribune* there was no question that Philby saw a CIA memorandum in October 1950, which reported that the Chinese Communists would move in to protect electric power installations along the Yalu River and a subsequent order to MacArthur not to advance upon them but to let them occupy that frontier.

''The Chinese Communists invaded on November 26, secure in the knowledge that they were protected from destruction of their sources of supplies.''

So it was that the U.N. forces were sent reeling — yet could not bomb airfields and Communist depots in clear sight across the Yalu. Communist MiGs could attack us, then hide on the other side. Anti-aircraft in China was employed with impunity against our vulnerable planes trying to bomb only the Korean side of bridges over the river — almost impossible in any event. At the time of the Red Chinese attack across the Yalu, Air Force Lieutenant General George Stratemeyer was to recall, we "had sufficient air, bombardment, fighters, reconnaissance so that I could have taken out all those supplies, those airdromes on the other side of the Yalu; I could have bombed the devils between there and Mukden, stopped that railroad operating and the people of China that were fighting could not have been supplied . . . . But we weren't permitted to do it. As a result, a lot of American blood was spilled over there in Korea." (*U.S. News & World Report*, February 11, 1955)

This policy was somehow supposed to placate the Red Chinese, who responded with a massive onslaught of their own. But even in retrograde the forces under MacArthur reacted valiantly. "The losses that we had in that withdrawal," the general said during Senate Hearings, "were less than the losses we had in our victorious attack at Inchon." Sadly, among those lost was General Walton Walker, killed in a road accident; General Matthew Ridgway was named his successor at the head of the 8th Army.

The first of January saw an all-out Communist offensive, with Seoul being recaptured by the Reds. Then it was counteroffensive; in March of 1951, our forces reoccupied the capital city. Still the enemy enjoyed sanctuary, and the Joint Chiefs even forbade the bombing of Racin, a North Korean city thirty-five miles from the Siberian border, because it was too close to the U.S.S.R.

At home, angry House Minority Leader Joseph Martin declared: "If we are not in Korea to win, then this Administration should be indicted for the murder of thousands of American boys." But, even while MacArthur pleaded for a freer hand, General Ridgway was indicating his own "acceptance of stalemate as one of the 'victories' possible in limited war. . . ." (*Conflict*) Ridgway was just what the appeasers were looking for, and they got MacArthur's head in April of 1951. The more compliant Ridgway replaced MacArthur as Supreme Commander, with General James Van Fleet appointed commander of the 8th Army. As MacArthur had said: "I've always been able to take care of the enemy in my front — but have never been able to protect myself from shafts from the rear."

In his autobiography, General of the Army Douglas MacArthur recalled a bomber pilot shot up by a fighter operating out of Manchurian sanctuary — from where he was even immune to "hot pursuit." The pilot, "wounded unto death, the stump of an arm dangling by his side, gasped at me through the bubbles of blood he spat out, 'General, which side are Washington and the United Nations on?' It seared my very soul."

The pro-Communist politicians had removed MacArthur just in time. By May our troops, "having handed the Chinese Communist Forces the bloodiest and most decisive beating in their history, were striking north again . . . ." (*Conflict*) General Van Fleet would later say: "So in June 1951, we had the Chinese whipped. They were definitely gone. They were in awful shape. During the last week of May we captured more than 10,000 Chinese prisoners." Whereupon Jacob Malik, "Russia's representative on the Security Council, proposed 'ceasefire' talks as a preliminary to 'peaceful settlement of the Korean problem.' (*The Chinese People's Liberation Army*, Samuel B. Griffith II, New York, McGraw-Hill, 1967)*

There would be no more major offensives as the Reds moved to gain by negotiations what they had not been able to secure on the battlefield. Our politicians eased the military pressure, allowed the Reds to dig in, and acceded to their demand for a truce line along the 38th Parallel. The wearying tactics, deceptions, delays, propaganda, and other Red tricks during the "talking war" are all ably described in *How Communists Negotiate*, by Admiral C. Turner Joy (New York, Macmillan, 1955). Our chief negotiator, Admiral Joy found that all the Communists respect is force. Indeed, talks were broken off at Kaesong and Russian MiG pilots attacked in strength from across the Yalu. When we retained air superiority, the Reds wanted to talk some more, this time at Panmunjom, where the talking continues to this day.

It was during this period that the Communists in Peiping blared their phony "germ warfare" charges,† a propaganda program masterminded by Huang Hua, Red China's Foreign Minister in the late Seventies, who was also in charge of brainwashing our P.O.W.s. The Reds used everything — from withholding medical care to torture and brainwashing — to demoralize or elicit "confessions" from P.O.W.s. Major General William F. Dean, an early captive and a winner of the Congressional Medal of Honor, tells about what he suffered in *General Dean's Story* (New York, Viking, 1954). It was *incredible*, yet Dean considered that he was not tortured as much as many other P.O.W.s.

Edward Hunter, who introduced the word "brainwashing" into the language, noted that the American military personnel in the Korean P.O.W. camps who were used most conspicuously in the germ-warfare campaigns "were not physically maltreated in the old-fashioned manner." (*Brainwashing*, New York, Pyramid, 1958) The psychological

---

*This book, by the way, was sponsored by the Communist-appeasing Council on Foreign Relations. It is anti-MacArthur and pro-Ridgway. The latter was a C.F.R. member who later used the C.F.R. journal *Foreign Affairs* to advocate U.S. withdrawal from Vietnam.

†The Communists were meanwhile employing chemical warfare, trafficking in narcotics. (See *Psycho-Chemical Warfare*, A.H. Stanton Candlin, New Rochelle, Arlington House, 1973.) Three hundred boxes of raw opium, for example, were found in the Ministry of Commerce during occupation of Pyongyang.

abuse they received was more insidious. Others were simply tortured. The enemy might proceed to tie a man tightly, reports Hunter, "so he cannot budge, then to rest a heavy stone on him and leave him for a long period. Sometimes pig bristles are used to agonize a 'stubborn' person's sensitive parts. In 'flying an airplane,' the victim is hoisted by the thumbs, then doused with cold water to revive him whenever he passes out. In the 'diamond-mine treatment,' he is forced to crawl back and forth on a plank covered with bits of broken glass. Sometimes he is roped and rolled back and forth over a plank studded with sharp nails. Innumerable variations of the 'ice bath' were used in Korea. In one version, the P.O.W. was stripped from waist down and put outside in subzero weather with his feet in a basin that soon froze."

Helping the Reds obtain "confessions" were Red newsmen including Britain's Alan Winnington and Australian Wilfred Burchett. Henry Kissinger years later entertained Burchett in the White House, and that journalist-agent died in 1983 at home, which was at the time in Communist Bulgaria.

Meanwhile, the Communists used their own men who were in our P.O.W. camps to continue the war in whatever way they could. They were under command of Nam Il, the top Communist negotiator at Panmunjom. Selected Chinese soldiers were actually ordered to surrender in order to get them inside the camps, where they rioted and intimidated non-Communist prisoners. Because of political restrictions on our military, the Reds virtually ran the camps — and on one occasion even captured the U.S. general ostensibly in charge of Koje Island. Threatening his death, they released him only after his replacement signed an outrageous statement falsely "admitting" that helpless Red prisoners had been killed by U.N. forces.

Discipline was so lax that the Red P.O.W.s carried out death sentences by their People's Courts against anti-Communists and those who did not wish to be repatriated. Again the politicians responded meekly. "Right after the Koje incident," reported General Mark Clark, who became U.N. Commander in May of 1952, "I had requested authority to bring to trial all of these ringleaders responsible for crimes in the prison camps. Washington delayed [*until too late*] acting on my request, presumably for fear that the trials might jeopardize the chances of an armistice." (*From The Danube To The Yalu*, New York, Harper & Brothers, 1954) Incredibly, prisoners who were known to have killed and committed atrocities against Americans were ordered returned home.

Syngman Rhee, President of the Republic of Korea, vehemently opposed the armistice. A brilliant and steadfast patriot, he had worked for more than fifty years to unify his country and could not bear the thought of the Communists occupying a single acre of it. President Rhee also meant to stop any chance of forced repatriation of North Koreans who wanted to stay in the Republic. President Eisenhower, after all, had been responsible for just such a repatriation in the shameless Operation Keelhaul after World War II. The North Koreans in the camps thus became a touchy issue. Plans were made to ship prisoners who feared repatriation to a "neutral" country where the Reds would "explain" to them why they should return to Communist slavery. Then the Comrades "conceded" that such P.O.W.s could remain inside R.O.K. But they required, observed General Clark, "that Communist Czech and Polish members of the five-nation neutral Repatriation Commission as well as Chinese and North Korean persuader teams be given freedom to travel into South Korea to persuade the nonrepatriates to come home."

General Clark, who had had experience with the Russian repatriation mission in Austria, was sympathetic to the Koreans. When he called on President Rhee, Clark reports, "I found him angrier and more anti-Armistice than ever. He declared he would never let this crowd of potential spies, saboteurs and agitators into his rear areas, and I couldn't blame him. As UN Commander, they were my rear areas, too."

To forestall the unwilling return of prisoners to the north, President Rhee unilaterally directed that 27,000 of these anti-Communists be freed. Hypocrites and Communists around the world decried this, but the move raised Rhee to the height of popularity in his own country. Former enemy soldiers were embraced and taken into the homes of the South Korean people, who hid and protected them from U.N. troops.

President Rhee now threatened to take the R.O.K. troops out from under U.N. command to prevent signing of the armistice. (The R.O.K. did not sign the eventual truce.) And, because of Rhee's steadfast anti-Communism, certain measures were taken to restrict his efforts. In his 1954 book, General Clark alludes to "an emergency plan ready for immediate execution." This, as it turns out, was Operation Everready, which became public knowledge only in 1975. Everready was a plan that the Joint Chiefs had directed General Clark to develop to stage a *coup* and overthrow Rhee should resistance to the armistice interfere too greatly with U.N. strategy.[*] It was as though we had prepared a plan to arrest Winston Churchill in World War II for not permitting Nazi occupation of half of Britain.

---

[*]It is thus not idle speculation that the State Department helped to overthrow Rhee in 1960, when it publicly "sympathized" with student rioters. Secretary of State Christian Herter rebuked Rhee for putting down the riots in which his own official residence was threatened by a mob. *Human Events* noted at the time: "Even State Department functionaries admitted that the note had no precedent in our diplomatic history."

President Rhee was right to resist appeasement, for after the armistice was signed and the exchange of P.O.W.s was made, General Clark admitted "we had solid evidence after all the returns were in from Big Switch that the Communists still held 3,404 men prisoner, including 944 Americans." But "when you have no gun threatening the Reds there is no way to demand and enforce compliance from them."

The tales our P.O.W.s brought back were harrowing. "Their replies provided the evidence from which the U.S. Defense Department concluded that more than 6,000 American troops and 5,550 other soldiers — most of the latter ROKs — had perished after falling into Communist hands. Half of these 11,500 men were the victims of Communist atrocities, and the other half died in imprisonment." (*Conflict*)

Knowing what faced them at home, three-quarters of the Red Chinese P.O.W.s refused to be repatriated to Mao's agrarian paradise.

In 1954 the Senate Permament Subcommittee on Investigations examined the extensive evidence which "conclusively proves that American prisoners of war who were not deliberately murdered at the time of capture, or shortly after capture, were beaten, wounded, starved, and tortured; molested, displayed, and humiliated before civilian populace and/or forced to march long distances without benefit of adequate food, water, shelter, clothing, or medical care to Communist prison camps, and there to experience further acts of human indignities." Human indignities like being abandoned by their own country.

Among the nine classes of brutality the Reds indulged in, the Subcommittee reported, were acts of torture including "perforating the flesh of prisoners with heated bamboo spears, burning prisoners with cigarettes and inserting a can opener into a prisoner's open wound."

So-called medical experimentation took place — such as the insertion of chicken livers in wounds which were then sewn shut. Sergeant Wendell Treffery told of fellow prisoners who were covered with maggots and blowflies, too weak to move, but were denied medical care. "Sergeant Treffery experienced treatment from his Communist captors equally as horrible. His toes, which were rotting, having been frozen when his combat boots were confiscated, were amputated with a pair of garden shears by a Chinese nurse without benefit of anesthesia. Later, in order to avoid being sent to the hospital where many of the seriously wounded were sent to die, he broke off his remaining two toes with his fingernails."

That was the Korean War. Of course there is no peace, and there have been literally thousands of violations by the Communists of the 1953 armistice, including the shooting down of American aircraft and the capture and torture of the men of the *Pueblo*. The R.O.K. capital city of

Seoul is still but a five-minute MiG flight from the demilitarized zone. Beyond that is Kim Il Sung — who invaded South Korea in 1950; who in 1968 sent infiltrators to attack the Presidential Blue House in an effort to kill President Park; and, who in 1974 again directed an attempt on President Park's life, this time killing the President's wife. Not to mention the shooting down of an unarmed U.S. helicopter, killing two; the bludgeoning and axe-murder of two U.S. officers supervising the trimming of a tree near Panmunjom; and, the repeated tunnelling by the Communists under the D.M.Z.

But what of all the charges we hear about the crackdown in South Korea on political dissidents? A South Korean professor was quoted a while ago in the "Liberal" *New Republic* as observing: "In the Viet Nam war, your government sent people to jail for destroying draft cards. The North Vietnamese were not 30 miles away from Washington at the time, but your government panicked. I'm prepared to admit that my government gets panicky, too, but the North Koreans are the same distance from here as Dulles Airport is from Washington."

The direct subordinate to the sixteenth United Nations Commander-in-Chief in Korea, Major General John W. Singlaub, meanwhile was recalled by Jimmy Carter for predicting what his fellow senior officers might then say only in private — that the proposed withdrawal of U.S. troops from Korea could only lead to war.

That plan was finally reversed by the Reagan Administration. But North Korea, in its turn, not long ago was responsible for a mass assassination of Seoul's officials in Rangoon — which followed in the wake of the Soviet murder of anti-Communist U.S. Representative Larry McDonald (D.-Georgia), outspoken Chairman of The John Birch Society, and 268 other innocents aboard Korean Air Lines Flight Seven. McDonald was *en route* to the thirtieth anniversary of the signing of the U.S.-Korean Defense Treaty.

No, there is no peace in Korea.

Chapter XXIV

Presidents Before "Watergate"

In 1972 a team of men later linked to the White House was caught attempting to wiretap Democrat Party headquarters in Washington. Nevertheless, electors in forty-nine of the fifty states voted to re-elect Richard Nixon as President of the United States. For the next two years, Nixon's political enemies and the mass media carried on an unrelenting vendetta against him on the grounds that he had conspired in the "crimes of the century" — by which they meant the break-in, bugging, and attempted cover-up of Watergate — finally forcing the resignation of the President.

It was obvious to some of us then, and is becoming much plainer with the passage of time, that even if Richard Nixon had been personally guilty of all that was charged in this chicken-stealing scenario, it amounted to little more than White House politics as usual. It is the relative insignificance of these Nixon transgressions, as compared to those of his immediate Presidential predecessors, that became the theme of a best-seller by Victor Lasky, *It Didn't Start With Watergate* (New York, Dial, 1977).

Of course, Mr. Nixon lied about it all. But Franklin D. Roosevelt, writes Lasky, "lied about not getting involved in foreign wars; Eisenhower lied about the U-2 flight; Kennedy lied about the Bay of Pigs; and Johnson lied about Vietnam. And in each of those cases far more was at stake than a third-rate political burglary. For, as the slogan had it at the time, 'No one died at the Watergate.' "

Veteran students of Presidential excesses are likely to find little that is new in the Lasky compilation, but his book is valuable in bringing together a picture of the sort of abuses of power that were for so long ignored or played down by a sympathetic press. One does wish that Victor Lasky had spent a bit more time on organization of the volume, and on Presidents Truman and Eisenhower, whose serious misbehavior is glossed over in favor of the exposures of Franklin Roosevelt, John Kennedy, and Lyndon Johnson. But the case of an outrageous double standard — one for Richard Nixon and quite another for everybody else — is nonetheless well made.

Consider the wiretapping that was at the heart of "Watergate." Franklin Roosevelt's son John remarked in the middle of the Nixon brouhaha: "I can't understand all the commotion in this case. Hell, my father invented bugging. Had them spread all over, and thought nothing of it." For instance, during peacetime, President Roosevelt tapped and otherwise abused the civil liberties of Americans who opposed our entry into World War II. He did this despite having been elected in 1940 on a platform stressing that he had kept us out of war. Even as he promised that he would not send America's sons into battle, he was secretly plotting to maneuver us into the conflict and illegally and surreptitiously abusing his powers by harassing members of the America First Committee, the powerful non-interventionist organization, who were correctly accusing him of deceit in the matter.

Meanwhile, F.D.R. viciously labeled his critics, especially Charles A. Lindbergh, as "copperheads." Thus, records Lasky, "the President called them 'traitors.' Not only that but . . . he ordered the wiretapping of their telephones; and he asked that telegrams criticizing his defense policies be sent to the FBI director for investigation, and correspondence endorsing Lindbergh's opposition to U.S. ships acting as convoy [*for the British*] be filed by Secret Service. Rarely had any legitimate movement of American citizens, none of whom had any links to any foreign power, faced such official hostility, abuse, and repression. But most liberals couldn't have cared less. In fact they happily joined in the witch-hunt."

Actively supported by Earl Warren, F.D.R. even locked up more than one hundred thousand Americans in concentration camps, solely because they had Japanese ancestry. Indeed, the President considered interning German-Americans, of whom there were perhaps six hundred thousand. "I don't care so much about the Italians," he said. "They are a lot of opera singers." Like Nixon, the man was a bigot; but his bigotry was carefully shielded from public view by an obedient press. In recent years our "Liberals" moaned to the heavens when Spiro Agnew was alleged to have referred to a "fat Jap" and Richard Nixon was said to have made slighting comments about Jews, but the "Liberal" press agreed to keep "off the record" F.D.R.'s remark about a man who objected to the "packing" of the Supreme Court. "What else," sneered Roosevelt, "could you expect from a Jew?" In fact, that outrageous slur was not put on the record until thirty years after Roosevelt's death, when upon retiring veteran *Chicago Tribune* reporter Walter Trohan cited it in *Political Animals.*

This was the same F.D.R., one remembers, who in 1939 turned away a thousand Jewish refugees attempting to escape Nazi Germany, many of them being returned to Hitler's camps and death. And F.D.R., recalls Trohan, "told Ibn Saud, during their wartime meeting, he would like to send the Arab king a half million or more Jews from New York . . . . [H]e made the statement with such anger that he failed to note or regard the presence of Henry M. Kannee, a White House stenographer who was taking down his words. I have often wondered whether Kannee let the words survive in press conferences records." One may be sure that famous "gap" in the Nixon tapes was not the first of its kind arranged to protect a President from embarrassment.

But the working press in the nation's capital played dead for President Franklin Roosevelt. As Mr. Trohan remembers it, Washington journalists knew very well that the President was carrying on sexual affairs with various women even as Mrs. Roosevelt was having a fling or two of her own. Missy LeHand was one of F.D.R.'s mistresses, recalls Trohan, and she was eventually dropped in favor of another, Crown Princess Martha of Norway. When the former took ill, the President called on her at the hospital. "We shook our heads over the fact that FDR took Mrs. R. with him on that visit, an incident of truth stranger than fiction — a man taking his wife to call on his mistress for whom he had betrayed their marriage, a mistress who was lying in illness partly because she had been betrayed in turn."

All of this is of course paled by Roosevelt's personal complicity in the attack on Pearl Harbor (after the Japanese code had been broken), and his betrayal and doublecross of the Poles, Czechs, and others. Duplicity was in his nature. "FDR's spokesmen were to boast," writes Walter Trohan, "that FDR was the architect of the appeasement of Hitler at Munich . . . . When the appeasement became a matter of shame, FDR was to deny any part in it." A compliant press let him get by with it.

And we should remember that the destruction of Richard Nixon, after all, was based upon the Watergate bugging and not on international piracy and conspiracy, areas in which he was even more guilty than Roosevelt. So let us return, with Victor Lasky, to the matter of political bugging:

"The various Roosevelt campaigns were rough indeed. Former GOP chairman John D.M. Hamilton contends, for example, that his office was bugged when he was campaign manager for Alfred Landon's presidential race in 1936. Hamilton claims that the bugging was ordered by FDR's Secretary of the Interior Harold Ickes, who was known to have a penchant for illegal eavesdropping. The bugging in Hamilton's office was quickly discovered by the GOP's security expert. 'We never announced anything or made any public charges,' Hamilton told the *National Observer*. 'We just used that phone to leak out wrong information to the Democrats to make them look silly, and when we wanted to say anything private we went to another phone.' ''

Or consider the experience of the *Chicago Tribune's* Walter Trohan who writes: "My home phones were tapped — I had two lines — and the *Tribune's* office phones were also tapped. I had a Washington police lieutenant, and expert on bugging, check the phones. He came from an examination of the lead box to my home, saying he had never seen such a setup, that I had taps on taps. He found that my telephones were being monitored by the FBI, military intelligence, naval intelligence and the Anti-Defamation League. This didn't concern me or my colleagues, although I made it known widely. Most of my colleagues felt it served me right for my opposition to the war. Today bugging seems to be the crime of crimes."

We have already complained that Mr. Lasky's *It Didn't Start With Watergate* all but ignores the scandals of the Truman Administration. But then Mr. Lasky's publisher limited him to a mere 438 pages. Finding appropriate space for "Give 'Em Hell, Harry" would have required at least another book. One remembers, for instance, that it was widespread charges of corruption that led Harry Truman, too, to appoint a special prosecutor, one Newbold Morris. But when Mr. Morris started asking questions of high-level personnel in the Administration, he was promptly fired by Attorney General Howard McGrath. Truman, in turn, fired McGrath. But nobody called it a "Saturday Night Massacre."

Truman owed his political career to the corrupt political machine of Tom Pendergast, a Missouri Boss Tweed capable of delivering the sixty thousand "ghost" votes which helped Harry win his Senate seat. (See Chapter XXII.) As a U.S. District Court Judge remarked of a Senate speech by Truman, it was an address "of a man nominated by 'ghost' votes, elected with 'ghost' votes, and whose speech was probably written by 'ghost' writers." Eventually a U.S. Attorney named Maurice Milligan gummed up the Pendergast machine and secured more than two hundred fifty convictions for vote fraud. Boss Tom was himself jailed for income-tax evasion. So Senator Truman attacked Milligan, claiming that a Jackson County Democrat could no more get a fair trial in federal court then could a Jew in Hitler's court. And, after Mr. Truman became President, he fired Milligan and pardoned a number of the members of the Pendergast gang. As President, Harry continued to work closely with the machine, and openly helped purge a Democrat Congressman named Roger Slaughter in a 1946 election involving massive vote fraud. More than seventy were indicted over that one, but the vault in Kansas City where the fraud evidence was stored was blown with nitroglycerin and the records stolen. Truman happened to be in a Kansas City hotel at the time, just three blocks away. Naturally the federal government dropped the case.

That was just small potatoes. When the Federal Bureau of Investigation told the President that Assistant Secretary of the Treasury Harry Dexter White was a Communist spy, it was definitely a more important matter. It became still more important when, well aware of the facts, Truman promoted White to the International Monetary Fund. But the Alger Hiss case and others proving Communist infiltration into the highest levels of his Administration were, said Truman, a "red herring." On the other hand, General of the Army Douglas MacArthur noted that his recall by the President came shortly after the General demanded that such subversive activity be exposed, explaining that U.S. military operations in Korea and elsewhere were being seriously jeopardized as a result.

This is not to say that Harry Truman was directly responsible for all the wrong-doing in his Administration, but who in the Establishment media gave Nixon the same benefit of the doubt? A prank by a Donald Segretti, say, was invariably reported as though it were performed on a personal order from Nixon. Now the historical revisionists *credit* Truman for his vulgar language, even in public, while Nixon is scored for similar expletives used in privacy to intimates.

Regardless of the phony cries of outrage, and morally corrupt as he was, Richard Nixon did not invent Presidential corruption, and did little more than other recent Presidents who are saluted by the Establishment press as heroes of the people. As Arthur Krock described it, the charges of corruption tolerated by President Truman escalated with the pardoning of members of the Pendergast gang from Harry's home county. "Later the President commuted the prison sentence of James J. Gavin, convicted of income-tax dodging in Indiana, for whom influential Democrats had interceded. There followed disclosures of the unwise friendships of Maj. Gen. Harry Vaughan, the President's military aide, in which gifts of deep-freezes, mink coats and other articles were made in the hope, often realized, of Government favors. In this category, was the naming to the American mission in Greece of John Maragon, friend of Vaughan, who later went to jail for crimes related to influence peddling. ✳✳✳

" . . . an unsavory procession of gamblers and gangsters contributed to the party fund and were honored guests at party dinners. The President denounced speculators on the commodity market only to discover that his own physician, Brig. Gen. Wallace H. Graham, was one; also one of his greatest favorites, Edwin W. Pauley. There were more murders in the Kansas City underworld linked to Democratic politics; the Kefauver

Committee unearthed ties between gangsters and Democratic local administrations; and then came in quick succession the disclosures of political manipulation of loans by the Reconstruction Finance Corporation to private persons, [*and*] of widespread irregularities in the Internal Revenue Service . . . .''

The buck stops where? In all of these cases it stops at the feet of Harry Truman.

The corruption of the succeeding Eisenhower Administration is also missing from Lasky's *It Didn't Start With Watergate*. Certainly there was ample material available.* Ike, after all, virtually stole the Republican nomination from Robert Taft through ''dirty tricks,'' even as he audaciously accused Taft of being the thief. If Nixon obstructed justice in the Seventies by not exposing members of his staff involved in a third-rate bugging attempt, what can be said of Eisenhower who in the Fifties covered up and sabotaged investigation of Communist penetration of the United States Government? Yet here the ''Liberal'' press is still on the side of the Presidential manipulator. The counsel to Senator Joseph McCarthy (R.-Wisconsin) was Roy Cohn, who has listed some of the omissions from a television ''documentary'' on McCarthy called *Tail Gunner Joe* that was in fact a network cover-up of Presidential misconduct in the *Eisenhower* Administration. First, writes Cohn, the charges that led to the Army-McCarthy Hearings: ''. . . were hatched under the aegis of the Anti-McCarthy cabal in the White House, headed by Sherman Adams, of vicuna coat fame! Their express purpose was the elimination of McCarthy; 2. The consequent attempted blackmail of Committee members by a White House staffer into killing subpoenas of Loyalty Board members on threat of exposure of any alleged intervention for [*G. David*] Schine; 3. Telephone calls secretly transcribed by Army Secretary Stevens, including one from supposedly 'impartial' Committee member Senator Stuart Symington, who urged adversary party Stevens not to use the 'Marquis of Queensbury' rules in dealing with McCarthy; 4. Perhaps the most important: when the behind-the-scenes activities of persons like Sherman Adams in the White House and White House dominated officials of the Justice Department began to surface, the whole complexion of the hearings changed. They began to look like a setup to get McCarthy. Shades of Watergate. Did the Eisenhower Administration rise to the challenge, and say we wish no cover-up, let the witnesses testify, and the truth come out? Don't you believe it. Such a reaction is expected only from Nixon. President Eisenhower issued an Executive Order prohibiting

---

*For a compendium of the most serious charges against Eisenhower, Lasky would have done well to have reviewed Robert Welch's *The Politician* (Belmont, Massachusetts, Belmont Publishing Company, 1963).

testimony at the hearings from any member of the Executive without prior permission — which of course was not given. It was known as the 'Eisenhower black-out order,' and it effectively prevented Senator McCarthy from establishing the facts at the hearings."

So we see that Richard Nixon didn't exactly invent "stonewalling" either.

The above-mentioned Sherman Adams was Ike's chief of staff, whose downfall came in the revelation that he had accepted as "gifts" an expensive coat and an oriental rug from financier Bernard Goldfine. As it happens, President Eisenhower, himself, received tens of thousands of dollars in expensive "gifts," a fact brought out in a study requested by the Impeachment Inquiry Staff investigating charges against Richard Nixon. Edited by C. Vann Woodward, the study was published by Dell in 1974 under the title *Responses Of The Presidents To Charges Of Misconduct*.

Eisenhower's press secretary James Hagerty denied that Ike was on the take from Goldfine. But a full account of one of these "gifts" then appeared in the *Washington Post*, establishing that Mr. Goldfine had not only given the chief of staff a vicuna coat, but also had given one to the President. After the story was published, "Hagerty conceded that Eisenhower had received vicuna material from Goldfine and sent him a 'thank you' letter. But, Hagerty went on, the President had not kept the material, giving it instead to a friend, whose name Eisenhower could not recall. Neither the press nor Congress followed up on the disclosure. . . ." Woodward and Bernstein, of course, were yet in swaddling clothes.

Richard Nixon is still being smeared for the alleged corruption of his underlings. What about Eisenhower? Here is the outline developed for the Impeachment Inquiry Staff:

"Between 1955 and 1960 Eisenhower was obliged to accept the resignation of a number of sub-cabinet officials whose conduct, under probing by congressional committees, raised ethical, if not legal, questions. These appointees included the Secretary of the Air Force (the use of his position to help direct business toward his own firm); the assistant secretary of defense for legislative and public affairs (impropriety in having firms controlled by his wife and brother-in-law bid for and receive military procurement contracts); the administrator of the General Services Administration (political favoritism in awarding of government insurance business); a member of the Federal Communications Commission (acceptance of loans and other favors from the attorney for a successful applicant for a television station license); and the chairman of the Federal Communications Commission (receiving of gratuities from the broadcast industry). In addition, a second-echelon, non-presidential appointee, the commissioner of public buildings, resigned under fire when it was disclosed that he had given federal contracts to firms which were clients of a company in which he held a 90% partnership. Generally, the White House staff, frequently Assistant to the President Sherman Adams, requested the official to resign when it appeared that the revelations might embarrass the President.''

Recalling that Richard Nixon was required to hand over the tapes that became the ''smoking gun'' in the Watergate affair, it is instructive to remember that Dwight Eisenhower refused to permit such ''fishing expeditions'' even when charges of misconduct were raised. Impeachment was not considered because President Eisenhower was able to deny Congress access to government papers. As the Inquiry Staff Report explained:

''The House Judiciary Committee raised [*the issue*] . . . of the denial of records to Congress by the executive branch. This occurred in the committee's 1955 investigation of charges that members of the Business Advisory Council of the Department of Commerce were using their position to influence government policy to the advantage of their own firms. Demands by the chairman of the committee that the council's files be turned over to the panel for study were discussed at the July 29, 1955, meeting of the cabinet. Reaffirming the principle of executive privilege he had laid down during the U.S. Army-McCarthy confrontation, Eisenhower said it was up to the departments involved to draw a line between what should and should not be made available to congressional committees . . . . Eisenhower told the cabinet that he wanted it clearly understood that he was never going to yield to the point where he would become known as a President who had practically crippled the presidency.''

But Richard Nixon was made to play by different rules. The reason why is best known to the Establishment which destroyed him.

The young man who followed Dwight Eisenhower to the White House, John F. Kennedy, has long been a favorite subject of Lasky research and does receive full treatment in *It Didn't Start With Watergate*. Where Nixon had his ''German Mafia'' and ''enemies list,'' Kennedy had an ''Irish Mafia'' and an in-house slogan that decreed: ''Don't get mad, get even.'' And as *Washington Post* editor Ben Bradlee, a Camelot intimate, acknowledged: ''My God, they wiretapped practically everyone else in this town.''

Victor Lasky provides evidence that Kennedy bugged Vice President Richard Nixon prior to their famous debates in 1960, and discloses that the Democrats also employed secret surveillance on the G.O.P. in that election year. Then there was former F.B.I. agent Carmine Bellino, who worked for the Kennedy family. Mostly, Lasky found, "Bellino's activities resembled those of the White House 'plumbers' of the Nixon era. Years later it was disclosed that, at President Kennedy's personal direction, Bellino had obtained the tax returns of numerous citizens."

Another dirty trickster for J.F.K. was a former Communist named Paul Corbin, who mailed out scurrilous anti-Catholic literature in order to prompt a sympathetic Catholic vote for Kennedy — who played strongly on the "religious issue" to assure the urban ethnic vote he needed for election. Donald Segretti was not alone. "Needless to say," comments Lasky, "Segretti served time in the slammer while Corbin — at the Kennedys' suggestion — was named an assistant to the Democratic National Chairman and later placed on the payroll of the Joseph P. Kennedy, Jr., Foundation."

Another sleazy Kennedy operation was directed against State Department security chief Otto Otepka, who earned the Kennedy animus by trying to do his job, which was to maintain security standards. But the Kennedy boys wanted to employ in the Administration a number of Leftists who could not be legally cleared. Otepka's office, accordingly, was broken into; he was illegally bugged; his safe was cracked; his burn bag searched; and, he was placed under personal surveillance. Witnesses hostile to Mr. Otepka were brought in by the Administration to give perjured testimony against the loyal security officer. "In the face of all this criminality," recounts Mr. Lasky, "including lying under oath, the Justice Department under Kennedy refused to take any action such as prosecuting outright perjurers. And what was the liberal reaction? Zilch. The media couldn't have cared less; there were no cries for the incarceration of the culprits, impeachment or, at the very least, resignation."

John Kennedy apparently did do some retiring. With Marilyn Monroe, for instance. Details can be found in Earl Wilson's *Show Business Laid Bare*. And while adultery may be a private (albeit criminal) matter, it did become something else when it went so far, and became so compulsive, that the Secret Service was fearful the K.G.B. would plant a spy in the Presidential bedroom. In July of 1962 the President and one of his mistresses, according to her diary account, actually got high on marijuana in the White House, laughing at the upcoming conference on narcotics to be held in a nearby suite. It took J. Edgar Hoover to get President Kennedy to end his affair with one Judith Campbell Exner, whose favors he "shared" with one of the top hoodlums in the country, "Momo" Giancana. Indeed, the Mafia chieftain claimed to their shared strumpet that he swung enough votes in the fraud-ridden 1960 elections in the Chicago area to have elected the King of Camelot.

Of course there were illicit affairs in King Arthur's Camelot as well; perhaps John Kennedy was trying to uphold the tradition of Sir Salacious. Walter Trohan describes a Georgetown woman who "was annoyed over the President-elect's trysts with a young woman neighbor. She took a flashlight photo of Jack leaving the neighbor's door at an early morning hour and threatened to publish it. I was approached and offered a copy of the photo, which was an interesting one, I must say. The *Tribune* was not interested in my report of the affair. The offer was withdrawn before I could turn it down, however. Later I learned that Joe had called on the woman who took the photo and bought a rather ordinary painting off her wall for a sum well into five figures. She got the message and he got the photo."

Nonetheless, as Lasky observes, President Kennedy's public image, "presented through an all-too-willing media, was that of a good husband, the kind family man, and the perfect father. Camelot was never sullied by stories of what really was going on behind the scenes, the sybaritic, hedonistic life led by a President who felt he could do anything and get away with it." Who can doubt that, had Richard Nixon so much as lusted in his heart, Woodward and Bernstein would have reported that he was holding orgies on the South Lawn? And *Washington Post* editor Ben Bradlee would have carried the story. Despite the fact that when Bradlee had personal knowledge that his own sister-in-law was regularly sleeping with President Kennedy in the White House he permitted himself to be used as cover for their trysts.

Lyndon Baines Johnson was yet another whose excesses were long ignored by the press. He moved into the big time with a fraudulent election to the Senate in 1948, personally arranging for the stuffing of a key ballot box, and moving on down the road to a fortune made from a federally licensed television station. As President, like Nixon later, Johnson used the F.B.I. to bring political pressure on private citizens and even Members of Congress. He employed other means as well. Joseph Califano, Jimmy Carter's Secretary of Health, Education and Welfare, has described how his former boss L.B.J. "even had one Senator's mistress contacted to have her persuade her lover to vote to break a filibuster."

Indeed, President Johnson ordered the F.B.I. to bug Republican candidates Barry Goldwater in 1964 and Richard Nixon in 1968. The same E. Howard Hunt who went to jail for his Watergate involvement was ordered in 1964 by his superior in the Central Intelligence Agency to spy on Republican candidate Goldwater. "Since I'd done it once before for the CIA," shrugs Hunt, "why wouldn't I do it again for the White House?"

Bill Moyers, who today moralizes about Presidential excesses, was the White House staffer who ordered the F.B.I. to gather information about any homosexuals who might be on Goldwater's staff. At the same time, the Johnson Administration was working to suppress the information that Walter Jenkins, a longtime close aide to the President, had once more been arrested on a morals charge in the pay toilet of a men's room at the Y.M.C.A., only two blocks from the White House. Johnson's personal lawyer, Abe Fortas, had "persuaded" the Washington newspapers not to run the story but the wire services refused to knuckle under.

Moyers was also instrumental in concocting the vicious campaign advertisement predicting that if Goldwater were elected President the world would be destroyed in a nuclear holocaust. And years later, as Lasky reports, this same Bill Moyers "proudly claimed to have 'hung the nuclear noose around Goldwater and finished him off.' By this time Moyers had left the White House to become publisher of Long Island's *Newsday*. Then he began pontificating on public television and writing a column for *Newsweek*. It was through these channels that the former 'hit man' of the Pedernales let it be known how appalled he was by the 'dirty tricks' of the Watergate era."

And it was also not until years later that the full story emerged of Democrat manipulation of the Federal Communications Commission, in which the F.C.C. was used to drive Conservative commentators off the airwaves by forcing broadcasters to carry opposition views at no charge. Stations around the country which could not afford a legal battle with F.C.C. and feared loss of their government licenses dropped Conservative programs challenging Johnson Administration policies. Fred W. Friendly describes the phony use of the so-called Fairness Doctrine in his book *The Good Guys, The Bad Guys And The First Amendment* (New York, Random House, 1976). Friendly, a former president of CBS News, quotes one anonymous Johnson Administration official who had been part of the plot: "If we did in 1974 what we did in 1964, we'd be answering questions before some congressional committee."

In any case, says Mr. Friendly, "Whatever lessons hindsight has taught, this campaign in 1964 against right-wing broadcasts was at the time considered a success by its creators. In a summary written during the closing days of the presidential election, [*attorney Martin Firestone, a former member of the F.C.C. staff*] pointed with pride to 1,035 letters to stations that produced a total of 1,678 hours of free time from stations carrying [*Reverend Carl*] McIntire, Dean Manion and [*Dan*] Smoot." According to Bill Ruder, a public relations man who had served as Assistant Secretary of Commerce under President Kennedy: "Our massive strategy was to use the Fairness Doctrine to challenge and harass right-wing broadcasters and hope that the challenge would be so costly to them they would be inhibited and decide it was too expensive to continue.''

White House strategists employed one Wayne Phillips, a former reporter for the *New York Times*, to coordinate a campaign to harass and/or silence Conservatives. Phillips in turn worked with longtime Democrat Party aide Wesley McCune, operator of a smear outfit called Group Research; McCune recalled that the ''Democrats gave me a large bundle, about ten thousand dollars.''

This attack on the First Amendment rights of Conservatives did not stop there. In fact a front organization headed by ''Liberal'' Eisenhower Republican Arthur Larson — the National Council for Civic Responsibility, later the N.C.C.R. of the Public Affairs Institute — was formed by the Democratic National Committee as an alleged ''nonpolitical'' organization. Fred Friendly describes the purpose of the N.C.C.R. as follows: ''A sum of some $250,000 was used to produce and sponsor anti-right-wing broadcasts, and to print and distribute literature exposing the John Birch Society and other extremist groups.'' As one of the leaders of this odious effort later commented: ''It was a seamy, sleazy operation . . . .'' Indeed it was. But the White House, under both J.F.K. and L.B.J., went ahead with it nonetheless.

Then there was the Bobby Baker scandal of 1963-1964, when L.B.J.'s close, longtime associate was found to have used his influence to line his pockets. As Vice President, Lyndon Johnson was so deeply involved that President Kennedy seriously considered whether to throw him to the wolves as Richard Nixon later did with Spiro Agnew. Many of the same Democrat Senators who voted to cover up the investigation of Baker were later to scream piously about the Agnew disasters and the cover-up of Watergate. Apparently hypocrisy and politics are synonyms.

The simple fact is that, in the case of Watergate, officials of the Democrat National Committee knew about the break-in weeks before it happened. But that part of the Watergate story was simply dropped from the record because of partisan objections by Democrats on the Investigating Committee. Such spying was commonplace. It is known, for instance, that Senator George McGovern used a spy against his opponent Senator Hubert Humphrey in 1972. As McGovern's erstwhile running-mate Senator Thomas Eagleton had admitted: ''All political parties spy on one another; the Republicans got caught at it.''

As we have pointed out, Richard Nixon's involvement in Watergate was penny-ante stuff, hardly constituting the crime of the century. And that is a *very* important point. The duly elected President of the United States was forced from office for chicken-stealing — doing exactly what every President had been doing since 1932 — to be taught the lesson that even the powers of the Presidency are subordinate to those of the insiders of the "Liberal" Establishment.

Establishment justice can be blind — or vengeful — as we have seen. This double standard must be recognized, and the hypocrites exposed when they employ it. The facts here show not only conspiracy but, equally important, they affirm the validity of the Conservative philosophy of limited government. Men are not perfect, and politicians are certainly not perfect men; power usurped by politicians corrupts, and absolute power corrupts absolutely. The simple solution is to reduce the power that the corrupt and their corrupters hold over us by actively working for more individual responsibility and less government control.

Chapter XXV

Human Cost Of Communism In Indochina

T HE "best solution" in Cambodia, testified Representative Bella Abzug in 1975, would be "to fly to safety Lon Nol and his supporters who are considered 'collaborationists' by the Khmer Rouge. If this is done there will be no occasion for a 'bloodbath.' . . . We must remember that this is a civil war in which brother fights brother, largely at the original instigation of a foreign power — the United States. So let us rescue those to whom we feel a commitment, and leave the others to settle their affairs in peace."

Ah, peace. The people of Cambodia, South Vietnam, and Laos have now experienced years of Communist peace. When the war finally ended in Laos, *Time* magazine exulted in an article entitled "Polite Revolution." In "true Laotian style," reported the Establishment slick, "last week's coup by the Communist Pathet Lao was a well-mannered affair, allowing for some touches of face-saving grace. ✻✻✻ In gradually seizing control of the country since mid-April, the Communists have managed to stay popular with their subjects by emphasizing such mass themes as anti-corruption and self-rule. They have made skillful propaganda use of traditional Laotian music, to the point that some foreign diplomats in Vientiane call it 'the song-and-dance revolution.' "

What did happen in the Seventies? The fall of Saigon to the Reds preceded that of Vientiane and followed the fall of Phnom Penh, and the headlines in the *New York Times* were again reassuring: "Indochina Without Americans: For Most, A Better Life." In South Vietnam, predicted the *Times* warmly: "Communist Rule Will Be Disciplined, Moralistic." Sydney Schanberg of the *Times* commented: "Some critics of American policy in Indochina have gone so far as to predict that the peninsula will become a virtual paradise once the Americans have gone."

So it went, as more than thirty million human beings were pushed like dominoes into the maw of Communism. And the Reds and our mass media — especially network television — created a great silence and called it peace. Terror descended; people disappeared never to be seen again; the concentration camps bulged; the firing squads killed hundreds of thousands; brainwashing flourished; and, for those Indochinese who could not escape their native land the choices were death or slavery. While the Free World stood all but mute.

Contrary to Bella Abzug's assurances, a bloodbath *was* imposed on Cambodia, claiming the lives of an estimated 1.2 million persons between April of 1975 and January of 1977. There were more massacres to follow. Dr. Ernest W. Lefever, who then directed the Ethics and Public Policy Program at the Kennedy Institute of Georgetown University, has described the reaction of the evening news programs on ABC, CBS, and NBC during the twenty months after "liberation" of Cambodia. These three leading network news programs, Lefever notes, "gave one minute of news a month to a purge that in terms of relative population exceeded the slaughter of Hitler's and Stalin's concentration camps. The attentive viewer — able to watch only one channel at a time — received only 20 seconds a month from the medium [*that*] American citizens rely on most for their news.

"Equally appalling was the skeptical and even apologetic tone of most of the early stories. The May 8, 1975 reporting was typical: ABC says bloodbath theory is widely believed by refugees, no confirmation; CBS says tales of executions are not confirmed; *New York Times* newsman Sydney Schanberg suggests Americans have stake in bloodbath theory; ABC and CBS report the Khmer Rouge troops are well-disciplined."

Never a word about the undisputed fact that Communist doctrine demands the use of terror in such circumstances. It is a concept which predates the Bolshevik Revolution. As V.I. Lenin wrote in 1908, it is necessary to institute the sort of "real, nationwide terror which reinvigorates the country and through which the Great French Revolution achieved glory." Ten years later, in 1918, dictator Lenin claimed "we can achieve nothing unless we use terror." The Red leader ordered: "The energy and mass nature of the terror must be encouraged." Which is why Russia's secret police chief Felix Dzerzhinsky, who is honored in Moscow to this day, acknowledged: "We stand for organized terror."

Just so. But the nature and vastness of that terror in Indochina was too long treated as a secret in the West. Arrest of a handful of Communist terrorists in Chile is considered news of monumental importance, worthy of angry complaint, while slave-labor camps throughout (say) Laos are afforded space only in the back of the largest newspapers, if at all. Yet the fact is that virtually the whole of Laos was turned into a concentration camp. Non-Communist Laotians, numbering in the tens of thousands, were placed in labor camps where they were denied medical attention and slowly starved to death. Attempted escape brings execution.

In 1976, the Pathet Lao announced a "cultural revolution" in the style of Mao Tse-tung and arrested all those who had resisted being "re-educated." The Red Government made a special target of religion and attempted to root out "reactionaries" and the "depraved" Western way of life. Meanwhile, Laos has been used both as the training and "rest and recreation" area for Red terrorists attacking neighboring Thailand, even as genocide by gas warfare was being used against the H'mong (Meo) people within the Laotian borders.

Some one hundred thousand Laotians fled their country in the wake of the Communist takeover, and nearly seventy thousand of them quickly became refugees in Thailand, as the Reds tightened control at home. Even back in 1975 the *New York Times* reporter in Vientiane, Fox Butterfield, was observing that "many Laotians are now afraid to talk openly in front of their own children." Planned famine and general scarcity were being imposed in this "more regimented, spartan society," wrote Butterfield. "Items ranging from flour and tomatoes to beer and ice cream have disappeared entirely, and gasoline has soared to the equivalent of $10 a gallon."

Mr. Butterfield reported: "All former opponents including army officers, policemen and bureaucrats, have been sent off to remote camps for re-education seminars. None have returned. The only man who publicly protested the re-education campaign was immediately arrested along with his whole family." By 1977 the *Times* began to report arrests and imprisonment without even the formality of a show trial, and cited the desperate hunger of the common people in the face of special privileges afforded the "new elite." In short, it has been business as usual for the Communists — whose leaders in Laos owe their loyalties to Hanoi and were protégés of Ho chi Minh.

Comrade Ho was of course a proponent of terror and torture who broke the back of North Vietnam as he consolidated his Communist regime there in the Fifties. Hoang van Chi, who served under Ho, described in *From Colonialism To Communism* some "typical tortures" used to elicit phony confessions or denunciations: "The victim was compelled to kneel down, supporting on his head a basket filled with heavy stones. He was forced to hang by his thumbs or feet from a rope thrown over a rafter. In this position he could be either beaten or, by pulling on the rope, jerked violently up and down. His thumbs were wrapped in a cloth soaked in oil which was then ignited.

"Since these tortures were widely used throughout the whole country, it is reasonable to assume that they had been carefully devised and sanctioned by the leadership of the party. It was the opinion of some people that such measures had already been employed in China two years earlier and imported into Vietnam by [*Red*] Chinese advisers.''

That account, remember, was from a man who was for years an active member of the Viet Minh.

Dr. Tom Dooley, an American missionary who helped half a million people escape North Vietnam, told in *Deliver Us From Evil* of a man accused by the Reds of teaching religion to seven young pupils: "Now two Viet Minh guards went to each child and one of them firmly grasped the head between his hands. The other then rammed a wooden chopstick into each ear. He jammed it in with all his force. The stick split the ear canal and tore the ear drum. The shrieking of the children was heard all over the village. Both ears were stabbed in this fashion. The children screamed and wrestled and suffered horribly. Since their hands were tied behind them, they could not pull the wood out of their ears. They shook their heads and squirmed about, trying to make the sticks fall out. Finally they were able to dislodge them by scraping their heads against the ground."

Those children, you see, had been charged with listening to "lies" about a just God in Heaven. Dr. Dooley also described the treatment afforded their Christian instructor. "As for the teacher," reported Dooley, "he must be prevented from teaching again. Having been forced to witness the atrocity performed on his pupils, he endured a more horrible one himself. One soldier held his head while another grasped the victim's tongue with a crude pair of pliers and pulled it far out. A third guard cut off the top of the teacher's tongue with his bayonet. Blood spurted into the man's mouth and gushed onto the ground. He could not scream; blood ran into his throat. When soldiers let him loose he fell to the ground vomiting blood; the scent of blood was all over the courtyard."

After the 1954 "cease-fire" the barbarity was for a time somewhat reduced as the Communists attempted to slow the flood of refugees into South Vietnam. But after a year or so, according to Hoang van Chi, the Communist Central Committee issued an order that the minimum number who must receive the death sentence in each village had been raised from one to five, resulting in probably one hundred thousand deaths. And, "apart from the number of people who were sentenced to death by the Special People's Tribunal and publicly shot, there still were people who died in jails and concentration camps, and those who committed suicide." Furthermore, "a far greater number of landlords' families — the majority of these being small children — died from starvation owing to the isolation policy." In all, an estimated half-million persons were killed in North Vietnam to consolidate control.

But, despite the Geneva agreement, the Reds were determined to inflict the same terror upon South Vietnam. As the residents of a small hamlet near Da Nang discovered. The following report is by John Hubbell from *Reader's Digest*:

"All were herded before the home of their chief. While they and the chief's pregnant wife and four children were forced to look on, the chief's tongue was cut out. Then his genital organs were sliced off and sewn inside his bloody mouth. As he died, the V.C. went to work on his wife, slashing open her womb. Then, the nine-year-old son: a bamboo lance was rammed through one ear and out the other. Two more of the chief's children were murdered the same way. The V.C. did not harm the five-year-old daughter — not physically; they simply left her crying, holding her dead mother's arm."

These are the monsters Henry Kissinger forced the South Vietnamese Government to accommodate. And, as the Reds swarmed toward Saigon in the spring of 1975, syndicated columnist Paul Scott reported: "The most vicious bloodbath in modern history is now going on in South Vietnam. Before it runs its bloody course, tens of thousands of South Vietnamese are expected to be martyred by the invading North Vietnamese Communists and their Vietcong comrades. The horrors of the massacre are so shocking that State Department officials handling the cabled reports from the U.S. Embassy in Saigon have become ill reading the accounts of the Communist treatment of people in the recently captured regions of South Vietnam."

The "liberators" reached Saigon in South Vietnam on April 30, 1975. They quickly captured an I.B.M. computer, whose top-secret data provided them with the names and records of more than one million members of the Armed Forces of South Vietnam, plus files on policemen, agents, double agents, and other members of Saigon's military security apparatus. The capture was confirmed by General Van tien Dung, North Vietnam's top field commander. Meanwhile, Paul Scott detailed Washington's reaction in the *Manchester Union Leader* for July 24, 1975:

"Secretary of State Henry Kissinger is orchestrating one of the biggest cover-ups in the history of U.S. foreign policy. While he assures audiences around the country that there has been no bloodbath in South Vietnam, U.S. intelligence reports on Vietnam passing across the Secretary of State's desk reveal a completely different story.

"The latest estimate of the Central Intelligence Agency is that the total number of persons killed or executed outright since the Communists started their takeover of South Vietnam in March has soared to more than 200,000. One CIA document puts the number at more than 250,000. The killings by North Vietnamese and Viet Cong troops match any of the highly played up massacres committed by Hitler during World War II. In one instance, more than 400 helpless orphans and at least five nuns in charge of the children were put to death at the Sacred Heart Catholic Orphanage in Da Nang and at an orphanage at China Beach . . . .

"Refugees from South Vietnam report that the Viet Cong attacks have been most vicious against anyone who has been associated with Americans in any manner and especially against any Vietnamese who assisted in the recent evacuation of refugees and orphans. In Da Nang, according to these confirmed reports, the Communists were particularly vengeful against any of the Vietnamese who had lived with Americans. 'They went into the police stations and took the co-hab records,' says one refugee doctor now here in Washington, 'and then went out and killed all those women and any of their children and then returned and chopped off the policeman's head.'

"Aerial photographs taken off the China Beach area in early April showed more than 30,000 bodies of South Vietnamese executed by the Communists. The region appears to be one of the main execution sites."

One recalls that Tom Wicker of the *New York Times* had declared in May of 1970 that not only had there never been wholesale reprisals in North Vietnam after 1954, but to predict that such terror would be visited upon the South amounted to raising an "historical hobgoblin" and using an "emotional argument" rather than relying upon evidence. Here are some early accounts of the liquidations in the south — the "historical hobgoblin" to which Tom Wicker referred — which we pieced together from occasional leaks through the thickening curtain of silence:

ASSOCIATED PRESS (April 20, 1975): Behind-the-lines reports quote "eye-witness accounts of macabre slayings, including the execution outside the Citadel in Hué of a government censor and the ceremonial beheading of a moderate political leader, Nyguyen ba Sau, 60, in the Chon Con market in Da Nang, after which his head 'was hoisted to the highest place and left there.' Some officials were also reportedly stoned to death in Da Nang."

HUMAN EVENTS (April 26, 1975): According to a Buddhist monk who fled Ban Me Thuot, the monks there were accused of helping people hide from the Vietcong "and were led to the market place the day after the fighting stopped. Several thousand other people were also assembled there. All were told to sit down. The local cadre walked through the crowd, pointing out South Vietnamese employees and police known to them. About 300, according to the monk, were taken to one side. After a presiding cadre delivered a lengthy harangue against these 'enemies' of the people, they were all taken out and killed."

WASHINGTON POST (May 3, 1975): The Reverend Joseph Nguyen quoi Hai, who escaped the Vietcong, is on his way to New York from Guam. "Late last December, he and many of his parishioners became captives of the Communists in the jungles and forests near the village of Tanhlinh. His escape, he explained, was planned after he learned he was slated for execution by a firing squad the next morning. During his captivity, he said yesterday, he witnessed more than 100 executions, was told of rapes of 15- and 16-year-old girls, and saw women given no time to rest after they gave birth on the march to the camp . . . . Many of the women and their newborn children died, he said, adding, 'there was so much blood.' "

TWIN CIRCLE (July 27, 1975): Captives of the Reds are sent to Saigon hospitals where they " 'give' blood for a grand blood plasma bank, thus atoning for their former ways by contributing to the Communist medical arts. But they are bled excessively; in a few days they are bled to death deliberately. Then the bodies are disposed of, after this form of Chinese torture; and our informant was driving a truck loaded with bloodless corpses until he escaped."

The terror continues. A group of Vietnamese who managed to flee in a small boat reached Texas, where they were quoted by United Press International as reporting that life under the Reds is "like being in Hell," and "ninety-nine percent want to escape." These refugees had drifted at sea for fifteen days before being picked up — while *fifty-one ships* ignored their S.O.S. flag. Many, after risking death to escape, have perished on the high seas while being ignored by the ships of nations already flooded with refugees from the Communists.

A group of thirty-eight escaped by boat from Vietnam and reached South Korea. Tran duc Phong, a member of that group, told reporters that the Reds are becoming even more vicious. "We could not live there any longer. Life there is terrible. Everybody thinks his days may be numbered." You might have seen his story, if you looked carefully, somewhere on the inside pages of your newspaper — perhaps back by the obituaries. You did not see it on the evening network news.

Another eyewitness to the Communist takeover was Father André Gelinas, a French-Canadian priest and Chinese scholar who was expelled from Saigon, now Ho chi Minh City, after the Reds had occupied the former capital for fifteen months. In the Parisian *L'Express* the priest described the pitiless executions, thousands of suicides, merciless beatings, forced mine-sweeping details, brainwashing, and mass exile of the former city workers to slave labor in "new economic zones."

A similar account appeared in *Worldview* magazine, this one by Theodore Jacqueney, a former critic of the South Vietnamese Government, who described the "Gulag-like" labor camps. Jacqueney reported that surviving prisoners in the camps "describe deaths from malnutrition, beriberi, dysentery, malaria, forced-labor-induced exhaustion, required minefield sweeping, and suicide." Former prisoners say that those in the camps commonly suffer from limb paralysis, blindness, and infectious diseases like scabies caused by long-term, closely packed, dark living conditions. "They also witnessed cases of re-education camp insanity brought on by a combination of oppressive living conditions and incessant demands for 'confessions.' "

Mr. Jacqueney testified about all of this before the House Subcommittee on International Organizations, as did Nguyen van Coi — a Vietnamese farmer who escaped to Thailand after nearly a year in a Communist concentration camp. Mr. Coi said conditions there were so terrible he "contemplated to put an end to my miserable life." For part of his incarceration (he had been in two prisons as well as a forced-labor camp), Coi said he was manacled in a cell which measured eleven feet by twenty-two feet . . . with *eighty-eight* other prisoners.

Testimony came also from Nguyan cong Hoan, who had been a critic of President Thieu, welcomed the "liberation" of South Vietnam, and had become a member of the puppet Hanoi Assembly. Mr. Hoan fled Vietnam in March of 1977, later explaining: "My first motivation was to help with the reconstruction of the country in 1975, but I realized that the Communists were worse than I imagined." Said Hoan: "No freedom of religion, speech or movement is allowed. In a word, there is no freedom at all except the freedom to obey the orders of the Communist Party. Otherwise you will be put into prison."

Perhaps one hundred thousand had been slaughtered outright in South Vietnam, Hoan estimated back in 1977, while as many as two hundred thousand more were being worked to death in the "Gulag" camps, and an additional three hundred thousand kept under some form of "house arrest." An additional million or so have been sent to the dreaded "new economic areas" to be worked to death at forced labor. The Vietnamese Reds seem to have paid more attention to public relations, said Mr. Hoan, than did their Comrades in Cambodia. "When the Khmer Rouge took over in Cambodia, they killed the opposition immediately on arrival. But the Vietnamese Communists are wiser. They compiled lists, classified people according to their importance, and sent them to different camps. Those who are killed are killed secretly."

While the slaughter and slavery continued, the Vietnamese Reds indoctrinated their captives about "American atrocities," seriously reporting the alleged delight of our soldiers in such practices as eating the flesh of Vietnamese babies. "After such a lecture," revealed Father Gelinas, "the audience is supposed to explain why they hate the

Americans. One evening a small old woman got up and started talking furiously: 'Yes, I hate them, they're odious, foul, and the proof is that they left, leaving us in the hands of the Communists!' '' We did, indeed, with terrified Vietnamese clutching pathetically at the underpinnings of our helicopters.

But if conditions under the Communists in Vietnam have been monstrous, and they have been, then the Khmer Rouge in Cambodia were absolutely demonic. Those responsible have much to answer for. One remembers columnist Frank Starr writing in the *Chicago Tribune* during March of 1975: ''All that's left to do now is turn our heads away, grit our teeth, and pull the plug. Then it's important only not to look back. Cambodia is nothing more than a mercy killing . . . .'' That same month Senator Mike Mansfield promised that ''peace will be forthcoming'' if Cambodian President Lon Nol could be forced to leave the country. ''We will enter into talks with those in the lower brackets,'' said the Montana Democrat, ''and there will be no bloodshed.''

So our ''Liberals'' forced Lon Nol to leave Cambodia, and *bloodbath* is too mild a term for the genocidal and cultural destruction that was wreaked on the Khmer Republic after mid-April of 1975. An estimated 1.2 million Cambodians, recall, were slaughtered in the first twenty months. There was scant word about it from Tom Wicker of the *New York Times*, who had repeatedly maintained that there was ''not much moral choice'' between Cambodia under Lon Nol and a nation fallen to the Khmer Rouge.

In Phnom Penh on the day of take-over, reports defected pilot Pech Lim Kuon, the streets of the capital were ''littered with corpses.'' Tens of thousands were forced at gunpoint from hospitals, along with some four million evicted from the big cities and driven into the countryside where at least ten percent died within days. It was as though more than thirty million Americans had been killed on a forced march.

The Khmer Rouge boasted in their radio broadcasts of beheading whatever Cambodian leaders were left in the country. Perhaps one hundred thousand were executed outright, and another twenty thousand killed in escape attempts. The wounded and dead were left to rot in the sun, and disease and starvation soon took their toll everywhere. The purposely restricted diet even in 1977, reported the *Washington Star*, ''contributes to widespread health problems. Malaria, cholera and dysentery have been particularly hard to control because anyone trained as a doctor is regarded as a class enemy.''

The leaders of the *Angka Loeu* or ''Organization on High,'' who became the rulers of the new Communist regime, announced the birth of a new country — and the death of another — claiming: ''More than

2,000 years of Cambodian history have virtually ended.'' So it seems. ''Books and archives have been burned,'' reported Stéphane Groueff in *France-Soir*. ''Pagodas, statues of Buddha, shops, museums, money itself — all have been physically destroyed. With the cold calculation of a surgeon, the authorities are trying to eliminate every last vestige or memory of the old ways in order to fabricate a new-model citizen.''

The horror has been so great as briefly to penetrate the pages of the Far Left *New York Review Of Books* in an article by Jean Lacouture. ''What Oriental despots or medieval inquisitors ever boasted of having eliminated in a single year,'' he asked, ''one-quarter of their own population?'' Indeed, in early 1976, the Communists began executing all of those who had been educated to the seventh-grade level or above. Another order went out requiring the slaughtering of all government workers, military and civilian — along with their families — as part of a blood debt. And, in the midst of all this, one of the top leaders of *Angka*, Ieng Sary, flew to a special session of the United Nations in New York to boast: ''We have cleansed the cities.''

Incredibly, the U.N. delegates burst into applause. Yes, you read that right. They burst into applause.

By May of 1977, intelligence experts believed that as many as two million Cambodians had been killed on orders of the Organization on High. Two million. If you find that unfathomable, consider some specifics and then multiply: Death proclaimed for being caught listening to a radio; a teacher hanged by his eight- to ten-year old pupils for being ''unfit''; a boy bludgeoned to death with a hoe, with his girl friend watching, because they had held hands. Elsewhere a mother is promised by the Reds that she will be given food for her month-old and three-year-old daughters — food she can't provide herself. The mother consents to let a soldier care for the children. Whereupon he batters them to death against a large tree.

This is Communist terror as usual. The kind that brings applause at the United Nations.

Some of these incidents are described in *Murder Of A Gentle Land*, by John Barron and Anthony Paul. (New York, Reader's Digest Press, 1977) It is a valuable and sobering volume, based upon interviews and reports from around the world, and all supported by accounts from hundreds of refugees who were eyewitnesses to the rape of Cambodia. Consider some more-or-less random selections of the reports of Communist behavior as gathered by Barron and Paul:

In Siem Reap frenzied troops ravaged civilian and military hospitals, slaughtering patients in their beds, smashing medical equipment and wrecking operating tables. With clubs, knives and bullets, they massacred approximately 100 patients, including women recuperating from child-birth . . . .

* * *

The seventeen officers in the government force defending Preah Net Preah, in Battanbang Province, were told that they were being sent to Angkor Wat, some 90 kilometers to the east, for courses in "the new communist theory." Instead, they were taken to a spot about 3 kilometers west of the district office in nearby Chuk village and battered to death with clubs. The district chief at Chuk was killed along with them.

* * *

[More than eighty Cambodian Air Force pilots had asked to be repatriated to their homeland from Thailand.] *The trucks had rear gates which could be narrowly opened so that only one person at a time could step down. As each pilot disembarked, soldiers bayoneted or clubbed him to death. In the trucks the pilots waiting their turn to die screamed in panic and hysteria. It took about two hours to kill them all. Afterward* Angka Loeu *through a domestic radio broadcast announced that the "traitors" had been executed.*

* * *

In the village of Thmei, Angka Loeu *uncovered a first lieutenant who disguised himself. Five soldiers took him, his schoolteacher wife, their two teenage sons and two daughters, ages nine and seven, and stripped them naked. They herded the family through the village beating them with a stick as if driving cattle. About a kilometer outside the village they opened fire with AK-47 automatic rifles, killing all.*

* * *

[Some sixty persons from Mongkol Borei — men, women, and children — were to be "purified" because the father "worked for Lon Nol."] *With military orderliness, the communists thrust each official forward one at a time and forced him to kneel between two soldiers armed with bayonet-tipped AK-47 rifles. The soldiers then stabbed the victim simultaneously, one through the chest and the other the back. Family by family, the communists pressed the slaughter, moving methodically down the line. As each man lay dying, his anguished, horror-stricken wife and children were dragged up to his body. The women, forced to kneel, also received the simultaneous bayonet thrusts. The children and babies, last to die, were stabbed where they stood.*

* * *

"Saray Savath tried to escape [testified a Buddhist monk]. *He was caught and given a first-degree execution. That meant he was to die slowly over some days. First the Red Khmers cut off his nose and ears;*

then they cut a deep gash into his arm. Thus, as he was bleeding to death, his arms were tied behind his back and attached to a tree. The rope was long, so the colonel could dance around the tree with pain, and the spectators were getting a better show. For two days and nights the colonel called for help by his tree, but nobody was allowed to go near him. On the third day he died."

In New York, you will recall, the United Nations delegates cheered those who did this.

And also in New York, on August 31, 1977, the *New York Times* responded with one of the most putrid "book reviews" we have ever seen. Under the byline of Paul Grimes it begins with a back-handed admission that John Barron and Anthony Paul have produced a work of near-monumental research, adding quickly that the reviewer sensed "embellishment." What do they expect the world to do? he asked. Perhaps, Mr. Grimes, they expected it not to applaud.

But the book, continues Grimes in his *New York Times* review, "is tarnished by a needless, meaningless appeal for moral force. It is tarnished by the propaganda implicit in the color of the book's cover and dust jacket — red. It is tarnished by propagandistic language: 'masters' (page 188) and 'pogrom' (page 191), to give two examples. It is tarnished by the title, 'Murder of a Gentle Land.' What, indeed is a 'gentle land,' and does the commitment of genocide necessarily mean that the perpetrators want to eliminate an entire country?"

What has happened to America that a book reviewer for our "most authoritative" newspaper can examine evidence of the death and torture of millions of human beings and respond by rebuking the color and title of the book!

Remember also that the next day, September 1st, that newspaper was reporting without "embellishment" that a "no man's land, heavily mined and booby-trapped, has been established for up to 20 to 30 miles into Cambodia, and it regularly takes a heavy toll. From parties of 20 to 30 men who started out [*for Thailand*] from villages in the border provinces, as few as two or three manage to make it across the line. Rarely are women or children taken along any more."

And rarely is so much as a complaint raised in the "world arena" of Establishment opinion about what is being done in Southeast Asia. Today's international squabble is manifested in the form of fighting over *which* Reds get to rule in places such as Kampuchea — Vietnamese Communists or Cambodian Communists. It is altogether the goriest conflict since World War II, with strife causing upwards of four million deaths in a decade. Yet, between August 1983 and March 1984, the three major U.S. television networks *combined* allowed for the war in Cambodia less than one minute of air time. Meanwhile, the grisly toll of the displaced and dead mounts daily as part of the price of "peace" and betrayal.

Chapter XXVI

Soviet Summit Synopses

SHORTLY before Soviet dictator Yuri Andropov's death was announced, President Ronald Reagan sent a secret letter to Moscow seeking a summit meeting. Perhaps Mr. Reagan had his ear to the political ground, for Presidential contender Walter Mondale had been making much of the fact that Reagan was the first U.S. President since Herbert Hoover not to sit down and "negotiate" personally with a Moscow leader. West German Chancellor Helmut Kohl also called for an early U.S.-U.S.S.R. summit between the President and Konstantin Chernenko, and Eastern European "diplomats" have been dropping hints that the new boss in Moscow wants to parley.

This spring, *Boston Globe* foreign policy correspondent William Beecher reported: "If quiet diplomatic explorations now under way show enough promise, top officials say, there is a possibility of a meeting between Secretary of State George P. Shultz and Foreign Minister Andrei Gromyko in the early summer to be followed by a summit between President Reagan and Soviet leader Konstantin U. Chernenko in late summer."

That timetable proved premature, but Democrat Walter Mondale in his party's 1984 nomination acceptance said we need to "meet in summits at least once a year," and kept the pressure on the President. Ronald Reagan, one recalls, came to national prominence for his vocal backing of Arizona Senator Barry Goldwater. Goldwater had just published his book *The Conscience Of A Conservative*, wherein he declared: "Every conference between East and West deals with some territory or right belonging to the free world which the Communists covet. Conversely, since the free world does not seek the liberation of Communist territory, the possibility of Communist concessions never arises."

That is as true today as when Ronald Reagan was citing it in his speeches for Goldwater twenty years ago. The purpose here is to review the history of personal summit meetings between American Presidents and Soviet leaders. Let us look at every one of them to see what they have produced and for whom.

Teheran, Iran, November 27-December 2, 1943: The first meeting of the "Big Three," (Stalin, Churchill, and Roosevelt) took place in the backyard of the Soviet tyrant whom F.D.R. called "Uncle Joe." The American President told the British Prime Minister he had been "begging" Stalin to meet him somewhere closer, but Stalin eventually had it his way. Secretary of State Cordell Hull observed in his *Memoirs*: "The President made his fourth unsuccessful attempt to meet with Stalin at the time of the Quebec Conference in August, 1943." Teheran was thus presented as a *Soviet* overture. And when F.D.R. sided with Stalin against Churchill at Teheran, the Soviet leader got from the Allies an even better deal than when he made his pact with Hitler in 1939.

World War II in Europe began when the free Western powers acted against the Nazi and Soviet division of Poland. But Roosevelt and Churchill now gave up to Stalin some forty-eight percent of that country, a fact so outrageous that it was judged prudent to keep it secret in the U.S. until after the 1944 elections. The Teheran minutes show that F.D.R. stated "there were in the United States from six to seven million Americans of Polish extraction, and, as a practical man, he did not wish to lose their vote." Franklin Roosevelt also noted that in the U.S. there were "a number of persons of Lithuanian, Latvian and Estonian origin," and he suggested to Stalin that it would be politically helpful if the Red dictator would declare elections for those captive lands. Stalin simply smiled enigmatically. "At Teheran," summarized Laurence Beilenson in *The Treaty Trap*, "Roosevelt gave up to the Soviet Union beyond hope of successful recall the Baltic States and the territory of Poland east of the Curzon Line." A month later, Stalin's puppet Lublin Gang was established as if it were the Government of Poland, eventually "agreeing" to cede half the land of their countrymen who were dying for the Allied cause.

Other topics at Teheran included giving more support to Communist Josíp Broz Tito in Yugoslavia at the expense of the loyal patriot General Mihailovic; Soviet participation in the United Nations (F.D.R. even brought up a plan for "Four Policemen" in the postwar world: Great Britain, the U.S.S.R., the United States, and China); the possible shooting of the entire German General Staff (raised by Stalin), then execution of fifty thousand Germans in reprisal, then a Roosevelt "compromise" calling for killing a few less; dismemberment of a conquered Germany; liberation of Prague by the Reds; splitting up the Italian fleet; and, in the East, an agreement for the Soviets to attack their treaty partner Japan after

Germany was defeated, as well as Roosevelt's reassurance to Stalin that he was pressing Chiang Kai-shek to include Communists in the Chinese Government.

During this period, F.D.R. was in secret communication with American Communist Party leader Earl Browder. As Browder said, Teheran changed the world . . . to the liking of the Reds.

Summits are heady stuff. Robert Sherwood bellowed in *Roosevelt And Hopkins*: "If there was any supreme peak in Roosevelt's career, I believe it might well be fixed at this moment, at the end of the Teheran Conference." But Teheran created a vacuum to be filled by the Communists in Central Europe and the Balkans. Teheran, concluded the forthright Chester Wilmot in *The Struggle For Europe*, was much more: It "not only determined the military strategy for 1944, but adjusted the political balance of post-war Europe in favor of the Soviet Union."

Yalta, U.S.S.R., February 3-12, 1945: A month before the "Big Three" were to meet for yet another summit conference in the Crimea, Churchill candidly wrote to Roosevelt: "I think the end of this war may well prove to be more disappointing than was the last." (*Triumph And Tragedy*) Roosevelt was ill, but against the advice of almost all his advisors he traveled to Soviet soil to avoid disappointing Stalin. Some two months later, F.D.R. was dead.

At F.D.R.'s side at the Yalta talks was Alger Hiss, the Soviet agent who testified that "it is an accurate and not immodest statement to say that I helped formulate the Yalta agreement to some extent." On the Soviet side of the table, beside Stalin, were the bloody-handed secret police chief Beria; Vishinsky, prosecutor of the infamous purge trials; and, Molotov, who had arranged the pact with Hitler's Germany that set World War II in motion. The dying Roosevelt said he thought this created an atmosphere like "that of a family." Well . . . he was married to Eleanor.

Roosevelt's advisor and later Secretary of State James Byrnes wrote in *Speaking Frankly* that at Yalta "more time was spent" on Poland than any other subject. The result? Ambassador Arthur Bliss Lane explained in *I Saw Poland Betrayed*: " . . . it was a capitulation on the part of the United States and Great Britain to the views of the Soviet Union on the frontiers of Poland and on the composition of the Polish Provisional Government of National Unity." Nevertheless it was publicly acclaimed. Poland's freedom was betrayed in the name of phony "elections" to be held after the Reds were in control in Warsaw. Admiral William Leahy commented to the President before the formula was signed that "this is so elastic that the Russians can stretch it all the way from Yalta to Washington without ever technically breaking it." (*I Was There*) Roosevelt responded that he was fully aware of it.

Among the secret deals at Yalta were protocols calling for forced German labor, in contravention of the Geneva Convention, resulting in the deaths in slavery of at least one million German soldiers in the Soviet Union; forcible repatriation of Soviet citizens from Western Europe; ceding to Stalin of the Manchurian railways, Dairen, Port Arthur, the Kurile Islands, and south Sakhalin; and, giving the U.S.S.R. three votes in the United Nations organization. The betrayal of China was also provided for in earnest, causing Senator Joseph McCarthy later to declare: "It is my judgment that we lost the peace in Europe at Teheran. It is even clearer that we lost the peace in Asia at Yalta." (*America's Retreat From Victory*) Historian John Lukacs reflected that, for six days of war against Japan, and for agreeing to join the postwar U.N., Stalin "was surprised to see how easily Roosevelt let him get what he wanted, if not more." Lukacs continued: "He would get an uncontested Russian zone of influence over the eastern half of Europe, over eastern Germany, and a restoration of the dominant position imperial Russia had had in the Far East before the Russo-Japanese War of 1904-5 . . . ." (*Outgrowing Democracy*) We even equipped Moscow's campaign to steal Manchuria.

In *Roosevelt's Road To Russia*, George N. Crocker offered a summary of what became a symbol of international immorality: "What followed Yalta was a mass expulsion which Churchill himself was impelled to allude to as 'tragedy on a prodigious scale.' Actually, never in history, even in the worst of pagan times has there been such a million-fold uprooting of human beings. By the fall of 1945, shocked voices in England were heard to say that it was the most enormous official atrocity in all the world's history . . . ."

A Philadelphia newspaper account, typical of the "Liberal" press in our country, described the conference as "the greatest United Nations victory of the war." Americans, safe behind their oceans, were fast asleep.

Potsdam, East Germany, July 17-August 2, 1945: As Vice President, Harry S Truman said of Yalta: "We are going to look forward to the most glorious period in the history of the world." Within months he was President and one of the new "Big Three" meeting west of Berlin at the former home of the German emperors. There was also a change in the British representation at these talks. With the European war over in May, the British electorate ousted Churchill in July and replaced him with Clement Attlee of the Labour Party. Attlee took over the Potsdam meetings in progress. Significantly, on the day before the conference opened, the first experimental atomic bomb was exploded at Alamagordo, New Mexico. And, just after the Allied victors adjourned, the bomb was dropped on Hiroshima. It was, to quote Truman, "the greatest thing in history.'' (*Meeting At Potsdam*) On July 24, 1945, the President ''mentioned to Stalin that the Americans had a powerful new weapon from which the Japanese could expect 'a rain of ruin from the air, the like of which has never been seen on earth.' The Russian dictator revealed no special interest.'' (*The War*) With his spies and agents riddling the American government, the new weapon was no surprise to Marshal Stalin.

Those atomic bombs were dropped despite the fact that the Japanese had been suing for peace and the American commanders in the war against Japan believed, as they had in 1944, that Tokyo could be made to surrender on our terms without invasion of the Japanese homeland. The Russian dictator even ''confided'' to Truman, reports John Toland, ''that the Japanese had requested him to mediate a peace but he had made no definite reply . . . .'' (*The Rising Sun*) Stalin naturally wanted booty in the Far East. As Churchill commented: ''Stalin is very amiable but he is opening his mouth very wide.''

Among ''reparations'' assigned to Stalin at Potsdam were German industrial equipment, basic materials, and other assets; the northern part of East Prussia, including the warmwater port at Königsberg; and, German assets in Bulgaria, Finland, Romania, and eastern Austria.

The postwar revenge known formally as the Morgenthau Plan had supposedly been killed earlier by Truman. Nevertheless, at Potsdam, the Morgenthau philosophy was strongly in evidence. Benjamin Colby summarized: ''Much of Germany's industrial plant was to be destroyed or carried off by the victors. Even factories making peacetime products were to be dismantled to hold general output down to a permitted low level. . . . Although actual boundaries were to be drawn at a 'peace conference,' the new Communist Poland was in effect permitted to keep seized German territory substantially in excess of that awarded at Yalta.'' (*'Twas A Famous Victory*)

An Iron Curtain, said Opposition leader Churchill in 1946, ''has descended across the Continent. Behind that line lie all the capitals of the ancient states of Central and Eastern Europe . . . .''

Geneva, Switzerland, July 18-23, 1955: At the old League of Nations building housing the European headquarters of the United Nations, representatives of the U.S., Great Britain, France, and the U.S.S.R. met and announced the birth of something called the ''spirit of Geneva.'' In fact, under orders from Moscow, the Communists in the U.S. had for two years been beating the drums for this summit conference. At these ''Big Four'' talks (*Conférence à Quatre*, said the Swiss), Eisenhower and British and French Premiers Eden and Faure met with Khrushchev and Bulganin of the U.S.S.R. The chief consequence was that U.S. policy ceased to be one of "containment" and embraced what was called "peaceful coexistence."

Nikita Khrushchev assured listeners that "neither side wants war," and rode around — in contrast to Ike — in an open and apparently unprotected car. "There were, of course, scores of KGB men on the streets," recounted Drew Middleton, "but comparison . . . inevitably favored the freewheeling, grinning, and gesticulating Khrushchev." (*Retreat From Victory*)

The Federal Bureau of Investigation was ordered not to arrest any Communist agents in the U.S. during the summit conference. Another grim omen, ordered hushed up until after the Geneva meeting, was the shooting down by the Soviets of a U.S. Navy plane over international waters off Alaska. The truth of this murderous action by the Soviets, wrote Robert Welch, "was that they wanted the whole world to know of the incident; to see what they could do to the United States with impunity and still have the U.S. President come smilingly to meet them at Geneva." (*The Politician*)

The unexpected development at the Geneva meeting was a proposal, announced by Ike, for East and West to exchange "blueprints" of military establishments and allow photo reconnaissance missions over national territories. In March of that year the President had appointed Nelson Rockefeller "chairman of a panel of experts in arms control and psychological warfare" to operate from the Marine base at Quantico. Wrote William Manchester: "The Quantico group's answer was a proposal for aerial inspection — in a felicitous phrase, 'Open Skies.' " (*The Glory And The Dream*) Nothing came of this, of course, but a feeling of being taken in by our own propaganda, and there were no formal agreements at Geneva. But a typical "Liberal" commentator called it "a peak" in the Eisenhower Presidency, "one of the great moments of the 1950s."

Charles L. Robertson points out that a main effect of the meeting was to create "an atmosphere of relaxation, an atmosphere the Russians exploited unsparingly in their propaganda during succeeding years: as the Western powers continued moves to maintain their chosen security posture, the Soviets charged them with violating the 'Spirit of Geneva'. . . ." (*International Politics Since World War II*)

Washington, D.C., and Camp David, Maryland, U.S., September 15 and September 25-27, 1959: On June 28, 1959, a Soviet Exhibition of Science, Technology and Culture opened in New York. During the succeeding months President Eisenhower invited the Butcher of Budapest to visit the United States, and within two weeks Vice President Nixon was in the Soviet Union (site of the "kitchen debate") as a return courtesy.

Nixon praised our "common love of sports," our mutual "love of humor," and "above all" our "desire for peace." Then, on September fifteenth, the Soviet Ambassador was at Andrews Field declaring: "Nikita Sergeyevich, I salute you on American soil." Khrushchev, the Soviet dictator, was a guest of the United States of America.

California Senator William Knowland expressed the widespread disgust at the time: "Whether we intend it or not [*Communists*] will by word and picture convey the idea that this gives to the Kremlin's leader, and to the Soviet Union, the moral support of the free people of the United States and their leaders . . . . Blood on the hand of Khrushchev is neither less red than that which covered Hitler's, nor are his threats to 'bury us,' meaning the United States and the free world, faded by the passage of a few months."

After three days of meeting with Eisenhower at Camp David, a joint statement was issued about the importance of disarmament. Ike expressed his "unshakable resolution" to put our faith in Soviet intentions — though, reported Arthur Krock in *Memoirs*, Eisenhower thought they would "probably cheat a bit" around the North Pole "where it would be difficult to catch them at it." It was also decided that the issue of Berlin should be reopened, said a joint statement, "with a view to achieving a solution which would be in accordance with the views of all concerned. . . . *etc.*"; and, that "all outstanding international questions should be settled not by the application of force but by peaceful means through negotiation." It was the signal for the beginning of unilateral disarmament by the United States.

President Eisenhower was supposed to go to the Soviet Union the next year.

Paris, France, May 15-19, 1960: DeGaulle, Macmillan, Eisenhower, and Khrushchev were to meet in a grand summit, but sixteen days before the scheduled event an American U-2 plane was brought down over the Sverdlovsk industrial complex in the Soviet Union. Khrushchev took this as an opportunity to declare that Eisenhower was "treacherous," an "aggressor," and a "bandit," withdrawing the invitation to the U.S.S.R. The Soviet dictator demanded an apology, punishment for those responsible, and on May seventeenth stalked from the Elysée Palace.

William Henry Chamberlain summarized: "The Summit That Never Was seems in retrospect very clearly the Summit That Never Should Have Been. May 16, 1960, should be remembered as a sorry day for the dignity and prestige of the United States. The bloody clown who heads the totalitarian Soviet state should never have been given the opportunity to heap guttersnipe insults on the President of the United States and to turn what was supposed to be a serious international conference into an obscene Communist propaganda circus.''

Vienna, Austria, June 3-4, 1961: On June 14, 1960, Senator John F. Kennedy spoke of the disruption of the "Big Four" meeting in Paris, asserting: "Our task is to devise a national strategy — based not on eleventh-hour responses to Soviet-created crises — but a comprehensive set of carefully prepared long-term policies designed to increase the strength of the non-Communist world. Until this task is accomplished there is no point in returning to the summit, for no President of the United States must ever again be put in the position of traveling across the seas armed only with vague speculative hopes.''

Indeed, J.F.K. criticized 1960 Presidential opponent Richard Nixon for promising to go to Eastern Europe, perhaps for another summit. Kennedy said *he* would go to Washington, if elected, "and get this country to work.'' Within a year, he was at a summit conference at Vienna, where *U.S. News & World Report* concluded that Khrushchev had found Kennedy a "pushover.''

As Victor Lasky outlined this summit: "The truth, as it later filtered out, was that Khrushchev had refused to withdraw any of his unreasonable demands — on Germany, nuclear testing, the U.N., Cuba, and Laos. In effect, Khrushchev demanded that Kennedy give in on every point. Unable to budge Khrushchev on a single item (except Laos, where both men agreed on a 'neutralist' coalition government), Kennedy said finally, 'It's going to be a cold winter.' '' (*J.F.K.: The Man And The Myth*)

The Chairman was quoted as bragging to East Germans: "I think that I have taught that young man what fear is.'' That was the summer that Khrushchev put up the Berlin Wall while Kennedy sat on his hands.

Glassboro, New Jersey, U.S., June 23 and 25, 1967: During a meeting of the U.N. General Assembly on the Israeli-Arab war, Soviet Premier Aleksei Kosygin flew to New York to address the U.N., having previously refused President Johnson's invitation to the U.S. There were two meetings between Kosygin and Johnson at Glassboro State College in Hollybush, New Jersey — chosen because it was halfway between the U.N. and Washington, D.C. The *New York Times* reported: "Little progress in settling substantive differences was achieved at the Glassboro meetings, but they afforded an opportunity for important personal contact.'' Here is all that L.B.J. could come up with: "It helps to try to reason together. That is why we went to Hollybush. Reasoning together was the spirit of Hollybush.''

Columnist James Reston captured the "Legacy of the Summit'' as follows: Kosygin "demanded preconditions on a settlement of both the war in Vietnam and the Arab-Israeli war. Get out of Vietnam, he said to the United States, and we will make progress on many things. Withdraw to the pre-war frontiers, he said to Israel, and we will negotiate. *** This was the fundamental and glaring difference between the two statements at the end. The President carefully avoided saying anything that could be used as a provocation or demand on the Soviet Union. Mr. Kosygin not only stated but constantly repeated his two major demands in provocative terms . . . .''

Nevertheless, summits being dear to the heart of the ''Liberal'' press, L.B.J.'s popularity soared. Kosygin flew on to Cuba to coordinate with Castro on subversion of the Western Hemisphere.

Moscow, Leningrad, Kiev, U.S.S.R., May 22-30, 1972: For two years Henry Kissinger worked with Soviet Ambassador Anatoly Dobrynin and Minister-Counselor Yuri Vorontsov on SALT and the 1972 summit. Among other things to come from this were the Anti-Ballistic Missile Treaty and an Interim Agreement on strategic delivery vehicles. We stopped our A.B.M. deployment at Malmstrom; the Soviets kept their ''Moscow'' Galosh system. And we guaranteed ''the Soviets a 40% edge in the number of ICBMs and a 34% edge in the number of Submarine-Launched Ballistic Missiles . . . .'' (*The Fateful Ends And Shades Of SALT*)

That SALT I A.B.M. Treaty, report Phyllis Schlafly and Admiral Chester Ward, ''crowned more than a decade of dedicated efforts to keep the American people subject at all times to a Soviet genocidal nuclear attack. It is difficult to believe, but the U.S. SALT delegation *rejoiced* that they had ensured that the American people could be killed by the scores of millions . . . . So help us God, despite their coy manner, they are serious. They really believe they converted the Soviet SALT delegates to the same immoral insanity.'' (*Kissinger On The Couch*)

Oh, it was all so gay on the way to *détente*. As William Safire recalled: ''Brezhnev and Nixon found common ground in making Kissinger the butt of jokes, a role Henry enjoys when conducted by heads of super-powers. 'Our people have instructions to settle SALT,' said Brezhnev, over a brandy. 'If not, it has to be Dr. Kissinger's fault.' The President, with some zest, suggested: 'We'll send him to Siberia — would you take him?' Brezhnev roared at this kind of sinister good humor, and said that if the negotiations failed, they would send Kissinger to Alma Ata (the Siberian town where Khrushchev had sent Malenkov after deposing him), and if he succeeded, to Lake Baikal, noted for its depth and frozen condition —not much of a choice either way.'' (*Before The Fall*)

So it went in the ''broad new relationship'' that Nixon and Kissinger arranged between the U.S. and the U.S.S.R. SALT I was then ratified by the Senate in August of 1972.

Washington, D.C.; Camp David, Maryland; San Clemente, California, U.S., June 18-26, 1973: Multiple independently targeted reentry vehicles (M.I.R.V.s) were not included in the 1972 Interim Agreement. Kissinger himself admitted that a ban on M.I.R.V.s could not be verified without "spot-checks on on-site inspection." Yet, as reported in *Kissinger On The Couch*, "at the Washington Summit on June 21, 1973, Kissinger sold us out to the Soviets. The price he committed the United States to pay was perfectly clear and absolutely specific: *no* effective inspection of the limitations on the Soviet Union. We would have to accept Soviet compliance on the basis of trust and nothing more."

In the second set of summit talks in thirteen months, accords were signed (prepared earlier) on joint ocean exploration, broader cultural exchanges, more agricultural and transportation research "sharing," and taxation of nationals in one country working in the other. Despite Watergate's pressures, said "Liberal" Senator Charles Percy of Illinois: "The promise of increased Soviet-American cooperation in reducing world tensions is too great to be postponed. The President has made the right decision in proceeding with the summit talks."

C.L. Sulzberger noted that, while Nixon was being cut up at home, Brezhnev had added to his Politburo his chiefs on foreign policy, armed forces, and the secret police. The Soviet dictator, said the *New York Times* analyst, "wants additional American economic and technological aid, a less expensive military balance in Europe, and some indication that the United States doesn't favor [*Red*] China over Russia in the intra-communist cold war." Indeed, Communist Party, U.S.A., chief Gus Hall boasted that Brezhnev's visit again demonstrated how "peaceful coexistence" is "a force against the policies" of the U.S.

Moscow, Minsk, Oreanda, U.S.S.R., June 27-July 3, 1974: A further Protocol to the A.B.M. Treaty of 1972 was signed in 1974 by Nixon and Brezhnev, reducing such sites to one each. We, however, got out of the missile defense business entirely, while the Moscow A.B.M. site protects its I.C.B.M. silos, the largest scientific-industrial concentration in the U.S.S.R., headquarters of the C.P.S.U., and the National Command Center.

There was a preplanned "nonagreement" during the 1974 arms negotiation that culminated in the summit, arguably more damaging than an agreement which would have faced scrutiny by an American Congress. "Unmitigated disaster" was the analysis proffered in *Kissinger On The Couch*: "As always, when the United States is represented by Henry Kissinger, the Soviets came out with *all* they wanted, and *exactly* what they wanted. In 1974 they fully attained their objective: a completely unconstrained opportunity to continue at full speed the 'staggering' momentum of their massive buildup of strategic offensive nuclear weapons systems to the force levels required to attain a first-strike capability against the United States. Coupled with this, they obtained guarantees that the United States would take no compensating action against the Soviet buildup, and would make no response whatsoever in the timeframe relevant to the Soviet threat.''

You see, while we act as though the Soviets want the *Mir* of peace, they show that they know the word's primary Russian meaning: "the world and those who live on it."

Vladivostok, U.S.S.R., November 23-24, 1974: Incredibly enough, the President of the United States flew to Vladivostok without any idea that he was to "negotiate" an agreement on strategic arms — the SALT II guidelines. Ford thought it was a "get acquainted" trip, and was then hit with nine and a half hours of facts and figures presented in arcane language. And there was a dangerous difference between the SALT I Interim Agreement and the one presented at Vladivostok, for the latter included limits on strategic bombers, of which we had a numerical advantage going into the talks. As James Dougherty concluded in *The Fateful Ends And Shades Of SALT*: "The inclusion of strategic bombers made the Vladivostok numbers seem equitable, even though they did not involve any substantial alteration of the U.S.-Soviet ratio for strategic missiles agreed upon in SALT I." Moreover, "Whereas SALT I had specified 'fixed' land-based ICBMs, the language of the Vladivostok Agreement left the way open for mobile ICBMs, something which the United States had earlier opposed."

It was quite a show. As described by *Time's* Hugh Sidey: "There was just a hint at Vladivostok that [*Kissinger*] was seducing Gerald Ford to walk the same primrose path of summitry that Nixon trod . . . . The Secretary had instructions for the President on how to talk and act. At the ramp in Vladivostok when the new President met the Russians it was like a movie scene. They were all there in their fur hats, shaking hands and slapping backs and grinning as if it were a class reunion. And it was, in a way. These were Henry Kissinger's boys . . . ."

The result was an agreement with no limits on launchers and M.I.R.V.s. Completely deluded, Gerald Ford claimed: "Brezhnev and I agreed that we first had to cap the arms race; both in launchers and in M.I.R.V.s." The President told a press conference in December of 1974: "At Vladivostok we put a firm ceiling on the strategic arms race which has heretofore eluded us since the nuclear age began. I believe this is something for which future generations will thank us." If so, they may say it in Russian.

Helsinki, Finland, July 29-August 2, 1975: In signing the Helsinki Final Act, Gerald Ford accepted the Red absorption of the Baltic States, half of Germany, and Central and Eastern Europe. In return, Moscow and its Warsaw Pact allies were supposed to allow increased cultural and human contacts and improve the rights of their captives. That has been a farce, despite the declarations by thirty-five heads of state on "Questions Relating To The Security Of Europe." Force, threat of force, or coercion against other states were declared to be in violation of Helsinki. All we had were the words of Leonid Brezhnev, as he affixed his signature in Helsinki to the document, laughing up his sleeve that "no one should try to dictate to other peoples . . . the manner in which they ought to manage their internal affairs."

The chief U.S. delegate to the European Security Conference looked back in 1982, saying "the Helsinki Final Act has been pummeled to near death by the Soviet Union. Yet we hear the chirping, 'Let's go back to work,' by those who have been demonstrating by their actions their utter contempt for the Final Act and for our process." He emphasized that "the only work I have seen is work represented by the invasion of Afghanistan, or the work of putting people in jail or psychiatric institutions. Are they offering more talk, more words on paper they will disregard? More promises they will not keep? Their words are useless in the face of their deeds against the Final Act. They are wrecking the Final Act."

Vienna, Austria, June 15-18, 1979: When Jimmy Carter sat down with Leonid Brezhnev he was informed that *"détente* has not abolished the class struggle." But Carter signed the SALT II Treaty anyway. Washington Senator Henry Jackson observed: "To enter a treaty which favors the Soviets, as this one does, on the ground that we will be in a worse position without it, is appeasement in its purest form." Fortunately it has not been ratified by the U.S. Senate, though President Reagan is acting as if it had been.

Retired General Daniel O. Graham, former Director of the U.S. Defense Intelligence Agency, shows how the thrust of the strategic-arms summits has affected the U.S. and its enemy in Moscow. In *Shall America Be Defended?*, General Graham observes: ". . . SALT and the hopes for SALT have seriously affected what the U.S. has and has not done in the field of offensive and defensive strategic weaponry. In a quite different way SALT has played a role in encouraging the Soviet buildup. The specific provisions of SALT II are consistent with the strategy and military building programs that have brought the Soviets to the brink of a decisive nuclear superiority and with the *non*-strategy of Mutual Assured Destruction that has driven the U.S. in the opposite direction, from preeminence toward impotence."

Nor should this be a matter of amazement since, on the one hand, we cannot expect Moscow to stand by any agreement not in its best interest and, on the other, those who would have us agree to SALT II and beyond are the same ones, or their progeny, who preached unilateral U.S. disarmament and Mutual Assured Destruction.

* * *

YET THE deadly game continues. Lenin's old friend Armand Hammer now says: "Mr. Chernenko has sent signals that he is ready to talk," perhaps by resuming START talks on the basis of a modified SALT II. In early 1984 "a senior Soviet official" suggested a limited START agreement could be reached by this summer. And not long ago the *Wall Street Journal* observed that Soviet Foreign Minister Gromyko had "delivered a speech attacking the Reagan administration as 'pathological,' 'piratical' and 'criminal.' Four hours later, Mr. Gromyko was talking about the weather with Secretary of State George Shultz as the two men began a lengthy private discussion of U.S.-Soviet relations."

And in the spring of 1984, a "top planner" for the U.S. was quoted as saying: "The President does not want a summit just to be having a summit. But if something could be solved at the summit or at least if progress could be made, that would meet our criteria." If so, it would be the first time in the history of such meetings that one produced anything but disaster for the Free World. The fact is, as Senator Goldwater put it in *The Conscience Of A Conservative*: For Communists, "negotiations are simply an *instrument* of political warfare. For them, a summit meeting is another battle in the struggle for the world."

Chapter XXVII
New World Order

" "WHEN in the course of history the threat of extinction confronts mankind, it is necessary for the people of the United States to declare their interdependence with the peoples of all nations and to embrace those principles and build those institutions which will enable mankind to survive and civilization to flourish. Two centuries ago our forefathers brought forth a new nation; now we must join together with others to bring forth a new world order."

That abominable parody of the U.S. Declaration of Independence was prepared by historian Henry Steele Commager as part of the so-called Declaration of INTERdependence, a project of the World Affairs Council of Philadelphia. Shamefully, this altered Declaration was signed by more than one hundred Members of Congress on the two hundredth anniversary of the proclamation of American independence.

The Declaration of INTERdependence was a part of the continuing drive to dilute, then dissolve, the sovereignty of the United States of America. The goal, we are repeatedly told, is a New World Order, a new international economic order, or any one of a half-dozen similar euphemisms. In any case, it would mean the end of the U.S. as we know it, and her submission first to regional and then world government. The proponents claim that achievement of their goal is inevitable; Americans can acquiesce and take their medicine, or have it shoved down their throats.

Those are totally false alternatives, of course, but they are being aggressively promoted. For instance, by the World Order Models Project (known as W.O.M.P.). Dr. Saul Mendlovitz, director of that important enterprise, contends that there "is no longer a question of whether or not there will be world government by the year 2000. The questions are how it will come into being (cataclysm, drift, more or less rational design), and whether it will be totalitarian, benign, or participatory (the possibilities being in that order)."

Mendlovitz is no nut. He is a professor of law at Rutgers University, a member of the Rockefeller-controlled Council on Foreign Relations, and definitely Big League. Indeed, he takes great pains "to thank the Carnegie Endowment for International Peace and the Rockefeller Foundation for the support which they gave to specific research within the World Order Models Project." Men like Mendlovitz might well be termed Establishment Revolutionaries, being funded by the great foundations for the purpose of attacking our way of life. It is of course Mendlovitz's task as a hired revolutionary to persuade (or scare) us into surrendering the freedom, liberty, and independence of our country. "I believe," declares the W.O.M.P. whopper, "that the most likely governance by the end of the century — compelled by the arms races and outbreaks of violence, the food, population and environmental imbalances as well as large-scale serious injustices — will be oligarchic and highly repressive." To forestall that, he contends, we will need "disarmament," a world police force (which, of course, should control all arms), and other internationalist machinery to assure World Government.

Fortunately, the American people are not that simpleminded, and the Establishment propagandists are having trouble selling their goods. Consider the aforementioned Declaration of INTERdependence. Its promoters, commented an angry Congressman John Ashbrook, have attempted "to undercut patriotic American values . . . ." The World Affairs Council, continued the late Ohio Republican:

". . . has even joined with the Philadelphia school system to develop a model fifth- and sixth-grade school program promoting the declaration of interdependence. Children are even asked to pledge themselves to the declaration's concepts, thus repudiating their own patriotic heritage, and to lobby for signatures from their friends and relatives for the declaration of interdependence.

"This so-called declaration of interdependence is a complete repudiation of the statement of our cherished American freedoms signed by our Founding Fathers 200 years ago. Unlike the Declaration of Independence, whose great hallmarks are guarantees of individual personal freedom and dignity for all Americans and an American Nation under God, the declaration abandons those principles in favor of cultural relativism, international citizenship, and supremacy over all nations by a world government.

"The declaration of interdependence is an attack on loyalty to American freedoms and institutions, which the document calls 'chauvinistic nationalism,' 'national prejudice,' and 'narrow notions of national sovereignty.' "

This was all part of a deliberate attack on the will of the American people to survive as a nation. It is but one such effort, and fell into justified disrepute when exposed by the Conservative newsweekly, *The Review Of The News*. Another such assailant has been the influential Aspen Institute for Humanistic Studies (long chaired by Robert O. Anderson, the Exxon mogul), which in December 1974 created the National Commission on Coping with Interdependence. This body, said its announcements, would "consider the implications for Americans of what Secretary of State Henry Kissinger has called 'the accelerating momentum of our interdependence.' " The succession of Cyrus Vance to head the State Department provided no respite. He was identified in the January 1977 issue of *Transition* (published by the Institute for World Order) as yet another "world order type." Pollster Daniel Yankelovich, who served on the Institute's board of directors, happily reported that Carter's Secretary "is concerned with those [*world order*] issues. He is in a very important position."

How does one go about "Coping with Interdependence"? The Aspen Institute spelled it out in a brochure, noting that "the most important changes will be modifications in attitudes which, in the nature of our pluralism, must first take place in the reasoning consciences of millions of individuals. The most important adjustment of all will be to blur, then erase, the psychic frontier between 'domestic affairs' and 'international affairs.' " Stripped of self-justifying verbiage, that simply means we are to be conditioned to forget that we are Americans and become men and women without a country.

School indoctrination is of course important, especially among those expected to become "leaders" in the New World Order. We are assured of this by no less an authority than C. Douglas Dillon — the former Undersecretary of State, former Secretary of the Treasury, C.F.R. Director, Brookings Institution Director, and Honorary Chairman of the Board of the Institute for World Order. Dillon has emphasized that it is essential "that we educate the intellectual elites so that thinking of this nature can come from a broad group of people." But even he agrees "it will take a while before people in this country as a whole will be ready for any substantial giving-up of sovereignty to handle global problems." Nonetheless, Douglas Dillon says, "global authorities will develop, possibly through the United Nations or parallel organizations."

To speed up this development, the Institute for World Order has established both School and University Programs to teach "world order." At the university level, according to program director Michael Washburn, "I think our success was somewhat spectacular. In 1960 there were virtually no courses being taught in this area. By 1963-1964, there were

500 colleges or universities with these courses; 50 or 60 had some kind of major or graduate studies program. In phase three, we set about to catalyze a much higher level of institutionalization for world order through our university-based world order centers. We were fortunate in getting support then from the Rockefeller Foundation, the James P. Warburg* family and from a number of smaller foundations in southern California, Minnesota and elsewhere. We have raised nearly $500,000 for our centers program in two years."

The barrage is falling upon our children from all sides. For instance, the director of the World Order School Program, Ms. Betty Reardon, happily reported that the National Education Association chose "Education for a Global Community" as its Bicentennial theme. In an interview with *Transition*, Ms. Reardon indicated what New World Order means. She offered Martin Luther King as a hero for schoolchildren, claiming that he "was a moral leader and a great teacher without being a 'moralist.' "

Never mind that the "Reverend" King was in fact a notorious libertine who was trained, backed, and advised by top Communists to provoke violence and build racial hatred as efficiently as any Grand Lizard of the Ku Klux Klan.

You see, says Ms. Reardon of the World Order School Program, "I consider him [*King*] to be part of the world order movement. He had a vision of a transformed society based on the principles of peace and justice and he had a transition strategy, nonviolent militant action, to get from the present to that preferred future. When the history of this period is written, he will be one of the greatest of those who symbolize the movement for community and the dignity and value of all human life."

It is not surprising that a pro-Communist like King would be a World Order favorite. Among the listed Sponsoring Institutions for the World Order Models Project, after all, is the Novosti "Press Agency" of Moscow,[†] a Soviet propaganda organ largely staffed by the Kremlin's Secret Police. In his authoritative book, *KGB*, John Barron described the director of Novosti, one Ivan Ivanovich Udaltsov, as "a KGB officer who, as minister counselor in Prague, participated in preparations for the Soviet invasion of Czechoslovakia. An entire division of Novosti, known

---

*James died in 1969. A member of the international banking establishment, with roots in the Schiff and Loeb families, James P. Warburg was a Communist-Fronter, a backer of the United World Federalists, and a proponent of universal disarmament. Warburg once told the U.S. Senate Foreign Relations Committee: "We shall have world government whether we like it or not. The question is only whether world government will be achieved by consent or by conquest." Recognize the line?

[†]The U.S.-based sponsor is the Woodrow Wilson School of Public and International Affairs, named for the champion of the ill-fated League of Nations. After the U.S. failed to join the League, Wilson's "alter ego," Colonel E.M. House, helped establish the Council on Foreign Relations to work toward World Government. It might not yet be One World, but it's a small world when the Wilson retinue and the K.G.B. are found openly supporting the same organization and goal.

as the Tenth Section, is staffed with KGB men, one of whom is the noted British traitor Harold A.R. ('Kim') Philby.'' Is Prague's recent past to become the world's future?

Indeed, in *Commentary* magazine for February 1975, Johns Hopkins professor of international relations Robert W. Tucker commented on the anticipated Communist role in the proposed New World Order. Professor Tucker observed that "the new equality is also likely to lead to an international system in which the relative power position of the Soviet Union will be considerably enhanced, for the Russians are neither dependent in any significant way on the new [*"developing"*] states nor disposed to view their claims in the manner of Western elites.''

But those "Western elites" are working with the Communists to siphon off our wealth. That is already in black and white in the United Nations Declaration on the Establishment of a New International Economic Order. In the New World Order, we are informed, the system must be changed because the poorer nations "which constitute 70 per cent of the world population, account for only 30 per cent of the world's income.'' Professor Tucker foresaw that "the world community will become a welfare community in roughly the manner that Western states have become welfare states.'' As former U.N. Secretary General Kurt Waldheim told the World Food and Energy Conference, "the time has come to think in terms of a redistribution of the wealth of the planet.''

All of this is to be handled in stages. Professor Richard N. Gardner, a top Carter advisor who became Ambassador to Italy, explained the strategy in the C.F.R. journal *Foreign Affairs* for April of 1974. The hope, announced Gardner, lies "not in building up a few ambitious central institutions of universal membership and general jurisdiction as was envisaged at the end of the last war [*World War II*], but rather in the much more decentralized, disorderly and pragmatic process of inventing or adapting institutions of limited jurisdiction and selected membership to deal with specific problems on a case-by-case basis, as the necessity for cooperation is perceived by the relevant nations.'' In short, said the Columbia professor, the " 'house of world order' will have to be built from the bottom up rather than from the top down . . . . an end run around national sovereignty, eroding it piece by piece, will accomplish much more than the old-fashioned frontal assault.''

This strategy also appears in the work of the other big names in the World Order business, among them Princeton professor Richard A. Falk, another member of the C.F.R. In the 1975 volume, *On The Creation Of A Just World Order* (edited by Saul H. Mendlovitz, New York, Free Press), Mr. Falk laid out a roadmap. The Seventies, he revealed, were to be the decade of "Consciousness Raising"; the Eighties, of "Mobilization"; and, the Nineties are to be the decade of "Transformation."

The piecemeal approach is to involve, to start, the transformation of the European Economic Community (E.E.C.) into a regional government. The leaders of the founding nine nations of the E.E.C. agreed in 1972 to a "European Union" by 1980. Plans were made in Paris for a preliminary political government with complete economic and monetary unity including one currency, budget, and central bank. Direct elections to a European Parliament have been held twice, in 1979 and June of 1984. The latest voter drive, waged under the slogan "United in democracy," had a $4.8 million television and print campaign by a French-based advertising agency that admitted it was "no different from persuading them to buy dog food." Somehow, that gullet-stuffer says it all.

While consolidation of Europe proceeds, regionalism is also going forward at other levels. David Rockefeller's Trilateral Commission has been set up to develop the next step, which is to make "partners" of Western Europe, North America, and Japan. Rockefeller selected his old college roommate and longtime director of the Council on Foreign Relations, George S. Franklin, as the Commission's first North American Secretary; meanwhile, Zbigniew Brzezinski, another C.F.R. member and protégé of David Rockefeller, became the first Director of the T.C. As is now well known to political observers, more than a dozen Trilateralists — about a quarter of the total American members — were soon holding top positions in the Carter Administration. They included President Jimmy Carter, Vice President Walter Mondale, National Security Advisor Brzezinski, Secretary of State Cyrus Vance, Secretary of Defense Harold Brown, United Nations Ambassador Andrew Young, and Secretary of the Treasury Michael Blumenthal.

Professor Richard Ullman commented of the T.C. in *Foreign Affairs* for October 1976 that the desired "result — to quote Zbigniew Brzezinski, the former Director of the Trilateral Commission — would be 'a community of the developed nations.' The path to that community, he wrote in this journal . . . , runs through intensive 'regular and ever more formal political consultation' and 'common political planning with regard to problems or areas of mutual interest' in order to achieve 'a shared political perspective among the governmental bodies of the three (trilateral) units.' Governor Carter used almost the same language in addressing the Foreign Policy Association last June."

Is this some kind of a conspiracy or plot? "If you like conspiracy theories about secret plots to take over the world," chortled the *Washington Post*, "you are going to love the administration of Jimmy Carter."

And, the *New York Times* for January 6, 1977, echoed: The "founding fathers of Trilateralism were members in good standing of the so-called Eastern Establishment. James E. Carter Jr., the former Governor of Georgia, joined the Trilateral Commission when he decided to make his run for the Presidency. Believers in the conspiracy theory of history will surely regard the Trilateral Commission as an Eastern Establishment front organization whose main purpose is to co-opt Jimmy Carter."

To co-opt Jimmy Carter? Hardly. Mr. Carter knew all about the objectives of the Trilateral Commission well before he became President. In March of 1976, for example, he told the Chicago Council on Foreign Relations how we should "coordinate" our policies with the Trilateral nations; in May of that year in Tokyo he told the American Chamber of Commerce that we need a "commitment" to Trilateralism; and, in June 1976 he informed the Foreign Policy Association: "*The time has come for us to seek a partnership between North America, Western Europe and Japan.*" (Italics in original prepared text.)

World Order is the order of the day, President Carter declared in his inaugural "Statement to the World" of January 20, 1977, announcing: "The United States will meet its obligation to help create a stable, just and peaceful world order." Mr. Carter did not deign (publicly) to endorse the plans of the World Order Models Project, as described by Professor Richard Falk: "WOMP accepts as self-evident the need to reorient American public and elite opinion; hopefully, this country can be encouraged to play a less domineering global role," writes Falk, "and to share its wealth and income with the world community on a far greater scale." (*A Study of Future Worlds*, New York, Free Press, 1975) Among other things, said Professor Falk, "To achieve this [*better world order*], central institutions would have to be equipped with police capabilities while national institutions would be substantially deprived of military capabilities."

Well, now. Mr. Carter actually aimed to eliminate all nuclear weapons from the earth, proposed Trilateralist Paul Warnke to bargain away our arms, and made his earliest major Budget reduction in defense. Meanwhile, on the domestic level, the F.B.I. was hamstrung and warned (under Carter) that the number of Soviet-bloc agents *legally* in the U.S. had doubled in the previous decade. Compare these developments with the comments of New World Order professor Richard Falk: "The first and central priority of the movement for a preferred world is to make progress toward *diminishing the role of the war system in international life*," writes Falk, "and toward *dismantling the national security apparatus in the major states of the world*." (Italics in original.)

Of course this could all be coincidence. Step right up and buy a tin of Dr. Carter's Little Sell-'Em-Down-The-River Pills. You will have to get in line. *America* magazine — published by the Jesuits of the United States and Canada — has been telling us it was not too early to speak of the Trilateral movement as a new "ism." Jeremiah Novak, formerly of the *Washington Post*, contends: The "trilateral world has the means to bargain in the same way the United States once did." Certainly the Trilateralist impact is already being felt. Novak wrote in *America* for February 5, 1977: "According to sources in the State Department, the trilateral papers have directly influenced the summoning of the Rambouillet and Puerto Rican conferences, the sale of IMF gold, the Law of the Sea conferences, the formation of the International Energy Agency, and steps to establish a new international currency, which replaces the U.S. dollar and gold. The commission's record and its powerful influence after the 1976 elections deserve a great deal of respect."

The Trilateral Commission has called for creation of a number of new institutions "to deal with planetary interest groups." New structures, reports Jeremiah Novak, "are recommended to meet the needs of oil users and producers and to 'bridge the economic systems' of Communist and non-Communist states. These interest-group institutions are seen as subordinate to a superstructure of planetary institutions."

And remember that we are no longer talking about the theories of impotent utopians. These planners are actually moving ahead. Take the strengthening of the World Bank and International Monetary Fund (I.M.F.). The Commission's "most immediate concern," observed Novak, "is the creation of a new world monetary system to replace gold and the dollar as the international exchange units with a new currency called special drawing rights (SDR's). In fact, as a move in this direction, the commission was instrumental in the IMF's sale of its gold and in the creation of a system of denoting all currencies in terms of SDR's as a first step in the push for a new world system." Trilateralism, remember, is only a way station on the road to the New World Order.

One by one, the bonds of internationalism are being wrapped around us in preparation for what Ford Foundation president Rowan Gaither admitted years ago is the ultimate goal — "so to alter our life in the United States that we can be comfortably merged with the Soviet Union." This is recognized by the Reds. As the Marxist *Guardian* noted some time ago: "In discussing the Trilateral group, the author of one commission report noted that 'it does not envisage a new anti-communist alliance; indeed, at some point in the future the more advanced communist states might choose to become partners.' "

That is the Establishment's offensive game plan. And patriots must attempt to intercept this lateral pitchout — this "end run around national sovereignty" — and again move the ball in the right direction. The lines and goals are clearly marked. As syndicated columnist Nicholas von Hoffman observed in late January of 1977: "Here at home it has been the John Birch Society and similar right-wing groups who first recognized a collusion between capitalists of the Rockefeller stripe and socialists like Willy Brandt and Helmut Schmidt. As a glance at the membership of the Trilateral Commission, the world ruling class's floating seminar, shows, Social Democrats and global capitalists have no trouble cooperating." Nor, he might have added, do Communist dictators who want Western technology to expand their hegemony by increasing the power of their military forces.

The Communists and World Order elitists are playing this game together. Thierry de Montbrial, an influential French economist, has written in the C.F.R. journal *Foreign Affairs* that "in an interdependent world sovereignty is always limited; hence we have already advocated the concept of management of the earth's natural resources for the general good and not for the benefit of a limited few." At this point, the author introduces what he calls a "relevant quotation" from Karl Marx's *Das Kapital*: "When our society reaches a higher level of economic organization, the right of ownership by a few individuals of land forming part of the planet will seem as absurd as the idea of man's ownership of man appears nonsensical to our society today. No nation, nor all the nations covering the globe, are owners of the land, but merely possessors, tenants, with the responsibility like diligent heads of families, of transmitting it, improved, to future generations."

Proponents of the New World Order go so far as openly to express admiration for the vast tyranny of Communist China. This is a recurrent theme, for instance, in *On The Creation Of A Just World Order*, where University of Michigan professor Ali Mazrui calls Occupied China "a major model of political and cultural engineering, with all its potentialities as a whole new civilization in the world." It is a "civilization" built, the admiring Michigan professor neglects to add, on the bodies of some *sixty-four million* dead Chinese. Peiping's tyranny, euphemizes Professor Mazrui of the World Order Models Project, really reflects Red "China's determined energy to transcend many of its problems through the energies of its own people and to mobilize a fifth of mankind in the quest for new social directions."

Elsewhere in *On The Creation Of A Just World Order*, McGill University professor Paul T.K. Lin, of the Centre for East Asian Studies, actually declared: "Red China's dynamic society today is indeed an *enormously instructive paradigm* of fundamental change along lines radically different from those of many other developing countries." So were the practices of Vlad the Impaler. And Professor Lin praised the following as "The 'end' values of [*Red*] Chinese development":

"1. Social justice based on freedom from exploitation, with human relations of egalitarianism, cooperation, and respect for work.

"2. Economic welfare for all in a society of abundance, with special attention to raising the level of life of marginalised groups (such as women and national minorities) and regions that have been resource-poor or historically oppressed. [*This of the butchers of Tibet!*]

"3. Maximum cultural and aesthetic fulfillment. This includes full popular participation in the production of culture.

"4. An esthetically and ecologically sound environment. This value is not posed *against* growth, but as part of development, fulfilling the same purpose of service to the people as growth."

This Red China, we are apparently to believe, is the very acme of the World Order ideal — or will be when the rest of the "class enemies" are executed or enslaved.* These minions of the anthill mentality are to be our ultimate partners in the New World Order — a scheme already being planned, for instance, by the Council on Foreign Relations. The Institute for World Order's honorary chairman, C. Douglas Dillon, has admitted the C.F.R. "is embarked on a major new program, looking ahead to the 80s. They call it the 80s Project. It's one of the largest projects they've ever undertaken, and it posits in their thinking the need for system improvement. They haven't as yet [*as of January 1975*] reached any answers, and they don't go as far [*publicly*] as the Institute for World Order, but they are now thinking and looking towards this."

As C.F.R. Director Dillon knows, the Council on Foreign Relations is a secret organization. It is not about to blare from the housetops that a world gestapo is in the making. The C.F.R. style is more subtle. But its 1980s Global Study is now under way, having been announced without fanfare on the day after Christmas 1976. A profusion of funding has been provided, reported the *New York Times*, "by the Ford Foundation, the German Marshall Fund of the United States, the Lilly Endowment, the Andrew W. Mellon Foundation and the Rockefeller Foundation. The unifying theme, according to [*Professor Richard H. Ullman of the*

---

*One must credit the New World Order boys with utopian presumption. There is a "disproportionate Western presence" in literature and law "in the global pool," according to Professor Ali Mazrui. Therefore, "In our new world we would require that every child in the world should learn three languages — a world language (e.g., English or French), a regional language (e.g., German or Swahili) and *either* a national language (e.g., Swedish, Persian) *or* a subnational language (e.g., Gujarati or Luganga)."

Woodrow Wilson School at Princeton], will be to suggest 'desirable, achievable conditions of international relations and specifying policy avenues leading toward such conditions.' " That is, dropping the euphemisms of the C.F.R., the objective is to plan how best to dupe the American rubes into the New World Order.

Meanwhile, Professor Ullman's fellow Ivy Leaguer and C.F.R. colleague, Marshall Shulman of Columbia, put out the word to the Establishment insiders in *Foreign Affairs* for January 1977, concluding: "It is therefore a central requirement that our actions serve to strengthen the international system, and that we seek as a long-term objective to draw the Soviet Union, [*Red*] China and other authoritarian regimes into constructive participation in that system, as they come to appreciate their self-interest in doing so."

Frankly, we are not enthused about fulfilling the Communists' self-interest, nor even that of the European Socialists — especially when it means surrender of American sovereignty through merger in a New World Order. We intend to see that there is no repudiation of the Declaration of Independence, wherein "with a firm Reliance on the Protection of divine Providence, we mutually pledge to each other our lives, our Fortunes, and our sacred Honor."

Chapter XXVIII

Admissions Of The Trilateral Commission

" "INAUGURATED in July 1973, the Trilateral Commission is a policy making organization" comprised of just three hundred "private" individuals from Japan, North America, and Western Europe. Yet Kiichi Miyazawa, former Foreign Minister of Japan, assures us: "Discussions within the Commission do affect the thinking of our governments." They do indeed. But then, from the very beginning, Commission founder David Rockefeller boasted of the Trilaterals that their "primary objective" is "to bring the best brains in the world to bear on the problems of the future." As a Rockefeller confidant puts it: "When David gets an idea, he does something about it."

Though its plenary sessions are closed to the public, more than a decade after its beginnings one can readily see that the Trilateral Commission is anything but a conspiracy of silence; it is in fact a relatively open collusion of the powerful, and brazen enough to own up to at least some of its aims. These admissions against interest need examining.

Not a plot against government *per se*, the Commission is comprised of individuals who see themselves *above* the mundane day-to-day activities of state affairs and determined to act as autocrats reigning from afar. Consider the 1980 broadcast of journalist Bill Moyers (a member of the Trilateral Commission's "parent" organization, the Council on Foreign Relations) commenting on Trilateral founder David Rockefeller (himself the C.F.R. Chairman):

"David Rockefeller is the most conspicuous representative today of the ruling class, a multinational fraternity of men who shape the global economy and manage the flow of its capital. Rockefeller was born to it, and he has made the most of it. But what some critics see as a vast international conspiracy, he considers a circumstance of life, and just another day's work."

We do not exaggerate in stating that such potentates have become creatures above the law. Moyers breathlessly reported: "Private citizen David Rockefeller is accorded privileges of a head of state . . . . He is untouched by customs of passport offices and hardly pauses for traffic lights. Rockefeller is the supreme example of how multinational companies do business." Moreover, you in essence paid for televising that Moyers celebration of David Rockefeller through public television; the Corporation for Public Broadcasting; the tax-exempt Ford Foundation, a major financial supporter of the Trilateral Commission; and, the tax breaks of the Weyerhaeuser Company, another T.C. backer headed by Commission member George Weyerhaeuser. Our guardians have indeed grown bold when they televise their might in the manner of Big Brother.

Certainly the Commission is not publicity shy. In 1976, for example, Number Eleven of "The Triangle Papers" was released to the public. Called *The Reform Of International Institutions*, its authors were heavyweight Trilaterals C. Fred Bergsten (Senior Fellow at the Brookings Institution), Georges Berthoin (former Chief Representative of the Commission of the European Communities in the United Kingdom), and Kinhide Mushakoji (Vice Rector for Programs at the United Nations University). This triumvirate contended: "History shows that an effective international system requires a custodian." Which of course leads one to the question: *Quis custodiet ipsos custodes?* Does this mean America First? Hardly. The Trilats explain our intended part in the world order of tomorrow as follows:

"America must still play a major role in managing the international system. It continues to provide the ultimate security of most of the other industrialized countries and remains the world's largest single economy, the home country of one-half the world's foreign direct investment, the major food supplier to international markets, and the least dependent of the large industrialized countries on imported energy and raw materials. However, both U.S. domestic politics — which increasingly inhibits it from shouldering a disproportionate economic burden — and the unwillingness of other countries to follow its lead rule out the same degree of American dominance which existed in the recent past."

If America is to be replaced as world leader, is the new order at least to be anti-Communist? In a word: No. The Trilateralists do "not envisage a new anti-Communist alliance; indeed, at some point in the future the more advanced Communist states might choose to become partners." Such is the totalitarian promise of the New World Order. As set forth in Number Thirteen of "The Triangle Papers," *Collaboration With Communist Countries In Managing Global Problems*, the Commissioners "desire to exploit any opportunities with the Communist countries for cooperative management of certain international problems.'' The historical fact that East-West complicity has only strengthened the Red bloc is deliberately down-played, as is the role of the West in building up our enemies by such actions. The Communist mass murderers, you see, are now to be our *partners*. Or, as it is blithely expressed in *Towards A Renovated International System*, Triangle Paper Number Fourteen:

''. . . the support for human rights will have to be balanced against other important goals of world order. Some Trilateral conceptions of détente with the Soviet Union and other communist states tend to conflict with a policy promoting human rights.''

Yes, the use of the Gulag is a mildly unsettling tendency of brutal dictators, but then one can't build a New World Order without breaking some eggs. So darkness at noon is apparently something with which Trilateralists can live. Indeed it is their avowed intention to do so. Leadership of the world must be ''collective,'' say the ''best brains'' on the globe, ''such as exists at the highest levels of the security system between the United States and the Soviet Union as they seek jointly to prevent nuclear war while competing actively at lower levels of international relations.'' (''The Triangle Papers,'' Number Eleven) In the midst of such ''security,'' remember, it has been openly admitted in Congress that the Soviets have with Western help developed the power to kill half the U.S. population in less time than it took to transmit a declaration of war in World War II.

This collective leadership, the Trilateralists note, must include ''dropouts'' from the international order. To wit: ''Most notable are the Communist countries, several of which (including the Soviet Union) were involved at the outset of the postwar international economic system but left before it began to function. They are now re-entering the world economy, particularly in such key individual markets as food (especially the Soviet Union) and energy (especially [*Red*] China).''

The butchers of Communist China have been pets of Zbigniew Brzezinski — for the first three years of the T.C.'s operations its central director and then U.S. National Security Advisor under President Carter, another Trilateral protégé. Brother Carter and Brzezinski called for a ''more just and equitable world order'' even if this meant selling out our Free China allies on Taiwan. As Zbig put it in the *Washington Star* in 1978: ''. . . we have to accommodate very broadly with the People's Republic of China. It represents [*sic*] one-fourth of humanity, and an extremely gifted and creative segment of humanity, with whom we have many common interests. These interests are long-term, not tactically anti-Soviet; they are much more connected with our fundamental view of a world of diversity and not a world dominated by this or that power.'"*

This is the view of the same Zbigniew Brzezinski who has written that Marxism "represents a further vital and creative stage in the maturing of man's universal vision." A man who espouses that a "needed change is more likely to develop incrementally and less overtly . . . in keeping with the American tradition of blurring distinctions between public and private institutions." (*Between Two Ages: America's Role In The Technetronic Era*, New York, Viking, 1970) That certainly is the declared Trilateral purpose, literally to propagandize "audiences in the three regions, so that the public opinion in Japan, North America, and Europe will come to reflect the private consensus." The "private consensus" being that of Brzezinski and Rockefeller and the other would-be masters.

So it came to pass that we were presented by the Trilateralists with a National Security Advisor who believed national sovereignty to be obsolete! And said so. Mr. Brzezinski maintained that "the old framework of international politics — with their spheres of influence, military alliances between nation-states, the *fiction of sovereignty*, doctrinal conflicts arising from nineteenth century crises — is clearly no longer compatible with reality." What, then, is real to this Trilateral founder? Bluntly, that the "nation state as a fundamental unit of man's organized life has ceased to be the principal creative force: International banks and multinational corporations are acting and planning in terms that are far in advance of the political concepts of the nation-state."

David Rockefeller agrees, but chooses to be coy about it. For example, in 1980 before the Los Angeles World Affairs Council, he disavowed being the "cabalist-in-chief" of a "coterie of international conspirators with designs on covertly ruling the world . . . ." In Rockefeller's speech, later reprinted in the *Wall Street Journal* for those who don't keep up on Trilateral affairs, he noted:

"To some extremists, the Trilateral Commission is pictured as a nefarious plot by an Eastern Establishment of businessmen in the service of multinational corporations, who will do almost anything including going into cahoots with the Kremlin for the sake of financial gain. The fact that many former members, including President Carter, are now members of the administration is hailed as proof of how devilishly well the conspiracy is working."

Golly, Dave, maybe our problems stem from believing what we read in the papers . . . the Triangle Papers. As for this fictional "coterie," our

---

*Such propaganda continues. In 1983, for instance, the T.C. proclaimed: "Security policies of trilateral countries should seek to strengthen China's ties to the West, possibly including some assistance to its military as well as its civilian modernization." We were saviors of the Bolsheviks, Stalinists, and post-Stalinists; then we saved Mao and are now expected to rescue the post-Maoists.

dictionary describes such a body as *an intimate often exclusive group of persons with a common interest or purpose.* That shoe fits. Commission publications formally describe "a series of concentric circles of international decision-making to provide the collective management which has become necessary for an effective international system: a small informal core group (which might differ in its precise composition from issue to issue), a broader group of all major countries, and formal implementation of agreed initiatives throughout existing or new universal institutions." Talk about coteries within coteries.

The growth of a New World Order will mean the death of the United States as we know it. Is that warning Extremist? The Trilateral Commission itself, in *The Problem Of International Consultations* (Triangle Paper Number Twelve) euphemizes as follows: "If a more effective and equitable economic order is to emerge, national policies and programs must be subject to moderation and adjustment to take into account probable adverse international ramifications. This can be accomplished only if powerful domestic agencies are brought under control and sensitized to the international consequences of their policies."

Control is the key. A major difficulty, in the Commission's view, is that the "public and leaders of most countries continue to live in a mental universe which no longer exists — a world of separate nations — and have great difficulties thinking in terms of global perspectives and interdependence." (*Toward A Renovated International System*) Trust the interdependents not to be parochial.

Take the energy "crisis" and the opportunities it afforded the manipulators of our society. A decade ago, the Trilateral Commission foresaw: "There can be little doubt that more serious shortages of energy and more drastic adjustment of economic patterns and social lifestyles lie ahead. Economic factors will by themselves induce certain changes. But the situation will call for a considerable degree of voluntary cooperation and of acceptance, voluntary and involuntary, of governmental regulation of an increased sector of personal life . . . . In essence, there will be a reallocation of capital, labor, technology, and available supplies of energy through the economics of scarcity." (As quoted in *Trilateralism*, edited by Holly Sklar, Boston, South End Press, 1980.) It was thus no surprise to the Trilats when Paul Volcker, the Trilateralist head of the Federal Reserve System under both Presidents Carter and Reagan, boldly declared in 1979: "The standard of the average American has to decline."

That same year, *New York Times* economic columnist Leonard Silk remarked: "Trilateralism survives, based on the need for a concentration of thought and power among those whose interests closely cohere in a disorderly world." Indeed it does. Four years ago the leading political tickets all had Trilateralists at or near the top — Jimmy Carter and Walter Mondale, George Bush, and John Anderson. Carter is gone but Trilateralist John Glenn joined the race with Trilateralists Mondale and Bush. And the Reagan Administration, which criticized the Carter elitists, includes (besides Vice President Bush) these "former" Trilateral members: William Brock, U.S. Special Trade Representative; Arthur Burns, U.S. Ambassador to West Germany; William Hewitt, U.S. Ambassador to Jamaica; Paul Volcker, Chairman, Board of Governors, U.S. Federal Reserve System; and, Caspar Weinberger, U.S. Secretary of Defense.

Even Trilateralist Henry Kissinger returned to head up the Reagan commission in Central America. The more things change, the more they stay the same. Remember the "Kissinger issue" of 1976 when he was being widely quoted as having declared: "The day of the United States is past and today is the day of the Soviet Union. My job as Secretary of State is to negotiate the most acceptable second-best position available." But of course Henry is a practiced master at surrendering with wit. When asked whether the T.C. was running the world, Herr Kissinger answered with a smile: "I am insulted. Why do I need the Trilateral Commission when I can run the world all by myself?"

Is this Commission really only a glorified gentlemen's club? Some would have you believe so. William Greider, writing in the "Liberal" Establishment's *Washington Post*, held that: "On paper they run the world. But, in the flesh, the Trilateralists get together and mostly talk about how the world ought to run, if only the world would cooperate." You see, the "best brains" in the world only get together for meetings of a David Rockefeller version of the Mystic Knights of the Sea. David is Amos, Zbig is Andy, Henry is the Kingfish . . . .

As we have pointed out, the Commission has been afforded less secrecy than such allied bodies as the C.F.R., which long urged building World Government through the United Nations. Theodore Jacobs, for example, chief counsel of a House Government Operations Subcommittee, observed in *Public Opinion* for April/May 1983:

"The Trilateral Commission has been the object of greater and more critical public and press attention than any other conference or group, partly because of its close association with David Rockefeller. Attention also stems from the skillful selection of ascendant politicians. Rockefeller and Brzezinski invited Jimmy Carter and Walter Mondale to join the group long before they were close to the White House. When Carter was elected in 1976, at least eighteen top-level executives in his administration were drawn from the Trilateral membership, giving rise to the most full-blown conspiracy theories. Trilateralists included Secretaries of State, Defense, and Treasury Cyrus Vance, Harold Brown, and Michael

Blumenthal. Jimmy Carter candidly admitted he learned a good deal about foreign policy from the Trilateral meetings and from its then director, Brzezinski. Vice President George Bush and Secretary of Defense Caspar Weinberger have been members. The Trilateral list has also included many of the Bilderberg participants, including George Ball, Henry Kissinger, and Paul Volcker. Commission members who join the government must resign, but they often rejoin when their official service ends . . . .

"After Jimmy Carter became president, he invited the commission to a White House reception and reportedly told the 200 visitors that if the Trilateral Commission had existed after World War I, there might not have been a World War II. ✳✳✳

"The conspiracy theory is fed by the secrecy of some of the gatherings and the interlocking network of rich and powerful participants. Indeed, the same people, sometimes called 'the old Council on Foreign Relations crowd,' do seem to be omnipresent."

But David Rockefeller says there is no conspiracy. And David is an honorable man. Just ask George S. Franklin, long a leader of the Trilateral Commission and C.F.R., who reports that criticism of (arguably) the world's most powerful man is "ridiculous." Franklin admits, "without him, we would have never gotten started . . . . But he [*Rockefeller*] doesn't attempt to control anyone on the Commission." Mr. Franklin should know, one gathers, since he roomed with young David at Harvard and would have picked up any hints that Rockefeller really wanted to rule the world. Moreover, as proof that D.R. was not behind Trilateralist Jimmy Carter, Franklin reports, the New York plutocrat voted for Gerald Ford in 1976 and Ronald Reagan in 1980. Never mind that Rockefeller did all in his power in 1980 to elect Mr. Bush, and that even George Franklin does not follow David into the voting booth. In any case, both Presidents Carter and Reagan offered Rockefeller a Cabinet position, though as always the man who *isn't* a cabalist-in-chief declined. Why accept a demotion?

While trying to play down the importance of the Trilateral Commission in 1981, the "Liberal" *Boston Globe* did acknowledge: "Part of the criticism that the commission is Rockefeller's cabal is attributed to the commission's funding. Ten percent of its funds — for the operation of the North America division — comes directly from Rockefeller, the Rockefeller Brothers Fund and the Rockefeller Foundation . . . . Charges of undue big business influence is [*sic*] attributed to some of the contributions made by a stellar list of almost 40 of the best-known [*"Liberal" Establishment*] companies in America, including Coca-Cola, Exxon, General Motors, IBM and Xerox." All do big business with the Reds.

What President Reagan refers to as the Soviet "evil empire" should be aided, says the Trilateral Commission. But of course the Commission is not in cahoots with the Kremlin, Mr. Rockefeller assures us. This despite reams of evidence, including a recent Heritage Foundation study showing, for instance, that the military balance is shifting in favor of the Kremlin because of "a virtual hemorrhage of technology in the past decade" from the U.S. to the U.S.S.R.

Why such aid? It is explained away with a variety of specious arguments. Take: *Energy: Managing The Transition*, a Trilateral study presented to the United Nations a few years ago, claiming "any global approach to energy issues must eventually involve the communist countries." Here is the scenario: "The Trilateral governments should, therefore, consider the advisability of providing capital and technical assistance (particularly in offshore drilling) to the Soviets as part of an overall energy agreement." Maybe *that's* why the Reagan Administration has cleared shipments of "drilling technology" to the U.S.S.R. despite strenuous objections from the Defense Department.

And remember Mr. Carter's "windfall profits" tax on oil? The Trilateral Commission put that bee in his bonnet in this same study, calling for raising prices above the world level through a higher federal excise tax on gasoline.

The "opinions" of the Trilateral Commission are often behind today's headlines. Consider, for example, 1983's Triangle Paper Number Twenty-Six, *Trilateral Security*, by Gerard C. Smith, Chief U.S. Negotiator, SALT I; Paolo Vittorelli, Chairman, Italian Institute for Defense Studies & Research; and, Kiichi Saeki, Chairman, Nomura Research Institute. Here is one of their findings: ". . . there is little reason to restrict general trade in the hope that such restrictions would be likely to affect Soviet policies or behavior in a desirable direction." You can bet the evil empire agrees.

On the one hand, the Trilateralists note the historical experience with that "dilemma of agreements concerning weapons which are inherently hard to monitor." In short, these Trilats are not ignorant of previously disastrous dealings with dictators. They observe: "The naval limitations agreed in the 1920s and 1930s had, on a sympathetic interpretation, only ambiguous results and insufficient strength to survive the conditions of the 1930s (Admiral Gorshkov once characterized them as the 'war of the diplomats for supremacy at sea'). The Geneva Protocol on Chemical Weapons and the Biological and Toxin Weapons Convention, while broadly subscribed to, have apparently been breached repeatedly when it has suited states to do so, most recently by the Soviets and their allies in Afghanistan and Southeast Asia."

Nevertheless, they stress: "The search for arms control and eventual disarmament remains basic to the health of the trilateral democracies." The Commission offers this advice concerning an enemy sworn to bury us: "We recommend that the *United States propose regular talks between senior U.S. and Soviet defense officials and military staffs,* which could promote better understanding of the concerns of the two countries." You see, the Trilaterals want to lead us down the road to East-West "accommodation," and in so doing they point to "weaknesses" of the Kremlin. We apparently are to be heartened by the following analysis:

"The Soviets are in a sense encircled by nations which are by now alarmed by the aggressive nature of the Soviet system. The invasion of Afghanistan has led to a seemingly indefinite military entanglement for the Soviets which is proving costly in men and resources, as well as in its prejudicial impact on world public opinion. The Soviet-sponsored repression in Poland has set back, perhaps for a generation, the Soviet aim of having a stable situation on its Western marches. And to the East, China gives every indication of remaining a strong rival of Soviet influence in Asia and elsewhere. Internally, many observers expect that the stagnation of the Soviet economy will deepen during the decade, and the shifting balance of nationalities will place non-Russians in the majority. These developments will increase the Soviet regime's difficulties in dealing with external problems."

Here are some other conclusions and recommendations in *Trilateral Security*: The U.S.S.R. has *not* acquired a meaningful position of superiority in offensive nuclear forces and, it is contended, the "efforts to maintain and increase the effectiveness of U.S. deterrence of the Soviet Union have been partially responsible for the decay of consensus on nuclear policy in some trilateral countries." This is the obverse of an Orwellian dictum that Weakness Is Strength.

More warheads for the U.S. is not the way to go, say these "best brains," who join the Soviets in opposing deployment of our MX missile. Ballistic missile *defense* is also to be avoided, supposedly because the U.S. and U.S.S.R. are mutually vulnerable — though this is untrue. Whereas the Soviets have a comprehensive and long-standing civil defense program, the Trilateralists argue that we should not try to protect our people in similar fashion: ". . . the prevailing political sentiment in most trilateral countries is very negative . . . . Many people have recoiled from such efforts because of the brutalizing effects that preparations to deal with nuclear war could have on the population and because they arguably make war somewhat more likely. There is little prospect that more ambitious civil-defense programs will be accepted by parliaments and publics as either desirable in principle or tolerable in cost." Not if the Soviets and the Commission have their way.

Similarly, the Commissioners contend that the U.S. would garner more benefits than the Soviets by *not* deploying tactical defenses. Common sense is turned on its head by our would-be rulers, who maintain: "There is a growing sense in Europe that [*American*] battlefield and tactical nuclear weapons may be more devastating for the Western European battlefield in case of sudden conventional attack than to the enemy." Yet, the Trilaterals admit that there has been a steady growth and modernization of the conventional Soviet forces to the point where "trilateral countries now find themselves faced by a situation in which the Soviets might think they could successfully execute non-nuclear offensive campaigns in Europe and in Asia." But never mind.

The Trilateral countries, claim the Commissioners, "should make a renewed effort to promote a CTB [*Comprehensive Test Ban*]. In the meantime, the United States should ratify the Threshold Test Ban and the associated agreement on Peaceful Nuclear Explosions (PNEs) and should seek to extend it to tests below the initial threshold of 150 kilotons. By bringing these agreements into force, the United States would give earnest of good intentions and consolidate useful steps toward stronger verification provisions in U.S.-Soviet agreements and towards tightening the international non-proliferation regime . . . ." Just how that will work the Trilateralists saith not.

With this as background, there should be little astonishment in noting that Western foreign ministers have been calling on the Kremlin to "moderate" its international behavior, promising that we won't seek military superiority, and asking the Reds to "work together with us" to end East-West friction. Meanwhile, U.S. disarmers went back on track with but a slight hiatus after the Soviet military shot down the unarmed civilian K.A.L. Flight Seven. The bodies of the innocent are not recovered, but the gravediggers are back at work.

We are of course also now being told by our Trilateral guides to be more generous with the "developing" world. This despite the fact that, according to a study by the Library of Congress, the U.S. has spent some $2.3 trillion on foreign aid since the Marshall Plan began in 1946 — a sum almost twice that of our National Debt. This vast sum is not enough, and much too slow, if one is to believe last year's Triangle Paper Number Twenty-Seven, *Facilitating Development In A Changing Third World*, by Takeshi Watanabe, founding president, The Asian Development Bank; Jacques Lesourne, Director, Organization for Economic Cooperation & Development Interfutures Project; and, Robert S. McNamara, former president, The World Bank.

We are informed in this Trilateral study that by the year 2000 eleven of the fifteen biggest cities will be in the developing world, and that before long a vast majority of mankind will live in the so-called Third World. Accordingly, these Commissioners instruct us: "Given the growth of interdependence and the diffusion of knowledge, it is impossible to imagine as viable in the long term a world order in which a relatively small fraction of the population (those who live in the trilateral countries) have average incomes some forty times that of the majority of mankind living in low-income countries. Such a situation — if existing within the boundaries of any one of our countries — would be regarded as socially, morally, and politically unacceptable."

Leave it to the Trilaterals to explain to us peons what is acceptable. Among other things, of course, we need a stronger World Bank and International Monetary Fund to bail out the big bankers, finance tin-pot dictators, and reschedule "loans"; trilateral countries "should take developing countries into account as much as they do their OCED partners"; and, "It is incumbent upon commercial banks to continue financing developing countries with major liquidity difficulties." And never mind that taxpayers are to guarantee that the Trilateralists profit from all of this without risk.

The Trilateral Commission wants the U.S. to get the international giveaway wagon going faster, deploring that our "foreign policy still does not reflect adequate recognition of the emergence of the developing countries as important participants in the international arena. The longer the disparity continues, the more opportunities will be missed, the higher the costs will be to this country, and the greater will be the risk of permanently losing the leadership role the United States has played for so long in international development cooperations." That is, in giving away money.

The trouble is that, thanks to Conservative exposure of such machinations, Americans don't care to be suckers any more. Indeed, as columnist Patrick Buchanan has aptly observed: ". . . it was because Americans were fed up with losing gracefully that they elected Ronald Reagan. On this count, the cowboy's record is decidedly uneven. When Reagan — despite the *New York Times* warning we would be an 'outlaw nation' — refused to sign the Law of the Sea Treaty, thereby aborting a wholesale rip-off of our mining technology, and a unilateral surrender of American rights to the sea beds, he vindicated the claims of those who elected him.

"When, however, his Treasury Department meekly signed on to yet another $750 million annual donation to the welfare window of the World Bank — providing 50-year, interest-free loans to such capitals as Delhi and Peking, Maputo and Luanda — the President's men actually toured Europe bleating apologies that we could not make it larger.''

But profitable brokerage of a vast redistribution of wealth and power is what the Trilateral Commission wants. The Trilateralists put it this way:

''The world has already entered its third post-war wave of institution-building. The first wave came immediately after 1945, with the creation of the United Nations system and its economic components — particularly the Bretton Woods institutions. The second came around 1960 and included the Common Market, the Organization for Economic Cooperation and Development, the regional development banks and — though it was barely noticed at the time — OPEC. The third wave began around 1973 and continues to this day. It has witnessed creation of a United Nations Environmental Program, a World Food Council, an International Energy Agency, a series of 'producers associations' of exporters of primary products, and . . . the CIEC [*Conference on International Economic Cooperation*] with its four standing commissions. The first and second postwar waves of international institution-building made the world safe for the explosion of interdependence of the last generation . . . .''

Behind all this, David Rockefeller reassures us, is simply ''a group of concerned citizens interested in fostering greater understanding and co-operation . . . .'' Which is, of course, transparent nonsense. The question is: Will the future belong to free peoples or to a would-be ruling elite? The answer lies in how effectively the goals of the conspiring elitists are exposed — goals which threaten our liberty, our treasure, and our very nationhood.

Selected Bibliography

Abels, Jules. *The Rockefeller Billions*. New York: Macmillan, 1965.

———. *The Truman Scandals*. Chicago: Regnery, 1956.

Adams, James Truslow. *The March Of Democracy*. New York: Charles Scribner's Sons, 1933.

Alexander, Holmes. *To Covet Honor*. Boston: Western Islands, 1977.

Allen, Gary. *None Dare Call It Conspiracy*. Seal Beach, California: Concord Press, 1971.

Allen, Robert S. and William V. Shannon. *The Truman Merry-Go-Round*. New York: Vanguard, 1950.

Ashton, E.B. *The Fascist*. New York: Morrow, 1937.

Asprey, Robert B. *War In The Shadows*. Garden City: Doubleday, 1975.

Ayling, S.E. *The Georgian Century*. London: Harrap, 1966.

Bailey, Thomas A. *Woodrow Wilson And The Lost Peace*. New York: Macmillan, 1944.

Baldelli, Giovanni. *Social Anarchism*. Chicago: Aldine Atherton, 1971.

Baldwin, Hanson. *Battles Lost And Won*. New York: Harper & Row, 1966.

———. *The Crucial Years: 1939-1941*. New York: Harper & Row, 1976.

Barnes, Harry Elmer. *The Genesis Of The World War*. New York: Knopf, 1927.

———, ed. *Perpetual War For Perpetual Peace*. Caldwell, Idaho: Caxton, 1953.

Barron, John. *KGB: The Secret Work Of Soviet Secret Agents*. New York: Reader's Digest Press, 1974.

——— and Anthony Paul. *Murder Of A Gentle Land*. New York: Reader's Digest Press, 1977.

Bassett, John Spencer. *The League Of Nations*. New York: Longmans, Green, 1928.

Beard, Charles A. *President Roosevelt And The Coming Of The War*. New Haven: Yale University Press, 1948.

——— and Mary Beard. *The Beards' New Basic History Of The United States*. Garden City: Doubleday, 1960.

Beckhart, Benjamin Haggott. *Federal Reserve System*. American Institute of Banking, 1972.

Beilenson, Laurence W. *The Treaty Trap*. Washington, D.C.: Public Affairs Press, 1969.

Bemis, Samuel Flagg. *A Diplomatic History Of The United States*. New York: Holt, Rinehart and Winston, 1965.

Bernstorff, Johann H. *My Three Years In America*. New York: Charles Scribner's Sons, 1920.

Beth, Loren P. *The Development Of The American Constitution*. New York: Harper & Row, 1971.

Bethell, Nicholas. *The War Hitler Won*. New York: Holt, Rinehart and Winston, 1973.

Beveridge, Albert J. *The Life Of John Marshall*. Boston: Houghton Mifflin, 1916.

Bird, Caroline. *The Invisible Scar*. New York: McKay, 1966.

Birdsall, Paul. *Versailles Twenty Years After*. New York: Reynal & Hitchcock, 1941.

Bizardel, Yvon. *The First Expatriates*. New York: Holt, Rinehart and Winston, 1975.

Blackstock, Paul. *The Secret Road To World War Two*. Chicago: Quadrangle, 1969.

Bohlen, Charles E. *Witness To History: 1929-1969*. New York: Norton, 1973.

Bonsal, Stephen. *Suitors And Supplicants*. New York: Prentice-Hall, 1946.

———. *Unfinished Business*. Garden City: Doubleday, Doran, 1944.

Borchard, Edwin and William Potter Loge. *Neutrality For The United States*. New Haven: Yale University Press, 1937.

Borkenau, Franz. *European Communism*. New York: Harper, 1953.

Bowers, Claude G. *The Party Battles Of The Jackson Period*. Boston: Houghton Mifflin, 1922.

———. *The Tragic Era*. New York: Blue Ribbon Books, 1929.

Boyle, Donzella Cross. *Quest Of A Hemisphere*. Boston: Western Islands, 1970.

Brant, Irving. *James Madison: Father Of The Constitution, 1787-1800*. Indianapolis: Bobbs-Merrill, 1950.

Brinton, Clarence Crane. *The Jacobins*. New York: Russell & Russell, 1961.

Browne, Harry. *How You Can Profit From The Coming Devaluation*. New Rochelle: Arlington House, 1970.

Bruckberger, F.L. *Images Of America*. New York: Viking, 1959.

Brzezinski, Zbigniew. *Between Two Ages*. New York: Viking, 1970.

Buckley, William F. Jr. and L. Brent Bozell. *McCarthy And His Enemies*. Chicago: Regnery, 1954.

Burger, Nash K. and John K. Bettersworth. *South Of Appomattox*. New York: Harcourt, Brace, 1959.

Burke, Edmund. *Reflections On The Revolution In France*. Garden City: Anchor Press, 1973.

Burlingame, Roger. *Henry Ford*. New York: Knopf, 1954.

Burner, David. *Herbert Hoover: A Public Life*. New York: Knopf, 1979.

Burns, James MacGregor. *Roosevelt: The Lion And The Fox*. New York: Harcourt, Brace, 1956.

———. *Roosevelt: The Soldier Of Fortune*. New York: Harcourt Brace Jovanovich, 1970.

Byrnes, James F. *Speaking Frankly*. New York: Harper and Brothers, 1947.

Candlin, A.H. Stanton. *Psycho-Chemical Warfare*. New Rochelle: Arlington House, 1973.

Carell, Paul. *Hitler Moves East: 1941-1943*. Boston: Little, Brown, 1964.

Carnegie, Andrew. *Autobiography*. Boston: Houghton Mifflin, 1920.

Carr, Albert Z. *John D. Rockefeller's Secret Weapon*. New York: McGraw-Hill, 1962.

Carroll, John Alexander and Odie B. Faulk. *Home Of The Brave*. New Rochelle: Arlington House, 1976.

Carson, Clarence B. *The Rebirth Of Liberty*. New Rochelle: Arlington House, 1973.

———. *Throttling The Railroads*. Indianapolis: Liberty Press, 1971.

Carson, Gerald. *The Golden Egg*. Boston: Houghton Mifflin, 1977.

Carter, Hodding. *The Angry Scar*. Garden City: Doubleday, 1959.

Carto, Willis A., ed. *Profiles In Populism*. Old Greenwich: Flag Press, 1982.

Caute, David. *The Fellow-Travellers*. New York: Macmillan, 1973.

Chadsey, Charles E. *The Struggle Between President Johnson And Congress Over Reconstruction*. New York: AMS Press, 1967.

Chamberlain, John. *The Enterprising Americans*. New York: Harper & Row, 1963.

———. *The Roots Of Capitalism*. Indianapolis: Liberty Press, 1976.

Chamberlain, William Henry. *America's Second Crusade*. Chicago: Regnery, 1950.

Chandler, Lester V. *Benjamin Strong, Central Banker*. Washington, D.C.: Brookings Institution, 1958.

Cheyney, Edward P. *An Introduction To The Industrial And Social History Of England*. New York: Macmillan, 1929.

Chodorov, Frank. *The Income Tax: Root Of All Evil*. Old Greenwich: Devin-Adair, 1954.

Churchill, Winston S. *Closing The Ring*. Boston: Houghton Mifflin, 1951.

———. *History Of The English-Speaking People*. New York: Dodd, Mead, 1957.

———. *The Aftermath*. New York: Charles Scribner's Sons, 1929.

————. *The Gathering Storm*. Boston: Houghton Mifflin, 1948.

————. *The Grand Alliance*. Boston: Houghton Mifflin, 1950.

————. *The Hinge Of Fate*. Boston: Houghton Mifflin, 1950.

————. *Their Finest Hour*. Boston: Houghton Mifflin, 1949.

————. *Triumph And Tragedy*. Boston: Houghton Mifflin, 1953.

Ciechanowski, Jan. *Defeat In Victory*. New York: Doubleday, 1947.

Clark, Alan. *Barbarossa: The Russian-German Conflict*. New York: Morrow, 1965.

Clark, Mark. *From The Danube To The Yalu*. New York: Harper & Brothers, 1954.

Cohen, Warren I., ed. *Intervention, 1917: Why America Fought*. Boston: Heath, 1966.

Colby, Benjamin. *'Twas A Famous Victory*. New Rochelle: Arlington House, 1974.

Cole, Wayne S. *Charles A. Lindbergh And The Battle Against American Intervention In World War II*. New York: Harcourt Brace Jovanovich, 1974.

Collier, Richard. *Duce!* New York: Viking, 1971.

Collins, J. Lawton. *War In Peacetime*. Boston: Houghton Mifflin, 1969.

Commager, Henry Steele, ed. *Living Ideas In America*. New York: Harper & Row, 1964.

Conquest, Robert. *The Great Terror*. New York: Collier, revised 1973.

Corey, Herbert. *The Truth About Hoover*. Boston: Houghton Mifflin, 1932.

Corwin, Edward S. *The Constitution And What It Means Today*. New York: Atheneum, 1969.

Coy, Harold. *The Americans*. Boston: Little, Brown, 1958.

Crocker, George N. *Roosevelt's Road To Russia*. Chicago: Regnery, 1959.

Current, Richard N., ed. *Reconstruction (1865-1877)*. Englewood Cliffs: Prentice-Hall, 1965.

Dangerfield, George. *The Era Of Good Feelings*. New York: Harcourt, Brace, 1952.

Davis, Kenneth S. *The Hero*. Garden City: Doubleday, 1959.

Dayton, Eldorous L. *Give 'Em Hell Harry*. New York: Devin-Adair, 1956.

Dean, William F. *General Dean's Story*. New York: Viking, 1954.

DeConde, Alexander. *Entangling Alliance*. Durham: Duke University Press, 1958.

Diggins, John P. *The American Left In The Twentieth Century*. New York: Harcourt Brace Jovanovich, 1973.

Donovan, Robert J. *Conflict And Crisis*. New York: Norton, 1977.

Druks, Herbert. *Harry S Truman And The Russians: 1945-1953*. New York: Speller, 1966.

Dufour, Charles L. *The Mexican War, A Compact History: 1846-1848*. New York: Hawthorn, 1968.

Dulles, Foster Rhea. *The United States Since 1865*. Ann Arbor: University of Michigan Press, 1959.

Durant, Will and Ariel. *Rousseau And Revolution*. New York: Simon and Schuster, 1967.

————. *The Age Of Napoleon*. New York: Simon and Schuster, 1975.

Earle, Peter. *Robert E. Lee*. New York: Saturday Review Press, 1973.

Eaton, Clement. *Henry Clay And The Art Of American Politics*. Boston: Little, Brown, 1957.

Ehrman, John. *The Younger Pitt*. New York: Dutton, 1969.

Eidelberg, Paul. *The Philosophy Of The American Constitution*. New York: Free Press, 1968.

Engelbrecht, H.C. and F.C. Hanighen. *Merchants Of Death*. New York: Dodd, Mead, 1934.

Esler, Anthony. *Bombs Beards And Barricades*. New York: Stein and Day, 1971.

Evans, M. Stanton. *Clear And Present Dangers*. New York: Harcourt Brace Jovanovich, 1975.

Fair, Charles. *From The Jaws Of Victory*. New York: Simon and Schuster, 1971.

Falk, Richard. *A Study Of Future Worlds*. New York: Free Press, 1975.

Farr, Finis. *FDR*. New Rochelle: Arlington House, 1972.

Fausold, Martin L. and George T. Mazuzan, ed. *The Hoover Presidency*. Albany: State University of New York, 1974.

Fehrenbach, T.R. *F.D.R.'s Undeclared War: 1939 To 1941*. New York: McKay, 1967.

Fisher, Antony. *Must History Repeat Itself?* Levittown, New York: Transatlantic Arts, 1974.

Fleming, Denna Frank. *The United States And The League Of Nations*. New York: G.P. Putnam's Sons, 1932.

Flexner, James T. *Washington: The Indispensable Man*. Boston: Little, Brown, 1969.

Flynn, John T. *As We Go Marching*. New York: Free Life, 1944.

——. *The Lattimore Story*. New York: Devin-Adair, 1953.

——. *The Roosevelt Myth*. New York: Devin-Adair, 1956.

Ford, Henry. *My Life And Work*. Garden City: Doubleday, 1923.

Forman, James D. *Anarchism*. New York: Franklin Watts, 1975.

Freidel, Frank. *America In The Twentieth Century*. New York: Knopf, 1960.

——. *The Triumph*. Boston: Little, Brown, 1956.

Friedman, Milton. *Capitalism And Freedom*. Chicago: University of Chicago Press, 1962.

—— and Anna Jacobson Schwartz. *The Great Contraction: 1929-1933*. Princeton: National Bureau of Economic Research, 1963.

Friendly, Fred W. *The Good Guys, The Bad Guys And The First Amendment*. New York: Random House, 1976.

Galbraith, John Kenneth. *The Great Crash, 1929*. Boston: Houghton Mifflin, 1972 (Third Edition).

Gardner, Brian. *Churchill In Power*. Boston: Houghton Mifflin, 1970.

Garraty, John A. *Henry Cabot Lodge*. New York: Knopf, 1953.

——. *The New Commonwealth: 1877-1890*. New York: Harper & Row, 1968.

Gehlen, Reinhard. *The Service: The Memoirs Of General Reinhard Gehlen*, translated by David Irving. New York: World, 1972.

Gies, Joseph. *Harry S Truman*. Garden City: Doubleday, 1968.

Gilbert, Martin, ed. *Churchill*. Englewood Cliffs: Prentice-Hall, 1967.

Gill, Brendan. *Lindbergh Alone*. New York: Harcourt Brace Jovanovich, 1977.

Gitlow, Benjamin. *The Whole Of Their Lives*. Boston: Western Islands, 1965.

Goldman, Emma. *Living My Life*. New York: Knopf, 1931.

Goldwater, Barry. *The Conscience Of A Conservative*. Shepherdsville, Kentucky: Victor, 1960.

Graham, Daniel O. *Shall America Be Defended?* New Rochelle: Arlington House, 1979.

Greene, Theodore P., ed. *Wilson At Versailles*. Boston: Heath, 1957.

Gregg, Pauline. *Modern Britain*. New York: Pegasus, 1965.

Gregory, Ross. *The Origins Of American Intervention In The First World War*. New York: Norton, 1971.

Griffith, Samuel B. II. *The Chinese People's Liberation Army*. New York: McGraw-Hill, 1967.

Grunfeld, Frederic V. *The Hitler File*. New York: Random House, 1974.

Guillebaud, C.W. *The Social Policy Of Nazi Germany*. London: Cambridge University Press, 1941.

Gunther, John. *Roosevelt In Retrospect*. New York: Harper & Brothers, 1950.

Hacker, Louis M. *The World Of Andrew Carnegie*. Philadelphia: J.P. Lippincott, 1968.

Haines, Lynn and Dora B. Haines. *The Lindberghs*. New York: Vanguard Press, 1931.

Halle, Kay, ed. *Winston Churchill On America And Britain*. New York: Walker, 1970.

Hamby, Alonzo L. *Beyond The New Deal: Harry S. Truman And American Liberalism*. New York: Columbia University Press, 1973.

Hammond, Bray. *Banks And Politics In America*. London: Oxford University Press, 1957.

Hammond, J.L. and Barbara Hammond. *The Rise Of Modern Industry*. New York: Harcourt, Brace, 1926.

Hansl, Proctor W. *Years Of Plunder*. New York: Harrison Smith and Robert Haas, 1935.

Hart, B.H. Liddell. *The Real War, 1914-1918*. Boston: Atlantic-Little, Brown, 1930.

Hayek, Friedrich A. *The Road To Serfdom*. Chicago: University of Chicago Press, 1944.

Haynes, George H. *The Senate Of The United States*. New York: Russell & Russell, 1960.

Heilbroner, Robert L. *The Making Of Economic Society*. Englewood Cliffs: Prentice-Hall, 1962.

——. *The Worldly Philosophers*. New York: Simon and Schuster, 1953.

Heinl, Robert D. Jr. *Victory At High Tide*. Philadelphia: J.P. Lippincott, 1968.

Henderson, Archibald. *Contemporary Immortals*. New York: Appleton, 1930.

Higgins, Trumbell. *Hitler And Russia*. New York: Macmillan, 1966.

Hinshaw, David. *Herbert Hoover: American Quaker*. New York: Farrar, Straus, 1950.

Hirschfield, Burt. *After The Alamo: The Story Of The Mexican War*. New York: Messner, 1966.

Hitler, Adolf. *Mein Kampf*, translated by Ralph Mannheim. Boston: Houghton Mifflin, 1942.

Hoffer, Eric. *The True Believer*. New York: Harper & Row, 1951.

Hofstadter, Richard, ed. *Great Issues In American History*. New York: Vintage, 1958.

Holbrook, Stewart. *The Age Of The Moguls*. Garden City: Doubleday, 1953.

Hoover, Herbert C. *The Memoirs Of Herbert Hoover*. New York: Macmillan, 1951.

Huddleston, Sisley. *France: The Tragic Years*. New York: Devin-Adair, 1955.

Hull, Cordell. *The Memoirs Of Cordell Hull*. New York: Macmillan, 1948.

Hunt, Frazier. *The Untold Story Of Douglas MacArthur*. New York: Manor Books, 1977.

Hunter, Edward. *Brainwashing*. New York: Pyramid, 1958.

James, Robert Rhodes. *Churchill: A Study In Failure, 1900-1939*. New York: World, 1970.

Johnson, Douglas. *The French Revolution*. New York: G.P. Putnam's Sons, 1970.

Johnson, Hugh. *The Blue Eagle From Egg To Earth*. New York: Doubleday, 1935.

Joll, James. *The Anarchists*. Boston: Little, Brown, 1964.

Josephson, Matthew. *The Politicos*. New York: Harcourt, Brace, 1963.

―――. *The Robber Barons*. New York: Harcourt, Brace, 1934.

Joy, C. Turner. *How Communists Negotiate*. New York: Macmillan, 1955.

Kershner, Howard. *Dividing The Wealth*. Old Greenwich: Devin-Adair, 1971.

Key, V.O. *Southern Politics*. New York: Vintage, 1949.

Keynes, John Maynard. *The Economic Consequences Of The Peace*. New York: Harcourt, Brace, 1925.

Kimball, Marie. *Jefferson: The Scene Of Europe, 1784-1789*. New York: Coward-McCann, 1950.

Kolko, Gabriel. *Main Currents In Modern American History*. New York: Harper & Row, 1976.

―――. *The Triumph Of Conservatism*. New York: Free Press of Glencoe, 1963.

Kraus, Michael. *The United States To 1865*. Ann Arbor: University of Michigan Press, 1959.

Krock, Arthur. *Memoirs*. New York: Funk & Wagnalls, 1968.

Kropotkin, Petr A. *Memoirs Of A Revolutionist*. Boston: Houghton Mifflin, 1899.

Kuehnelt-Leddihn, Erik von. *Leftism*. New Rochelle: Arlington House, 1974.

Ladenburg, Thomas J. and Samuel Hugh Brockunier. *The Prosperity And Depression Decades*. New York: Hayden, 1971.

Lane, Arthur Bliss. *I Saw Poland Betrayed*. Indianapolis: Bobbs-Merrill, 1948.

Lansing, Robert. *War Memoirs Of Robert Lansing*. Indianapolis: Bobbs-Merrill, 1935.

Larson, Bruce L. *Lindbergh Of Minnesota*. New York: Harcourt Brace Jovanovich, 1973.

Lash, Joseph P. *Roosevelt And Churchill: 1939-1941*. New York: Norton, 1976.

Lasky, Victor. *It Didn't Start With Watergate*. New York: Dial Press, 1977.

―――. *J.F.K.: The Man And The Myth*. New York: Macmillan, 1963.

Leahy, William D. *I Was There*. New York: Whittlesey House, 1950.

Leckie, Robert. *Conflict*. New York: G.P. Putnam's Sons, 1962.

Lee, Clark and Richard Henschel. *Douglas MacArthur*. New York: Holt, 1952.

Leeds, Christopher. *Italy Under Mussolini*. London: Wayland, 1972.

Leuchtenburg, William E. *Franklin D. Roosevelt And The New Deal*. New York: Harper & Row, 1963.

Lindberg, Charles A. *The Spirit Of St. Louis*. New York: Charles Scribner's Sons, 1953.

―――. *The Wartime Journals Of Charles A. Lindbergh*. New York: Harcourt Brace Jovanovich, 1970.

―――. *We*. New York: G.P. Putnam's Sons, 1927.

Link, Arthur S. *Woodrow Wilson And The Progressive Era*. New York: Harper & Brothers, 1954.

Lodge, Henry Cabot. *George Washington*. Boston: Houghton Mifflin, 1898.

Loewenheim, Francis L., Harold D. Langley, and Manfred Jonas, ed. *Roosevelt And Churchill: Their Secret Wartime Correspondence*. New York: Saturday Review Press, 1975.

Lopez, Claude-Anne and Eugenia W. Herbert. *The Private Franklin*. New York: Norton, 1975.

Loucks, William N. and J. Weldon Hoot. *Comparative Economic Systems*. New York: Harper & Brothers, 1948.

Lundberg, Ferdinand. *America's 60 Families*. New York: Vanguard Press, 1937.

Lukacs, John. *Outgrowing Democracy*. Garden City: Doubleday, 1984.

Lyons, Eugene. *Herbert Hoover: A Biography*. Garden City: Doubleday, 1964.

———. *The Red Decade*. New Rochelle: Arlington House, 1971.

MacArthur, Douglas. *Reminiscences*. New York: McGraw-Hill, 1964.

McCarthy, Joseph R. *America's Retreat From Victory*. New York: Devin-Adair, 1951.

———. *McCarthyism: The Fight For America*. New York: Devin-Adair, 1952.

Malin, James C. *The United States After The War*. Boston: Ginn, 1930.

Malkin, Maurice. *Return To My Father's House*. New Rochelle: Arlington House, 1972.

Manchester, William. *The Glory And The Dream*. Boston: Little, Brown, 1974.

Marburg, Theodore. *Development Of The League Of Nations Idea*. New York: Macmillan, 1932.

Marshall, S.L.A. *The Military History Of The Korean War*. New York: Franklin Watts, 1963.

Martin, Rose L. *Fabian Freeway*. Santa Monica: Fidelis, 1968.

Medvedev, Roy A. *Let History Judge*. New York: Knopf, 1972.

Mee, Charles L. Jr. *Meeting At Potsdam*. New York: M. Evans, 1975.

Meltzer, Milton. *Brother, Can You Spare A Dime?* New York: Knopf, 1969.

Mendlovitz, Saul H., ed. *On The Creation Of A Just World Order*. New York: Free Press, 1975.

Merk, Frederick. *Manifest Destiny And Mission In American History*. New York: Knopf, 1963.

———. *The Monroe Doctrine And American Expansionism*. New York: Knopf, 1966.

Methvin, Eugene H. *The Rise Of Radicalism*. New Rochelle: Arlington House, 1973.

Michon, Georges. *The Franco-Russian Alliance*. New York: Macmillan, 1929.

Middleton, Drew. *Retreat From Victory*. New York: Hawthorn, 1973.

Mikolajczyk, Stanislaw. *The Rape Of Poland*. New York: Whittlesey House, 1948.

Miller, Clarence F. *et al. The Federal Income Tax: Its Sources And Applications*. Englewood Cliffs: Prentice-Hall, 1968.

Miller, Martin A. *Kropotkin*. Chicago: University of Chicago Press, 1976.

Millis, Walter. *Road To War: America 1914-1917*. Boston: Houghton Mifflin, 1935.

Minnigerode, Meade. *Certain Rich Men*. New York: G.P. Putnam's Sons, 1927.

Mises, Ludwig von. *Human Action*. Chicago: Regnery, 1963 (Third Edition).

———. *Planned Chaos*. Irvington-on-Hudson: Foundation for Economic Education, 1947.

———. *Theory And History*. New Rochelle: Arlington House, 1969.

Mitchell, Broadus and Louise Pearson. *A Biography Of The Constitution Of The United States*. New York: Oxford University Press, 1964.

Monaghan, Frank. *John Jay*. New York: Bobbs-Merrill, 1935.

Morison, Samuel Eliot. *The Oxford History Of The American People*. New York: Oxford University Press, 1965.

——— and Henry Steele Commager. *The Growth Of The American Republic*. New York: Oxford University Press, 1937.

Morris, Gouverneur. *The Diary And Letters Of Gouverneur Morris*. New York: Charles Scribner's Sons, 1888.

Morris, Robert. *No Wonder We Are Losing*. Plano, Texas: University of Plano Press, 1958.

Mosley, Leonard. *Lindbergh*. New York: Doubleday, 1976.

Muggeridge, Malcolm. *Chronicles Of Wasted Time: The Infernal Grove*. New York: Morrow, 1974.

Myers, Gustavus. *History Of The Great American Fortunes*. New York: Modern Library, 1909, revised 1936.

Myers, William Starr and Walter H. Newton. *The Hoover Administration*. New York: Charles Scribner's Sons, 1936.

Myrdal, Gunnar. *An American Dilemma*. New York: Harper & Row, 1944.

Neilsen, Waldemar A. *The Big Foundations*. New York: Columbia University Press, 1972.

Nevins, Allan and Frank Ernest Hill. *Ford: Expansion And Challenge, 1915-1933*. New York: Charles Scribner's Sons, 1957.

———. *Ford: The Times, The Man, The Company*. New York: Charles Scribner's Sons, 1954.

Nicolson, Harold. *Peacemaking*. Boston: Houghton Mifflin, 1933.

Nitze, Paul H., James E. Dougherty, and Francis X. Kane. *The Fateful Ends And Shades Of SALT*. New York: Crane, Russak, 1979.

Nock, Albert Jay. *Our Enemy, The State*. New York: Free Life, 1935.

O'Connor, Richard. *Gould's Millions*. Garden City: Doubleday, 1962.

———. *Iron Wheels And Broken Men*. New York: G.P. Putnam's Sons, 1973.

Paine, Thomas. *The Rights Of Man*. Garden City: Anchor Press, 1973.

Parkinson, C. Northcote. *The Law And The Profits*. Boston: Houghton Mifflin, 1960.

Parmat, Herbert S. and Marie B. Hecht. *Never Again: A President Runs For A Third Term*. New York: Macmillan, 1968.

Parton, James. *Life And Times Of Benjamin Franklin*. Boston: Ticknor and Fields, 1867.

Payne, Robert. *The Great Man*. New York: Coward, McCann & Geoghegan, 1974.

———. *The Life And Death Of Adolf Hitler*. New York: Praeger, 1973.

Perrault, Gilles. *The Red Orchestra*. New York: Simon and Schuster, 1967.

Peterson, H.C. *Propaganda For War*. Norman: University of Oklahoma Press, 1939.

Porter, Katherine Anne. *The Never-Ending Wrong*. Boston: Atlantic-Little, Brown, 1977.

Quigley, Carroll. *Tragedy And Hope*. New York: Macmillan, 1966.

Rae, John B., ed. *Henry Ford*. Englewood Cliffs: Prentice Hall, 1969.

Rauch, Basil. *Roosevelt From Munich To Pearl Harbor*. New York: Creative Age Press, 1950.

Read, James Morgan. *Atrocity Propaganda*. New Haven: Yale University Press, 1941.

Reed, John. *Ten Days That Shook The World*. New York: Vintage, 1960.

Reiners, Ludwig. *The Lamps Went Out In Europe*. New York: Vintage, 1960.

Richards, William C. *The Last Billionaire*. New York: Charles Scribner's Sons, 1948.

Robbins, Lionel. *The Great Depression*. New York: Macmillan, 1934.

Roberts, Stephen H. *The House That Hitler Built*. New York: Harper & Brothers, 1938.

Robertson, Charles L. *International Politics Since World War II*. New York: John Wiley & Sons, 1966.

Roche, George. *The Bewildered Society*. New Rochelle: Arlington House, 1972.

Rockefeller, John D. *Random Reminiscences Of Men And Events*. New York: Doubleday, Doran, 1909.

Rogge, Benjamin. *Can Capitalism Survive?* Indianapolis: Liberty Press, 1979.

Romasco, Albert U. *The Poverty Of Abundance*. London: Oxford University Press, 1965.

Roosevelt, Franklin D. *Public Papers And Addresses Of Franklin D. Roosevelt, 1928-36*, New York: Random House, 1938.

Rothbard, Murray. *America's Great Depression*. Los Angeles: Nash, 1963.

Rowe, Vivian. *The Great Wall Of France*. New York: G.P. Putnam's Sons, 1959.

Rozwenc, Edwin C., ed. *The Meaning Of Jacksonian Democracy*. Boston: Heath, 1963.

Rublowsky, John. *After The Crash*. New York: Crowell-Collier, 1970.

Safire, William. *Before The Fall*. Garden City: Doubleday, 1975.

Sanborn, Frederic R. *Design For War*. New York: Devin-Adair, 1951.

Schlafly, Phyllis and Chester Ward. *Kissinger On The Couch*. New Rochelle: Arlington House, 1975.

Schlesinger, Arthur M. *A Thousand Days*. Boston: Houghton Mifflin, 1965.

———. *The Coming Of The New Deal*. Boston: Houghton Mifflin, 1958.

————. *The Crisis Of The Old Order*. Boston: Houghton Mifflin, 1958.

Schumpeter, Joseph. *Capitalism, Socialism And Democracy*. New York: Harper & Row, 1950.

Sears, Louis Martin. *George Washington & The French Revolution*. Detroit: Wayne State University Press, 1960.

Seward, William Henry. *The Jacksonian Era, 1828-1848*. New York: Harper & Row, 1959.

Seymour, Charles. *The Intimate Papers Of Colonel House*. London: Ernest Benn Limited, 1926.

Shatz, Martin, ed. *The Essential Works Of Anarchism*. New York: Bantam, 1971.

Shenton, James P. *The Reconstruction*. New York: G.P. Putnam's Sons. 1963.

Sherwood, Robert. *Roosevelt And Hopkins*. New York: Harper & Brothers, 1948.

Shirer, William L. *The Rise And Fall Of The Third Reich*. Greenwich: Fawcett Crest, 1959.

Simonds, William Adams. *Henry Ford*. Indianapolis: Bobbs-Merrill, 1943.

Simpson, Colin. *The Lusitania*. Boston: Little, Brown, 1972.

Sklar, Holly, ed. *Trilateralism*. Boston: South End Press, 1980.

Smellie, K.B. *Great Britain Since 1688*. Ann Arbor: University of Michigan Press, 1962.

Smith, Adam. *The Wealth Of Nations*. New York: Modern Library, 1937.

Smith, Gene. *The Shattered Dream*. New York: Morrow, 1970.

Smith, Page. *John Adams*. Garden City: Doubleday, 1962.

Snell, John L., ed. *The Outbreak Of The Second World War: Design Or Blunder?* Boston: Heath, 1962.

Snyder, Louis. *The War, A Concise History*. New York: Messner, 1960.

Solzhenitsyn, Aleksandr. *The Gulag Archipelago, I-II*. New York: Harper & Row, 1973.

Sorensen, Charles E. *My Forty Years With Ford*. New York: Norton, 1956.

Speer, Albert. *Inside The Third Reich*. New York: Macmillan, 1970.

Stenehjem, Michele Flynn. *An American First*. New Rochelle: Arlington House, 1976.

Stevenson, William. *A Man Called Intrepid*. New York: Harcourt Brace Jovanovich, 1976.

Stuart, Jack, ed. *Succession or Repudiation? Realities Of The Truman Presidency*. New York: Simon and Schuster, 1975.

Sullivan, Mark. *Our Times*. New York: Charles Scribner's Sons, 1932.

Suskind, Richard. *By Bullet, Bomb And Dagger*. New York: Macmillan, 1971.

Sutton, Antony. *Wall Street And FDR*. New Rochelle: Arlington House, 1975.

————. *Wall Street And The Bolshevik Revolution*. New Rochelle: Arlington House, 1975.

————. *Wall Street And The Rise Of Hitler*. Seal Beach, California: '76 Press, 1976.

Tansill, Charles Callan. *America Goes To War*. Boston: Little, Brown, 1938.

————. *Back Door To War*. Chicago: Regnery, 1952.

Tarbell, Ida M. *The History Of The Standard Oil Company*. New York: Macmillan, 1904.

Taylor, A.J.P., *et al. Churchill Revised*. New York: Dial Press, 1969.

Taylor, George Rogers, ed. *Jackson Versus Biddle: The Struggle Over The Second Bank Of The United States*. Boston: Heath, 1949.

Theobald, Robert A. *The Final Secret Of Pearl Harbor*. Old Greenwich: Devin-Adair, 1954.

Thompson, R.W. *Generalissimo Churchill*. New York: Scribner's, 1973.

————. *Winston Churchill: The Yankee Marlborough*. Garden City: Doubleday, 1963.

Thomson, George Malcolm. *Vote Of Censure*. New York: Stein and Day, 1968.

Tocqueville, Alexis de. *Democracy In America*. New York: Vintage, 1945.

Toland, John. *Adolf Hitler*. Garden City: Doubleday, 1976.

————. *Infamy: Pearl Harbor And Its Aftermath*. New York: Doubleday, 1982.

————. *The Rising Sun*. New York: Random House, 1970.

Trohan, Walter. *Political Animals*. New York: Doubleday, 1975.

Tuchman, Barbara. *The Proud Tower*. New York: Macmillan, 1966.

Twight, Charlotte. *America's Emerging Fascist Economy*. New Rochelle: Arlington House, 1975.

Utley, Freda. *The China Story*. Chicago: Regnery, 1951.

————. *Odyssey Of A Liberal*. Washington, D.C.: Washington National Press, 1970.

Vandenberg, Arthur H. Jr., ed. *The Private Papers Of Senator Vandenberg*. Boston: Houghton Mifflin, 1952.

Van Deusen, Glyndon G. *The Jacksonian Era, 1828-1848*. New York: Harper & Row, 1959.

Veale, F.J.P. *Advance To Barbarism*. New York: Devin-Adair, revised 1968.

Viereck, George S. *The Strangest Friendship In History*. New York: Liveright, 1932.

Wall, Joseph Frazier. *Andrew Carnegie*. New York: Oxford University Press, 1970.

Walther, Daniel. *Gouverneur Morris: Witness Of Two Revolutions*. New York: Funk & Wagnalls, 1934.

Wanniski, Jude. *The Way The World Works*. New York: Simon and Schuster, 1978.

Weaver, Richard M. *The Southern Tradition At Bay*. New Rochelle: Arlington House, 1968.

Webster, Nesta H. *The French Revolution*. Hawthorne, California: Christian, 1969.

Wedemeyer, Albert C. *Wedemeyer Reports!* New York: Holt, 1958.

Welch, Robert. *The Politician*. Belmont, Massachusetts: Belmont Publishing Company, 1963.

Wellman, Paul I. *The House Divides*. Garden City: Doubleday, 1966.

Werth, Alexander. *Russia At War*. New York: Dutton, 1964.

Wertham, Fredric. *A Sign For Cain*. New York: Warner, 1966.

Whaley, Barton. *Codeword Barbarossa*. Cambridge: M.I.T. Press, 1973.

Whitney, Courtney. *MacArthur: His Rendezvous With History*. New York: Knopf, 1956.

Willoughby, Charles A. and John Chamberlain. *MacArthur: 1941-1951*. New York: McGraw-Hill, 1954.

Wilmot, Chester. *The Struggle For Europe*. London: Collins, 1966.

Wilson, Joan Hoff. *Herbert Hoover: Forgotten Progressive*. Boston: Little, Brown, 1975.

Winterbotham, F.W. *The Ultra Secret*. New York: Dell, 1974.

Wise, Jennings C. *Woodrow Wilson: Disciple Of Revolution*. New York: Paisley Press, 1938.

Woodcock, George. *Who Killed The British Empire?* New York: Quadrangle, 1974.

Index